KU-203-757

Russia's Crony Capitalism

*The Path from
Market Economy to
Kleptocracy*

ANDERS ÅSLUND

Yale UNIVERSITY PRESS/NEW HAVEN & LONDON

Published with assistance from the foundation established in memory of Philip Hamilton McMillan of the Class of 1894, Yale College.

Copyright © 2019 by Anders Åslund.

All rights reserved. This book may not be reproduced, in whole or in part, including illustrations, in any form (beyond that copying permitted by Sections 107 and 108 of the US Copyright Law and except by reviewers for the public press), without written permission from the publishers.

Yale University Press books may be purchased in quantity for educational, business, or promotional use. For information, please e-mail sales.press@yale.edu (US office) or sales@yaleup.co.uk (UK office).

Set in Minion type by IDS Infotech, Ltd.
Printed in the United States of America.

Library of Congress Control Number: 2018957954

ISBN 978-0-300-24309-3 (hardcover : alk. paper)

A catalogue record for this book is available from the British Library.

This paper meets the requirements of ANSI/NISO Z39.48-1992 (Permanence of Paper).

10 9 8 7 6 5 4 3 2 1

Contents

Acronyms and Initialisms

APEC	Asia-Pacific Economic Cooperation
BRICS	Brazil, Russia, India, China, and South Africa
CBR	Central Bank of Russia
CEO	Chief executive officer
CIS	Commonwealth of Independent States
CMEA	Council of Mutual Economic Assistance (also called COMECON)
CPSU	Communist Party of the Soviet Union
DCFTA	Deep and Comprehensive Free Trade Agreement
EAEU	Eurasian Economic Union
EBRD	European Bank for Reconstruction and Development
ECB	European Central Bank
EU	European Union
ECHR	European Court of Human Rights
FATF	The Financial Action Task Force
FCPA	Foreign Corrupt Practices Act
FDI	Foreign direct investment
FSB	Federal Security Service
FSO	Federal Protection Service

FSU   Former Soviet Union

G-7   Group of Seven (Canada, France, Germany, Italy, Japan, United Kingdom, and United States)

G-8   G-7 plus Russia

G-20   Group of Twenty biggest economies in the world

GATT   General Agreement on Tariffs and Trade

GDP   Gross domestic product

GNP   Gross national product

Gosplan   State Planning Committee

GRU   Main Intelligence Directorate

IFI   International financial institution

IMF   International Monetary Fund

IPO   Initial public offering

KGB   Committee for State Security

NATO   North Atlantic Treaty Organization

OECD   Organization of Economic Cooperation and Development

OSCE   Organization for Security and Cooperation in Europe

PPP   Purchasing power parities

Rosatom   Russian State Atomic Energy Corporation

Rostec   Russian Technologies

SCO   Shanghai Cooperation Organisation

SIPRI   Stockholm International Peace Research Institute

SVR   Foreign Intelligence Service

USAID   United States Agency for International Development

USSR   Union of Soviet Socialist Republics

VAT   Value-added tax

VEB   Vnesheconombank

VTB   Vneshtorgbank

WTO   World Trade Organization

Russia's
Crony
Capitalism

Introduction

On December 3, 1991, I received my own office in the former Central Committee headquarters of the Communist Party of the Soviet Union, at the Old Square beside the Kremlin in Moscow. It was an exhilarating moment: Russia had never been so free and open, and I was an economic adviser to the new government. Two years of intense reforms ensued in Russia, but it was only after the financial crash in 1998 that the market reforms were completed and economic growth resumed.

A quarter of a century has passed since the Soviet Union collapsed on December 25, 1991, and few now remember how free Russia was in the 1990s.

On New Year's Eve 2000, the ailing president Boris Yeltsin resigned and appointed Prime Minister Vladimir Putin his successor. In March 2000, Russia held an early presidential election, which Putin won. It was Russia's last competitive election.

Putin took his seat at the head of a table that was already laid with macroeconomic stability and high economic growth. His government continued reforms from 2000 to 2003, and for a golden decade, from 1999 to 2008, Russia enjoyed an impressive average annual growth of 7 percent, and the standard of living grew even more. After 1999, Russia ran budget surpluses, and the public debt dwindled.

But this happy state of affairs was not to last. In 2008, the global financial crisis hit Russia hard, and since then Russia's economy has barely grown—its average growth since 2009 has been just 1 percent. Putin's eighteen years of rule comprise nine years of high growth and nine years of near stagnation. By the end of 2017, Putin had ruled Russia for as long as Leonid Brezhnev led the Soviet Union, and although a sense of political and economic stability prevails, so does stagnation.

Why did the Russian economy switch from seemingly sustained high growth to lasting stagnation? The standard answer is oil. Russia is a petrostate. When oil prices were high, from 2011 to 2013, oil and gas accounted for roughly two-thirds of Russia's exports, half of its state revenues, and one-fifth of its GDP. But oil can be managed in many ways, by the state or by competing private entrepreneurs, and part of the answer lies in the way Putin has managed Russia's vast oil and gas revenues.[1]

At the World Economic Forum in Davos in January 2000, the US journalist Trudy Rubin famously posed the question to a panel of prominent Russians, "Who is Mr. Putin?" Wisely, nobody answered. The interpretation of Putin's objectives remain disputed, but increasingly less so. Everyone has noticed his great respect for the old Soviet security service, the KGB. Early on, many saw him as a fiscal conservative and a free marketer. While he has stayed fiscally conservative, he has become an advocate of state capitalism. A rising view is that he is a kleptocrat. Each of these observations provides part of the explanation for why Russia's economy went from high growth to stagnation.[2]

My argument in this book is that Putin has usurped Russia's large energy rents to build his crony capitalism. Energy rents have made that possible, but the choice has been his. Putinism is authoritarian kleptocracy, and his economic policy, or Putinomics, as historian Chris Miller has named it, is a combination of macroeconomic stability with kleptocracy.[3]

I have followed the Russian economy closely ever since I arrived in Moscow in 1984 for three years' service as a Swedish diplomat. Having lived with perestroika, I published the book *Gorbachev's Struggle for Economic Reform* in the fall of 1989. My assessment at the time was that the most likely scenario for Russia's future was "radicalized economic reform with far-reaching democratization. As Soviet reformist economists are waking up from their imposed lethargy, they are becoming ever more radical, because they realize that the state of the economy was worse than they had imagined and that half-measures do not offer any results."[4]

Following this experience, from November 1991 until my resignation in January 1994, I had the honor to work as an economic adviser to the reform government effectively led by Yegor Gaidar, spending a large part of my time in Moscow. Immediately afterward I wrote the book *How Russia Became a Market Economy* (1995), making the point that a market economy had been born.

As reforms slowed, the drama dissipated. I waited to write my third book about the Russian economy until 2007, when my key observation could once again be found in the title: *Russia's Capitalist Revolution: Why Market Reform Succeeded and Democracy Failed.* The oil boom was about to reach its peak. The regime of Vladimir Putin had ended democracy, but the market economy was still holding sway, even if the state sector was expanding.

Today, Russia has passed another milestone. On March 18, 2018, Putin was reelected to the presidency with 77 percent of the vote in an authoritarian procedure in which no serious opponent was permitted to stand for election. President Putin has now started his formal fourth—and actual fifth—term in office. As in the mid-1980s, the Russian economy is again caught in stagnation, and there is little hope for improvement so long as the current regime lasts. The Russian political and economic systems are too petrified to meet the future successfully. This appears a propitious time to take the measure of the Russian economy.

My aim in this book is to analyze how the Russian economic system has developed under Putin's leadership, how it actually works, and how it may evolve in the future. I do not to try to understand Vladimir Putin's psychology but instead record in these pages what he has actually done. Although great and radical reforms of the 1990s have not continued, Russia's system has been transformed. The changes have been gradual but carried out with great determination, as has been characteristic of Putin's policy making. They have not been well understood because Putin has skillfully operated by stealth.

Far too often, people claim, "Russia has always been like that," but during the past three decades the changes in Russia have been monumental. In 1984, Moscow was a gray and dark place. The broad consensus was that the Soviet Union, though stagnant, was perfectly stable and could not possibly change in the foreseeable future. I never believed that. The backwardness and ossification of the Soviet system were all too evident. Within months Mikhail Gorbachev became secretary general of the Communist Party of the Soviet Union (CPSU), and six years later the Communist Party and the Soviet Union were history.

Just before Gorbachev's elevation to power, two articles summed up the situation with great foresight. The outstanding strategic thinker Zbigniew Brzezinski noted that the Soviet Union was a Third World country with nuclear arms. The great historian of Russia Richard Pipes emphasized the petrification of the communist system and concluded that the Soviet Union was in a crisis "camouflaged by massive disinformation and saber-rattling, [and that it] fits very well the concept of a 'revolutionary situation' as defined by Lenin," when the ruling elite could no longer rule and the population would no longer follow.[5]

Today, Russia's physical appearance is better than ever. It is modern, colorful, and clean, thanks to a decade of high economic growth. But the mood in Moscow is remarkably reminiscent of 1984. Russia has gone through a systemic and political reversal. The British journalist Ben Judah has eloquently summarized the state of affairs: "After Yeltsin a regime was built in Russia that was both highly sophisticated and deeply backward at the same time. . . . The Kremlin tried to build institutions that were outdated and inefficient even when they were young— a vertical of power restoring the Soviet chain of command."[6]

Yet Russia's reversal is not to the Soviet Union but to the bygone era of the tsars. After two years of economic contraction in 2015–2016, a new stability has emerged. The expected economic growth is minimal, but the fear of economic destabilization has eased. Just as in the time of Brezhnev, secretary general of the CPSU from 1964 to 1982, domestic politics have evaporated as Russia has become increasingly authoritarian. The general expectation is that Putin will remain president forever and that little will change. I beg to differ, but change requires a new regime.

The aims of this book are manifold. My focus is on the Russian economic system rather than the people, even if we cannot ignore them. What kind of a beast has the Russian economy become? How does it really work? What are its strengths and weaknesses? How much growth can it produce? Is it sustainable? Can it reform? A second group of questions pertains to the likely choices of the Russian leaders. How will they act? Will they opt for reform, austerity, or international action? A third cluster of issues concerns how Russia can change its economic policy. Last, how can and should the outside world deal with Russia?

Vladimir Putin has designed the current Russian system with great skill. As the dominant decision-maker, he has built a system to his liking: an authoritarian kleptocracy. The outstanding Russia scholar Karen Dawisha summarized its essence in the title of her book *Putin's Kleptocracy*. In this compelling work, Dawisha offers ample evidence that the current ruling Putin circle can be best understood as an organized crime gang. She concludes "that the group now in power . . . [is] committed to a life of looting without parallel. This kleptocracy is abhorrent."[7]

Russia's development under Putin was not ordained by history, culture, or circumstance—it is Putin's deliberate choice. He has built an elaborate and consistent political and economic system. His great sophistication in implementing these policies has no positive meaning. Putin outlined many of its features in his 2000 book of interviews, *First Person*. He has constructed a system that offers him full control and great security.

Some analysts, such as the Russian journalist Mikhail Zygar, have argued the opposite view, that "Putin, as we imagine him, does not actually exist. It was not Putin who brought Russia to its current state." Zygar insists that Putin did not wish, for example, to shut down Russia's independent television channels, concluding that "today's image of Putin as a formidable Russian tsar was constructed by his entourage, Western partners, and journalists, often without his say." But to take over the top television channels was clearly a major aim of Putin's policy from the outset. Moreover, Putin has selected all his close collaborators himself and has done so with great care, emphasizing personal trust. There can be no doubt that Putin knows what he has been doing and has done so intentionally. The only question is how detailed his design is. In this book I will try to clarify to what extent Putin has had clear ideas from the outset and how they have evolved.[8]

Putin has built his regime on men loyal to him. He has picked these men along his career path starting as a teenager in Leningrad, through university, to the KGB in Leningrad and Dresden, among business friends, and to the mayor's office in St. Petersburg. After moving to Moscow in 1996, he became more reserved with acquaintances and embraced new followers more cautiously. One can divide the men loyal to Putin into three categories: KGB officers, technocrats, and cronies. Moreover, Putin clearly requires three essential personality traits: trust, obedience, and secrecy. Merit, effectiveness, and ideological bent are all subordinate characteristics.

Putin's system consists of four circles. His friends from the St. Petersburg KGB form the first circle. They have successfully seized control of the Federal Security Service (FSB), other security agencies, the state apparatus, and the judiciary. Putin has built his "vertical of power" and "dictatorship of law" while eliminating all checks and balances except rivalry among the security services.

The second circle comprises the state enterprises, which are run by Putin's close associates, who are absolutely loyal to their boss. The chief executives control vast resources, and they possess multiple ways of transferring assets to private beneficiaries.

Putin's cronies, private businessmen who are his longtime friends from St. Petersburg, form the third circle. All have become billionaires through preferential deals with the Russian government, mainly by receiving large no-bid procurement orders from Gazprom and by buying Gazprom assets cheaply. This system, set up in 2004–2006, generates large capital outflows to their personal benefit.

The fourth circle is less noticed. It consists of the Western offshore havens, mainly in the United States and the United Kingdom, where companies with anonymous owners are allowed to thrive. Strangely, this circle is the least known and discussed because of the great secrecy that prevails in the Anglo-American offshore.

These four circles compose the Putin system of authoritarian kleptocracy, one that is strikingly similar to Russian tsarism before Tsar Alexander II's reforms of the 1860s. Putin is often called the new tsar, and for good reason. Legally, his power is unlimited. With his loyal aides he controls the state apparatus, security services, judiciary, and state enterprises. Because of supreme state powers and a far-reaching deinstitutionalization, Putin's Russia lacks any real property rights. Rather than developing a meritocracy, Putin has built a new aristocracy. The sons of his close friends have become vice presidents of state companies in their twenties.[9]

How strongly ideology motivates the Putin regime is up for debate. A certain nationalism and orthodoxy are present, and definitely Russian traditionalism. The dominant ideology is statism, but the true aims of this regime are personal enrichment and power. In chapter 6 I analyze what we know about Putin's personal wealth and propose a probable range of $100–$160 billion, making him the richest man in the world, but this assessment is based on several assumptions that may be questioned. With such a focus on personal enrichment, it would be surprising if Putin could attain many other objectives.[10]

The Kremlin attitude to the Russian revolution is indicative of the current official mood. Usually Russia celebrates major anniversaries more than other nations, but the centenary of the Russian revolution in 1917 was almost ignored. This deeply conservative authoritarian regime favors stability and abhors revolutions. The February revolution was liberal and led to chaos, while the October revolution was communist. The current conservative regime rejects both liberalism and socialism and all the more so revolution and opposition to the rulers. Instead, the Kremlin decided to celebrate the seventy-second anniversary of the victory in the Great Patriotic War all the more. As Tony Barber of the *Financial Times* put it: "For Mr Putin, 1917 stands out as a time of tremendous political and social disorder. The state was weak and unable to exert control. In Mr Putin's eyes, this makes 1917 an inappropriate year to celebrate." Indeed, it sounds like the "damned nineties."[11]

This book focuses on the functioning of the Putin regime's economic system and economic policy. Rather than offering a chronological narrative, it is thematic, concentrating on the main systemic features.

Chapter 1 offers the reader a brief picture of the richness of Russia's historical inheritance and thought and a periodization of the Putin reign. Even if Putin's reversal to authoritarianism and statism can be seen as a natural postrevolutionary and postimperial development, the changes between his different terms have been substantial. They were based on his choices and were by no means inevitable.

How Putin consolidated political power and seized control over the state apparatus from 2000 to 2003 is the subject of chapter 2. Putin possessed a base in the KGB and relied on trusted associates with whom he had long worked. On becoming president, he started to build his "vertical of power," restoring federal control over Russia's various regions. His greatest challenge came not from Russia but from attempts at democratization in Ukraine. In the judicial system, Putin established his "dictatorship of law," which implied Kremlin control over the courts. Putin developed a plethora of competing law enforcement agencies that obtained far-reaching mandates. Today Russia's supreme body is the Security Council.

Chapter 3 records Russia's conservative macroeconomic policies. The financial crash of 1998 was a major shock to the country's policy makers, including Putin. Their lesson was that macroeconomic stability is a sine qua non for political and economic stability, and these policies prevail today.

The major endeavor of Putin's second term was to build state capitalism, the topic of chapter 4. The turning point was the regime's confiscation of the oil company Yukos in 2004–2005, which initiated a steady expansion and consolidation of the big state enterprises. Close associates of Putin run the biggest state companies, and they are responsible only to him. Four of these big state enterprises are showcased: Gazprom, Rosneft, Vnesheconombank, and Rostec.

The cronies and their enterprises form a more exotic part of Putin's system. A small group of private businessmen who are old personal friends of Putin from St. Petersburg have flourished immensely under his reign, thanks to preferential deals with the government and with state enterprises, and their sons have been given privileged starts in life through early promotions. Putin's four most important cronies and their businesses—the pinnacle of Russia's new crony capitalism—are analyzed in chapter 5.

In chapter 6, I report on and assess information of the wealth of Putin's friends as well as of Putin himself. This chapter illuminates the role of the fourth circle, the Anglo-American offshore, where most of this great wealth is stored. It also presents a number of Putin's lesser-known friends, who might hold wealth for him.

Chapter 7 scrutinizes how Russia's foreign economic policy has changed. Until 2009, Russia embraced globalization, manifested in its ambition to join the World Trade Organization. Then, however, it turned around, preferring limited regional economic cooperation within the Eurasian Economic Union, the five member states of which are Russia, Kazakhstan, Belarus, Armenia, and Kyrgyzstan. Russia's aggression against Ukraine since 2014 has provoked significant Western sanctions on Russia, which have reinforced its protectionist tendencies.

The Putin period has been characterized by a continuous ideological strife over economic policy between liberals and statists, described in chapter 8. Former finance minister Alexei Kudrin stands out as the leader of the market economic wing, while Putin's adviser Sergei Glaziev is the most prominent statist. In practice, the systemic liberals have won on macroeconomic policy, while the statists have been victorious in all other fields. The rising opposition leader Alexei Navalny is instead focusing on corruption, as a new nonideological paradigm has evolved, reform versus corruption.

Chapter 9 concludes with an assessment of what the Russian economy has become and offers a policy outlook. The Putin regime is an extreme form of plutocracy that requires authoritarianism to persist. Because of its poor institutions Russia is stuck in a middle-income trap. Its assets are substantial but unbalanced, with far more military than economic power. The regime can no longer base its legitimacy on economic growth so it has switched to small victorious wars. The West needs to face up to Russia's new asymmetric warfare. It should respond with greater demand for transparency. The last section suggests what reforms Russia should prioritize the next time it becomes serious about reforms.

Fortunately, many sources of high quality are available for a study of this nature. The literature on Russia in the 1990s is substantial, though surprisingly little attention has been devoted to the Russian economy from 2000.[12]

The amplest source is actually President Vladimir Putin himself. In early 2000, he published a revealing book of interviews, *First Person*, which appears his most honest account of his actual views. For all his years as president, Putin offers extensive documentation on his website, www.kremlin.ru, which has a good search engine. Few political leaders have published so much about themselves and provided it in such an accessible form. All Putin's big speeches and many meetings are documented there. Twice a year, Putin makes three-to-four-hour-long television appearances: one international press conference and one call-in program. On these occasions, he comments on many controversial issues, which is an effective technique to minimize the publicity about them, but Putin is on the record on all these topics. This book contains numerous quotations by Putin. Most are taken from his website. The references are made to the English version, though I have sometimes improved the translations from the Russian version, and some materials are available only in Russian.

A few people have done eminent research on Putin and his economic activities in the 1990s. Yuri Felshtinsky and the late Vladimir Pribylovsky have documented Putin's economic activities in St. Petersburg in great detail. In parallel, my late friend Boris Nemtsov and Vladimir Milov studied how Putin's friends tapped Gazprom for money and who obtained those funds. Nemtsov was murdered outside the Kremlin's wall on February 27, 2015. The late Russia scholar Karen Dawisha elaborated further on this analysis in her pathbreaking book *Putin's Kleptocracy*. Alexei Navalny and his Fund for the Fight against Corruption have pursued outstanding studies of top-level Russian corruption.[13]

The vast journalistic Organized Crime and Corruption Reporting Project has taken investigative financial journalism to a new height. It got plenty of air under its wings in April 2016 with the leak of the Panama Papers, from the Panamanian law firm Mossack Fonseca; suddenly, 11.5 million financial documents, containing substantial revelations about Russian offshore funds. In Russia, the fiercely independent *Novaya Gazeta*, whose investigative team is headed by Roman Anin, has taken the lead, while Luke Harding at the *Guardian* has carried out heroic efforts.

Edward Lucas of the *Economist* has exposed Putin's friend Gennady Timchenko and his business practices. A Reuters investigative team led by Stephen Grey has worked wonders. Ben Judah has unmasked the kleptocracy in Britain. Other excellent sources are *Novoe Vremya* and its editor Evgeniya Albats. The business newspapers *Kommersant*, *Vedomosti*, *Forbes*, and Russian Business Consulting publish plenty of interesting economic news. Of course, a researcher needs to stick to known sources because the web is full of strange disinformation.

In the early 2000s, Paul Klebnikov of *Forbes*, an acquaintance of mine, started assessing the wealth of Russian tycoons. He did so until he was murdered in 2004. Fortunately, Russian *Forbes* has continued his valuable work, giving us some relevant assessments of the wealth of important Russians.

Ordinary statistics are pretty straightforward. My preferred source is the International Monetary Fund's World Economic Outlook database. The main Russian statistical sources remain good, notably the Central Bank of Russia and the Ministry of Finance, but also Rosstat (the Russian Federal State Statistics Service). The Bank of Finland Institute for Economies in Transition offers an excellent service by elaborating and compiling these key statistics. In most cases, I have recalculated ruble sums into dollar sums at the exchange rate of the given date. Opinion polls are often of dubious character, and so I use only one source, the independent Levada Center, where I know the main people and trust their integrity.

The Origins of Putin's Economic Model

T he continuity in Russia's economic policy since 2000 is easily exaggerated because Vladimir Putin has ruled all along and he has emphasized stability, but the Russian economy has gone through major structural changes under his rule. Each of Putin's terms represents a distinct economic policy. Since 1999 macroeconomic policy has been conservative, aiming at stability, whereas the economic system has deteriorated from a reasonably competitive market economy to crony capitalism, which has resulted in nine years of high growth being followed by nine years of near stagnation.

A common view is that Putin's consolidation of authoritarian power was the only natural outcome of his leadership, but this is hardly true. Russia has many different traditions. The liberal Moscow journalist Arkady Ostrovsky has emphasized the intellectual metamorphosis back and forth in the past thirty years in Russia. Few countries have seen such great intellectual and real changes. Vladimir Mau, who was an influential adviser to Russia's great reformer Yegor Gaidar, and his coauthor Irina Starodubrovskaya view the Russian drama as a revolutionary process, anticipating reaction. The prominent political scientist Michael McFaul's thoughts run on the same line: Russia had gone through a revolution but it had not been completed; the reversal to authoritarian political power was neither surprising nor inevitable.[1]

Russia has a rich historical inheritance, and interpretations of that history vary greatly. Some scholars emphasize how peculiar Russia is, whereas others see the country as basically European. Conversely, in the nineteenth century, Russian intellectuals were divided between Slavophiles and Westernizers.

The preeminent historian of Russia, the late Harvard professor Richard Pipes, has pursued one dominant line in his historiography: the patrimonial state in which the tsar owns both the land and its inhabitants. In his classic work *Russia under the Old Regime*, Pipes emphasizes as major features of this model the weakness of all social groups, the absence of property rights, and the prevalence of a strong secret police. More recently he summarized: "The dominant strain in Russian political thought throughout history has been a conservatism that insisted on strong, centralized authority, unrestrained either by law or [by] parliament."[2]

This system reached its perfection under Tsar Nicholas I (1825–1855). In 1833, his minister of education, Count Sergei Uvarov, formulated the famous conservative triad: "Orthodoxy, Autocracy, Nationality." In 2006, Minister of Defense Sergei Ivanov alluded to this triad, claiming that "the new triad of Russian national values is sovereign democracy, strong economy, and military power." Today, nobody talks about "sovereign democracy," and the economy is weak. The Russian Orthodox Church is dominated by the state and not allowed to assume a life of its own. What remains of the old triad is autocracy and a strong secret police. Russia's nationalism, like most European nationalisms, is divided between two major streams. One is exclusive, favoring ethnic or linguistic Russians over Central Asians and Caucasians. The other is Eurasianist or imperialist, maximizing the size of the Russian Empire. Putin toys with both without committing himself to either.[3]

Russia has also a strong liberal tradition. The late Berkeley professor Martin Malia produced the most comprehensive argument, in his book *Russia under Western Eyes,* that Russia was a part of Europe's politics and culture, fully involved with the Enlightenment from 1700 until World War I. The Russian aristocracy consisted largely of Poles and Germans and spoke French. The Russian exile Alexander Herzen was one of the great mid-nineteenth-century liberal thinkers. And the liberal tsar

Alexander II (1855–1881) carried out impressive reforms and liberated the serfs two years before Abraham Lincoln ended slavery in the United States.[4]

During the two last decades before World War I, capitalism flourished in Russia, delivering high growth. The war devastated not only the Russian Empire but also the German and Austro-Hungarian Empires, all facing communist revolutions. Until 1917, Russia's exceptionalism from continental Europe must not be exaggerated.[5]

The Russian revolution, the civil war, and communism brought about terrible destruction of people and institutions. At the end of the Soviet Union, Russians saw the year 1913 as the ideal. The late comedian Arkady Raikin quipped: "If it is better than in 1913 than it is already good." Accordingly, one of the first private restaurants to open in Leningrad was named "1913." The outstanding director Alexander Sokurov made his monumental film *The Russian Ark* about the last great Tsar's Ball in the Winter Palace in 1913. Television advertisements for banks in the early 1990s displayed the buildings as they looked just before World War I to engender trust. The leading new business newspaper *Kommersant* presented itself as a continuation of a prerevolutionary newspaper that had "temporarily" ceased publication in 1917 but reemerged in 1989. Russians saw themselves as natural risk takers. An old Russian saying was revived: "Who does not take risks, does not drink champagne."[6]

The foremost student of the communist economic system, Hungarian professor János Kornai, has eminently summarized its key economic features. This was the most thoroughly politicized system the world had seen, with undivided centralized political power of the ruling Communist Party and the suppression of all opposing forces. All means of production were nationalized. This near-complete nationalization was a poison pill supposed to render impossible the restoration of capitalism. The market was replaced with centralized bureaucratic allocation carried out by the State Planning Committee (Gosplan), which focused on physical output. Prices were regulated below a market clearing level, guaranteeing permanent shortages. No real money existed, and currency played no active role, being reduced to a unit of account. The ideal was autarky, insulating the domestic economy, but because foreign trade was necessary, the state monopolized foreign trade.[7]

The socialist economy aimed at building a strong military industry rather than boosting living standards. The Soviet government held back both wages and private consumption to the benefit of investment and military expenditures. Soviet leaders prided themselves on full employment, which was facilitated by low regulated wages and high investment.

The main drawback of the communist economy was a permanent shortage of goods and services. Shoddy work, poor quality, low efficiency, and demoralization became natural consequences and the system's hallmarks. Real socialism was popularly summarized in the phrase, "They pretend to pay us, and we pretend to work." The most positive aspects of communism were full employment and that it provided good education, general literacy, good mathematics, and plenty of engineering; for ideological reasons, the social sciences, law, and languages were intentionally neglected, leading to extraordinary parochialism. Health care was miserable.

It is difficult to countenance today that once upon a time people actually believed that communism would deliver equality and welfare. When neither welfare nor freedom materialized, Marxism-Leninism perished, but slowly. Repression eased after the death of Joseph Stalin in 1953, and from the 1960s economic growth started to decline. Eastern Europe saw a series of popular uprisings against communist rule: in East Berlin in 1953, in Poland and Hungary in 1956, in Czechoslovakia in 1968, and in Poland in 1980–1981. The Soviet squashing of the Prague Spring of 1968 put an end to the belief that communism could be reformed. The formation of the anticommunist trade union Solidarity in 1980, and its crushing by the Polish military in December 1981, reconfirmed that Soviet communism was no viable ideology.[8]

After the ideology had died, the Soviet regime preached the benefits of stability, just as Putin does today. The long reign of Leonid Brezhnev, secretary general of CPSU from 1964 to 1982, became later known as the period of stagnation (*zastoi*). The overcentralized economic and political institutions could not handle the challenges of information technology. Price distortions and industrial structure grew worse over time, leading to greater shortages and poorer quality with minimal technological progress. Yet thanks to enormous new oil and gas fields in Western Siberia and a global oil price boom from 1973, the Soviet Union sailed through the 1970s without reforms.

The demise of communism was as protracted as its collapse was sudden. As Ernest Hemingway put it in his novel *The Sun Also Rises*, "How did you go bankrupt? Two ways. Gradually, then suddenly." During the second half of the 1980s, the Soviet Union experienced a perfect storm. All but the oil price decline was homemade.[9]

From 1981, the price of oil started falling, and in 1987–1988 Soviet oil production peaked out. The declining oil revenues posed a major challenge to the Soviet economic system. Russian reform leader Yegor Gaidar argued that the oil boom had made the Soviet leadership so arrogant and ignorant that the slumping oil price unleashed the collapse of the USSR. Observing the oil boom in the 2000s, Gaidar expected the Putin regime to go through a similar development.[10]

By the mid-1980s, the collapse of communism was overdetermined and long overdue, but Mikhail Gorbachev unleashed it by trying to reform the system. In March 1985, he became secretary general of the gerontocratic CPSU. His starting point was: "We cannot go on living like this any longer." His three early slogans were *glasnost'* (more openness), *perestroika* (economic reform), and new thinking (in foreign policy). In January 1987, he added the revolutionary term *democratization*. But as the Polish philosopher Leszek Kolakowski told a seminar I attended at the University of Oxford: "Reformed communism is like a baked snowball." The more Gorbachev reformed the system, the more inconsistent it became, and the worse the economic outcome.[11]

Today it is difficult to countenance that in the late 1980s the Soviet leaders still harbored illusions about keeping up with the United States in an arms race. Until 1988, the USSR steadily increased its defense expenditures, which probably reached one-quarter of GDP, while the United States spent only 6 percent of its GDP on defense. President Ronald Reagan's Strategic Defense Initiative, popularly dubbed Star Wars, might not have been realistic, but it scared the Soviets, exposing their technological and economic weakness.[12]

Initially, Gorbachev justified his perestroika with the arms race: "Only an intensive, highly developed economy can safeguard a reinforcement of [our] country's position on the international stage and allow it to enter the next millennium with dignity as a great and flourishing power." But the Soviet economy was unable to stand up to this challenge, lacking both economic and technological strength. The information revolution was in its infancy, and the Soviet system could hardly have survived the Internet. Its secret police demanded complete public control and secrecy, even prohibiting photocopying. Nor could the Soviet hierarchical command structure handle small enterprises, entrepreneurship, or creative destruction.[13]

The outer Soviet empire went first. Gorbachev did not seem interested in maintaining it. He disliked the stultified dictatorships in Eastern Europe that the Soviet Union subsidized. At the Soviet-led invasion of Czechoslovakia in 1968, the Soviet Union had initiated the "Brezhnev doctrine," claiming its right to intervene to "defend socialism" in any part of the socialist commonwealth. In December 1988, Gorbachev declared the contrary at the United Nations: "For us the necessity of the principle of freedom of choice is clear. Denying that right of peoples, no matter what the pretext for doing so, no matter what words are used to conceal it, means infringing even that unstable balance that it has been possible to achieve. Freedom of choice is a universal principle and there should be no exceptions."[14]

This speech ended the Brezhnev doctrine, and one year later all the communist regimes in Eastern Europe (East Germany, Poland, Czechoslovakia, Hungary, Bulgaria, and Romania) were gone. In 2000, Vladimir Putin expressed his regrets: "We would have avoided a lot of problems if the Soviets had not made such a hasty exit from Eastern Europe."[15]

Gorbachev's greatest political weakness was that unlike previous Soviet leaders he had little understanding of nationalism. In his book *Perestroika*, Gorbachev stated: "If the nationality question had not been solved in principle, the Soviet Union would never have had the social, cultural, economic and defense potential it has now. Our state would not have survived if the republics had not formed a community based on brotherhood and cooperation, respect and mutual assistance."

Gorbachev allowed forbidden questions about national repression to be raised, but he had no good answers. In 1990 and 1991, a "war of laws" erupted between the Soviet Union and the republics, and the republican laws were perceived as more legitimate than the union laws, because key republics were more democratic. Seven out of fifteen Soviet republics wanted to leave: the three Baltic republics, the three Caucasian ones, and Moldova. If Ukraine were to join, they would form a majority.[16]

Gorbachev's fatal mistake was never to contest a democratic vote, depriving himself and the Soviet presidency of democratic legitimacy. Boris Yeltsin understood this, and as an outstanding political campaigner he fought for direct democratic elections of a Russian president. On June 12, 1991, he won that contest as an outsider with 57 percent of the votes against a former communist, Prime Minister Nikolai Ryzhkov.

In 1991, the Soviet Union faced a horrendous economic and financial crisis with all conceivable causes: large budget deficits, uncontrolled wage hikes, shortages, inflation, large foreign debt, ballooning public expenditures, collapsing public revenues and uncontrolled credit issue. From 1990, the republican parliaments legislated huge, populist social expenditures but refused to send their tax revenues to Moscow, starving the Soviet treasury. Meanwhile the USSR lost control over nominal wage increases. The Soviet budget deficit ballooned to probably 34 percent of GDP by the end of 1991, guaranteeing hyperinflation. The economy was in free fall. At the end of 1991, the Soviet international reserves were depleted, and GDP fell by about 10 percent in 1991. Presumably, these catastrophic events taught Putin the importance of macroeconomic stability.[17]

The end of an empire is usually accompanied with major bloodshed, but in this regard the collapse of the Soviet Union shines. World War I finished off the Austro-Hungarian, German, Russian, and Ottoman Empires. France pursued bloody colonial wars in Vietnam and Algeria. As the British departed from India, more than one million died in bloodletting when Pakistan and India partitioned. The breakup of Yugoslavia in the 1990s led to long wars, costing some two hundred thousand lives. By comparison, the end of the Soviet Empire was remarkably peaceful.[18]

In 1991, Russia was in a revolutionary situation. Russian scholar Leon Aron observed: "The political 'centre' . . . disappeared. This was a revolution, and in revolutions there is no centre." The old institutions no longer functioned, and people no longer wanted to be ruled by their old rulers, who often abandoned their offices. The economic and financial crisis was profound with massive shortages, triple-digit inflation, plummeting output, and a large public debt. Strangely, the situation was perfectly peaceful. At this time, I spent much of my time in Moscow, which was kinder than ever before.[19]

Putin observed the Soviet collapse from Dresden with dread: "'Moscow is silent'—I got the feeling then that the country no longer existed. That it had disappeared. It was clear that the Union was ailing. And it had a terminal disease without cure—a paralysis of power."[20]

While petrified, the old communist institutions had not disappeared. They were dormant and would come back with a vengeance. Russia had a constitution from 1978 that had only been amended. It had an unwieldy unrepresentative parliament elected in semidemocratic elections in March 1990. President Yeltsin, who had just been elected in fully democratic elections, was the only truly legitimate institution.

Boris Yeltsin's two presidential terms, 1991–1999, left a complex legacy that will likely be subject to multiple reevaluations. Russia was never as free, open, and colorful as in the 1990s. Everything was possible, but it was also a time of economic misery. The introductory words of Charles Dickens's classic novel *A Tale of Two Cities* fit this time perfectly: "It was the best of times, it was the worst of times, it was the age of wisdom, it was the age of foolishness, it was the epoch of belief, it was the epoch of incredulity, it was the season of Light, it was the season of Darkness, it was the spring of hope, it was the winter of despair."[21]

For Russian liberals, it was the best of times. Russia enjoyed more freedom than ever. For a newspaper reader, Moscow was a Mecca, with a score of daily newspapers representing all conceivable political views. A handful of outstanding television channels, spearheaded by Vladimir Gusinsky's NTV, quickly raised the level of television to a global top level.

For Russian statists and imperialists, it was the worst of times. In Putin's Russia, the 1990s are called "the damned nineties." Opinion polls show that Russians are confused. In 2016, 55 percent of the Russians regretted the collapse of the Soviet Union in 1991, but 50 percent acknowledged its inevitability. This tension between regret and sense of inevitability also reflects the Russian attitude to the 1990s. This decade left many legacies, both good and bad.[22]

After the three-day failed coup of August 1991, Russian president Boris Yeltsin was the unquestioned leader, and he was the most impressive man I ever saw. When he entered a room, he filled it with his large, warm, and loud personality. As a truly great leader, he was at his best in extreme crisis. When the situation was impossible, he stood up and did what he had to do, but most of the time he did far too little. Yeltsin focused strategically on three tasks: securing his power, peacefully dissolving the Soviet Union, and resolving the rampant economic crisis.[23]

Yeltsin prohibited the antidemocratic CPSU and transferred its assets to the state, but he did not opt for major political reform, such as an adoption of a new constitution or the dissolution of the old parliament. He did not abolish the repressive KGB, though he split it into five agencies, reducing its staff by about half. It went through name changes, and since 1995 the bulk of it has been the FSB.[24]

As a history buff, Yeltsin was acutely aware of the chaos that had arisen after the Russian revolution in February 1917, when the provisional government had dissolved the tsarist imperial service. Therefore, he did not want to carry out any major reform of the state service. He argued: "It would have been disastrous to destroy the government administration of such an enormous state. Where it was possible to put in experienced 'old' staff, we did. And sometimes we made mistakes."[25]

The most daring step Yeltsin took was to abolish the Soviet Union. He understood that it was unsustainable. In his memoirs, he wrote: "I was convinced that Russia needed to rid itself of its imperial mission." But he had to do so in a way that was politically acceptable to Russians. On December 1, 1991, such an opportunity arrived. In a Ukrainian referendum 90 percent of its inhabitants voted for independence. Yeltsin acted instantly. Together with Ukraine's newly elected president, Leonid Kravchuk, and the reformist speaker of the Belarusian parliament, Stanislav Shushkevich, he met secretly one week later at a desolate Belarusian hunting lodge (Beloveshskaya Pushcha).[26]

These three heads of the states that had created the Soviet Union dissolved it. As a replacement, they set up the loose Commonwealth of Independent States (CIS), inspired by the British Commonwealth. Yeltsin made no claims on territories of other former Soviet republics. All borders were to remain as they were, and all union property would belong to the republic where it was located. The three Baltic countries, Estonia, Latvia, and Lithuania, had departed after the aborted Moscow coup in August 1991 and stayed aloof, insisting that they had never belonged to the Soviet Union.

In the fall of 1991, the overriding concern was the rampant economic crisis. Soviet shops were empty, and even so Russia had triple-digit inflation. It needed to stop inflation and build a market economy. In November 1991, Yeltsin appointed a new government with Russia's best and brightest young economists, led by Deputy Prime Minister Yegor Gaidar and Minister of Privatization Anatoly Chubais, who were the ideological leaders of the market economic reforms. In his great reform speech to the Russian parliament on October 28, 1991, Yeltsin clarified that the two central economic tasks were to establish economic freedom and financial stabilization: "We have a unique opportunity to stabilize the economy within several months and start the process of recovery. We have defended political freedom. Now we have to give the people economic [freedom], remove all barriers to the freedom of enterprises and entrepreneurship, offer the people possibilities to work and receive as much as they earn, after having relieved them of bureaucratic pressures."[27]

The most important reform was the deregulation of prices in January 1992. Gaidar explained why it was necessary: "There *were* no reserves to ease the hardships that would be caused by setting the economic mechanism in motion. Putting off liberalization of the economy until slow structural reforms could be enacted was impossible. Two or three more months of such passivity and we would have economic and political catastrophe, total collapse, and a civil war." Imports, too, were liberalized immediately, which was popular as all kinds of goods quickly became available in the shops.[28]

The other major reform was privatization. From 1988, state enterprise managers had gradually been taking ownership of the enterprises they were supposed to manage. Yeltsin concluded: "For impermissibly long, we have discussed whether private property is necessary. In the meantime, the party-state elite has actively engaged in their personal privatization. The scale, the enterprises, and the hypocrisy are staggering. The privatization in Russia has gone on, but spontaneously, and often on a criminal basis. Today it is necessary to grasp the initiative, and we are intent on doing so."[29]

In August 1992, Yeltsin announced a program for voucher privatization that was quickly implemented. Until the summer of 1994, 16,500 enterprises with more than 1,000 workers were privatized. A critical mass of private enterprise had been built. In 1995, Russia claimed 920,000 private enterprises. This was the biggest privatization the world ever saw.[30]

But many things did not work out, because the liberal forces lacked the necessary political strength. As early as in November 1991, the not very reformist parliament appointed a chairman of the Central Bank of Russia, Georgy Matiukhin, who favored large monetary emissions. Nor could the reformers break up the ruble zone or liberalize energy prices and energy exports. As a consequence, rent seeking became the name of the game. In 1991, a skillful operator could buy oil in Russia at an official price of one dollar per ton and sell it abroad at one hundred dollars per ton. The early big fortunes were being made at the expense of the state.

The budget deficit lingered at 8 percent to 9 percent of GDP from 1993 to 1998. Only the financial crash of August 1998 convinced the Russian polity of the need for fiscal restraint. In this way the financial stabilization failed. Russia suffered inflation of 2,500 percent in 1992. Russia's GDP plummeted precipitously until 1998, officially by about half, but in fact perhaps by half as much, but we shall never learn the truth because of many statistical complications. Registered income inequality rose sharply from 1989 to 1994 from a low European level almost to the US level.[31]

Whatever Yeltsin's true intentions, he had no good grasp on political institutions, though he persistently defended the freedom of the media. Initially, he tried to rule by decree, which resulted in haphazard and contradictory rulings with a brief shelf life. After the parliament had declared war on him, Yeltsin called for a referendum on its dissolution on April 25, 1993. He won it hands down, but he failed to exploit this opportunity. Waiting for too long, in September 1993 he was compelled to dissolve by decree the predemocratic parliament, which responded by instigating a military revolt that Yeltsin quashed with great bloodshed on October 3–4. Yeltsin promoted a new constitution with strong presidential powers that was adopted in a December 1993 referendum, but he and the reformers failed to gain a majority in the new State Duma in the 1990s.[32]

The darkest stain on Yeltsin's rule was the war in Chechnya that the Kremlin's "party of war" started in December 1994. It was both bloody and unsuccessful, ending in the summer of 1996 with Chechnya becoming an autonomous but lawless zone.[33]

To ordinary Russians, the worst transition shock was the explosion of violent crime starting in 1989, as the old order broke down. Protection rackets asked budding entrepreneurs to pay for protection, or *krysha* ("roof"), in return for a share of their turnover. The eminent St. Petersburg political scientist Vadim Volkov noticed: "Since the actions of the state bureaucracy and of law enforcement remain arbitrary and the services provided by the state tend to have higher costs, private enforcers (read: the mafia) outcompete the state and firmly establish themselves in its stead." St. Petersburg was named Russia's crime capital and was compared with Al Capone's Chicago during Prohibition.[34]

By 1994, the great mob war started to fade. New big businessmen, commonly called oligarchs, had set up their own security services, becoming "powerful enough to ignore the old gangsters." The oligarchs were everything the Soviet Union was not, fast and innovative, unconventional and conspicuous. Most of all, they were opportunists prepared to take any risk. They were self-made men, most of them young, bright, and educated in the best Soviet engineering schools. After having imported computers in the late Soviet years, they concentrated on oil exports from 1990 and moved into banking, profiting from cheap credits from the Central Bank of Russia and high-yielding treasury bonds. From 1995 to 1999, they purchased oil, mines, and metallurgical companies to make great fortunes on the ensuing commodity boom in the 2000s. To facilitate their businesses, they got deeply involved in policymaking and media.[35]

Two issues rendered the oligarchs infamous. Before the presidential elections in the summer of 1996, seven top oligarchs threw all their

money and media power behind President Yeltsin and probably managed to turn the election to his advantage. This intervention was widely
seen as a big step toward the demise of Russia's democracy. The seven
oligarchs were Boris Berezovsky, Vladimir Gusinsky, Mikhail Khodorkovsky, Alexander Smolensky, Vladimir Potanin, Mikhail Fridman, and
Petr Aven. Berezovsky and Gusinsky controlled media companies and
were forced out by Putin in 2000. Smolensky's big SBS-Agro Bank went
bankrupt in the crash of 1998, and he disappeared. Khodorkovsky was
arrested in 2003 and sentenced to eleven years' prison in Putin's showcase trial. Potanin remains the dominant owner of Norilsk Nickel, and
Fridman and Aven are co-owners of Alfa Group, Russia's biggest private
holding company.[36]

The other controversy concerned the so-called loans-for-shares
privatization in 1995, which many perceived as the oligarchs' original sin.
At the time, it was politically impossible to sell large enterprises to foreigners, but the government was desperate for cash. Moreover, the reformers wanted to tie the new businessmen to reform and the reelection
of Yeltsin in 1996. In the end, only twelve companies were privatized in
that fashion, and merely three changed principal owners: Yukos, Norilsk
Nickel, and Sibneft. Oneximbank of Vladimir Potanin and Mikhail
Prokhorov bought Norilsk Nickel for $170 million. Mikhail Khodor-
kovsky's Menatep purchased 86 percent of Yukos's shares for $309 million.
Boris Berezovsky and Roman Abramovich acquired a majority of Sibneft
for $100 million. These were privileged insider privatization, but nothing
else was sold for more. Forty percent of Gazprom was sold for $100 mil-
lion, although Gazprom was worth ten times more than Sibneft.[37]

These three companies were economically extraordinarily successful. Economist Andrei Shleifer and political scientist Daniel Treisman
noticed: "Between 1996 and 2001, the reported pretax profits of Yukos,
Sibneft, and Norilsk Nickel rose in real terms by 36, 10, and 5 times, respectively." The stock market valuation of Yukos and Sibneft surged
more than thirty times in real terms. Their economic success led to the
conspicuous enrichment of their young owners, which Russian society
could not stomach.[38]

Several important events concluded the 1990s. On August 17, 1998,
Russia experienced a shocking financial crash, which in hindsight may

be seen as the completion of the building of a market economy. In August 1999, President Yeltsin named Vladimir Putin his prime minister. Soon afterward, Putin launched a second war in Chechnya. On December 19, 1999, Russia held a new Duma election, and the new government party Unity gained 23.8 percent of the votes cast. Together with like-minded parties Unity could form a parliamentary majority in support of the government for the first time since 1991. On December 31, Yeltsin resigned to the benefit of Putin.[39]

President Putin's first term, 2000–2004, stands out as Russia's happiest. The economic policy was better than ever, and Russia was still quite a free society. Cunningly, Putin exploited the economic success to consolidate his political power.[40]

Russia's finances had finally stabilized, and from 1999 to 2008 the economy grew as never before, at an average of 7 percent a year (fig. 1.1). Russians' standard of living surged even faster. The private sector boomed, peaking at 70 percent of GDP in 2003. This was also a period

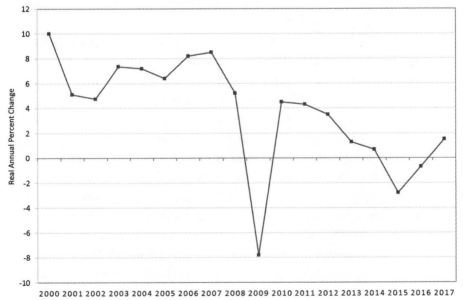

Fig. 1.1 Real GDP growth, 2000–2017. *Source: BOFIT (2018)*

of great structural reforms. The federal state was back, and the big losers were the regional governors and the oligarchs, but also the communists. The Russian state imposed its rules on the whole country, centralizing federal finances and leveling the playing field.[41]

In 1999, when people asked whether the Russian economy could survive, the worldwide management consulting firm McKinsey Global Institute published a study of great foresight. It concluded that Russia had sufficient physical and human capital for a sustained growth rate of 8 percent a year. The main hurdles were a distortional tax system, a dysfunctional government, the subsidization of inefficient companies, and the absence of a land market. Neither the banking system nor the legal system posed significant impediments to high growth.[42]

The Russian government pursued this line of reform. After having assumed power in early 2000, Putin appointed Herman Gref, a young liberal lawyer from St. Petersburg, minister of economic development and trade, while his liberal St. Petersburg colleague Alexei Kudrin was appointed minister of finance. In the early 1990s, Gref and Kudrin had worked closely with Putin in St. Petersburg. They continued the economic reforms of their friends Gaidar and Chubais. Mikhail Kasyanov, who had been minister of finance and was seen as close to the Yeltsin family, succeeded Putin as prime minister.

Putin asked Gref to write an operative reform program. Gref gathered the best and brightest liberal economists in Moscow, and in July their program was adopted. The Gref program is a bureaucratic document of about two hundred pages with instructions to officials to compose hundreds of legal acts on structural reforms. Impressively, much of this program was legislated and implemented in 2000–2003.[43]

The big question was how Putin would handle the oligarchs. On July 28, 2000, he convened a much-anticipated meeting with twenty-one leading Russian businessmen in the Kremlin, telling them in no uncertain terms: "You stay out of politics and I will not revise the results of privatization." The two media oligarchs Vladimir Gusinsky and Boris Berezovsky were already out of favor and did not attend. The state was back and the old Yeltsin oligarchy was over. The Kasyanov government functioned as a coalition government of liberals and big business, being the most effective government Russia ever had.[44]

Tax reform was key. The Russian tax system was an unwieldy, arbitrary, and inefficient mess. Russia had two hundred taxes, and multiple agencies competed over the same revenues. A draft tax code had been lying in the Duma since 1997. From 1998 to 2003, it was adopted in steps. Small, inefficient nuisance taxes were abolished as the number of taxes was slashed to sixteen. Four different payroll taxes were merged into one unified social tax. All tax collection was concentrated to one tax service. The tax rates were reduced and loopholes eliminated. The sensation was the replacement of a progressive income tax, peaking at 30 percent, with a flat personal income tax of 13 percent. The tax reform boosted tax revenues.[45]

The 1993 constitution had guaranteed the right of Russian citizens to own land, but until the 1999 elections the communists and agrarians in the State Duma had blocked the adoption of a land code, which was needed to legalize private land ownership. Publicly Putin avoided this sensitive issue, but he tacitly supported the liberal Union of Right Forces that drove this law through the Duma in October 2001. In July 2002, the Duma legalized the sale of agricultural land. Other important economic reform laws were a civil code reinforcing private property rights, a new bankruptcy law, a new labor code, a pension reform introducing compulsory private pension savings, and substantial deregulation for small enterprises.[46]

The years 2000–2003 encompassed Russia's most successful period of economic reform, and the economic results were stellar. Putin had successfully satisfied multiple constituencies to consolidate his power. Veteran Kremlinologist Lilia Shevtsova assessed: "Putin was simultaneously a stabilizer, the guardian of the traditional pillars of the state, and a reformer. He was a statist and a Westernizer. He appealed to all strata in the society."[47]

Putin showed his political genius and opportunism in his selection of national symbols. He stuck to the liberal tricolor flag while bringing back the tsarist double eagle as the coat of arms, and he rehabilitated the magnificent old Soviet national anthem with new words. Although these choices might have appeared ideologically inconsistent, each enjoyed a popular majority.

Putin's second term, 2004–2008, was characterized by the oil price boom, which helped him breed state capitalism in Russia. Thanks to the economically successful loans-for-shares privatization, the new private companies drove up oil production by an astounding 50 percent from 1999 to 2004. In late 2003, global oil prices started rising sharply. The economy seemed to be on autopilot, delivering high growth, a large budget surplus, and a reassuring current account surplus. Having now consolidated power, Putin could cast aside his mask and proceed to what he really wanted. His new goal was state capitalism, but he waited to clarify that until 2006.[48]

By and large, structural reforms ended in 2003 and have not been resumed. Putin's last attempt at a serious structural reform was the monetization of social benefits in January 2005. It was poorly explained, and the public understood it as their loss of social benefits. As a consequence, old-age pensioners started large-scale street protests around the country. The government made certain concessions, and it dropped the idea of further structural reforms. Why bother with reforms when economic success seemed guaranteed?

The turning point foreshadowing Putin's second presidential term was the arrest of Mikhail Khodorkovsky, the main owner and CEO of the Yukos oil company, on October 25, 2003. Khodorkovsky was the richest man in Russia, with a wealth assessed at $15 billion. The initial official accusation was a dubious privatization of the mineral fertilizer company Apatity, but the prosecution moved on to tax fraud, although that case never seemed plausible. The Kremlin's real aim was to confiscate Yukos, although Putin denied it repeatedly. In 2004–2005, Yukos was expropriated and its assets were transferred largely to Rosneft in closed auctions at low prices.[49]

The Yukos confiscation was a pivotal political event. It preceded the State Duma elections in December 2003 and the March 2004 presidential elections, and it helped Putin to gain complete political control. The Yukos confiscation also marked the end of privatization and structural reforms and a much more negative attitude to international economic interaction.

The president continued to speak in favor of a free market economy, but his policy had changed. After three failed attempts to privatize Rosneft, the government decided to keep it. Rosneft also fought off several merger challenges. In July 2004, Putin appointed his former personal assistant Igor Sechin chairman of the supervisory board of Rosneft, which became the leading purchaser of oil companies. Gazprom tried to keep up with the competition. It bought Sibneft in 2005 and forced Royal Dutch Shell and its partners to sell 51 percent of their Sakhalin II project at a price set by Gazprom in 2007. It also ousted TNK-BP from its giant Kovykta gas field in Eastern Siberia.[50]

Putin and his men were building a new state capitalism. In 2006–2007, several large state companies and corporations were formed. The idea was that Russia needed "national champions," meaning national monopolies. In several sectors, a state monopoly was to be formed with Gazprom as the model. In 2006, the United Aircraft Corporation was created, as were the United Shipbuilding Corporation and the Atomic Energy Industry Complex (Rosatom) in 2007. Some seven hundred armament companies were merged into the state corporation Rostec. The new state enterprises were confusingly similar to old Soviet industrial ministries. Their chief executives were longtime friends of Putin.[51]

The Orange Revolution in Ukraine in November–December 2004 delivered a major shock to Putin. He seemed convinced that the United States had instigated this grassroots revolt. He grew increasingly suspicious of the West, favoring less economic cooperation. In early January 2006, Gazprom's chairman and Russia's first deputy prime minister Dmitri Medvedev turned off the gas tap to Ukraine in a macho display on Russian television because of a pay dispute. But 80 percent of Gazprom's exports to the European Union passed through Ukraine, prompting not only the Ukrainian government but also the EU and the United States to protest. Although a settlement was reached within a few days, Gazprom repeated the trick in January 2009 for two weeks.[52]

Putin had persistently advocated sound market economic policy, but in a televised question-and-answer session on October 25, 2006, he abruptly changed tone, returning to former Soviet rhetoric. He favored industrial policy, extensive state intervention, centralized micromanagement, state investment, subsidies, trade and price regulation, protectionism with higher custom tariffs, export taxes, and import substitution, as well as ethnic discrimination. In characteristic fashion, Putin adjusted his rhetoric to the policy he had in fact adopted three years earlier.[53]

In May 2008, Putin's second presidential term expired. Before he departed, his government produced a policy agenda called "Strategy 2020." It was supposed to be a follow-up to the Gref program of 2000 and guide his chosen successor, Dmitri Medvedev. Strategy 2020 was full of lofty reform ideas, but it was never taken seriously because its proposals differed so markedly from Putin's actual policies, and it proved to be of little significance.[54]

After the arrest of Mikhail Khodorkovsky in 2003, Russia could no longer be called an oligarchy. The centralized state had returned with a vengeance. Putin ruled with the assistance of his security police, ministers, and state enterprise managers. A popular anecdote showed how times had changed: a young woman was advised that it was better to marry a high state official than an oligarch, because the money was the same, but the state official enjoyed a much more secure tenure. Big private businessmen started talking about their companies as their temporary loans, expecting that the state could take them over at any time.

Putin's third informal term, 2008–2012, saw the rise of asset stripping and crony capitalism. In 2008, its tenth year of high economic growth, the Russian elite was blinded by hubris. In current US dollars, Russia's GDP had skyrocketed from a miserable $200 billion in 1999 to $1.9 trillion in 2008 to become the sixth biggest economy in the world (fig. 1.2).

The possibilities seemed unlimited. In May 2008, Gazprom became the most valuable listed company in the world, with a market capitalization of $369 billion. In June, Gazprom CEO Alexei Miller predicted that oil prices would rise to $250 per barrel by 2010 and that Gazprom would become the first company in the world to reach the value of $1 trillion. On July 11, the price of oil hit the unprecedented level of $147 per barrel.[55]

Although democracy was gone, hopes for modernization persisted. By serving just twice, Putin showed respect for the limit of two consecutive terms set by the 1993 constitution. On December 10, 2007, Putin announced that First Deputy Prime Minister Dmitri Medvedev was his preferred successor. The Kremlin's four obedient Duma parties instantly endorsed him. In March 2008, Medvedev was "elected" president in tightly controlled elections, and he obediently appointed Putin prime minister.

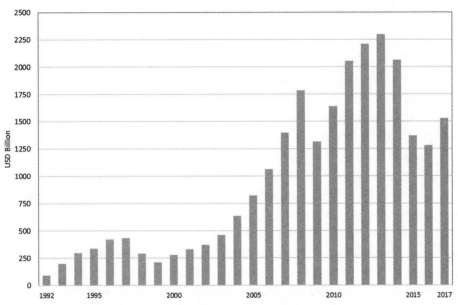

Fig. 1.2 GDP in current US dollars, 1992–2017. *Source: IMF (2018)*

All along, Medvedev was considered a weak underling to Putin, but he was younger and more reformist, and he did not come from the KGB. Instead Medvedev had taught law at St. Petersburg University before becoming Putin's assistant in 1991. The runner-up for president had been the other first deputy prime minister, Sergei Ivanov, who was a KGB general of Putin's age from St. Petersburg.[56]

Medvedev presented his manifesto "Forwards Russia!" which was a creed for modernization. His key question was, "Should a primitive economy based on raw materials and endemic corruption accompany us into the future?" US president Barack Obama took Medvedev seriously as a modernizer and launched a "reset" of US policy to Russia soon after his inauguration in January 2009.[57]

Alas, little came out of the anticipated modernization. Putin retained ultimate power, so these years should be seen as his third informal term as ruler. Seemingly in contradiction to his endeavor to build state capitalism, Putin spearheaded a swift stripping of assets, generating a new dimension of crony capitalism. Several friends of his from St. Petersburg now assumed outsized roles. The most important are Gennady Timchenko, Arkady Rotenberg, and Yuri Kovalchuk. The main object of their asset stripping was Gazprom, where Putin functioned as the real chief executive. Rotenberg and Timchenko owned the main subcontractors that built Gazprom's new pipelines in privileged no-competition contracts. Timchenko became the main trader of Russian oil. Kovalchuk controlled Bank Rossiya, which was the financial hub of Putin's St. Petersburg friends, and it purchased Gazprom's ample financial and media assets. Putin's travels abroad as prime minister focused on promoting Gazprom pipeline construction in the European neighborhood, especially South Stream.[58]

The opposition politicians Boris Nemtsov and Vladimir Milov have estimated that the total value of assets removed from Gazprom and placed into the private hands of Putin's friends from 2004 to 2007 at about $60 billion. Not surprisingly, Gazprom's market value has sunk from a high of $369 billion in May 2008 to some $46 billion in August 2017 because shareholders know that they do not really own the stock. They receive only dividend yields. Putin and his friends established their network in the early 1990s, but only in his second term did their larceny become truly astounding.[59]

The global financial crisis came as a rude surprise to the Kremlin. As late as September 2008, Putin exuded arrogance, calling Russia a "safe haven" in the budding crisis, although both stock market and oil prices had been falling from May and July, respectively. This time, Russia had accumulated substantial reserves. The state spent generously, but to no benefit, bailing out big bad companies rather than forcing them into bankruptcy as in 1998. Russia's GDP plunged by 7.8 percent in 2009, more than in any other G-20 economy, and its future productivity had been deflated.

In June 2009, President Medvedev hosted Western leaders in St. Petersburg to complete Russia's accession to the World Trade Organization. At this time, however, Putin had lost interest in the WTO, and he upstaged everyone by proposing a customs union among Russia, Kazakhstan, and Belarus a couple of days before Medvedev's grand event. Medvedev and his ministers were openly stunned. Putin's message was clear: he, and not Medvedev, called the shots. Putin did so, even though this delayed Russia's entry into the WTO by some two years. Unlike many prior Russian initiatives on cooperation among former Soviet states, the Kremlin stayed focused on this project and gradually expanded the customs union to Armenia and Kyrgyzstan, upgrading it to the Eurasian Economic Union (EAEU).

In September 2011, Putin and Medvedev announced that they were "castling," switching portfolios, at a United Russia Party Congress. Putin declared: "I want to tell you directly that we have long since reached an agreement on what we will be doing in the future. That agreement was reached several years ago." Medvedev proceeded to nominate Putin: "I think it's right that the party congress support the candidacy of the current prime minister, Vladimir Putin, in the role of the country's president." This obviously untrue charade came as a shock to Russia's liberals, who had hoped that Putin would allow Medvedev to stay as president.[60]

Although few thought Medvedev had much power, Russia's liberal upper middle class had hoped for liberalization and modernization. Suddenly they realized they were facing the opposite. Putin dressed Medvedev down as a nonentity, showing that he was in charge. The December 2011 Duma elections were blatantly forged, which provoked the largest public protests in Russia since 1991. Cleverly, the Kremlin labeled the protests the "mink revolution," suggesting that the protesters were too wealthy. This period of unrest occurred after the Arab Spring had erupted in Tunisia, Egypt, Libya, and Syria.

Putin rarely showed himself for one and a half months, until mid-January 2012. Then, for the first time, he pursued an American-style election campaign with major public appearances every day, and he published seven big, programmatic newspaper articles. Before his inauguration in May 2012, the police had ended the protests with force. When Putin was driven to his inauguration in the Kremlin, the police had emptied the streets. Putin had restored order, but he had seen that the middle classes were ungrateful, despite all the wealth they had gained, and that he had to reach out to the lower classes and the country beyond the capital.[61]

Moscow sociology professor Natalia Zubarevich divides Russia into four groups. "Russia 1," consisting of Moscow and St. Petersburg, is too well off to rise in opposition to the government. Together with their hinterland, they account for 20 percent of Russia's population. But she warns of coming social instability in "Russia 2," the large industrial cities with 250,000 to 1 million inhabitants that make up 30 percent of Russia's population. "Russia 3" constitutes 40 percent of the population, small towns and the countryside, which are dominated by old and politically passive people. These three groups make up 90 percent of the population. The final 10 percent, ethnic minority territories, mainly in the Northern Caucasus, is of little concern to the rest of Russia, allowing the Kremlin to use unlimited force. Since the election of 2012, Putin has abandoned Russia 1 and focused on Russia 2 and 3, while he enjoys nearly 100 percent of the votes in Russia 4.[62]

After Putin was inaugurated, he issued eleven reform decrees on May 12, 2012, but this was little but liturgy. They were sanctimoniously treated as Putin's reform program. Nobody expected them to be implemented, and they were not. Putin has systematically rolled back Medvedev's few reforms.

Russians call Putin's current rule from 2012 "manual management" (*ruchnoe upravlenie*), because he micromanages without principles. Not surprisingly, the outcome has been minimal growth. The main institutional change is that the council of ministers has lost significance, because Medvedev chairs it and he has minimal authority. Putin makes the main economic decisions together with a top official visiting him or a select group of ministers. The Security Council has replaced the council of ministers as the most important policy-making forum. It is eerily reminiscent of the old CPSU Politburo, with twelve permanent members, who are mainly *siloviki*, representatives of the armed services, and they meet almost weekly.

Putin's enhanced dominance has facilitated the parallel development of state capitalism and crony capitalism. To Putin, loyalty and trust seem to be everything. Ever more corporate power is being concentrated into the hands of a limited number of state and crony executives. At the highest level, Kremlin interference is overwhelming. All business deals over $1 billion have to be confirmed with the Kremlin, which has capped the Russian stock exchange at a very low price-earnings ratio. The old large private corporations from the 1990s are gradually being squeezed out, bought by large state corporations or cronies. Most old oligarchs do not mind retiring with their fortunes abroad, where they have educated their children.

With its occupation and annexation of Crimea in February–March 2014 and its later military aggression in eastern Ukraine starting in April 2014, the Kremlin violated all relevant international laws from the end of World War II, including the UN Charter, the Helsinki Charter of 1975 and ensuing Helsinki agreements, and the Treaty on Friendship, Cooperation, and Partnership between Ukraine and the Russian Federation of 1997. Nor did the Kremlin offer any explanation to all these violations of fundamental international law.

The United States and the European Union reacted as one could expect, by imposing major sanctions on Russia: first individual sanctions on people and companies involved in the occupation of Crimea and then sectoral sanctions in finance, oil, and military industry. In September 2014 and February 2015, Ukraine, Russia, Germany, and France concluded two cease-fire agreements in Belarus's capital, Minsk, but the Russian-backed forces have not maintained the cease-fire, and artillery and hot trench warfare continues. So have the Western sanctions, which are gradually being ratcheted up as Russia does nothing to comply with its prior international commitments.

On March 18, 2018, Putin was "reelected" as president for a fourth term of six years, with 77 percent of the votes cast. This was no real election, since no real opponent was allowed and state control of the media was at its most extreme. Not even the swearing in of Putin on May 7 in the Great Kremlin Palace was joyful. Putin looked remarkably bored. This time he limited his car trip to a drive inside the Kremlin.

As he had done in all previous elections, Putin had refused to participate in any election debates. The only time he ever campaigned was in 2012 in an apparent response to the public protests. This time around, Putin barely paid attention to the elections. While he had published seven big programmatic articles before the 2012 election, in 2018 he presented no program. His public appearances, including his annual address to the Russian Federal Assembly on March 1, were emptier than ever, reminiscent of Leonid Brezhnev, though without ideology.

The same was true of his postelection appearances. After the 2012 election, Putin had issued eleven decrees with tasks for his six-year term, though little was achieved. This time around, he presented just one decree, itself exceedingly vague, almost without relevant numbers, though with such catchphrases as "ensure sustainable growth of real wages, as well as the growth of pensions above inflation level."[63]

Putin kept Medvedev as prime minister, even though the opposition leader Navalny had revealed that Medvedev had taken $1.2 billion in bribes and been highly ineffective. On May 18, a new government was appointed. Half the ministers were new, yet the new cabinet suggested no new political initiatives or ideas. The positions appeared more like an exercise in musical chairs, though the few Medvedev loyalists were eliminated. Before the election, some people had speculated that former finance minister Alexei Kudrin would be given a major reform role. In the end, he was appointed head of the Auditing Chamber, an irrelevant role, which clarified that no reform was intended.

Without saying so, Putin made clear that he had no intention of making any significant policy changes or pursuing any economic reforms. A broad economic consensus predicts an annual growth rate of 1.5–2 percent in Russia for the next several years and a nearly stagnant standard of living. The old policy of macroeconomic stability combined with kleptocracy appeared set to continue. The two main questions were whether more repression and adventurous foreign policies were to be expected.

Russia's economic situation in 2018 can be summarized in two words: stability and stagnation. The collapse of the Soviet Union and the financial crash of 1998 left a deep imprint on Putin and the Russian elite, teaching them the importance of macroeconomic stability for the sake of political stability. A typical recent Putin statement is: "I note that we have achieved sustainable macroeconomic stabilization over these last few years. . . . Considering the current economic challenges, we must preserve the health and stability of the Russian economy, which is our priority." Conservative fiscal and monetary policies have assumed the status of dogma.[64]

For the rest, Putin had great leeway, and he chose state and crony capitalism. Russia had inherited a strong sentiment in favor of statism, which Putin exploited. The crash of half the private banks in 1998 brought about state dominance in banking, while rising oil production and increasing oil prices beginning in 2003 made the enrichment of the owners of oil companies look automatic, which facilitated Putin's large renationalization drive from 2004, but it was no political necessity.

Putin's fondness of fast-growing emerging economies might have blinded him to the benefits of good governance. His logic appears to be: if China and India grow so much faster than Western countries, why should we bother about good governance? Not only is Russia's crony capitalism blocking growth, but it is undermining the weak existing institutions, driving a far-reaching deinstitutionalization. China scholar Minxin Pei has written on China's crony capitalism, and the qualitative similarities are striking.[65]

At present, Putin seems to be stuck in a kleptocratic system. The three dominant circles are his friends atop the FSB, his friends running the big state companies, and his private business friends from St. Petersburg, who tap the economy on so much money, but Putin rules. This system does not permit any reform, and the question is not whether it will reform but how long it can stay reasonably stable. For how long will Russian society accept a stagnant standard of living?

Putin's Consolidation of Power

I n his first term, 2000–2004, President Vladimir Putin methodi-
cally consolidated his power. In so doing, he revealed certain clear
values, but at the same time he was skillfully everything to everybody while not necessarily revealing his real positions to the public. Now that he has been in power for eighteen years, most of his aims
appear obvious, but that was not the case during his first term as president.
Russia experts Fiona Hill and Cliff Gaddy have probably nailed Putin's
nature: "Vladimir Putin is a fighter and he is a survivalist. He won't give
up, and he will fight dirty if that's what it takes to win."[1]

Putin's many public statements can guide us to his thinking, but
they must be checked against his actions, because as a clever politician
he has said many nice things that were popular but he did not believe in
them. Notably, Putin has repeatedly praised democratic values and freedom, yet his rule has tended in the opposite direction. Like most skillful
politicians, Putin shows some strong values, while he appears opportunistic in many regards.

Throughout Putin's career, the KGB and now the FSB have been his
mainstays, endowing him with specific ideas. Putin has persistently cherished the FSB and its values, using the security service as his main ruling
lever. This means that Putin was antidemocratic from the outset, even if
he tried to hide his values with many statements praising democracy and

freedom. In particular, Putin has adamantly opposed a free media, especially when it mocks him, as the NTV television program *Kukly* (Puppets) successfully did. Further, Putin has insisted on centralized Moscow rule over the whole country.

A couple of Putin tenets have been less obvious. His enduring lesson from the Russian financial crash of 1998 was that financial stability and fiscal conservatism were vital to sustain his political rule. More disturbingly, Putin appears to have been so entrenched in organized crime since the early 1990s in St. Petersburg that it has become part of his very being, as Boris Nemtsov and Vladimir Milov, Yuri Felshtinsky and Vladimir Pribylovsky, and Karen Dawisha have shown.[2]

Naturally, Putin could not have had strong views on every important matter, and sometimes he has changed his view, most strongly in the sphere of foreign policy. What he saw as a matter of convenience, others saw as a matter of values. His most difficult political moment was probably Ukraine's Orange Revolution in 2004. Hill and Gaddy make the crucial point that we Westerners have failed to appreciate "how dangerously little Putin understands about *us*—our motives, our mentality, and, also, our values."[3]

Another area in which Putin's positions have evolved somewhat opportunistically was economic policy. Like all intelligent people, Putin also has learned from crises. His great formative moments are probably three: the collapse of the Soviet Union, the Russian financial crash of 1998, and Ukraine's Orange Revolution.

When Putin came to power on New Year's Eve 1999, the obvious question was what ideas he stood for. During most of his first term, Putin evidenced great skills as a politician trying to be everything to everybody, opportunistically telling almost all what they wanted to hear. Some thought he was a hard-core nationalist, while others perceived him as a liberal Westernizer, and most thought he was something in between. Unlike his predecessor, he was definitely sober. In hindsight, Putin's views are pretty clear, and most were evident in his interview book, *First Person,* hastily composed in 2000.

Putin loved the KGB. From his youth he had cherished this repressive agency, and he aspired to join it as soon as he could. From the outset

Putin was antidemocratic, but as deputy to the leading liberal Anatoly Sobchak, mayor of St. Petersburg from 1991 to 1996, he had to pay lip service to democracy, so he did.

Putin "wrote" a doctoral dissertation in the 1990s, but it was plagiarized, drawing extensively on the American textbook *Strategic Planning and Policy*, by William King and David Cleland. Vladimir Litvinenko, the rector of St. Petersburg Mining Institute, where Putin defended his dissertation, received 10 percent of the shares of Phosagro, a company previously owned by Yukos, in compensation for his consultancy. Still, the dissertation is interesting, reflecting Putin's appreciation of state ownership of natural resources, national champions, and state capitalism.[4]

In the early 1990s, when Putin was St. Petersburg's first deputy mayor for international economic relations, the city was renowned as the crime capital of Russia, and Putin dealt with the most criminal part of that economy. A report by an investigative commission chaired by the liberal politician Marina Sal'e offers overwhelming evidence that Putin was deeply involved in organized crime at least from late 1991, though he did not make a great deal of money. Crony capitalism is an original part of his system.[5]

Putin claims to admire two philosophers, Ivan Ilyin and Lev Gumilev. Both are antidemocratic Russian nationalists, but of opposite kinds. Ilyin had a narrow linguistic outlook, while Gumilev preferred imperialist outreach. Putin has quoted each of them publicly, Ilyin five times and Gumilev six times. Ilyin, however, he has mentioned on major occasions, whereas he has cited Gumilev as sops to the Kazakhs and Kyrgyz and not all too deeply felt.[6]

Ilyin was an anticommunist and a white philosopher who was expelled from Russia together with many other prominent intellectuals on "the philosophers' ship" in 1922. He favored monarchy and autocracy, advocating, as historian Walter Laqueur writes, "a strong central power for post-Communist Russia, with few rights for non-Russian regions such as Ukraine or the Caucasus." Though not quite a Nazi, he was close to it. Laqueur writes that Ilyin "considered Nazism a positive phenomenon that with some modifications could serve as a model for the future Russia."[7]

Historian Tim Snyder sees Ilyin as a key to understanding Putin. Ilyin "believed that individuality was evil" and that "the purpose of politics is to overcome individuality and establish a 'living totality' of the nation."

He aspired to a fascist Holy Russia to be ruled by a "national dictator." Putin had Ilyin's body exhumed from Switzerland and reburied at a monastery in Moscow, laying flowers on Ilyin's grave. Putin suggests that he shares a kindred ideology with Ilyin. Like Ilyin, Putin favors a strong central power, autocracy, orthodoxy, Russian dominance in the region, and state capitalism. In an opposing view, Marlene Laruelle has objected that "Ilyin saw Russia's essence in autocracy, statehood, messianism and cultural exceptionalism," arguing that this is not really fascist even if Ilyin was a rabid anti-Semite and anti-Bolshevik with an attraction to fascism.[8]

Still, Putin has been careful not to become attached to any specific branch of nationalism. He has repeatedly praised Lev Gumilev, who was the father of Eurasianism, the imperial form of Russian nationalism, and was strongly opposed to the narrow ethnic or linguistic nationalism of Ilyin. Gumilev was an authoritarian statist, although he spent the years 1938–1956 in Soviet labor camps. Putin has invoked Gumilev to appeal for cooperation among the former Soviet republics. In his greeting to an international academic congress honoring the centenary of Lev Gumilev in 2012, Putin expressed his confidence that it would "contribute to further promoting integration processes within the Commonwealth [of Independent States] and strengthening trust and mutual understanding in the region."[9]

Among Russia's historical leaders, Putin seems most attracted to Nicholas I, the founder of the tsarist secret police who tightened authoritarian order after the liberal Alexander I and the Decembrist uprising. In 1848–1849, Nicholas I culled uprisings all over Eastern Europe. His tragic finale, however, was the Crimean War, 1853–1856, which dealt a devastating blow to Russia's rising great power ambitions.[10]

In 2017, Putin made an uncommon historical diversion. In July, he quoted the famous motto of the conservative Alexander III (1881–1894), "Russia has only two allies: the army and the navy," and in November he unveiled a monument to Alexander III in Crimea. Also in July, Putin tried to rehabilitate Ivan the Terrible, lamenting negative historical myths about Russia:

> Take for example the famous legend that Ivan the Terrible killed his son. It remains unknown in fact whether he really

killed his son or not. Many researchers believe that he did not kill anyone at all and that the Pope's nuncio made it up when he visited Russia for talks with Ivan IV and tried to turn the Orthodox Rus into a Catholic Rus. . . . He was made Ivan the Terrible, an extremely violent individual. Although, if one examines other countries in this period of time, everything was the same everywhere.

Russian history, by contrast, considers Ivan IV (1547–1584) the most frightful of Russia's rulers. Before Putin, Stalin was the last Russian ruler who attempted to rehabilitate Ivan the Terrible, promoting Sergei Eisenstein's famous film about him. Putin avoids mentioning liberal tsars, notably Alexander II.[11]

Values do not seem particularly important to Putin, while power is. He appeals to the existing values of his chosen electorate as a seasoned politician and draws on arguments that justify his rule.

During the years 1991–1994, I visited St. Petersburg a couple of times a year for high-level events attended by the city's political stars. Mayor Anatoly Sobchak was an outstanding speaker. The darling of the Western community (including myself) was First Deputy Mayor Alexei Kudrin.

But no. 3 in St. Petersburg also attended. His name was Vladimir Putin, though few paid attention to him. Nor did he so desire. He behaved like a security guard who was not to be seen rather than an official. Because of his creepy manners, the local Scandinavian diplomats strongly disliked him, and they warned me that he was a KGB officer. Somewhat more softly, Hill and Gaddy observe that "Vladimir Putin managed to keep a remarkably low public profile during his time as deputy mayor of St. Petersburg." He loved secrecy and had no need to show himself.[12]

Although Putin was a relative failure as a KGB officer, retiring with the rank of major, he has displayed extreme loyalty to this odious organization. Putin gave his most relevant thoughts on the KGB in his book *First Person*. When questioned about Stalin's Great Terror: "When you agreed to work in the agencies, did you think about 1937?" Putin responded, "To be honest, I didn't think about it at all. Not a bit."[13]

Putin disclosed a similar attitude to the East German Ministry of Security, in charge of the severe repression in that country. "There were all kinds of people who worked there, but the people I knew were decent people. I was friends with many of them, and I think that the way they are now being castigated isn't right. . . . Yes, there were probably some [Ministry of Security] agents who engaged in persecution of people. I didn't see it. I don't want to say that it didn't happen. But I personally did not see it." Putin showed that he focused on his friends, not on abstract principles. He did not mind torture, at least as long as he did not have to see it.[14]

When asked what he wanted to do in the KGB, Putin seemed more human: "Of course I wanted to go into intelligence. Everyone did. We all knew what it meant to be able to travel abroad." Putin's cellist friend Sergei Roldugin delivered the final nail in the coffin of the "nice" KGB, by recalling having told Putin: "There's no such thing as a former intelligence agent."[15]

Putin is obsessed with information. During his three-to-four-hour phone-in programs and press conferences twice a year, he displays an amazing knowledge of facts. At a press conference in 2001, Putin emphasized, in a response to the journalist Christian Caryl, the importance of being able "to work with a large amount of information. That's a skill that is cultivated in the analytical services and special services, the skill of selecting what is most important from a huge flood of information, of processing information and being able to use it."[16]

When Putin became prime minister in 1999, he changed the information flow. Previously, three or four competing agencies had delivered their information and analysis to the top independently of one another. Desiring only one version, Putin put four FSB generals in charge of the information flow. Similarly, the journalist Ben Judah has reported: "The master begins his work day by reading three thick leather-bound folders. The first—his report on the home front compiled by the FSB, his domestic intelligence service. The second—his report on international affairs compiled by the SVR, his foreign intelligence. The third—his report on the court complied by the FSO," or Federal Protection Service.[17]

All the material comes from his three favorite intelligence services, and nothing is open information. Apparently, Putin pays little attention to economic information. Neither the Central Bank nor the Ministry of Finance is a daily supplier of information. Putin's reliance on intelligence reports makes him vulnerable to internalize their biases and conspiracy theories.

Putin is an outstanding influence agent who knows how to "work with people," as he puts it. He elaborated on this theme in 2001: "In order to work with people effectively you have to be able to establish a dialogue and bring out the best in your partner. If you want to achieve results you have to respect your partner. And to respect means to recognize that he is in some way better than you are. You should make that person an ally, make him feel that there is something that unites you, that you have some common goals. That skill I think is the most important skill." Putin has repeatedly excelled in these skills. Putin likes everything about the KGB: its secrecy, its skills, its intelligence, analysis, and values.[18]

One of Putin's outstanding features is his reliance on old friends. Putin has been extremely careful in his choice of associates, and this is probably one of his greatest strengths. He selects people he can really trust, drawing on a narrow circle of past contacts from the KGB and St. Petersburg. He is very loyal to his top appointees, rarely dismissing anybody and, when he does, allowing them to decline in rank over time.

Early on in Putin's administration, Russian sociologist Olga Kryshtanovskaya and British political scientist Stephen White presented their thesis that Putin was building a "militocracy" of primarily KGB officers, or *siloviki*, men from the power services. The rising prominence of secret police as well as military officers is undisputable, but as scholars Sharon Werning Rivera and David W. Rivera have argued, the siloviki have not become overly dominant. The Russian state administration abounds with ordinary technocrats.[19]

Putin's selection of cadres looks traditionally Soviet. The key to advancement has been trust, gained through working closely with Putin for years early in his career. Trust and loyalty have had outsized importance, as in the Soviet system under Leonid Brezhnev. His loyalty to old associates has been as great as his negligence of merits. Putin's selection of top associates seems quite natural, describing his career. Only one man of significance has known Putin since they were teenagers, his judo partner Arkady Rotenberg. Yet in his financial dealings two childhood friends have popped up, the cellist Sergei Roldugin and butcher Petr Kolbin.[20]

Karen Dawisha has carefully documented Putin's acquaintances. His great coming of age was his entry into the KGB, where he met many key associates in Leningrad and the Higher School of the KGB, such as Sergei Ivanov, Nikolai Patrushev, Alexander Bortnikov, Vladimir Yakunin, and Viktor Ivanov. Some have retired, notably Yakunin and Viktor Ivanov, but Sergei Ivanov, Patrushev, and Bortnikov remain heavyweights on the Security Council.[21]

Putin's life in Dresden in 1985–1990 appears to have been quite boring. Only three current top people are known to have become closely connected with him there: his KGB colleagues Sergei Chemezov and Nikolai Tokarev and his East German Stasi colleague Matthias Warnig. Chemezov is now the CEO of the state armaments corporation Rostec, Tokarev is the CEO of the state oil pipeline company Transneft, and Warnig is one of Putin's favorite corporate board directors.[22]

From 1991 to 1996, Putin surged as first deputy mayor of St. Petersburg. During this time he developed two circles of close associates. One comprised friends mainly in private business in Bank Rossiya and the Ozero dacha cooperative. Key members here were the future cronies Gennady Timchenko, the brothers Arkady and Boris Rotenberg, Yuri Kovalchuk, and Nikolai Shamalov, as well as future top government officials Yakunin, later CEO of the Russian Railways, and Andrei Fursenko, later education minister.[23]

The other Putin circle in St. Petersburg was located in the mayor's office, from which he selected many later ministers, such as Prime Minister Dmitri Medvedev, longtime finance minister Alexei Kudrin, economy minister Herman Gref, and Deputy Prime Minister Dmitri Kozak, as well as current CEO of Gazprom Alexei Miller and CEO of Rosneft Igor Sechin. Among these, only Sechin is identified as from the security services.[24]

Putin's key associates can be divided into three groups: KGB officers, technocrats, and cronies. The three characteristics that Putin clearly requires are trust, obedience, and secrecy; merit, efficiency, and results are of subordinate significance.

Anyone who has stepped out of line and criticized other members of the elite has been accused of washing the elite's dirty linen in public and ousted. The prime example is Putin's KGB colleague from St. Petersburg Viktor Cherkezov. He surged with Putin, but when he published an article criticizing FSB colleagues for corruption in October 2007, he was quickly demoted.[25]

The only women in high positions are the Federation Council chair Valentina Matvienko, who is also a member of the Security Council, the chair of the Central Bank Elvira Nabiullina, and a few ministers. Ethnicity does not appear to be a consideration, reflecting great tolerance in that regard.

Putin's personnel policy appears pretty standard: he appoints and trusts whomever he knows well, and he does not rely on strangers. In this regard, Putin acts like Soviet leaders Mikhail Gorbachev and Leonid Brezhnev, while Boris Yeltsin differed, by being remarkably detached from his environment. Yeltsin appointed many young and highly qualified people whom he barely knew to top positions. Not having worked for a long time in Moscow, Putin broke the traditional Moscow dominance, which offended the Muscovites. Ideology does not seem to have played any role. The current Russian saying is that the country is ruled by *ponyatie* (understanding), which is a Mafia term, implying that everybody knows what to do.[26]

A new feature of Putin's third presidential term was the nationalization of the elite. In his annual speech to the federal assembly in December 2013, Putin called for "deoffshoreization," asking Russia's large companies to move their registrations from offshore havens to Russia and bring home their profits for taxation. In practice, this policy has not brought private Russian companies back to the motherland. Instead, it has divided the elite into a nationalized state and security elite staying in Russia while it has driven private companies and their owners and families out of the country. Like wealthy Chinese, well-to-do Russians have opted for excellent European and North American education for their children, but Putin has gradually adopted the policy of discriminating against foreign education and prohibited millions of men in uniform from traveling abroad. The natural consequence is a declining level of qualifications and increasing parochialism and isolation of the Russian elite.[27]

Putin's personnel system can be seen as three circles. The first circle comprises the top national security officials, Sergei Ivanov, Nikolai Patrushev, and Alexander Bortnikov. A second also very wealthy circle consists of the top loyal state enterprise managers, Igor Sechin, Sergei Chemezov, and Alexei Miller, discussed in chapter 4. A third circle is the cronies, the foremost and richest of whom are Gennady Timchenko, Arkady Rotenberg, Yuri Kovalchuk, and Nikolai Shamalov, all discussed in chapter 5. All these men are close Putin associates, while they compete among themselves.

Putin's authoritarian orientation was evident from the eruption of the second war in Chechnya in 1999. His intention from the outset was to build a vertical state power. His two first objectives were to seize media control and to restore centralized state power.

In September 1999, somebody blew up four Russian apartment buildings: two in Moscow, one in southern Volgodonsk, and one in Buynaksk in Dagestan. Altogether 293 people were killed. The authorities blamed Chechen terrorists, but since the government failed to investigate these events convincingly, the contrarian view—that they were carried out by the FSB—appears more likely, though the case remains open. Putin used these terrorist acts as an excuse to start a second devastating Chechnya war, which served as his election campaign in 1999–2000. The journalist Anna Politkovskaya, who was murdered on Putin's birthday in 2006, reported the horrors of this war.[28]

Putin started his presidency with a major attack on the leading media oligarch, Vladimir Gusinsky, and forced him to give up his outstanding television channel, NTV, in the summer of 2000. Putin presented it as a case of bankruptcy. Next, he took over another leading television company, ORT, from Boris Berezovsky, claiming that he had privatized it unlawfully. Gradually, Putin consolidated his control also over other television channels, but he never acknowledged this as his purpose, always claiming mismanaged finances as the cause of state takeover. He developed a powerful propaganda apparatus, which the Soviet-born British journalist Peter Pomerantsev has elegantly characterized as "Nothing is true and everything is possible." Putin and his propagandists have become the masters of fake news. Initially, they maintained the high quality of Russian television news of the 1990s, but increasingly they omitted unpleasant news, and at present Russian official television is nothing but aggressive propaganda.[29]

Putin's foremost goal was to reinforce federal power, to build a strong "*vertikal*" of power. As he put it in 2000: "From the very beginning, Russia was created as a supercentralized state. That's practically laid down in its genetic code, its traditions, and the mentality of its people." When becoming president, Putin formulated his key task: "It was clear to me that work with the regional leaders was one of the most important lines of work in the country. Everyone was saying that the *vertikal*, the vertical chain of government, had been destroyed and that it had to be restored."[30]

Six days after his inauguration in May 2000, Putin strengthened central control over Russia's eighty-nine regions by decree. He eliminated the regional governors from the Federation Council, the upper chamber of Russia's Federal Assembly, allowing the governors and chairs of the regional legislatures to appoint the senators, who in practice became obedient to the Kremlin, rendering the Federation Council a rubber-stamp body.

He also introduced a new administrative level of seven federal districts, each headed by a presidential envoy. Federal law was thus imposed on the whole country, leveling the playing field and increasing the federal share of tax revenues. Putin's objective was to restore a strong and effective state power or statism (*gosudarstvenost'*). In 2004, Putin took a further step, replacing elections of regional governors and in effect appointing them.[31]

Putin has built up the state administration and modernized it. The number of civil servants has increased greatly, and in 2005 he multiplied senior officials' wages, which was highly justified because until then public salaries had been pitiful. It became popular to join the state service. Putin personally has paid great attention to the World Bank Ease of Doing Business index and demanded that Russian state administration improve greatly, and it has done so. Russia has surged from number 124 in the world in 2010 to number 35 out of 180 countries in 2017. E-government has been brought in on a big scale. Ordinary Russian state administration functions quite well today.[32]

During his many years in Moscow, Putin has transformed the government slowly and deliberately. In the spring of 2001, he made two major moves, cleaning out the leadership of the ministries of defense and interior as well as of Gazprom, but his moves were against people he clearly could not trust. In the winter of 2003–2004, Putin carried out a major personnel change. He ousted Prime Minister Mikhail Kasyanov and the head of the presidential administration Alexander Voloshin, who were top officials that he had inherited from President Yeltsin's administration. While in Moscow, Putin has coopted and promoted many holdovers, including Minister of Defense Sergei Shoigu, First Deputy Prime Minister Igor Shuvalov, Moscow Mayor Sergei Sobyanin, and Duma Chairman Vyacheslav Volodin. None of them is known to have a KGB background, but none seem as close to Putin as his prime St. Petersburg associates.

Russia's democratic transition was haphazard and incomplete. The former US ambassador to Russia Michael McFaul lamented as early as 2001 that because its "illiberal institutions and norms exist, Russian democracy is more susceptible to collapse than are liberal democracies. The institutional defenses against authoritarianism such as a robust and independent media, a developed party system, and a vibrant civil society do not exist." Yet, he concluded rather optimistically: "That the Soviet Union and then Russia experienced two breakdowns in the past decade suggests that a third breakdown is likely." Putin is painfully aware of that possibility, which he is determined to prevent.[33]

The deinstitutionalization and personalization of state power have proceeded far under Putin. The State Duma and the Federation Council as well as their regional counterparts are no longer legislative bodies but merely administrative organs, because they do not represent the people in any meaningful way, while the state administration writes laws and decrees.[34]

The greatest problem in postcommunist transition has been to establish the rule of law. Without it, no property rights can exist. Businesses have to defend their property with extrajudicial means, such as private security and political connections. In the Soviet system, judges had a low status and were subordinate to prosecutors.[35]

When the Soviet Union collapsed, legal chaos existed, and protection rackets ruled over the many budding entrepreneurs. In an excellent book on property rights in Russia, the political scientist Jordan Gans-Morse emphasizes the great developments in judicial reform in the 1990s under Yeltsin. Commercial courts were established in 1992. The 1993 Constitution enshrined the principle of an independent judiciary. Two parts of the Civil Code were adopted, as were laws on bankruptcy, the security market, and joint stock companies. As early as 1997, the legal scholar Kathryn Hendley concluded that "for the most part, the legal infrastructure needed for a market economy has been created—at least on paper."[36]

Putin is a lawyer by training, and in 2000 he presented judicial reform as a key goal: "First, we need to guarantee property rights. I believe that one of the main purposes of the state is to create rules—universal rules—in the form of laws, instructions, and regulations. And secondly, to comply with these rules, and guarantee their compliance." He emphasized that "the state should not command business."[37]

A problem, however, was that Putin ambiguously called his judicial reform "dictatorship of law." He elaborated on this concept in his first presidential address to the Federal Assembly on July 8, 2000:

> State functions and state institutions differ from entrepreneurial ones in that they should not be bought or sold, privatized or transferred for use or lease. Professionals are needed in state service, for whom the only criterion of activity is the law. Otherwise, the state is opening the path of corruption. And the moment may come when it is simply transformed, and ceases to be democratic. This is why we insist on a single dictatorship—the dictatorship of the Law. Although I know that many people do not like this expression. This is why it is so important to indicate the limits of the area where the state is the full and only owner.[38]

He asked one of his closest aides, Dmitri Kozak, a deputy head of his presidential administration and a fellow lawyer from St. Petersburg, to lead a presidential working group of judicial reform. In December

2001, Russia adopted a package of new judicial laws that came into effect in 2002. They improved the status of judges and the financing of the courts as well as renewed all procedural legal codes. One goal was to strengthen the independence and autonomy of courts and judges. As a part of the reinforcement of federal power, judges became independent of regional authorities. They had already tenure, but the law on their status of December 2001 eliminated the requirement to consult regional legislatures when appointing or promoting a judge. Judges were still appointed without term limit, though they were forced to retire at fixed ages (sixty-five on regular courts and seventy on the top courts). Their protection from prosecution for criminal offenses was weakened.[39]

The 2002 Criminal Procedure Code reinforced the powers of the judges, entitling them to sign arrest and search warrants and to decide on pretrial detention. Finally, they were supposed to become superior to prosecutors. With the powers of the prosecutor's office trimmed, the chances of frivolous arrest and detention had been reduced. Further, the practice of sending cases back to the law-enforcement authorities for additional investigation was stopped under the new code, raising a defendant's chances of being acquitted.[40]

All this sounded good, but the main effect of the judicial reforms was centralization, making the judges dependent on the presidential administration rather than the regional governors. Gans-Morse concludes that Russia's legal defense of property rights was at its best between 1999 and 2003.[41]

The Yukos affair put the whole judicial reform into doubt (see chapter 3). The origins of this court case were political, spiced up with the opportunity for someone to seize valuable assets cheaply. The main accusation against the oil company was that it had followed the letter of the new tax code and used a big loophole. Nevertheless, the government won all court judgments, proving that these courts were not independent from government.[42]

The Yukos affair marked the end of Putin's apparent ambition to build the rule of law and secure property rights. From the late 1990s, Russian private companies had faced "illegal corporate raiding" (*reiderstvo*), which implied that law enforcement officials stole private companies with the use of state powers. As Gans-Morse writes, "From the mid-2000s onward, countless entrepreneurs faced arrest on trumped-up charges as law enforcement officials ... sought to acquire firms' assets at below-market rates." Similar affairs were to follow with Russneft, Euroset, Bashneft, and many others of less significance. Corporate raiding with the help of the courts became ever more audacious, and the victims more obedient. The rising impression was that the omnipotent law enforcers enjoyed free rein and even billionaires could not defend themselves.[43]

Deinstitutionalization has further damaged the judicial system. Until 2014, Russia's economic courts were considered professional and fair, often judging against state agencies, notably the tax authorities. In 2014, however, Putin signed a law merging the economic courts with the ordinary court system, whose quality was far inferior. The whole judicial system was now put under full political control, being deprived of integrity and independence.[44]

In 2010, Columbia University professor Timothy Frye concluded that "strengthening the rule of law requires changes in political relations that level the playing field between the powerful and the powerless, and on this front Russia has made far less progress. Indeed, some argue that Russia has moved from state capture by private business to capture of private business by the state." Since those words were written, the state capture has become evident.[45]

Occasionally Putin speaks sharply about the need to fight corruption, especially when he appears before law enforcers. In March 2015, he stated that "the policy of cleaning out all state agencies, including the Interior Ministry, will continue consistently and firmly. The statistics show that the measures we have taken have already helped to bring down the level of corruption, but ... this problem is still far from being solved. ... Last year, more than 11,000 corruption-related cases were sent to the courts."[46]

Increasingly, however, Putin tends to dismiss concerns about corruption as exaggerated, using Ukraine as the showcase of corruption. In July 2017, he stated to a group of students: "Corruption should not be a matter of speculation, since it exists across the world. ... Look at what has happened with our neighbors. The current [Ukrainian] government was voted into power on promises to fight corruption. ... Unfortunately, they chose to do it by staging a government coup. Now that they have the power, what are the results? There is even more corruption. Ukraine is choking with corruption from the top to the very bottom."[47]

In recent years, several senior officials have been arrested or prosecuted for corruption, notably Minister of Defense Anatoly Serdyukov in 2012, Economy Minister Alexei Ulyukaev in 2016, a few regional governors, state enterprise managers, and quite a few law enforcement generals. Ulyukaev was sentenced to eight years in prison for allegedly having taken a bribe of $2 million from Igor Sechin, Putin's close associate and the CEO of Rosneft, who refused to appear in court. Even in these cases, the actual reason for the arrest is perceived to have been not corruption but conflicts with senior people in Putin's entourage. Many of his protégés appear to have legal immunity. They include nearly all the top state officials, the big state enterprise managers, Putin's cronies, and Chechnya's president Ramzan Kadyrov, who has been sanctioned by the United States for violations of human rights.[48]

Each year, the Kremlin publishes an extensive and detailed list of the property, incomes, and expenditures of the president and leading members of his administration and their families, but these lists have no relation to reality. Nor are the filings amended when independent media or anticorruption activists uncover major unreported assets of the truly powerful.

A decade ago, a prominent US chief executive who had done extensive business in Russia and around the world told me that to his mind Russia was the most corrupt big country in world history. According to Transparency International, Russia ranked 135 out of 180 on its Corruption Perceptions Index for 2017, lower than any other G-20 country.[49]

In few areas has Putin changed his policy more than in foreign affairs. As newly elected president in 2000, Putin went out of his way to be helpful and accommodating to other great powers, including the United States. He ignored the NATO bombing of Yugoslavia in 1999, which had marked a low point in postcommunist US-Russia relations. In 2000, Putin was quite positive on NATO, stating, "I don't see any reason why cooperation between Russia and NATO shouldn't develop further; but I repeat that it will happen only if Russia is treated as an equal partner."[50]

Former deputy secretary of state Strobe Talbott summed up the situation: "Putin wanted to join the West, but on terms that were more respectful of Russia's national interests and national anxieties." The fundamental problem is that the West tends to believe that foreign policy should embrace certain values, whereas Putin has adopted an extreme position of pure realpolitik.[51]

Before the G-8 summit in Okinawa in July 2000, Putin made a flashy, unprecedented visit to North Korea, presenting himself as a global fixer. Putin started off well with George W. Bush when they met in June 2001. Bush uttered: "I looked the man in the eye. I found him to be very straightforward and trustworthy. . . . I was able to get a sense of his soul, a man deeply committed to his country and the best interests of his country." On September 11, 2001, Putin was the first foreign leader who managed to call Bush after the Al-Qaeda terrorist attacks in New York and on the Pentagon. He offered logistical support for the US military in Afghanistan.[52]

The war in Afghanistan suited Putin perfectly because it was a war against international terrorism, which was how Putin saw the domestic Chechen rebellion in southern Russia, while others considered his policy in Chechnya to be domestic repression and human rights violations. Putin has persistently driven this theme with his Western counterparts, and George W. Bush showed a great deal of understanding.

Soon, however, a series of events permanently altered Putin's foreign policy outlook and his view of the United States. The three most significant incidents were probably the US unilateral withdrawal from the Anti-Ballistic Missile (ABM) Treaty in July 2002, the US initiation of the war with Iraq in March 2003, which Russia opposed together with Germany and France, and the Orange Revolution in Ukraine in November–December 2004.

Time and again, Putin has returned to the ABM Treaty as the breaking point in his relations with the United States. In his presidential address in March 2018, Putin stated: "Back in 2000, the US announced its withdrawal from the Anti-Ballistic Missile Treaty. Russia was categorically against this. . . . We did our best to dissuade the Americans from withdrawing from the treaty. All was in vain. The US pulled out of the treaty in 2002. Even after that we tried to develop constructive dialogue with the Americans. . . . All our proposals, absolutely all of them, were rejected." The US ambitions to build missile defense in Eastern Europe became a permanent bone of contention.[53]

Before the United States launched the war in Iraq in 2003, Putin spoke like a peacenik, underlining "the new quality of Russia as a country peace-loving and oriented toward solving all the disputes arising in the world solely by peaceful means and on the basis of international law. . . . The same applies to the situation around Iraq." After the war and the execution of President Saddam Hussein, Putin became embittered: "Everyone remembers well what happened to Iraq and Saddam Hussein. Hussein abandoned the production of weapons of mass destruction. Nonetheless, under the pretext of searching for these weapons, Saddam Hussein himself and his family were killed during the well-known military operation. Even children died back then. His grandson, I believe, was shot to death. The country was destroyed, and Saddam Hussein was hanged." He lamented the Western intervention in Libya and the killing of President Muammar Gaddafi in 2011 in a similar tone. That Gaddafi and Hussein had killed thousands of their own citizens was of no interest to Putin.[54]

For a long time, President Bush avoided responding to Putin's criticism of the United States. In September 2003, for example, Bush stated: "I respect President Putin's vision for Russia: a country at peace within its borders, with its neighbors and with the world, a country in which democracy and freedom and rule of law thrive." Putin made his first anti-American statement after the Beslan massacre in southern Russia in September 2004.[55]

Ukraine's Orange Revolution in November–December 2004 probably delivered the greatest shock Putin has experienced as a ruler. He claimed that "our European and American partners decided to support the orange revolution even against the Constitution," presenting it as a Western political conspiracy. Putin saw the uprising as an attempted Western coup against a fellow authoritarian ruler, and he feared that he would be the next victim. He saw the Orange Revolution as the greatest democratic challenge facing his rule, fearing that Russians would follow the Ukrainians' example and rise in protest against the Kremlin's authoritarian power and usurpation of Russia's wealth, even though

Ukraine did not commit any hostile acts against Russia. In 2005, Putin responded by prohibiting all conceivable preconditions for an Orange Revolution in Russia, adopting strict laws against nongovernmental organizations.[56]

His attitude to the West deteriorated radically. He had expressed nostalgia about the Soviet Union all along, but in his famous Munich speech in February 2007, Putin displayed his anti-Americanism in full: "Today we are witnessing an almost uncontained hyper use of force—military force—in international relations, force that is plunging the world into an abyss of permanent conflicts. One state and, of course, first and foremost the United States, has overstepped its national borders in every way." He lashed out against the United States: "Incidentally, Russia—we—are constantly being taught about democracy. But for some reason those who teach us do not want to learn themselves. I consider that the unipolar model is not only unacceptable but also impossible in today's world."[57]

The Orange Revolution was not the only popular uprising worrying Putin. In 2003, Georgia had its Rose Revolution, that brought Mikheil Saakashvili to the presidency, and in March 2005 Kyrgyzstan had its Tulip Revolution. Putin was reviled by the Arab Spring movement, which started in Tunisia in December 2010 and spread through Libya, Egypt, Yemen, and Syria in 2011. Putin steadfastly and vocally supported the "legitimate" incumbent rulers.

The Munich speech was followed by a more aggressive foreign policy. In May 2007, Russia pioneered cyber warfare with a big attack on Estonia's government and its commercial banks. Since 2008, Russia has increased its military expenditures and modernized its military, hardware, and tactics. It has broadened its military toolbox, putting more emphasis on intelligence, insurgents, disinformation, and cyber warfare.

In January 2008, President George W. Bush suddenly started campaigning for NATO Membership Action Plans for Ukraine and Georgia to be adopted at the April NATO summit in Bucharest. The United States presented this idea too late to be able to persuade the other member states. The Bucharest April 2008 NATO summit communiqué concluded boldly: "NATO welcomes Ukraine's and Georgia's Euro-Atlantic aspirations for membership in NATO. We agreed today that these countries will become members of NATO." But NATO did nothing to make this commitment credible, rendering the declaration harmful.[58]

This communiqué provoked the Kremlin while leaving Georgia and Ukraine without security guarantees. Absurdly, Putin was invited to the NATO summit. In a closed meeting he made a militant statement, disqualifying Ukraine's right to sovereign statehood and territorial integrity. "This is a complex state formation. If the NATO issue is added there, along with other problems, this may bring Ukraine to the verge of existence as a sovereign state.... Ukraine is home to as many as 17 million ethnic Russians. Who will dare to claim that we don't have any interests there?"[59]

Putin called the transfer of Crimea to Ukraine in 1954 illegal: "Crimea was simply given to Ukraine by a CPSU Politburo decision, which was not even supported with appropriate government procedures that are normally applicable to territory transfers." Immediately after this near declaration of war, President George W. Bush went to a friendly meeting with Putin at his residence in Sochi, which Putin could only interpret as a US acceptance of his stand. Within six years, Russia had attacked both Georgia and Ukraine, calling NATO's bluff, and NATO did very little. In August 2008, Russian troops entered Georgia for a five-day war, and on August 26, Russia recognized the sovereignty of the small autonomous territories in Georgia, Abkhazia and South Ossetia, which were occupied by Russian troops.[60]

In the winter of 2013–2014, Ukraine posed a new challenge to Putin's regime. Once again Putin faced a popular democratic revolt in his East Slavic neighborhood. This time, the Kremlin was prepared. Domestically, it had tightened the screws with antidemocratic legislation, and it had prepared its military with contingency plans for Ukraine. After Ukraine's president Viktor Yanukovych had failed to impose a Putinlike regime in Ukraine despite killing some 125 people in Kiev, he fled to Russia on February 22, 2014.

The Kremlin acted instantly. Starting on February 27, Russia surprised the world with "small green men": Russian special forces without insignia started occupying Crimea from Russia's leased naval base in Sevastopol, and they encountered no armed resistance. They swiftly occupied Crimea before anybody realized what was going on. Their medals and an official Russian propaganda film date the start of their operation as February 20, two days before Yanukovych's ouster.

On March 18, Russia surprisingly annexed the occupied Crimea, killing two birds with one stone. National euphoria erupted over Russia's regaining of the popular Soviet holiday resort peninsula. The independent Levada Center measured 88 percent approval, including many liberals. Ukraine had been transformed into an enemy. As a consequence, Russians no longer discussed Ukraine as a democratic experiment but instead called it a failed state, serving the Kremlin's desire for stability at home.[61]

In its exuberance, the Kremlin sent limited Russian special forces without insignia into much of eastern and southern Ukraine to arouse unrest. In one appearance on April 17, 2014, Putin presented Russia as the defender of the rights of ethnic Russians and Russian speakers in a "*Novorossiya,*" reviving an old, long-forgotten tsarist concept:

> The essential issue is how to ensure the legitimate rights and interests of ethnic Russians and Russian speakers in the southeast of Ukraine. I would like to remind you that what was called Novorossiya (New Russia) back in the tsarist days—Kharkov, Lugansk, Donetsk, Kherson, Nikolayev and Odessa—were not part of Ukraine back then. These territories were given to Ukraine in the 1920s by the Soviet government. Why? Who knows. They were won by Potyomkin and Catherine the Great in a series of well-known wars. The center of that territory was Novorossiysk, so the region is called Novorossiya. Russia lost these territories for various reasons, but the people remained.[62]

Even at this moment of exuberance, Putin was careful not to go all out as a neo-imperialist, and he soon dropped the term *Novorossiya*. He continued with a caveat: "The key issue is providing guarantees to these people." The Kremlin-instigated uprising failed except for in parts of the two most eastern provinces of Luhansk and Donetsk, but when the Ukrainian military carried out a major offensive against the separatists and Russian volunteers, the Kremlin sent in regular Russian forces in July, safeguarding the separatist territory and causing Ukraine major losses.[63]

The hot war in eastern Ukraine has continued. Russia has used all conceivable unconventional military means, including insurgency, sabotage, disinformation, trade war, economic sanctions, and cyber in Ukraine. It has tested its considerable nonconventional capabilities that can reinforce its military might.

Putin had gone full circle from a pro-Western stand to a staunch anti-Americanism. With his intervention in Ukraine, he had alienated the United States, the European Union, and all the former Soviet republics. Russia has become marginalized, having little but China, India, the Middle East, and Venezuela to turn to.

Like all successful authoritarian leaders, Putin devotes great attention to his law enforcement agencies, and he has nurtured their strength as well as their competition. Major changes of personnel and organization are rare, but when they occur, he has acted fast and hard.

Putin's two favorite agencies have been the FSB (the domestic arm of the old KGB) and the FSO (the presidential security arm of the old KGB). Top Putin loyalists have headed these two agencies, and Putin has poured resources and privileges on both organizations. While the FSO is a small elite force, the FSB has grown very large. The FSB continues to operate throughout the former Soviet Union, and in recent years it has also been allowed to expand abroad, previously the territory of the foreign intelligence agency, or SVR.

In the Soviet Union, the foreign intelligence main directorate of the KGB competed with the military intelligence directorate, the GRU. In 1991, Yeltsin cut the foreign intelligence directorate off from the KGB, forming the SVR. The SVR and GRU continue their rivalry, and both agencies are considered highly competent. The much stronger FSB, however, has entered this competition abroad.

The Ministry of Interior led the Soviet police force. It was generally seen as corrupt and incompetent, which is still the case, and it is outflanked by all other branches of law enforcement in official ranking and resource allocation. Putin waited until April 2001 to replace the ministers of interior and defense, who were not his people. Since then, Putin has enjoyed great control over all law enforcement agencies.

The Prosecutor General's Office has long been accused of extensive corporate raiding. In January 2011, its investigative arm was made independent as the Investigative Committee under the leadership of Putin's friend from law school and St. Petersburg KGB Alexander Bastrykin. These two organizations have competed in predation, leaving businesspeople their victims. None of them wants to abandon their rich loot.[64]

In April 2016, Putin ambitiously created a National Guard of four hundred thousand paramilitary security forces. He put it under the command of his longtime chief bodyguard General Viktor Zolotov, while retiring a whole row of old KGB generals. Most of the National Guard's 400,000 troops were taken from the Ministry of Interior. While its public aim is to fight terrorism, its formation has been seen as a preparation to fight domestic opposition.[65]

Russia has many law enforcement and security agencies with vast resources and power. A standard practice of Russian law enforcement agencies is to detain businesspeople for pretrial detention on the flimsiest of grounds to shake them down. In 2010, the *Washington Post* reported that "according to court records, 404,333 people were convicted of economic crimes, but only 146,490 received prison terms. The rest paid fines or got suspended sentences. At the same time, 59 people died in Moscow's pretrial prisons, half a dozen more than the year before."[66]

One of the most notorious, and best-investigated, cases is that of the lawyer Sergei Magnitsky, who accused officials of having stolen $230 million from the tax authorities. Instead, Magnitsky was charged by those same officials for their crime, and in 2009, he died in pretrial detention in Moscow's Matrosskaya Tishina prison at the age of thirty-eight under dubious circumstances. Thanks to the fund manager Bill Browder's exposure of this case, the US Congress adopted the Sergei Magnitsky Rule of Law Accountability Act in December 2012, under which a total of forty-nine Russian culprits have been sanctioned. One of the offenders sanctioned by the United States was the head of the Investigative Committee, Putin's law school friend from St. Petersburg Alexander Bastrykin.

The Magnitsky case illustrates how Russian law enforcement agencies persecute businesspeople on a large scale and how sadly absent their protection is. In December 2016, the US Congress adopted the Global Magnitsky Act, and in December 2017 the US Treasury named the first designations. The only Russian on that list was Artem Chaika, son of the Russian prosecutor general Yuri Chaika. Young Chaika had been exposed as a major organized criminal using his father's subordinates for his extortion of enterprises from innocent victims in a film by the anticorruption activist Alexei Navalny in December 2015.[67]

Putin has repeatedly complained about how the police deal with business. In his annual address to the Federal Assembly in December 2015, he embraced free market values: "I believe free enterprise to be the most important aspect of economic and social well-being. Entrepreneurial freedom is something we need to expand to respond to all attempts to impose restrictions on us." He went on to pronounce his harshest critique ever of lawless law enforcers:

> During 2014, the investigative authorities opened nearly 200,000 cases of so-called economic crimes. But only 46,000 of 200,000 cases were actually taken to court, and 15,000 cases were thrown out during the hearings. Simple math suggests that only 15 percent of all cases ended with a conviction. At the same time, the vast majority . . . 83 percent of entrepreneurs who faced criminal charges fully or partially lost their business—they got harassed, intimidated, robbed and then released. This certainly isn't what we need in terms of a business climate. This is actually the opposite, the direct destruction of the business climate. I ask the investigative authorities and the prosecutor's office to pay special attention to this.[68]

Anybody reading these lines would presume that the president intended to change policy, ending the laissez-faire policy toward the law enforcement divisions to discipline them, but he did not indicate any follow-up. While 212,316 criminal cases had been opened against businesspeople in 2014, the number rose to 255,250 in 2015. Although Putin continued to promise defense against the "law enforcers," he allowed the corporate raiders to continue to indulge in the riches of Russia's private entrepreneurs. By attacking the Magnitsky Act, he defended them.[69]

As Jordan Gans-Morse concluded in his fine empirical study of property rights in Russia: the country has reversed itself from a certain degree of the rule of law to "state predation." The organized crime of the early 1990s was defeated in the mid-1990s, and a relative rule of law took hold in the early 2000s, but that has now given way to state predation.[70]

In February 2016, the prominent business newspaper *Vedomosti* sadly noted that "the fundamental problems of the interaction between law enforcers and business—the absence of guaranteed property rights, as well as independent and just courts, and the corporate raiding of law enforcement—have been preserved, and the current crisis has grown worse."[71]

A Russian journalist observed in 2014 that "paradoxically the more successful a business is, the greater are the risks." A survey by the global accounting firm PwC showed that 57 percent of Russia's businesspeople wanted to sell their firms, as compared with 17 percent in Europe as a whole, clarifying the dismay of Russian entrepreneurs. In the years 2009–2013, no fewer than 670,000 cases were opened against Russian businesspeople for "fraud." Of these just 146,000 went to court. This small share indicates the prevalence of corporate raiding or extortion.[72]

Nor does a court sentence necessarily imply guilt in Russia. In 2017, a survey among managers of big and medium-sized enterprises showed that almost 60 percent of the managers reckoned that in a conflict with a bigger company their only defense would be official administrative support, showing no trust in the law or the courts. When Medvedev was president, 2008–2012, he had two laws adopted to stop this practice, but they had little impact. Repeated official proposals to curb pretrial detentions of businesspeople, for example, by the Supreme Court in 2016, have had no effect.[73]

By defending his law enforcement agencies against accusations of corruption more frequently than he criticizes corruption itself, Putin shows that he accepts this behavior of Russia's purported law enforcers. Rather than trying to rein them in, he continues to expand their powers. In May 2017, Putin issued a decree that entitled the FSB to "take decisions within its authority regarding seizure of land and (or) property . . . for the needs of the Russian Federation." Nothing was said about possibilities for private individuals or companies to appeal if the FSB confiscated their property. This is reminiscent of Ivan the Terrible's exceptional rule, or *oprichnina,* in the sixteenth century, when he let the secret police carry out mass repressions and confiscate land from the aristocrats.[74]

In 1996, Russia joined the Council of Europe, an all-European interparliamentarian body that promotes human rights, democracy, and the rule of law, because Yeltsin had such an aspiration. It has fifty-seven members and is separate from the European Union. Its court, the European Court of Human Rights, verifies whether a member country complies with its own laws. Soon Russia became a major customer with thousands of cases every year, and it validated its verdicts. In 2015, however, Russia's Constitutional Court decided that it would no longer do so. The tipping point was a 2014 decision by the European Court of Human Rights to award shareholders of the now-defunct oil company Yukos €1.9 billion in compensation.[75]

The practically unlimited powers of the Russian law enforcement agencies are a foundation of the Putin system. The competition among the law enforcers has been intense, but currently the dominant verdict among Russian experts is that the FSB has gained the upper hand against the other agencies. If their rivalry goes too far, it could cause a destabilizing split among the security forces.[76]

The old adage remains valid that the severity of Russia's laws is alleviated by the state's inability to enforce them. The FSB wants to be omniscient and perfectly informed, while repression is quite limited. Dozens of Russian journalists have been murdered, but human rights organizations count only just over one hundred political prisoners in Russia, though the many people sentenced for or in pretrial detention for economic crimes form a large gray group. The political situation is reminiscent of the pre-perestroika years, when many intellectuals went into "internal exile," avoiding politically sensitive topics, indulging in culture instead. Moscow's theaters are flourishing.

The scholar of Russian intelligence services Mark Galeotti has summed up the situation: "Moscow has developed an array of overlapping and competitive security and spy services. The aim is to encourage risk-taking and multiple sources, but it also leads to turf wars and a tendency to play to Kremlin prejudices." An illustration of this rivalry is that the US authorities accused both the GRU and the FSB of having hacked the Democratic National Committee in 2016, presumably in independent competition. Galeotti argues that this is a reflection of the FSB expansion abroad, the decline of the SVR, and the competition between the intelligence agencies.[77]

The FSB and FSO are the two top elite services favored by Putin in high state appointments. An additional force is the *kadyrovtsy*, the independent security forces of Chechnya's president Ramzan Kadyrov, who operate also in Moscow, indulging in violent crimes to the great irritation of the FSB. Symptomatically, five members of these forces were sentenced for the February 2015 murder of Boris Nemtsov.[78]

Putin's rule has been characterized by far-reaching deinstitutionalization. Many state bodies that used to be important are no longer relevant. During his third term, Putin largely abandoned collegial consultations.

Previously, the council of ministers made most economic policy decisions, but since the weak Dmitri Medvedev chairs this council, Putin prefers to make decisions in meetings with a limited group of ministers or one-on-one between him and a CEO of a state company or a minister, as is regularly reported on his website.[79]

The Russian parliament, the Federal Assembly, has become a mere transmission belt for the government's legislation. The real legislative work takes place inside the ministries and the presidential administration. Because the president appoints regional governors, regional governments have little freedom. Putin spends a lot of his time meeting governors one by one.

The only relevant official collegial body is the Security Council, which appears to have become the new Politburo. Its meetings are always chaired by Putin. Its twelve permanent members generally meet slightly more often than every second week, usually in the middle of the afternoon on a Friday or Thursday, though their meetings can take place at any time, as it suits Putin. During the first half of 2018, the Kremlin website reported fourteen meetings of the permanent members of the Security Council.[80]

Eleven of the permanent members are there ex officio: President Putin, Prime Minister Medvedev, Chairman of the Federation Council Valentina Matvienko, State Duma Speaker Vyacheslav Volodin, Head of the Presidential Administration Anton Vaino, National Security Council Secretary Nikolai Patrushev, Foreign Minister Sergei Lavrov, Interior

Minister Vladimir Kolokoltsev, Defense Minister Sergei Shoigu, Director of the Federal Security Service (FSB) Alexander Bortnikov, and Director of the Foreign Intelligence Service (SVR) Sergei Naryshkin. Curiously Putin's former chief of staff, Sergei Ivanov, is still a permanent member, even though he was demoted to special presidential representative for environmental protection, ecology, and transportation in August 2016. Half of the permanent members are generals.[81]

An oddity is that Putin's favorite and long-time chief bodyguard, General Viktor Zolotov, is not a permanent member but a mere member of the Security Council. In early April 2016, Putin appointed Zolotov commander of the newly formed National Guard and a permanent member of the Security Council by decree, but a few days later this decree was amended, excluding Zolotov. For months, a disparity prevailed. Putin's website claimed that Zolotov was a permanent member of the Security Council, whereas the website of the Security Council did not list him. After several months, Putin's website dropped Zolotov. To judge from the official Kremlin bulletins, Zolotov has never attended a meeting of the permanent members of the Security Council.

Both these circumstances raised eyebrows. Until 2016, Sergei Ivanov was widely seen as Putin's deputy, so both his demotion and his tenacity on the Security Council are noteworthy. It is also remarkable that Putin cannot appoint the general widely seen as his favorite to the Security Council. Is Putin fully in charge of the Security Council, or is it a real collective decision-making body? The evidence suggests the latter.

Each time the Security Council meets, it issues a brief statement about who has attended and what topics were discussed. It meets before all major international events and discusses primarily foreign policy, but often the members also discuss "current issues of the domestic socioeconomic agenda." Thus, the main economic decisions are being made without any economic official at the table.[82]

The Security Council is reminiscent of the old Soviet Politburo, which ruled the Soviet Union. It met more regularly, once a week, always on a Thursday, and had about a dozen full members along with candidate members. It even issued similar bulletins about what topics it had discussed each time. It was the Politburo that ousted Nikita Khrushchev in October 1964 and launched a failed coup in August 1991.

If any top-level body can threaten Putin, it is the Security Council. The Kremlin, which was quite open in the 1990s, is now closed, and much of the information that slips out is disinformation. As in Soviet days, researchers need to turn to hard data such as official photos, statements, appearances, and appointments. Two recent periods of top-level crises have been apparent. One was immediately after the murder of Boris Nemtsov on February 27, 2015, after which Putin did not appear in public for ten days. The other was in August 2016, when Sergei Ivanov was removed as head of the presidential administration.

During his eighteen years in power, Putin has accomplished an impressive consolidation of power. He has built up a centralized personal authoritarian system. He has toyed with multiple values, but they are too many and contradictory to be taken seriously. His statements about ideas appear more like opportunistic image-making. Putin's two central goals appear to be political power and the enrichment of himself and his friends.

Putin is undoubtedly deeply committed to the KGB, but his enchantment seems to be with its methods, information, and power rather than with its values. Putin's selection of top officials appears based on one criterion: trust. He prefers men whom he has worked with for many years. He does not care much about their views, as long as they obey. Until his rejuvenation of top cadres started in 2015, Putin clearly preferred men of his own age. His new cadres tend to be technocrats in their forties without strong political views but highly obedient.

The three closest aides of Putin in the national security sphere appear to be Sergei Ivanov, Nikolai Patrushev, and Alexander Bortnikov, who are all KGB generals. One after the other has served as chairman of the FSB following Putin, forming a tight FSB circle. These three men form one of Putin's rings of power. They are all the same age and from the KGB in Leningrad and are on first name terms with Putin.

Yet these three men could challenge Putin's political power. The members of the FSB circle are living very well, but they might not be profiting from the great larceny around Putin as much as the cronies and the state enterprise managers. They have strong views on foreign policy, which they show in their rare publications, and the rumor is that these three men together with Putin decided the annexation of Crimea. When things are not going well, they might object to Putin.

The dossier composed by the former British intelligence officer Christopher Steele contains very interesting information. On August 5, 2016, Sergei Ivanov was reported to be "angry at the recent turn of events. He believed that the Kremlin 'team' involved, led by presidential spokesman Dmitriy PESKOV, had gone too far in interfering in foreign affairs" with the hacking of the Democratic National Committee server and the wider pro-Trump operation. Ivanov "was determined to stop PESKOV playing an independent role in relation to the US going forward." On August 10, Ivanov was reported to have expressed his dismay that "PUTIN was generally satisfied with the progress of the anti-CLINTON operation to date." Two days later, Ivanov was sacked as Putin's chief of staff, but he has managed to survive politically as the Russian hacking scandal has mounted in the United States. It would be strange if his sacking were not connected with this conflict over interference in the US election campaign in the Kremlin.[83]

Putin's two big political tasks have been to build a *vertikal* of power and a dictatorship of law. He has done so successfully, subordinating both the executive and judicial powers to him. Like many authoritarian leaders, he encourages competition among his law enforcement agencies, so that they cannot overthrow him, but rivalry could split and destabilize the security forces. The big drawback is that systematic deinstitutionalization has created a political and judicial system that does not allow secure property rights and thus cannot lead to significant economic growth.

Clearly, Putin is in charge. It is not credible that he is just manipulated by his aides, because few select their aides more carefully than Putin. The Security Council remains the only authoritative top-level policy forum.[84]

Conservative Fiscal and Monetary Policy

C ontemporary Russians have experienced many shocks. The greatest was the collapse of communism and the Soviet Union. The financial crash of August 17, 1998, delivered a second great blow. In 2008, the global financial crisis hit them again, and the halving of the price of oil in 2014 amounted to a fourth crisis.

Russia is particularly prone to crisis because of its dependence on oil and gas. When prices were high, they accounted for two-thirds of its exports, half of its federal revenues, and about one-fifth of GDP. A reasonable assessment is that when oil prices were high, they contributed about half of the economic growth. Russians talk a lot about the need for diversification of the economy to make it more resilient, but the country's comparative advantages in oil and gas production are indisputable. The best way to diversify the economy is to grow so that other industries, notably the service sector, expands.[1]

Since the Russian economy is so prone to crisis, the population greatly values macroeconomic stability. Few people understand that better than Vladimir Putin, who praises economic stability almost constantly. The collapse of the Soviet Union and the Russian crash of 1998 taught him that macroeconomic stability is vital for political stability.

After the financial crash of August 1998, the Russian economy experienced an extraordinary turnaround. In a single year, it was transformed from an apparent basket case with steadily falling output to one of the most dynamic economies in the world. Many changes occurred simultaneously, rendering it difficult to distinguish the cure, and answers depend on preconceptions.

Fiscal conservatives argued that the switch from a loose to a conservative fiscal policy cured the economy. All macroeconomic indicators improved—budget balance, public debt, inflation, trade balance, and current account balance. At long last, a critical mass of markets, financial stability, and private enterprises had been attained. As enterprises faced hard budget constraints and a more level playing field, growth took off.

Another idea was that commodity prices were the dominant cause. The world of crude oil rose from a low of less than $10 a barrel in 1998 to a peak of $147 per barrel in 2008, generating an enormous windfall for Russian oil producers and, through taxation, the Russian state (fig. 3.1). Natural gas and metal prices surged in parallel.[2]

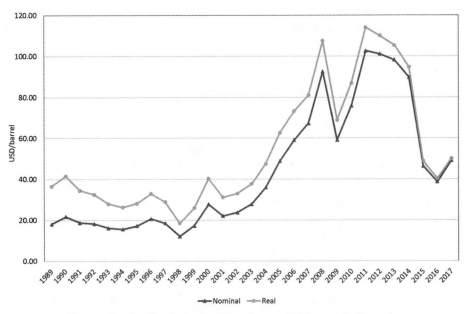

Fig. 3.1 Crude oil price, 1989–2017. *Source: US Energy Information Administration, Short-Term Energy Outlook April 2018*

A third related view was that the large devaluation that cut the dollar value of the ruble by three-quarters in the fall of 1998 jumpstarted the Russian economy. Exporters of commodities benefited the most and drove Russia's economic recovery.[3]

A fourth suggested cause was that the crisis itself created opportunities for the political resolution of the underlying economic problems. Society came together only when it realized how costly a steady large budget deficit was and slashed it. What had been politically impossible suddenly became conventional wisdom.[4]

Fifth, Yegor Gaidar argued that Russia had arrived at the end of its revolution and was ready for postrevolutionary stabilization and recovery. After the revolutionary passion of the 1990s had abated, politics would allow sensible economic policy, and plenty of free capacity was at hand.[5]

A sixth explanation is that economic reforms instigated and promoted by President Vladimir Putin turned Russia around, but the strong growth started in 1999, before Putin was appointed prime minister, so he cannot have caused the initial growth. All these explanations have some merit, and they are largely complementary. Many factors coincided and contributed to high economic growth.

Since Putin came to power in 2000, great stability has prevailed on the top financial posts. His close associate from the mayor's office in St. Petersburg, Alexei Kudrin, was finance minister from 2000 until 2011. His like-minded deputy Anton Siluanov succeeded him. Kudrin's former first deputy Sergei Ignatiev was chairman of the Central Bank of Russia (CBR) from 2002 to 2013. When Ignatiev retired, former minister of economy and Putin aide Elvira Nabiullina, who harbored similar views, took his place. All these people are respected as competent professionals and people of integrity. They have been strong supporters of market economic reforms and are called "systemic liberals," that is, liberals who work within the system.

The crash of 1998 had an extraordinary impact on Russian society, economy, and politics. After the voucher privatization in the early 1990s, the Russian stock market had boomed prematurely, multiplying six times in 1996 and 1997, although the economy had not started growing. On August 17, 1998, the Russian economy crashed monumentally. The ruble was suddenly devalued, soon to one quarter of its prior dollar value; the government defaulted on high-flying domestic treasury bonds; and bank payments were frozen for three months.[6]

The fundamental cause of the financial crash was a stubbornly large budget deficit of 8–9 percent of GDP from 1993 to 1998. The government was politically unable to cut this large budget deficit, but international donors, led by the International Monetary Fund (IMF), realized that the public finances were unsustainable and refused to provide financing. Weirdly, private investors kept the Russian government afloat with large international portfolio inflows into Russian domestic treasuries, whose real yields were obscenely high, reaching at 100 percent, at great cost to the Russian treasury, reminiscent of a Ponzi scheme. In 1997, Russia received no less than $46 billion in private portfolio inflows, or 10 percent of GDP. Although this was legal, it was speculation at its worst. The situation was obviously untenable, but the purchasers of domestic Russian treasury bonds could make fortunes as long as they got out before the crash.[7]

The cause of Russia's large budget deficit was political. In October 1997, an unholy alliance of Prime Minister Viktor Chernomyrdin, representing the old state enterprise managers, the leading oligarch, Boris Berezovsky, and the communists in the State Duma, agreed to increase the budget deficit to 8 percent of GDP at the worst possible time. Days later contagion from the East Asian financial crisis spread to the Russian stock market like a viral outbreak. On October 28, 1997, the Russian stock market plummeted by 19 percent. Since the government had just expanded the budget deficit, it was too embarrassed to retreat.[8]

In early 1998, the crisis seemed to have abated. In March, President Boris Yeltsin finally sacked the inert Chernomyrdin, but it took another month before his successor, the young technocrat Sergei Kirienko, was confirmed as prime minister by the Duma. Kirienko, thirty-five, looked even younger and was known as *kinder surpriz* (literally, child surprise, or prodigy). However smart he was, he lacked authority and needed another month to form a government. At the end of May, Russia was hit by a full-fledged financial crisis. Foreign investors no longer wanted to purchase risky Russian treasuries, but the youthful government did not understand the severity of the crisis.

In 1996–1997, the IMF had been rendered redundant by the large private capital inflows, but when private funds dried up, it reentered the stage with force. In July 1998, together with the World Bank and Japan, the IMF composed a stabilization package with credits totaling $22.6 billion. Its key condition was that the regional governments accepted to pass on a larger share of their revenues to the federal government, but the cabinet was too weak to persuade the Duma. On July 18, the State Duma decided to refute such legislation. The IMF made one big disbursement of $4.8 billion but then dropped Russia like a hot brick. The financial crash was only a matter of time, but the young newly appointed ministers did not understand that and went on vacation.[9]

In the first half of August, the crash was obviously coming. The business magnate George Soros understood that perfectly well. We communicated daily before the crash. When Soros failed to get relevant Russian policy makers to listen, I encouraged him to publish an article in the *Financial Times* to clarify the depth of the crisis. He did so. On August 13, the *Financial Times* published his letter. Market panic erupted, and four days later the Russian financial crash was a fact. Soros had acted to salvage Russia, but speculators thought he was in the market, which he was not. Thanks to Soros's letter, Russia did not run out of reserves as it had in 1991, which facilitated its recovery. The reserves of more than $10 billion were sufficient to stop a free fall of the ruble and hyperinflation.[10]

On August 17, all hell broke loose. The ruble collapsed. The Russian banks closed their doors to people desperate to get cash, and half the banks went bankrupt. The Central Bank halted international bank payments for three months, but all bank payments stopped. The government defaulted on some $70 billion of domestic treasuries, though not on its external debt. The immediate economic effects were devastating. Once again middle-income Russians lost two-thirds of their bank savings in the absence of deposit insurance. Inflation surged with the sharp devaluation, arousing fears of renewed hyperinflation, though it stopped at 48 percent for 1998.[11]

In the middle of September, I organized a high-level international conference in Moscow. We had to carry $40,000 in cash to pay for rooms in an American hotel and for restaurants, since credit cards no longer

worked. President Boris Yeltsin was forced to appoint a government under the old-style communist Yevgeny Primakov with a few communists
in leading economic positions. The *New York Times Magazine* published
an article by veteran Moscow correspondent John Lloyd with the devastating headline "Who Lost Russia?" blaming the reformers. Were market
reforms over?[12]

In September 1998, somebody put up anonymous billboards in
Moscow with the text: "Nobody will save Russia apart from ourselves." In
jest one of the posters had been signed "Michel Camdessus," the forceful
managing director of the IMF. Russia's self-confidence had hit a low.[13]

But something unexpected happened. Since nobody was ready to
lend the Russian government any money, it had no choice but to cut expenditures sharply, because the population could not be forced to pay
significantly more taxes in the short term. Russia switched from more
than a decade of excessive budget deficits to a decade of budget surpluses.

The sudden tightening of fiscal and monetary policy had a major
positive impact on the economy. Output fell by 4.8 percent in 1998, but
then it bottomed out. Inflation leveled off faster than expected. Half of
the banks closed for good, though after three months of actual bank
holidays, the surviving banks started working again. The state established a bad bank facility for selling off the assets of bankrupt banks. It
took years to settle the defaulted treasury bonds, but the final outcome
was a write-off of about $60 billion, sharply reducing Russia's public
debt. Since the bonds were subject to Russian jurisdiction, foreign investors could not sue the government.

Contrary to general expectations, the crash of 1998 initiated a decade of high growth. It had leveled the playing field and imposed hard
budget constraints on all enterprises. The large distortive subsidies and
nonpayment of taxes were wiped out. The period 2000–2003 represented the height of Russia's market economy. This was a time of macroeconomic balance and competitive markets. The private sector thrived as
never before or after. State subsidies were minimized, and the result
was a high growth rate averaging 7 percent a year from 1999 to 2008 (see
fig. 1.1). Russia had never grown faster.

The financial crash brought about Joseph Schumpeter's famous
creative destruction. From 1988 to 1994, young new businesspeople had

made their fortunes on commodity trading, buying oil for 1 percent of the world market prices and selling it abroad for the global market prices. They financed their trade by establishing banks, which borrowed money cheaply from the Central Bank, while inflation eliminated their interest costs. Before the crisis, they had bought high-yielding Russian treasuries.[14]

Now they were punished both for holding large amounts of Russian treasuries and for having borrowed in foreign currency. Eight of the ten biggest private banks went under, notably Menatep, Oneximbank, SBS-Agro, Bank Rossiisky Kredit, Inkombank, and Most Bank. The only exceptions were Alfa Bank and MDM, which had wisely sold their domestic treasuries in the summer of 1998, sensibly using their returns to pay off their foreign loans.[15]

The oligarchs had bought many enterprises at the voucher auctions without knowing what to do with them. Now they sold most of them. The foremost oligarchic group, Menatep, headed by Mikhail Khodorkovsky, had set up a holding company called Rosprom (an abbreviation for Russian industry), controlling some two hundred old, mismanaged companies in 1994–1995. After the crash of 1998, Menatep sold them at almost any price to concentrate its resources on the jewel in its crown, the oil company Yukos. The loss to the oligarchs was also reputational. In the years of budding capitalism, many ordinary Russians admired the oligarchs for their apparent smartness. Suddenly, they did not seem all that clever, only arrogant, upsetting people over their usurpation of state power.[16]

Most old state enterprise managers had carried out insider privatization of the companies they had managed in Soviet times, having no clue how to operate in a market economy, while being too proud to ask for advice. They went bankrupt on a massive scale, which eliminated barter and most arrears, while their assets were sold off.

Productive assets that had been petrified by unimaginative state enterprise managers were taken over by daring young entrepreneurs, such as Mikhail Khodorkovsky (Yukos), Roman Abramovich (Sibneft), Oleg Deripaska (Rusal), and Andrei Melnichenko and Sergei Popov (SUEK). Young men in their thirties revived Soviet giants that were competitive in raw material production. The new low ruble exchange rate and rising commodity prices helped them, but their success was based on ruthless enterprise restructuring with the assistance of the foremost international consulting companies, notably McKinsey.[17]

In parallel, the newly enriched Russian consumers drove consumer demand. Swiftly, new large private Russian retail chains developed, confusingly similar to Western department stores. Some Western companies also made it big, notably French Auchan, Swedish IKEA, German Metro, and Austrian Billa. The Russian mobile phone market developed briskly, with three private mobile phone companies, Vimpelcom, MTS, and MegaFon, competing hard by offering excellent service and prices.

The regional governors had thrived on barter, in collusion with businesspeople who could extract public contracts from regional governments, while diverting tax revenues from the federal government. Until August 1998, barter had increased persistently, but then it collapsed, when the federal government insisted on cash payments of taxes. The elimination of these subsidies leveled the playing field for Russian business. When the federal government was strong enough to insist on payments in cash, it could also ensure that a larger share of total taxes went to the Federal Treasury. Minister of Finance Mikhail Kasyanov and his first deputy Alexei Kudrin were the authors of this policy.[18]

The liberals also lost in the crash of 1998. They were blamed for the "damned nineties," as the Russian shorthand of that decade later became. The many opinion polls help us understand the public view. Most Russians forgot that it was the communist leadership that had brought about the collapse of the Soviet Union and its economy. Instead, they cherished the Soviet Union as a respected superpower, sparring with the United States. They blamed Yeltsin for the collapse of the Soviet Union, Gaidar for hyperinflation, and Chubais for the emergence of the oligarchs, and all three for corruption, while they gave them no credit for building the market economy that delivered the decade of unprecedented growth. As Lev Gudkov, director of the renowned Levada Center, writes: "The people can neither forget nor forgive the reformers, whom they blame for the catastrophic collapse of living standards, loss of savings, unemployment, and months-long delays in wages in the 1990s."[19]

The big winners of the crash of 1998 were the state, the federal government, and Putin, who happily arrived at a laid table, as well as benefiting from the commodity boom that took off in 2003. As the independent political analyst Dmitri Oreshkin observed in 2017: "We liberals of the Gaidar type have fulfilled our function, to form a liberal market economy, and society has no need for us any longer." Centralized political power returned, and the Federal Treasury assumed control over public finances.[20]

The lasting policy effect was a strong commitment to macroeconomic stability among the ruling elite. The state was back, and Putin as its leader received great freedom of action, which he used with cunning political skill. He had learned the wisdom of conservative macroeconomic policies: "A competent macroeconomic policy remains one of the state's most important regulatory functions." Although he has abandoned most promarket positions, he continues to defend a conservative macroeconomic policy.[21]

After the crash of 1998, the weakened President Boris Yeltsin had little choice but to sack the reformist but hapless Kirienko government. In came a government consisting mainly of left-wing old-timers, led by former communist intelligence chief Yevgeny Primakov. In spirit, however, the Kirienko program survived, because little money was available for expensive public investment programs, industry, or social transfers. Moreover, some liberals remained in the government, particularly Mikhail Zadornov, who was minister of finance from 1997 to 1999.

The default forced severe expenditure cuts and vital reforms on the country. Russia's prior political inability to balance its budget ended because the alternative was hyperinflation, which was unpalatable to all. The Russian government focused on two major expenditures: enterprise subsidies and pensions. It cut direct subsidies and quickly eliminated indirect supports by demanding that everyone pay taxes in cash rather than in services. More controversially, the government reduced real pensions by not indexing them to the high inflation. In contrast to the young reform ministers who preceded him, the old communist Primakov was politically able to cut pensions, which slumped by about half in real terms from the summer of 1998 to early 1999.

Russia cut public expenditures in an extraordinary fashion. In spite of falling output, the government slashed total consolidated government expenditures by no less than 17 percent of GDP in three years, from 48 percent in 1997 to 31 percent in 2000. Russia went from public expenditures on a Western European level to less than in the United States, and it has continued to maintain these levels. Thanks to the large expenditure cuts, Russia switched from chronic budget deficits to persistent budget surpluses until 2008 (fig. 3.2).[22]

A group of World Bank economists calculated that in 1998 the Russian government spent the extraordinary amount of 16.3 percent of GDP on enterprise subsidies, of which 10.4 percent were direct subsidies and 5.9 percent were indirect subsidies through barter. The new government responded by forcing all taxpayers to pay their taxes in real money. It eliminated the individually negotiated taxes that oil and gas companies had enjoyed. The government started pursuing its claims with a new aggressive bankruptcy law passed in 1998. The novel hard budget constraints cleared up chains of arrears, leading to creative destruction. The enterprise surveys of the *Russian Economic Barometer* show that

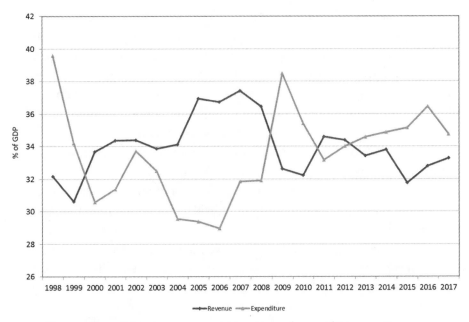

Fig. 3.2 Consolidated government revenues and expenditures, 1998–2017.
Source: IMF (2018)

barter payments between Russian industrial enterprises fell precipitously from a peak of 54 percent of all inter-enterprise payments in August
1998 to 14 percent in the fall of 2001. Barter ceased to be a problem.[23]

The financial crash reinforced the economic power of the federal
government. The monetization made it possible for the central government to collect its lawful share of taxes. The devaluation of the ruble
raised the value of foreign trade taxes in rubles, and the government
hiked export tariffs on natural resource companies, resulting in the
windfall from rising global oil prices going to the Federal Treasury. Federal revenues more than doubled, from 9 percent of GDP in 1998 to 20
percent in 2002, approximating the US level.[24]

The Federal Treasury had been established in 1992, but only beginning in 1999 did it acquire real powers of budgetary oversight reinforced by
the new Budget Code of 2000. The government also improved its financial
control by banning the placement of public money in interest-bearing
commercial bank accounts, demanding that all government agencies make
all their transactions from one account at the Federal Treasury.[25]

Of all the reforms carried out under President Putin, none has been
more acclaimed than the radical reform of the tax code. Since the early
1990s, the Russian reformers had wanted to introduce a comprehensive
new tax code, but the recalcitrant Duma blocked all significant reforms.

Until 1999, taxation was almost arbitrary. Russia's tax system was
unwieldy, inefficient, and poorly enforced. The country had more than
200 taxes: approximately 30 at the federal level and more than 170 at the
local and regional levels. In the absence of an effective federal government, the regions had invented strange local taxes. The proliferation of
taxes and high tax rates encouraged both exemptions and tax evasion.
Multiple tax agencies were competing with one another over the same
revenues.[26]

The enforcement of the tax laws was as haphazard as it was brutal.
Until the reforms, the tax inspection agency and the tax police were the
state organs causing businesses the greatest suffering, pursuing actual
tax farming. The more taxes a businessperson paid voluntarily, the
greater risk he or she ran of being extorted. The notorious tax police
often preyed on the most honest or weakest businesses to extract addi-

tional payments. A rational business operator responded by cutting a corrupt deal with the tax authorities.

A draft tax code had been lying in the State Duma since reform attempts in 1997. Key provisions of tax reform were incorporated into the government-IMF crisis plan of July 1998, but the Duma promulgated only parts of it. In January 1999, the first procedural part of the tax code came into effect. Tax reform was a key part of the Gref program of 2000. The second part of the tax code, comprising major reforms of key federal taxes, such as the value-added tax (VAT), the personal income tax, the excise tax, and the new unified social tax, came into force in 2001. Last, the new corporate income tax was introduced in 2002. The principles were clear: the tax system should be fair, simple, stable, predictable, and efficient.[27]

The number of taxes was slashed, eliminating small and inefficient nuisance taxes. Another ambition was centralization. Ten of the remaining sixteen taxes (down from the former two hundred) were federal. This reform reduced the far-reaching regional autonomy that had developed during the Yeltsin years. The Kremlin secured steady federal revenues, liberalized the Russian economy, and strengthened federal control over the state.[28]

The most popular tax reform was the abolition of the progressive personal income tax of up to 30 percent. Russians knew that the really wealthy did not pay taxes. In the summer of 2000, the progressive personal income tax was replaced with a flat income tax of 13 percent, notwithstanding opposition from the IMF, which feared that tax revenues would fall. The inspiration came from Estonia, which had introduced a flat personal income tax in the 1994, though Estonia's was twice as high at 26 percent. The flat income tax was a major breakthrough. It eliminated the disincentives to work and encouraged citizens to reveal their earnings, reducing illegality and corruption. Its positive shock expanded the tax base. The revenues from personal income tax rose from 2.4 percent of GDP in 1999–2000 to 3.3 percent in 2002. Over one year, wrote several economists in the *Journal of Political Economy*, "the Russian economy grew at almost 5 percent in real terms, while revenues from the personal income tax increased by over 25 percent in real terms."[29]

In 2001, Russia reduced the corporate profit tax from 35 percent to 24 percent. Far more important for taxpayers was the expansion of deductible business costs. Previously, only "material costs," wages, amortization, insurance, and other production and sales costs, had been deductible in a Marxist fashion, but not repairs, technical services, natural resource exploration, research and development, advertising, and personnel training costs, as well as interest paid on loans. Thus, according to the Institute of the Economy in Transition in Moscow, "practically all necessary business expenses are considered deductible from the tax base." As the tax burden on companies fell, their interest in exemptions declined, and taxation became more equal for all companies.[30]

The social payroll taxes paid by the employer had been the highest taxes, and they had been collected by four separate extrabudgetary funds. The small Employment Fund was eliminated, while the three remaining funds (Pension Fund, Medical Insurance Fund, and Social Insurance Fund) were combined into a unified social tax, which was to be collected by the Tax Ministry. Problems created by ineffective and competing tax authorities disappeared. In 2001, the payroll tax of 39.5 percent became a unified Single Social Tax, which was reduced to 26 percent in the mid-2000s, though it has varied since then.[31]

Before the reform of the tax code, the tax inspection and the tax police were the state organs that posed the greatest hazards for businesses. A presidential decree of March 2003 abolished the tax police, which had represented the arbitrary power of the bureaucracy over business. The stated motivation for the elimination of the agency was that the tax police were not "detecting, preventing or interdicting tax crimes" but instead were extorting money from businesses that paid taxes. The abolition of the tax police and the other tax reforms removed taxation from businesses' chief complaints.[32]

The fewer, lower, and simpler taxes left less room for discretion for the authorities, and the tax burden became bearable. Small-scale tax violations were decriminalized and became subject to civil rather than criminal law and were punished with moderate fines. The tax system became effective in raising revenue, without placing undue burden on individuals or companies. The lower tax rates actually raised public revenues as a share of GDP, since Russians were happy to pay taxes legally.

However, "large" and "especially large" violations of tax laws still resulted in criminal proceedings under the Russian criminal code. A company executive found guilty of "especially" large-scale tax evasion could face imprisonment for up to six years. This left a large loophole, and the Yukos affair numbed the tax police reform.[33]

Russia's decade of high economic growth greatly improved public finances. The consolidated budget recorded persistent surpluses from 2000 to 2008 (fig. 3.3). The main advocate of using these large budget surpluses to pay off the public debt was Putin's economic adviser Andrei Illarionov, and Putin accepted his view. As a result, Russia saw a stunning decline of its public debt. In the spring of 1999, the debt corresponded to Russia's GDP in US dollars, but by 2008 it had plummeted to just 6 percent of GDP, thanks to a combination of the write-off of the domestic treasury bonds, the appreciation of the ruble, high economic growth, and steady budget surpluses (fig. 3.4).

Russian consumers benefited amply. The Russian middle class measures its income in US dollars because of the far-reaching dollarization of the Russian economy, and the average monthly wages rose, incredibly, twelve times from just $79 in 2000 to a high of $946 in 2013 (fig. 3.5).

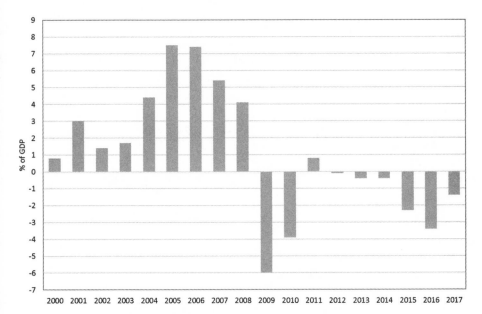

Fig. 3.3 Consolidated government budget balance, 2000–2017.
Source: BOFIT (2018)

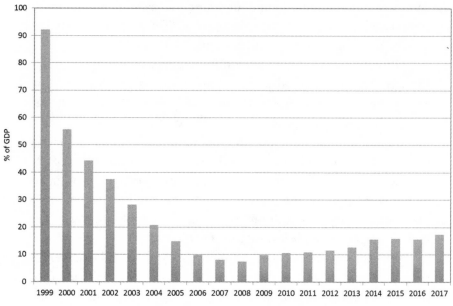

Fig. 3.4 Public debt, 1999–2017. *Source: IMF (2018)*

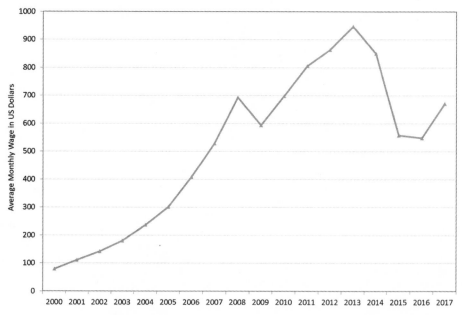

Fig. 3.5 Average monthly US dollar wage, 2000–2017. *Source: BOFIT (2018)*

Employment patterns in the former Soviet Union have differed from those in the Western world. Russian workers in the provinces tend to stick to their places of work, even when they are not being paid or real wages plummet. As a consequence, unemployment has never been dramatic, and it varies surprisingly little over time. It fell from 10 percent in 2000 to 6 percent in 2007, and in recent years it has lingered around 5.5 percent (fig. 3.6).

Russians went through hyperinflation in the early 1990s, and inflation remains a much greater concern than unemployment. Inflation has been somewhat high by international comparison, falling from 20 percent in 2000 to 2.2 percent in early 2018 (fig. 3.7).

Another idea that arose from the crash of 1998 was that Russia needed large international currency and gold reserves. In March 1999, the reserves hit rock bottom at a paltry $10.8 billion. They gained momentum in 2000, rising to $28 billion. The reserves continued to grow apace, reaching $77 billion at the end of 2003 (fig. 3.8).[34]

The Russian liberals had started thinking of institutionalizing the reserves that resulted from the high oil price windfall. They looked at

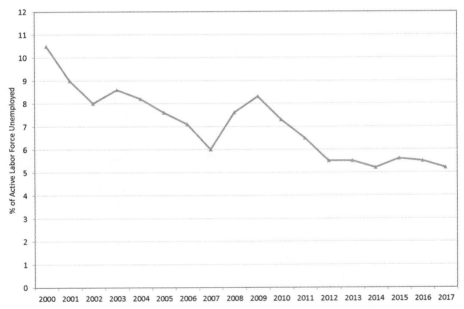

Fig. 3.6 Unemployment rate, 2000–2017. *Source: BOFIT (2018)*

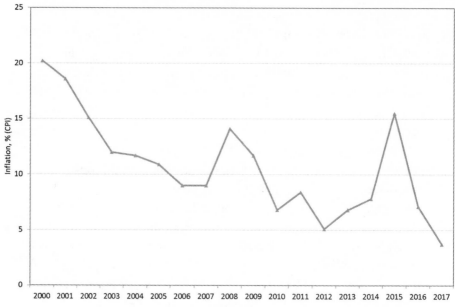

Fig. 3.7 Inflation, Consumer Price Index, end of year, 2000–2017.
Source: BOFIT (2018)

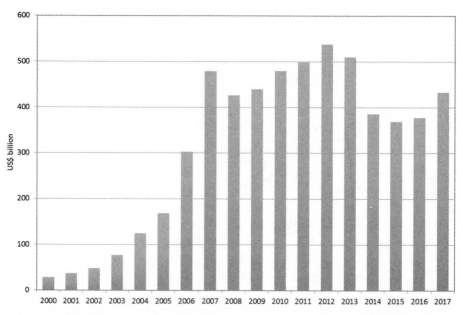

Fig. 3.8 Foreign currency and gold reserves, 2000–2017. *Source: BOFIT (2018)*

the sovereign wealth funds of various oil-rich countries, chiefly Norway's pension fund. Putin's economic adviser Andrei Illarionov and Kudrin cherished this idea, and Putin pushed it through. On January 1, 2004, the Russian government established a Stabilization Fund under the Ministry of Finance. It was meant to be a "rainy-weather" fund for budget support when the oil price fell. All fiscal revenue above a certain oil price level was passed on to the Stabilization Fund.[35]

As the price of oil continued to rise, the Stabilization Fund grew. By February 1, 2008, when it had accumulated $157 billion, the Ministry of Finance divided it into two funds, aspiring to get better returns on the reserves. The new Reserve Fund had the same function as the old Stabilization Fund, with highly liquid international bonds yielding poor returns. Initially, it contained $125 billion, peaking at $143 billion on September 1, 2008, but it plunged to $25 billion in January 2012 because of the lower price of oil and budget stimulus spending. Yet it peaked at $92 billion in September 2014. After the fall in oil prices and Western financial sanctions, the Reserve Fund was nearly depleted, and it was merged with the National Welfare Fund at the end of 2017. The variations in this fund were considerable, but it was designed to compensate for low oil prices.[36]

The aim of the other sovereign wealth fund, the National Welfare Fund, was to deliver higher returns through riskier long-term investments. In practice, it has become a budget support fund that is used for dubious Kremlin investments, such as the recapitalization of the notoriously loss-making Vnesheconombank (VEB). The National Welfare Fund rose quickly from $32 billion in February 2008 to $88 billion on January 1, 2009, but since then it has hovered around a similar level, declining to $67 billion on December 1, 2017, 4.2 percent of GDP. These assets are not liquid, and presumably they should be written down because of losses.[37]

In 2016, a subsidiary of VEB, the Russian Direct Investment Fund (RDIF), was transformed into a third sovereign wealth fund with $10 billion, but its orientation is quite different, being geared toward attracting foreign private equity investments. Increasingly, it has been drawn into the same kind of funny state operations as VEB and VTB (Vneshtorgbank of Russia), which led to its Ukraine-related designation by the US Treasury in July 2015.[38]

The Reserve Fund and the National Welfare Fund have granted the Russian government more security and flexibility, as was intended. They have not become particularly large, but is this a sensible way of keeping national wealth? The funds have generated minimal returns and enabled the government to maintain poor economic policies that should be reformed. Most countries do not have sovereign wealth funds, and Russia's public debt is uniquely low, giving the country plenty of room to increase its indebtedness.

In September 2008, Russia was hit by the global financial crisis. In hindsight, the Russian government had managed the fiscal crisis of 1998 eminently economically, though not politically. This time, the opposite was true. The crisis was a rude surprise to the Kremlin, blinded by hubris. As late as early September, Putin had called Russia a safe haven, even though Russian stock prices had fallen sharply since May and commodity prices had been dropping since mid-July.

On September 15, all hell broke loose in global financial markets, as the American investment bank Lehman Brothers went bankrupt, leading to a global liquidity freeze, which hit Russia hard. Suddenly the Russian leaders realized how exposed their corporate sector was to large credits from foreign banks. The international price of oil plummeted to $34 per barrel in December 2008, and the Russian stock market plunged by 80 percent in dollar terms from May to December.

Unlike the situation in 1998, the Russian government had built up large reserves. In August 2008, its international currency and gold reserves reached $598 billion, making Russia's the third largest in the world after China and Japan (see fig. 3.8). Confident that these large reserves would carry Russia through the liquidity squeeze, the government opted for an extreme Keynesian policy of overbridging the crisis with fiscal stimulus, as China and India did. Russia launched the largest fiscal stimulus program of all the G-20 countries, turning a budget surplus of 4.1 percent of GDP in 2008 to a deficit of 6.0 percent of GDP in 2009.[39]

The government channeled $50 billion in bailout money to both state-owned and private companies through VEB. In total, it spent $104 billion from the Reserve Fund on budget support from September 2008 until June 2010. Its greatest support, however, was spending $200 billion of its international currency reserves. The Central Bank maintained an overvalued exchange rate, pursuing a gradual devaluation for three months from November 2008 to February 2009. This policy was evident, but not explicit, effectively allowing the wealthy and well connected to profit on speculating against the ruble. The Russian government thus bailed out big companies.[40]

While this Keynesian stimulus might have seemed sensible, its outcome was miserable. Russia's GDP plunged by 7.8 percent in 2009, more than in any other G-20 economy, and its future productivity had been aggravated. Much of the capital injection flew out of the country. The IMF assessed Russia's capital flight in 2008 at a record $119 billion (table 6.1, p. 166).[41]

The government pursued the opposite course of the creative destruction of 1998. It bailed out big, inefficient companies owned either by the state or by oligarchs, which crowded out more efficient enterprises. Of 481 state-owned firms deemed "strategic," 79 received state support. Enterprises with low profitability that had quickly increased their debt before the crisis were likelier to receive government assistance during the crisis. The "average productivity ... declined among the treated firms, while it grew among the control firms in the post-bailout period." In short, "firms that received government assistance performed worse than matched firms that did not receive such assistance." Not only did the government spend money on the worst enterprises, but its help further aggravated their performance. Still, by supporting the old, big companies, the government kept up real wages, which was a major objective.[42]

The Russian government had freedom of action with its ample funds, and it made this deliberate policy choice, which was widely celebrated as a wise stimulus until the poor economic outcome became apparent. In 1998, the government had fewer options, but the crash delivered a catharsis. During 2010–2012, Russia's economic growth looked good in comparison with the stagnant eurozone, and its macroeconomic stability remained stellar, but with a deteriorating economic structure and minimal reforms, economic growth was set to gradually decline, even if oil prices stayed high.

By 2014, Putin's policy of state and crony capitalism had eliminated economic growth. Then, two big blows hit the Russian economy. The price of oil fell by half from June 2014 to February 2015, and in July 2014, the West imposed financial sanctions on Russia because of its aggression in Ukraine. Each produced negative effects, and they reinforced each other.

The conventional wisdom was that Russia would manage well since its total foreign debt was not large—$732 billion in June 2014, about one-third of GDP. Its share of GDP rose with the depreciation of the ruble, whereas Russia's problem was not solvency but liquidity. Western sanctions caused a "sudden stop" of all refinancing of Russian foreign debt.[43]

In December 2014, a monetary crisis hit Russia with a furor. The CBR decided to let the exchange rate float freely, suddenly moving to inflation targeting. An obvious aim was to conserve currency reserves that had been sharply reduced in 2014. Traditionally, the ruble-dollar rate and the oil price in dollars have followed each other closely, but now the ruble plummeted much further. Society was shocked. Panic erupted. People ran to the shops to buy whatever they could before new, higher import prices were introduced and many imports had become prohibitively expensive.

As a consequence, inflation shot up. With the exchange rate plunge, inflation surged from 7 percent to 16.9 percent on a year-over-year basis in March 2015. The CBR refused to intervene with currency sales. Instead, it hiked the interest rate to 17 percent and waited for the panic to recede. The alarm eased after a couple of weeks, and the inflation rate declined gradually. The CBR maintained high nominal interest rates, tightening actual monetary policy. By mid-2017, inflation had sunk to the target rate of 4 percent, and it continued to fall to 2.2 percent in early 2018.

During the financial panic of December 2014, Putin made two major public appearances, but he said a minimum about economic policy, reassuring his audiences that the economic situation was quite good. Putin avoided the word "crisis," blaming the outside world while avoiding any analysis of the effect of falling oil prices and sanctions, respectively. He argued that "the current situation was obviously provoked primarily by external factors," expressing a bland hope that things would get better, as if Russian policy was irrelevant. He was vague about future policy: "What do we intend to do about this? We intend to use the measures we applied, and rather successfully, back in 2008. In this case, we will need to focus on assistance to those people who really need it. . . . We would certainly be forced to make some cuts."[44]

In early 2015, Putin held meetings with senior economic officials, resulting in the government adopting a package of sixty anticrisis measures. Still avoiding the word "crisis," the program was called the Plan for Sustainable Economic Development and Social Stability in 2015 (though it was popularly called the anticrisis plan). Again, Putin claimed that the government should repeat its anticrisis policy of 2008–2009:

> This is not the first situation of this kind that we are going through. In 2008–2009 we went through the same thing. Then it was also a crisis that came from outside. Let me remind you that it started with the collapse of the mortgage system in the United States and then it touched other countries, including ours. Now as well, one of the main causes of the situation in the economy is the situation on foreign markets, in this case for raw materials, which is seriously reflected also here.[45]

In mid-February, Putin clarified his policy: "Overall, the agenda is clear. . . . Our tasks include diversifying the economy, creating conditions for faster growth, creating the right environment, improving management at every level of power . . . stabilizing the currency and of course keeping our macroeconomic indicators on course." He avoided the tough questions of allocation of resources and said nothing about reform.[46]

Although Putin insisted that Russia would repeat its policies of 2008–2009, he did not do so. Instead, in its new anticrisis plan the Kremlin economized on reserves through a floating exchange rate, and the budget cost was small, focusing on the recapitalization of banks. Yet Putin has nixed all proposals of structural reform.

A great improvement was the altered exchange rate policy, moving Russia from a pegged exchange rate to a floating exchange rate policy with inflation targeting. This has helped the CBR to save reserves. Russia's reserves have gradually recovered and stabilized around $400 billion, which seems to be the Kremlin's target. That corresponds to 30 percent of the current GDP, or two years of current imports. After the month of panic in December 2014, the ruble exchange rate recovered. It floats freely but has stabilized at about half the dollar value of June 2014.[47]

This anticrisis plan was supposed to have a total cost of $38 billion, or 3 percent of a GDP of $1.2 trillion, compared with the bailout of $200 billion in 2008–2009, which was then 10 percent of the GDP of $1.9 trillion. This drop reflected the tighter fiscal situation. Two-thirds of the anticrisis package was sensibly devoted to the recapitalization of twenty-seven big banks. Admittedly, 199 "strategic" companies, irrespective of ownership or efficiency, were singled out for assistance and loan guarantees, similar to 2008–2009, but because of the falling exchange rate they did not need much financing.

The large depreciation of the ruble also helped the government to limit the budget deficit because oil revenues remained almost constant in ruble terms, whereas they plunged in dollar terms. The government's goal was to keep the budget deficit low, around 3 percent of GDP, and it did. Federal government debt has stayed minimal, at 13 percent of GDP. The Kremlin has responded ruthlessly by slashing expenditures on education and health care and, in 2016, even pensions. Russia has maintained practically full employment, with an official unemployment rate vacillating between 5 percent and 6 percent.

In the aftermath of the 2014 crisis, Russia went through a new bank crisis. In three years, more than three hundred banks were closed down, leaving more than five hundred banks. The CBR has been widely lauded for cleaning up the Russian banking system, but the results are dubious. The Russian banking system is not developing but shrinking, and its structure is not improving but turning worse. The big state banks have become more dominant than ever. The five biggest state banks, led by Sberbank and VTB, account for almost 60 percent of banking assets.

In the second half of 2017, three of the five biggest private Russian-owned banks, Bank Otkritie, Binbank, and Promsvyazbank, went under with horrendous losses, raising doubts about the sustainability of most of the private banking sector as well as the quality of the central bank supervision. They were taken over by the Central Bank after having been outcompeted by the large state banks, which benefited from cheap funding while becoming ever more monopolistic, focusing on big, mainly publicly owned clients. The few foreign banks primarily serve foreign companies, and Russian medium-sized and small private companies are now left with little access to credit. The Central Bank had used Bank Otkritie and Binbank as consolidators of multiple smaller failing banks, raising doubts about the quality of bank inspections. Moreover, banking requires strong property rights and a well-functioning judicial system, which Russia lacks. Russia's malfunctioning banking system is a serious bottleneck for the development of the economy.[48]

The falling oil prices sharply reduced Russia's export revenues. Russia's merchandise exports fell by almost half from 2013 to 2016, from $522 billion to $282 billion, but so did imports, because of the falling exchange rate, from $341 billion to $192 billion (fig. 3.9). As a consequence, Russia managed to maintain a significant current account surplus even at the worst of times (fig. 3.10). Both exports and imports recovered significantly with rebounding oil prices in 2017.

Something had to give, and that was the standard of living, investment, and GDP. In the two years 2015–2016, real disposable incomes slumped

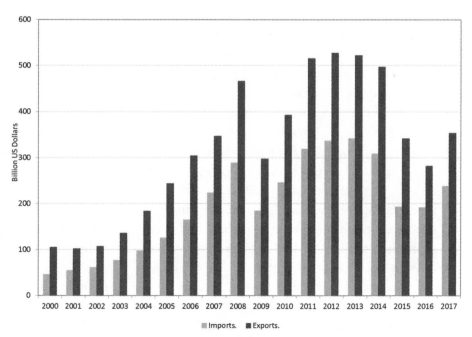

Fig. 3.9 Merchandise exports and imports, 2000–2017. *Source: BOFIT (2018)*

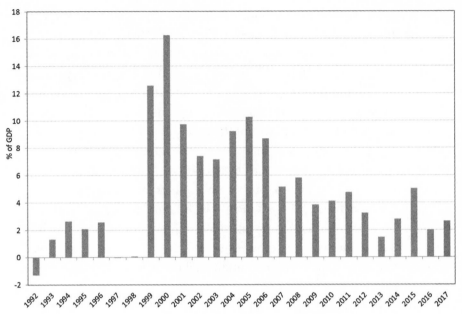

Fig. 3.10 Current account balance, 1992–2017. *Source: IMF (2018)*

by 16 percent, and retail sales, also reflecting the standard of living, plummeted by 15 percent; investment fell by 9 percent. Real disposable incomes continued to fall in 2016–2017.[49]

Social scientists have argued that Putin established a social contract with the Russian people, granting them stability and a steadily increasing standard of living, while he took care of politics. Since 2014, Putin has abandoned this social contract. The question is how long the Russian people will accept a lower or even falling standard of living.[50]

For the future, one of Russia's big negatives is its demography. Russia's working-age population peaked at 90 million in 2003–2006, and it is now falling continuously. By 2016, it had dropped to 83 million, and it is expected to shrink by about 700,000 a year, or almost 1 percent of the labor force, until 2030. This implies a corresponding decline in GDP, all other things being equal.[51]

The Russian government does little to the benefit of its human capital. The two key health statistics are life expectancy and infant mortality. Life expectancy for men has been remarkably low in Russia for decades, and it decreased further during the collapse of the Soviet Union and the early transition period, hitting a low of 58 years in 1994. The main cause was increased mortality in cardiovascular diseases, suggesting that Russian men found it exceedingly difficult to live through the stress of the postcommunist transition. Many of the deaths reflected increased drinking. Male life expectancy started rising steadily from 2006, but it remains very low by international standards at 66 (fig. 3.11). By contrast, Russian women live eleven years longer than their men. In 2016, the overall life expectancy in Russia was just 71.6 years, according to the World Bank World Development Indicators, putting Russia in the worst half, at number 108, of 186 countries in the world.[52]

Russia's infant mortality rate was mediocre until the late 1990s, but then it started to improve every year. Even so, Russia's infant mortality remains twice the EU average and is three times as high as in the Czech Republic, which is the best-performing postcommunist country (fig. 3.12). The far greater improvement of infant mortality in the Central European countries is best explained by their democracy, which forces the authorities to take better care of their citizens.

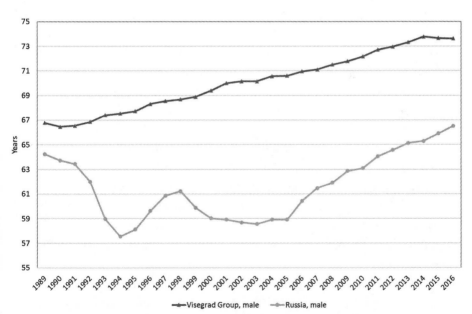

Fig. 3.11 Male life expectancy at birth, Russia and the Visegrad Group, 1989–2016. *Source: World Bank (2018)*

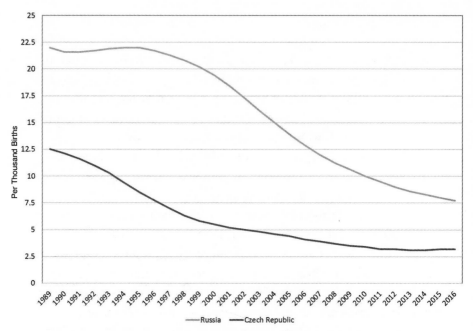

Fig. 3.12 Infant mortality, Russia and the Czech Republic, 1989–2016.
Source: World Bank (2018)

Socially, Russia is underperforming badly according to all relevant international comparisons. The situation was far worse in the Soviet Union, but the Russian government devotes strikingly little attention and resources to the improvement of social conditions.

At first glance, Russia's combination of crony capitalism and very conservative macroeconomic policy may appear odd, but it makes a lot of sense. The Kremlin's big lesson from the crash of 1998 was that a severe financial destabilization is dangerous for political stability so it must be avoided. Therefore, it has shunned large budget deficits and substantial public debt. The Kremlin sees large international reserves as a matter of sovereignty.

From 2000 to 2008, Russia maintained significant budget surpluses, almost eliminating its public debt. After public finances had stabilized, Russia could carry out major tax reforms, taking its cue from Estonia, reducing the number of taxes sharply, cutting tax rates, and adopting sensible rules for deductions. The most popular policy was the flat income tax of 13 percent. Value-added taxes and the unified social taxes have varied slightly, but the new tax system has been quite stable.

As Russia's public debt dwindled and its international reserves rose, the idea arose of strengthening the country's financial stance further with sovereign wealth funds. The first fund was introduced in 2004. The Reserve Fund and the National Welfare Fund grew until the crises of 2008 and 2014. They have served as buffers, but they have also reduced the urgency for reform. At the end of 2017, their combined size had shrunk to 5 percent of GDP. The government made the logical decision to abolish the Reserve Fund in February 2018. The sovereign wealth funds have attracted more attention than they deserve. It is more important that Russia's public debt is minimal and that its international currency reserves are substantial. The Russian Ministry of Finance can easily borrow from the Central Bank reserves when the sovereign wealth funds have been depleted without expanding the money supply.

In 2008–2009, when ten years of high growth had bred a sense of hubris, the Kremlin did the opposite of 1998. Rather than cutting expenditures, it opted for the largest fiscal stimulus package of any G-20 country. It rescued large and inefficient companies regardless of ownership, crowding out more efficient enterprises. It used $200 billion of currency reserves to bail out the establishment through a gradual devaluation during three months. The outcome was a decline in GDP of almost 8 percent, a less efficient enterprise structure, large capital outflows, and much smaller reserves, but the standard of living was maintained even in 2009.

Although the Kremlin did not admit that this policy was a failure, its response to the crisis of 2014 showed that it had learned its lesson. Russia at last adopted a floating exchange rate and opted for inflation targeting, saving its reserves and quickly reducing inflation after a large depreciation in a textbook fashion. The budget deficit was kept below 3 percent of GDP. Russia had arrived at a macroeconomic policy that is likely to stick, and highly professional systemic liberals maintain it. However, the Kremlin ignores any growth-oriented policies.

In an article on Russia after the global financial crisis, the eminent economists Sergei Guriev and Aleh Tsyvinski concluded that if "economic reforms are not implemented, Russia is likely to enter a new decade of

Brezhnev-style stagnation." They foresaw a "'lost decade' as in the 1990s Japan, when the acute phase of the crisis was mostly over but the economy grew very slowly for more than 10 years." After its financial crash in 1990, Japan got zombie banks encumbered with excessive nonperforming loans, and today Russia has got zombie companies. Guriev and Tsyvinski observe that "Russia still has an ossified, corrupt, and inefficient economy built during the fat years of the oil boom." Their prediction of stagnation and zombie companies has been remarkably accurate, and current forecasts suggest that their words will stay true.[53]

The Rise of State Capitalism

A major trend under Putin has been the renationalization of large private companies. Renationalization started with the arrest of Mikhail Khodorkovsky on October 25, 2003, and was soon followed by the state company Rosneft seizure of Khodorkovsky's oil company, Yukos. Big state enterprises have expanded, mainly by purchasing good private companies on the market, but also through corporate raiding, in which private enterprises have been seized with the unlawful assistance of law enforcement agencies. The state sector has expanded because of privileges granted by the state, including cheap and plentiful state funding, as well as the unique right to buy big companies, and not because of economic efficiency.

This chapter shows how state capitalism has developed and functions in Russia, showcasing four key state enterprises in four major industries: gas (Gazprom), oil (Rosneft), banking (VEB), and armaments (Rostec).[1]

Russia lacks accurate statistics on the size of the private and public sectors, and assessments of the state sector vary to an amazing degree. According to analysis by the European Bank for Reconstruction and Development (EBRD), the private sector peaked in 2003, when it generated 70 percent of GDP. It fell to 65 percent of GDP in 2005, but soon afterward the EBRD stopped publishing these statistics because there was no reliable methodology behind that or any other assessment.[2]

The Russian Antimonopoly Committee has claimed that the state share of Russia's GDP has increased from 35 percent in 2005 to 70 percent in 2015, but this widely cited assessment does not appear to be based on any profound analysis.[3]

In 2017, Russia's Statistical Committee (Rosstat) finally published assessments of how much of value was added in each sector. Rosstat did not offer a sum, and some sectors are missing, such as defense and security services, presumably corresponding to a residue of 10.2 percent. Summing these up offers a public share of GDP of about 45 percent in 2016. Given that this first official attempt at estimating the public sector was partial and clearly aimed at playing down the public sector, it needs to be taken with a big grain of salt.[4]

The best analytical assessment available has been elaborated by a group of researchers led by Alexander Radygin of the Gaidar Institute for Alexei Kudrin's Center for Strategic Research. They divide public economic activity into three elements: public service sector, enterprises with state participation, and state unitary enterprises (the old type of Soviet enterprises). Their assessments cover the period from 2006 to 2016. By this assessment, the overall size of the public sector went from 39.6 percent of GDP in 2006 to 51.7 percent of GDP in the financial crisis year of 2009 and then down to 46.0 percent of GDP in 2016. These appear to be the most reliable numbers on the size of the public sector in the Russian economy.[5]

The financial crisis of 2009 with its massive state bailout increased the public sector by 11 percent of GDP in a single year, whereas the many state purchases of big private companies in other years did not really register. Yet this makes sense if we think of how the public enterprise sector is composed and functions. Russian state enterprises tend to be monopolistic, each dominating a big sector of the economy. They usually do not compete with private enterprises, apart from on the margins. The industries dominated by state enterprises are energy, transportation, banks, and armaments production, while metallurgy, mining, and telecommunications, which are often state owned in other countries, are predominantly private. The retail sector and most consumer services are entirely private. Thus, the state sector consists primarily of the declining industries, whereas private enterprise dominates the dynamic industries.

State capitalism is a common phenomenon around the world, but its nature varies greatly from country to country. Russia's state capitalism appears particularly inefficient and dysfunctional. Joshua Kurlantzick has eloquently summed up the peculiarities of Russian state capitalism:

> Unlike Brazil or China or Singapore, Vladimir Putin's Kremlin has not used the state's sizable currency reserves to invest in young Russian companies, promote new industries, or even make new investment in oil and gas extraction technology. Neither has Russia forced state firms to compete with each other and with foreign firms operating in their domestic markets. . . . Instead, in Russia, state companies throttle any potential private-sector competitors. Under Putin, the Kremlin has allowed just one or two state firms to dominate nearly every leading industry, with each company staffed by Putin loyalists. Companies that have resisted state takeover have been sacked with enormous tax bills until they sell out. Many of the most promising young entrepreneurs in Russia simply have fled the country.[6]

Radygin and his coauthors offer a similar assessment: "The share of state ownership in a company reflects negatively on efficiency." The degree of inefficiency of state companies they record is truly astounding. In the 1990s, most of the old, inefficient state unitary enterprises went through corporatization, which both facilitated privatization and corporate governance. In 2016, state unitary enterprises generated only 1.5 percent of GDP, while companies with state participation delivered 25.3 percent of GDP. Many but not all of these companies have private shareholders. Yet since 2003 corporate governance has hardly improved.[7]

The problem is thus not only state capitalism but how the Kremlin pursues it. It ignores competition, investment, technological development, and entrepreneurship. The state enterprises have many other purposes—political control, social mitigation, and personal enrichment of the Putin elite—as Boris Nemtsov, Vladimir Milov, Leonid Martynyuk, Karen

Dawisha, and the Panama Papers have documented so well. Each big state enterprise is managed by a close associate of Putin, and the top state managers are subordinate to the president rather than the state.[8]

Rosneft's seizure of Yukos was the epic battle of state capitalism versus private ownership. It marked the end of the Yeltsin oligarchs. Rosneft was a state company composed of remaining state firms, often with substantial private minority shares. Its many assets were spread out and difficult to manage. From 1998 to 2002, three attempts were made to privatize Rosneft, but the government failed to sell on each occasion because the expected prices were deemed too low.

The main reason for Rosneft's survival as a state company was its strong chief executive, Sergei Bogdanchikov, who wanted to avoid privatization and strengthen the company. He received political support from Igor Sechin, one of Putin's closest aides.[9]

Rosneft illustrates how state companies evolve in Russia. The seed is a remnant of state property. The next element is a strong executive. The third factor is a man close to Putin, who wants to promote a certain renationalization in his own material interest. Decisive, however, is whether the president finds reason to get into the act. When he does, money is not a problem, which also means that the state does not care about efficiency or profitability. Cheap public funding or low private asset prices are usually at hand. This shows why full privatization was so important. If no significant state company exists in an industry, a renationalization drive is much less likely. Good examples are the Russian steel and cement industries, which remain private, while such industries are owned by the state in many other countries.

Rosneft's battle with Yukos took place in 2003–2004. The preeminent expert on Russian oil, Thane Gustafson, sets the start in 2002: "In 2002 ... the hard-line silovik wing of the Kremlin—led behind the scenes by Putin's chief assistant Igor Sechin—joined forces with Sergei Bogdanchikov in the campaign against Mikhail Khodorkovsky and Yukos."[10]

On February 19, 2003, Putin held his annual meeting with a score of oligarchs in the Kremlin. The theme chosen by the Kremlin was corruption in Russia. Putin declared that his aim was "to liquidate the very basis of corruption": "During the last two years, new laws were adopted to de-bureaucratize the state apparatus. Unfortunately, so far we see no real improvement. . . . And today I would like to hear your views."[11]

Mikhail Khodorkovsky, the CEO and biggest owner of Yukos, took Putin at his word. He made a presentation in the televised meeting showing that the state-owned oil company Rosneft had purchased the small oil company Severnaya Neft for $600 million, although Severnaya Neft had been privatized for $7 million to a former deputy minister of finance named Andrei Vavilov two years earlier. Implicitly, Khodorkovsky accused the Rosneft management of corruption. Later that year, when I asked Khodorkovsky privately about this, he claimed that they had reliable information that Vavilov had paid a kickback of $200 million.[12]

Furiously, Putin exclaimed that Khodorkovsky, of all people, had no business complaining about corruption. Referring to Khodorkovsky, he stated: "Having made their billions, they spend tens, hundreds of millions of dollars to save their billions. We know how this money is being spent—on what lawyers, PR campaigns and politicians it is going, and on getting questions like these asked." Previously, Khodorkovsky had presumed that the kickback went to Sechin and Bogdanchikov. Now the thought struck him that Putin might have been in on the act.[13]

In July 2003, Khodorkovsky's first deputy, Platon Lebedev, was arrested, and on October 25, Khodorkovsky himself was arrested. The original legal complaint was the privatization of one subordinate company, the fertilizer plant Apatity (now called Phosagro and owned by Putin cronies), but the prosecutor general and the tax administration eventually prosecuted Khodorkovsky and Yukos for major tax crimes. Profit taxes varied greatly between different Russian regions, and Yukos had used domestic regional tax havens. Both Khodorkovsky and Lebedev received long prison sentences. In May 2005, Khodorkovsky was sentenced to nine years in prison for tax evasion. In 2007, additional charges were brought against Khodorkovsky for embezzlement and money laundering, implausibly for having stolen the oil for which Yukos had not paid tax, and his prison sentence was extended to eleven years. Many other Yukos managers were sentenced to prison or fled abroad.[14]

Putin's rationale was obvious. Aspiring to consolidate political power, he targeted one man, the wealthiest and most outspoken big businessman, to teach all the others who was the boss. If he crushed Khodorkovsky, he had defeated all the big business leaders. Khodorkovsky did many things that could enrage Putin, and opinions over the trigger vary. Khodorkovsky sponsored scores of candidates from various parties for State Duma elections in December 2003. He donated about $100 million a year through his Open Russia Foundation to build Russian civil society. He called for the construction of private pipelines to both China and the Arctic Sea, attempting to break the Transneft state export pipeline monopoly. In the summer of 2003, Yukos lobbyists defeated Putin's government in the State Duma when the government tried to hike taxes on oil companies. In the fall of 2003, Khodorkovsky was close to selling a majority stake in Yukos to Chevron or ExxonMobil. Presumably, Putin's main problem with Khodorkovsky was that he was the most daring big private businessman. If Putin took him down, the others would fall into line. Political scientist Stephen Fortescue issued the verdict: "Above all it was designed to put all the oligarchs in their place by making a victim of the most independent-minded of them." It worked.[15]

Meanwhile, Yukos was confiscated. The tax authorities seized the company and sold off its parts to Rosneft for a pittance. In December 2004, Rosneft took over Yukos's main oil field, Yuganskneftegaz, at a bargain price in a farcical executive auction before Christmas on December 19, 2004. The Russian authorities had scared away all other companies, so it was open only to Gazprom and Rosneft. Gazprom withdrew at the last minute because of international legal concerns, but Rosneft had no foreign assets to bother about. As Thane Gustafson recorded: "Two people claiming to represent Baikalfinansgrup (they were later identified as being employees of Surgutneftegaz) submitted the sole bid for Yuganskneftegaz, at $9.37 billion. The hammer went down, and 76.8 percent of the shares of Yuganskneftegaz had changed hands."[16]

This "auction" price was far lower than any assessment. In October 2004, the "Ministry of Justice valued [Yuganskneftegaz] at $14.7 billion to $17.3 billion. J.P. Morgan, hired by Yukos, valued the company at $16 billion to $22 billion." Nor was Baikalfinansgrup a real enterprise. It was an unknown shell company, registered in a broken-down wooden shack in the provincial town of Tver, close to Moscow. At a press conference on December 21, Putin revealed that he was initiated: "The shareholders of [Baikalfinansgrup], as is well known, are exclusively physical persons, but ones who have done business in the energy sector for many years." The next day, Rosneft announced that it had acquired Baikalfinansgrup, underlining that this was not an auction but a charade.[17]

Repeatedly, Putin stated that he opposed the nationalization of Yukos and relied on the rule of law, although the politicized legal proceedings suggest that he had favored confiscation all along. On October 27, 2003, Putin claimed: "But there will be no meetings and no bargaining over the law enforcement bodies and their activities, so long, of course, as these agencies are acting within the limits of Russian legislation. . . . Neither the executive authorities nor even the Prosecutor's Office can deprive someone of their freedom, even for the period of pre-trial detention. Only the court has this power . . . and before the court, as before the law, all should be equal."[18]

In an Italian interview in early November, Putin declared: "I am categorically against re-examining the results of privatization. . . . There will be no deprivatization or a re-examination of the results of the privatization, but everyone will have to learn to live according to the laws." On June 17, 2004, Putin told reporters: "The Russian administration, government and economic authorities are not interested in bankrupting a company like Yukos. . . . The government will try to ensure that this company does not go bankrupt." On September 6, he said: "I don't want to bankrupt Yukos. . . . Give me the names of the government officials who want to bankrupt Yukos and I'll fire them." In spite of all these statements by Putin, the confiscation of Yukos proceeded apace and Putin appeared to do nothing to stop it or even slow it down.[19]

Through the Yukos confiscation, the Kremlin had declared its preference for state ownership of major enterprises. As will become evident, whenever a manager of a major state enterprise found an excuse for taking over a well-run private company, he could count on the president's tacit blessing. The general prosecutor's office or the tax service initiated a corporate raid, and one or two state banks provided the financing needed for the takeover. Unlike in the Yukos case, the former owner usually received some payment. Whether it was high or low appears to have depended on the owner's personal relations with top officials. Some were forced into fire sales while leaving the country, whereas others received good prices.

Incredible as it appears in hindsight, many foreign investors believed that Putin was establishing law and order in Russia and that Khodorkovsky was a crook. The stock price of Yukos held up for a year before it collapsed, causing US investors losses as large as $12 billion. In December 2013, Putin pardoned Khodorkovsky, which seemed to be connected with Putin wishing to do something positive before the Sochi Winter Olympics in early 2014. Khodorkovsky left Russia immediately. In December 2015, the Russian prosecutors opened a new case against Khodorkovsky, now accusing him of murder of the mayor in Nefteyugansk in June 2008.[20]

Russia's development of state capitalism might appear paradoxical. From 1991 to 2002, the country carried out the greatest privatization the world has ever seen. Why did this policy reverse itself into rampant renationalization? The Russian government never announced any reversal, but the real turning point was the Yukos case. In 2006–2007 the official policy toward ownership changed in favor of state enterprises, promoting big national champions that each dominated their industry.[21]

The restructuring of the banking sector after the financial crash of 1998 lay the foundation for the future renationalization. Half of the private banks went under, including all the big oligarchic banks except for Alfa Bank. Only the old Soviet savings bank, Sberbank, offered deposit guarantees, thus attracting much of ordinary people's savings. The five big state banks—Sberbank, VTB, VEB, Gazprombank, and Rosselkhozbank—had state guarantees, which granted them cheap market funding. The government's reliance on state banks was reinforced during the financial crisis in 2008–2009.

Enterprise financing falls into three separate segments. The big Russian state banks give preferences to large state enterprises, whereas large private Russian companies have raised much of their funding abroad and small and medium-sized firms turn to small private banks. As the big state banks have gradually gobbled up small and medium-sized banks, small enterprises have had ever less access to credit. The playing field has become increasingly tilted to the benefit of state-owned enterprises.[22]

In late 2006, overt government policy changed. During Putin's annual call-in program, a lumberjack in Northern Russia queried Putin about his view of the transfer of forests to private hands, suggesting that it would "damage the interests not only of the logging companies but also of ordinary people, who won't be able to just go into the forest to gather mushrooms and berries." Putin took the opportunity to distance himself from "liberal economists" who "think that putting the forests into private hands is a more radical and economically efficient method of developing the sector. . . . In our current situation it is still too early to transfer such an important national resource as our forests to private hands, and I will not sign such a law." With this answer, Putin distanced himself from privatization in general.[23]

Russian government policy changed accordingly. With a minimum of public discussion, the Kremlin decided to merge whole industrial sectors into conglomerates enjoying near monopolies in 2006–2007. The new idea was to create national champions. The government had successfully taxed the oil rents of private oil companies, but the Kremlin preferred to channel these rents through state enterprises.

Two close KGB friends of Putin promoted alternative schemes, First Deputy Prime Minister Sergei Ivanov, one of Putin's KGB friends from St. Petersburg, and Sergei Chemezov, a former KGB colleague of Putin's from Dresden and head of Russia's arms exporter Rosoboronexport. Both wanted state-owned companies to become more independent from the ministries, which supervised the old "unitary" state enterprises, and to give them independent supervisory boards. Ivanov and Chemezov proclaimed that the concentration of resources would lead to faster technological development.[24]

Ivanov, who oversaw for the military-industrial complex, favored standard Western open joint-stock companies with majority state ownership. His two creations were the United Aircraft Corporation, which he chaired, and the United Shipbuilding Corporation, chaired by Igor Sechin.[25]

Chemezov proposed an original scheme called state corporations. Legally the state corporations were strangely set up as nongovernmental organizations (*nekommercheskie organizatsii*). In 2007, six such state corporations were set up. Each was formed with a separate law. Since they were nongovernmental organizations, their formation amounted to the privatization of their assets to the benefit of the president, who appointed the boards of these state corporations. The political scientist Vadim Volkov has calculated the production assets transferred to these nongovernmental organizations at $80 billion, and the government topped up this amount with a capital infusion of another $36 billion.[26]

Chemezov formed Russian Technologies (Rostec), an armaments company, whose chief executive he remains. All nuclear facilities were transferred to the newly founded state corporation Rosatom, which re-created the old Soviet Ministry of Atomic Energy. The old Soviet foreign trade bank, Vnesheconombank (VEB), was a third important state corporation. The other three were Olimpstroi, responsible for the construction of the Sochi Olympics, the Communal Services Reform Fund, and the Russian Corporation for Nanotechnologies (Rusnano), which was later transformed to an ordinary state-owned open joint-stock company. For the rest, ordinary state-owned companies prevailed.[27]

Curiously, Putin hardly said anything in public about state corporations, as if his closest men were doing this on their own initiative, although Putin undoubtedly drove this development. He holds about one publicized individual meeting with each of the heads of the big state enterprises every year.

The governance of both the state companies and state corporations changed. Overtly, the Kremlin's aim was to improve corporate governance and make these enterprises autonomous from the ministries, but in reality Putin secured direct control. He appointed the supervisory boards of both state corporations and state companies and their chief executives were his men, answering only to him. Ministers and senior presidential administration officials dominate their boards, but the president appoints them. An apparent series of accidents bred state capitalism, but tacitly Putin has pursued a policy of deliberate renationalization.[28]

The real aim of state corporations appears to be twofold. First, they concentrate political and economic power into the hands of Putin and his trusted friends. Second, the state corporations are also supposed to enrich this circle of friends, as will become evident in the following chapters. Surprisingly, neither competitiveness nor economic efficiency appears important. Thanks to substantial defense expenditure, the national champions were supposed to promote technological development. By contrast, the old Soviet military-industrial complex had insisted on competition, for example, among half a dozen sophisticated airplane producers.

President Dmitri Medvedev clearly opposed the state corporations. In August 2009, he asked the prosecutor general to investigate them. In November, he daringly issued an instruction to Prime Minister Putin to present proposals on the reform of state corporations "after the audit of state corporations' activities showed that the current legislation does not set common criteria for defining a state corporation as a form of legal entity's incorporation. In a number of cases, the lack of proper oversight of state corporations' activities has led to them making ineffective use of the state assets transferred to their control."[29]

Evidently, Putin refused to follow this instruction. In March 2011, Medvedev challenged Putin's scheme more specifically, prohibiting state officials from sitting on the boards of state corporations. Instead, Medvedev promoted independent directors, particularly university professors. He encountered loud resistance from disadvantaged officials, notably Sechin. Medvedev's initiative would have undermined Putin's power structure. This might have been a major reason for Putin's decision to return to the presidency half a year later. Surely this was far more important to Putin than Medvedev's stand on Libya in the United Nations Security Council, which has widely been seen as the tipping point because Putin complained about it publicly.[30]

The renationalization has been a gradual and drawn-out process. Usually, state corporations have bought big, good private companies when they have come up for sale. Many business leaders who made their fortunes in the 1990s saw themselves as opportunistic private equity investors rather than industrialists. One of them quipped to me: "We are prepared to sell everything apart from our family silver, if the price is right." They were more interested in money and a good life than in what their enterprises produced. Many of Russia's billionaires have quietly sold out their assets in Russia and emigrated to London, France, or Monaco.

Roman Abramovich is an extreme example. Coming from a poor family, he became an orphan before he was four. He made an early fortune on oil trading and managed to develop close relations with the Yeltsin family and later Putin. As a favored insider he made it big through the privatization and restructuring of the oil company Sibneft, in which he acquired a majority, together with Boris Berezovsky, in the loans-for-shares privatization in 1995 for $100 million. In September 2005, Gazprom bought the private Russian oil company Sibneft from Roman Abramovich and his partners for $13.1 billion, according to the *Financial Times*. This was seen as a high price by market commentators. At the advanced age of thirty-eight Abramovich retired to the pleasures of London, where he had bought the Chelsea Football Club. Abramovich is rumored to have been one of five people who picked Putin.[31] In 2018, Abramovich failed to renew his UK residence permit in time, so he adopted Israeli citizenship.

Unlike his former partner Boris Berezovsky, Abramovich avoided the limelight and was unknown to the Russian public until 1998. No political statement of his has ever been published. From 2000 to 2008, he was governor of the northeastern region of Chukhotka, where he spent vast amounts of money on charity to develop the region. Stephen Fortescue has shown that his Sibneft benefited from even more aggressive tax planning than Yukos. Presumably thanks to his close relations with Putin and complete discretion, the Kremlin raised no objection. The discreet Abramovich lives seemingly happily in outstanding luxury with four giant yachts and one large private jet. Renamed Gazprom Neft, Sibneft remains one of Russia's best oil companies, just as the recently renationalized Yukos and TNK-BP are excellent parts of Rosneft.[32]

As the biggest gas producer in the world, accounting for 11 percent of global production, Gazprom is the gift that keeps on giving. It is a highly profitable cash cow, extracting Russia's plentiful gas in Western Siberia at a low cost. In 2011, Gazprom recorded the highest net profit of any company in the world. Even so, its market valuation is small and its free cash flow is minimal, because its large energy rents are sunk into not very profitable capital investments such as pipelines. Arguably, Gazprom is the worst-managed big company in the world. In 2012, the still-private Moscow investment bank Troika Dialog stated: "Over the past five years, Russia's Gazprom has indeed been the worst stock in the sector globally." It has deteriorated further since then.[33]

Gazprom was formed out of the old Soviet Ministry of Gas Industry, whose last minister was Viktor Chernomyrdin. From 1985 until 2001, Chernomyrdin and his associates controlled Gazprom. Its legal status changed in 1989 from a Soviet ministry to an industrial association, and from 1993 on, it was gradually partially privatized. Gazprom maintained ownership of all the ministry's assets, including production, transportation, distribution, sales, and regulation. It has persistently been a state in the state. It has fulfilled many functions—gas production, transportation, domestic supplies, and export sales—but it has also had many social responsibilities, such as delivering gas without being paid to poor people, regions, and enterprises.[34]

Gazprom's unique position arises from its old boss Chernomyrdin, who was prime minister from 1992 to 1998, and from the nature of the gas industry. Chernomyrdin carried out the corporatization and partial privatization of Gazprom from 1992 to 1994. In November 1992, he transformed Gazprom into a joint stock company by presidential decree. The company was partially privatized in a unique fashion in 1993–1994. Its management used voucher auctions to privatize almost 40 percent of Gazprom shares for an implied price of about $100 million. Of all Russian privatizations, this was by far the biggest giveaway, as its market capitalization peaked at $369 billion, almost four thousand times more, in May 2008.[35]

After Chernomyrdin was ousted as prime minister in April 1998, he and Gazprom's CEO Rem Vyakhirev allegedly indulged in gross asset stripping, transferring large assets to their children. The *Washington Post* reported: "Two sons of former prime minister Viktor Chernomyrdin are major shareholders in Stroitransgaz, as is the daughter of Gazprom's chief executive, Rem Vyakhirev. . . . The foreign investors have also alleged that hundreds of millions of dollars' worth of Gazprom assets, mostly rich gas fields, have been transferred to another fast-growing Russian gas company, Itera, either without adequate compensation for Gazprom or in questionable stock deals."[36]

In the spring of 2006, I took two young investors to meet Russian ambassador Chernomyrdin in Kyiv. We had an enjoyable conversation, but then one of the young men asked Chernomyrdin: "What would you invest in in Ukraine if you had $100 million of spare cash?" Chernomyrdin grew quite upset because of a misunderstanding and retorted, "$100 million!? I have $5 billion!" That amount corresponded at that time to 5 percent of Gazprom's market value.[37]

In May 2001, President Vladimir Putin sacked the Chernomyrdin-Vyakhirev group from Gazprom. Putin appointed as CEO his former assistant from the St. Petersburg's mayor's office, Alexei Miller, in place of Vyakhirev, and his chief of staff Dmitri Medvedev as chairman of the supervisory board. Miller, a young economist, had no experience of the energy sector. My late friend and former Russian finance minister Boris Fedorov, who was a member of the board of Gazprom from 2000 until his premature death in 2008, thought that Putin would clean up Gazprom from massive corruption. Gazprom did recover some assets, but it soon became clear that the nature of the regime had not changed, only the beneficiaries. Miller remains CEO of Gazprom, but the outstanding independent Moscow energy analyst Mikhail Krutikhin notes that "Gazprom has one manager: Putin."[38]

Gazprom has a supervisory board with eleven members, chaired by Viktor Zubkov, a former prime minister and a long-standing close friend of Putin. All are Russian citizens apart from Timur Kulibayev, the billionaire son of Kazakhstan's president Nursultan Nazarbayev. The German energy company E.on used to have one board member, Burkhard Bergmann, 2000–2011, but it sold its shares in Gazprom and gave up its board seat over disappointment with the company's poor performance. The Gazprom board that is elected annually varies little and is dominated by its managers.[39]

Gazprom enjoys multiple monopolies, including on trunk pipelines, exports through pipelines, development of new offshore fields, and the regulation of pipeline transportation. It decides independently whether another company will be allowed to transport gas through its pipelines, compelling a large share of Russia's gas to be flared.

Gazprom is profoundly conservative. Its international business is traditionally to export natural gas on long-term contracts to Europe through pipelines, and it has resisted novelties of all kinds, such as liquefied natural gas, shale gas, spot sales, and exports to China and the Far East. It probably opposes shale gas for good commercial reasons, since it has ample supplies of cheap ordinary gas, but it has been conservative also in its contract policy, insisting on decade-long contracts with prices fixed to oil prices and specific volumes. Customers have been compelled to pay even if they have not taken delivery of contracted volumes, so-called take-or-pay conditions.

In spite of its administrative clout, Gazprom has lost out to two competitors on the domestic market, the privately owned and far more efficient Novatek and Rosneft. Russia's gas production has been roughly constant since the late 1980s (fig. 4.1), whereas Gazprom's production of natural gas has fallen steadily by 25 percent from 562 billion cubic meters (bcm) in 2009 to 419 bcm in 2016, and its share of Russia's gas production has fallen from 85 percent to 65 percent. In 2017, however, Gazprom managed to reverse this trend by increasing its production by 12 percent to 472 bcm, thanks to larger sales to Europe. Unable to sell at capacity, Gazprom is considered to have a monumental surplus of some 100 bcm annually. In 2014, Gazprom lost its export monopoly on liquefied natural gas when Rosneft and Novatek gained the right to export the gas. Novatek is a crony company, in which Putin's friend Gennady Timchenko owns 23 percent, while Putin's close associate Sechin runs Rosneft.[40]

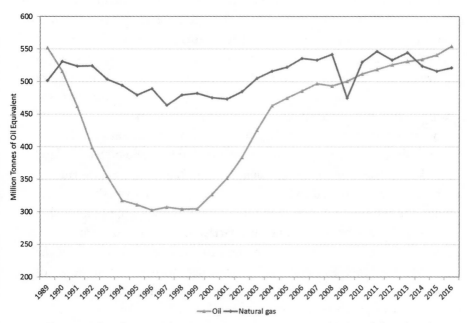

Fig. 4.1 Oil and gas production, 1989–2016. *Source: BP historical data (2018)*

Gazprom's first liquefied natural gas project was the Sakhalin II development, initiated by a group of foreign companies led by Royal Dutch Shell independently of Gazprom. In 2007, Gazprom imposed itself on this project, taking over 50 percent at a price set by Gazprom. The first liquefied natural gas plant was commissioned two years later. Beginning in 1997, the reform of Russia's public utility UES was a welcome improvement, but Gazprom reversed the attempt to establish an electricity market after it had purchased a large share of Russia's power assets.[41]

Before December 2005, the trade in Gazprom shares was highly restricted even on the domestic market, but that month Putin issued a decree permitting foreigners to trade freely in Gazprom stocks. The price of Gazprom stocks multiplied. The government kept state ownership of 50 percent plus one share, allowing the rest of the stocks to be traded freely. Gazprom shares are mainly traded in London. For a couple of years, international investors loved Gazprom, driving its market capitalization to $369 billion in May 2008. Since then, it has slumped precipitously by 86 percent, lingering around $50 billion for the past couple of years. By contrast, the market capitalization of other international oil majors has fallen only moderately with lower oil prices.[42]

The Gazprom stock is traded entirely on the basis of its high dividend yield, at 5.7 percent in August 2018—that is, not as a normal stock but rather as a bond. The shareholders do not consider themselves as owners but rather as subject to state decisions about the dividends. Yet the miserably low stock price does not bother the Gazprom management. In 2015, JP Morgan Cazenove concluded: "Weak corporate governance which has been a drag for Gazprom investment case is now compensated by stronger commitment to dividend and better dividend yield. . . . The looming budget deficit makes the [Russian] government much more aware of the Gazprom dividend. The minority shareholders and the state are now finally in same boat in terms of requiring higher payout." The finance company summarized its view of Gazprom: "Owning Gazprom has been a challenging experience for investors over the last several years. The stock underperformed the market and the sector and is currently trading near a 12-year low. There are internal and external reasons for this. First, the company, which employs almost half a million people, is seen as relatively slow and inefficient in decision making. Second, Gazprom is heavily involved in political developments related to Ukraine gas suppliers." This situation has not changed.[43]

Gazprom has many objectives, most of them of dubious motive, and dysfunctional decision-making. Its foremost objective is the enrichment of the Putin circle. Its second goal is Russian geopolitics. Its third aim is an array of social objectives, notably making sure that the whole country is supplied with gas, but also the support of employment in remote company towns. Last, Gazprom is not altogether oblivious of commercial considerations.[44]

Throughout the years Gazprom has been accused of larceny, though the nature of the accusations has changed. In the 1990s and 2000s, the main concern was privileged arbitrage between different regulated prices and nonpayments. While these concerns linger, liberalization of gas trade has limited them. Boris Nemtsov and Vladimir Milov have detailed four kinds of corruption in Gazprom: privileged procurement, asset stripping, exclusive trade agreements, and stock market manipulation.[45]

For geopolitical reasons, Gazprom's overwhelming ambition has been to avoid gas transit through Ukraine by building pipelines through the Baltic Sea—Nord Stream and later Nord Stream 2—as well as Turkish Stream.

But overinvestment in no-bid contracts, or capital procurement at excessive prices, is also the most important source of overpricing or undue enrichment. In a fine analysis, Troika Dialog assessed $37 billion or 70 percent of Gazprom's capital investment in 2011 as "value destruction." Most of these value-destructive activities amounted to "building capacity that cannot possibly be utilized in the foreseeable future," both production and pipeline capacity.[46]

Gazprom's capital expenditures vary swiftly with net profits. The most extreme year was 2011. Initially, Gazprom had planned for $27 billion of capital investment, but as revenues unexpectedly skyrocketed with rising gas prices, Gazprom eventually "invested" $53 billion, almost twice as much. No efficient investment planning is possible with such short notice. It is difficult to avoid the impression that the Gazprom management was just shoveling money out of the door, as one investor saw the situation.[47]

Gazprom has regularly overinvested in pipelines that are not commercially viable. These contracts have been awarded to companies controlled by a few close friends of Putin (see chapter 5: Arkady Rotenberg and Gennady Timchenko). The excellent Russian investigative journalist Yulia Latynina, who has been forced to flee Russia, notes that Gazprom is planning a loss of $15 billion for 2017–2019, largely to pursue overinvestment in pipelines to be built by Rotenberg and Timchenko. When Gazprom built Blue Stream in the late 1990s, Hermitage Capital Management showed that Gazprom's cost per kilometer of pipeline was 119 percent higher than on the Turkish side. The comparative costs have risen substantially since then and appear now to be three times higher.[48]

In spite of poor commercial performance, Gazprom's managers are handsomely remunerated. According to Russian *Forbes*, Miller's salary alone has been $25 million a year for many years, and he enjoys plenty of fringe benefits. The eminent opposition newspaper *Novaya Gazeta* published photos of "Millerhof," the palace allegedly built for Miller in the Moscow region in 2008–2009. It is so called because of its reminiscence of Peter the Great's palace Peterhof outside of St. Petersburg. Presumably to salvage Miller from the scandal, a big businessman closely connected with the Kremlin claimed it as his property.[49]

From 2000 to 2015, the international accounting firm PwC audited Gazprom, and it signed off on its annual reports without revealing anything of real interest. In 2015, Gazprom chose a Russian auditor instead, presumably to liberate itself from Western insight following the Western sanctions against Russia after its aggression against Ukraine starting in 2014.[50]

No CEO in the world has overseen such value destruction as Gazprom's Miller, but even after seventeen years of disastrous management, Miller's tenure appears secure, reinforcing the perception that he is a transmission belt for Putin's decisions about crony enrichment and geopolitics. In 2013, *Forbes* quoted an anonymous banker saying, "If Miller goes, the stock price of Gazprom will rise by 15% the same day." The *Economist* summarized the situation at Gazprom at around the same time: "Gazprom is not a normal company.... As a firm that issues shares to outside investors, it should in theory strive to maximise profits in the long run. But since it is majority-owned by the Russian state, it pursues political goals too. ... As President Vladimir Putin consolidated his power in the early 2000s, he built Gazprom into a main instrument of Russia's new state capitalism. He appointed allies to top positions. He used Gazprom as a tool of foreign policy."[51]

Even at Gazprom there are healthy parts arising from private companies it has bought. Gazprom Neft, formerly Sibneft, bought by Gazprom in 2005, is still considered the most efficient and modern oil company in Russia, thanks to the modernization pursued under Roman Abramovich. Gazprom's ultimate advantage is its vast resources of cheap gas, while its drawback is that it has damaged its reputation for reliability so beyond contempt that it is unable to sell its plentiful gas even at rock-bottom prices.

Gazprom is probably Russia's foremost geopolitical tool in the former Soviet Union and Eastern Europe. In the 1990s, Gazprom often allowed its customers to run up large arrears but then called for debt-equity swaps and seized control of the pipeline system in several countries— Belarus, Moldova, and the Baltic countries.

Gazprom has been notorious for cutting supplies for flimsy reasons in Eastern Europe. A study by the Swedish Defense Research Agency established that Russia used "coercive energy policy," such as supply cuts, coercive price policy, and sabotage, fifty-five times from 1991 until 2006. Of these incidents, thirty-six had political underpinnings and forty-eight had economic foundations. Gazprom was the dominant actor in sixteen of these cases. The main targets have been Lithuania, Georgia, Belarus, Ukraine, and Moldova. The two biggest and most famous incidents of cuts to gas supply were to and through Ukraine in January 2006 and January 2009.[52]

Gazprom claims to be reliable and generous, but the Kremlin has pursued a combination of self-dealing and geopolitics. The Russian-Ukrainian gas trade is a case in point. Reuters revealed how it functioned. From 2002, the Ukrainian gas trader Dmytro Firtash, one of pro-Russian president Viktor Yanukovych's main backers, dominated this trade. "Gazprom sold more than 20 billion cubic metres of gas well below market prices to Firtash" from 2010 to 2013. The price he paid was so low that companies he controlled made $3.7 billion on the arrangement, and Gazprombank "granted Firtash credit lines of up to $11 billion." In 2014, Firtash was arrested in Vienna at the request of the US Department of Justice for corruption in India, but a Russian businessman close to Putin "loaned the Ukrainian businessman $155 million for bail." Thus, Firtash appears to have been a Kremlin influence agent rather than a businessman.[53]

Gazprom's blatant cuts of gas supplies through Ukraine for four days in 2006 and especially for two weeks in 2009 greatly upset the European Union. It responded by demanding a different trading regime. In 2009, the European Union adopted its third energy package, compelling the unbundling of supply and production from networks. In February 2015, the European Commission went further, proposing an energy union. European Commission president Jean-Claude Juncker declared that the free movement of energy would become a fifth freedom of the European Union, in addition to the free movement of goods, services, people, and capital.[54]

Gazprom has allied with the big energy companies in Western Europe, often being accused of oligopolistic aspirations. The main victims have been East European countries and the consumers of gas. In August 2012, the European Commission opened an investigation for anticompetitive behavior against Gazprom's pricing and trading policies. In April 2015, the commission expressed its preliminary view that Gazprom had broken EU antitrust rules by pursuing an overall strategy to partition Central and Eastern European gas markets. The European Commission established that "6 EU Member States are dependent on one single external supplier for all their gas imports." These countries are Bulgaria, Estonia, Finland, Latvia, Lithuania, and Slovakia, whose sole supplier is Russia, and all but Finland had suffered multiple politically motivated supply cuts.[55]

The commission had three major concerns: Gazprom's prohibition of the reexport of gas, unduly high gas prices in monopolized markets, and Gazprom's use of its pipeline monopolies to seize markets. The European Commission alleged that Gazprom had used monopolistic power in Central and Eastern Europe for geopolitical purposes. Gazprom decided to cooperate. In March 2017, the commission acknowledged that Gazprom had made sufficient concessions on all three points, adopting a market-economic approach with free trade of gas.[56]

In May 2018, the European Commission finally issued its verdict, imposing on Gazprom "a detailed set of rules that will significantly change the way Gazprom operates in Central and Eastern European gas markets." Gazprom had "to remove any restrictions placed on customers to re-sell gas cross-border," enabling "gas flows to and from parts of Central and Eastern Europe that are still isolated from other Member States." Gazprom had to render pricing transparent and was prohibited from taking advantage of its control of gas infrastructure. Yet the energy giant did not have to pay any fines.[57]

Ukraine has the greatest troubles with Gazprom. Traditionally, it was Gazprom's biggest customer, but this gas trade has been notoriously corrupt, involving both Russian and Ukrainian gas traders, as Margarita Balmaceda has documented so well. In early April 2014, one month after President Yanukovych had fled the country, Russia hiked Gazprom's gas price to Ukraine by 80 percent from $268.50 per billion cubic meters to $485 per bcm. Naturally, Ukraine's Naftogaz objected and stopped accepting Russian gas, for which Gazprom sued it. Because of Gazprom's arbitrary pricing and erratic supplies, Ukraine stopped importing gas from Russia from November 2015.[58]

In June 2014, Gazprom filed a lawsuit against Naftogaz at the Stockholm International Arbitration Court, claiming that Naftogaz owed it some $75 billion for not having bought all the gas it had contracted for ten years in January 2009. Naftogaz countersued the same day. In 2017, Naftogaz won on all the three counts, which largely coincide with the issues raised by the European Commission. The arbitration court dismissed Gazprom's claim that it should be paid for gas that Naftogaz had not purchased. The court also revised the price formula, tying the price to market prices at European gas hubs. Finally, the court ruled against the ban on gas re-export. Later on, Naftogaz won an award from Gazprom in a separate case about Gazprom underpaying for gas transit through Ukraine and won a net award of $2.6 billion. Gazprom responded by refusing to pay.[59]

Gazprom continues its battle for market dominance in Europe. It is proceeding with the construction of two big pipelines: Nord Stream 2, from Russia to Germany through the Baltic Sea, and Turkish Stream. Its obvious aim is to monopolize transportation of gas from the east to the European Union. Since Gazprom offers attractive conditions to several large European energy companies, they bank on Gazprom. The opposing forces are parts of the European Commission, which favors energy security and a well-functioning energy market, the East European countries, and the United States, which is facilitating the exports of liquefied natural gas to Europe. For the time being, the market is winning, as natural gas sold on the spot market has become the price setter in Europe, and some of the gas comes from the United States.

Gazprom has not been sanctioned by any Western country because of European resistance, whereas the United States sanctioned Novatek, Rosneft, and Gazprombank on July 16, 2014, and Miller on April 6, 2018. As the *Financial Times* has stated, "Dealing with Gazprom is a delicate matter. This is no ordinary parastatal enterprise, being as much a tool of geopolitics as an energy company. Vladimir Putin . . . made clear his hostility to the [EU] probe from the outset, passing a law forbidding state companies from passing information to foreign regulators without Moscow's consent."[60]

Together with Gazprom, Rosneft, which produces half of Russia's crude oil, is Russia's prime cash cow. It stands out as Russia's most aggressive corporate raider. Because its average production costs are low, it generates large rents. Like Gazprom, however, Rosneft's free cash flow is usually small because of excessive capital expenditures, mainly on acquisitions of other oil companies but also on capital investment. Rosneft is generally considered more modern than Gazprom because most of its assets were acquired relatively recently from excellent private companies—Yukos, TNK-BP, and Bashneft. Furthermore, it has hired many Western managers for senior positions. Its development, too, has differed from Gazprom's, because from the outset Rosneft was much smaller, but it has compensated by being more aggressive. Over time, Rosneft appears to be becoming more monopolistic and less efficient, as its poor stock price reflects.

In the early 1990s, the Russian reform government broke up the Russian oil industry into many independent companies. From 1992 to 1999, they were first privatized and then consolidated into large, vertically integrated oil companies—Yukos, Lukoil, TNK, Surgutneftegaz, Sibneft, and a handful of others. From 1999 to 2004, the oil industry went through a major recovery, and oil production surged by 50 percent. The three oil companies that had been privatized by financial outsiders—Yukos, TNK, and Sibneft—led the surge (fig. 4.1, p. 111).[61]

Rosneft originally comprised various remaining state-owned oil assets, but two men drove its expansion: Sergei Bogdanchikov, its CEO until 2010, and Igor Sechin. Both benefited from Putin's energetic but understated assistance. Sechin has been one of Putin's closest aides since 1991. Putin has described him as "a philologist by training. He knows Portuguese, French, and Spanish. He worked abroad, in Mozambique and Angola." He presumably worked for military intelligence (GRU) in Africa. As probably Putin's closest aide in the Kremlin in the early 2000s, Sechin seized control over Rosneft soon after 2000. From 2004 to 2012, he was chairman of Rosneft's board of directors. He maintained control over the company as deputy prime minister for energy policy, 2008–2012, and since 2012 he has been the CEO of Rosneft, despite having worked previously only in the public sector.[62]

In a complex series of maneuvers from 2004 to 2005, almost all Yukos assets were expropriated to the benefit of Rosneft, which acquired the assets at prices far below their market level in "auctions" without competition. Thanks to these Yukos assets, Rosneft tripled its oil production and became one of Russia's biggest oil companies, roughly equal to the privately held Lukoil.

Rosneft's second major expansion occurred in October 2012, when it acquired TNK-BP for the high price of $55 billion. From its formation as a joint venture in 2003, TNK-BP had been the most successful big oil company in the world measured on return on investment. In March 2013, BP stated: "BP initially invested around $8 billion in its 50 per cent interest in TNK-BP in 2003. Since then TNK-BP has grown its production by 41 per cent [and] has replaced its reserves by an average of 125 per cent a year." BP received net $12.5 billion in cash and 18.5 per cent of Rosneft shares, then valued at $14.5 billion. In addition, BP received dividends exceeding its initial investment of $8 billion. Thus, in a decade BP made an extraordinary gain of nearly 350 percent on its initial investment of $8 billion.[63]

When asked about Rosneft's purchase of TNK-BP soon after the deal, Putin offered no commercial rationale, but his detailed response revealed considerable involvement: "It is true that the Cabinet and I had mixed feelings ... [about] Rosneft's purchase of BP's interest." Putin claimed not very credibly that he opposed nationalization as "there was concern that . . . the Russian part of TNK, could also be absorbed by Rosneft, a state company. . . . That does not correspond to our trend of curbing government sector growth." He continued: "We had a difficult choice to make. But ultimately, we nevertheless agreed with Rosneft and BP's suggestion, their joint suggestion that they could work together." He welcomed BP to "the board of directors, this will ensure additional transparency in activities of our biggest oil company, Rosneft, which incidentally is the world's biggest crude oil producer."[64]

Despite the company's excessive debt, Sechin wanted to continue Rosneft's expansion. In 2014, he announced that he wished to buy Bashneft. In 2009, when Dmitri Medvedev was president, the Russian state had sold Bashneft to the private Russian company Sistema, controlled by the apolitical businessman Vladimir Yevtushenkov. Sistema quickly turned Bashneft from a mediocre company to Russia's fastest-growing oil company. In the summer of 2014, Sechin claimed, as did a Moscow court, that Sistema had paid too little, so it renationalized Bashneft, and Yevtushenkov was arrested. Moscow's business community feared a new Yukos affair. The arrest was perceived as particularly unfair, since few were as cautious and detached from politics as Yevtushenkov. After a few months, Yevtushenkov was acquitted, having lost Bashneft and most of his wealth. In the fall of 2016, Rosneft bought Bashneft for $5.3 billion in an "auction." It was supposed to be a privatization without the participation of state companies, but Putin changed the rules, allowing Rosneft to gobble up another excellent private oil company.[65]

Adding insult to injury, in May 2017 the indefatigable Sechin claimed damages, alleging that Sistema had stripped assets from Bashneft, although Sistema had invested heavily and developed the company profitably. As a result, Sistema's stock prices fell by 37 percent in one day, and in the ensuing month the broader Russian stock market fell by 14 percent. The *Financial Times* reported that "some international investors say the lawsuit is the most worrying aspect because a private enterprise has not only been stripped of its asset, but the Kremlin-controlled beneficiary is also seeking further compensation." In August, the Bashkortostan arbitration court in Ufa awarded Rosneft $2.3 billion in a case with no merit. Sistema had lost more than half of its stock price. One Western portfolio investor commented: "For anyone wondering why the Russian market trades on giveaway multiples, Sistema's sorry saga is a salutary tale." This case illustrates how Putin allows Sechin to damage Russia's national economic interests for what seems to be lawless self-indulgence.[66]

In December 2016, Rosneft carried out an unusual financial operation that was labeled "privatization." The first announcement of the deal came from Putin's press secretary Dmitri Peskov, who stated that 19.5 percent shares of Rosneft had been sold to "a consortium of Glencore and Qatar's sovereign fund." Putin met with Sechin, who claimed that "this amounts to over 1 trillion rubles, which will come to the budget, including 10.5 billion euros for Rosneft's 19.5 percent stake." Putin concurred: "It is the largest privatization deal, the largest sale and acquisition in the global oil and gas sector in 2016."[67]

But nothing was what it seemed. Glencore had contributed only €300 million, and it benefited from a trading agreement with Rosneft, which might have covered the whole cost. Qatar contributed €2.5 billion, and the rest came as bank loans from Italy's biggest bank, Intesa Sanpaolo, Gazprombank, and other Russian banks. Rosneft had just sold $10.8 billion in domestic ruble bonds, which had been purchased by Bank Otkritie and appear to have financed most of the "privatization." The mystery deepened when Putin awarded the three main foreign participants in the deal the prestigious Order of Friendship.[68]

The actual beneficiary owners of these stocks remain to be identified, but formally the Rosneft shares are owned by Singaporean QHG Shares Pte, which belongs to British QHG Invest, which is controlled by QHG Holding, which is owned by the Cayman offshore company QHG Cayman Limited. Evidently, someone is trying to hide the real owners through a large number of shell companies. In June 2017, Rosneft announced that it wanted to renationalize the stake it had just sold, raising further suspicions about the real beneficiary owners.[69]

In September 2017, the puzzle of ownership increased when this shell company sold off 14 percent of Rosneft to a little-known private Chinese company. The owner of that company was arrested by the Chinese authorities in an anticorruption drive, and the deal was canceled in May 2018.[70]

Rosneft prides itself on having all the paraphernalia of good corporate governance, such as published annual reports that are internationally audited, independent directors, and, like Gazprom, a listing on the London Stock Exchange. Sechin possibly enjoys more direct access to Putin than anybody else, having had his office next to Putin's from 1991 to 2012. In September 2017, Germany's former chancellor Gerhard Schröder became chairman of Rosneft's supervisory board. Of its eleven members, no fewer than seven are foreigners, but the Putin circle maintains full control, and Sechin is in charge.[71]

Rosneft's oil production increased significantly between 2005 and 2012, but this was largely thanks to the Yukos assets and their good production management. At present, it accounts for roughly half of Russia's oil production, nearly five million barrels a day, which makes it the largest listed oil company in the world in terms of oil production, but it is so inefficient and focused on the interests of the state and managers rather than its shareholders that its market capitalization was $68 billion in 2018, and ExxonMobil is five times more valuable. Rosneft is also overindebted, with a total debt that is twice as large as its market capitalization.[72]

Its stock prices and market evaluations speak a different language. In July 2006, Rosneft carried out an initial public offering of $10.7 billion, which was largely bought by big foreign energy companies that wanted to develop business alliances with Rosneft. Just after the TNK-BP acquisition, Rosneft's market capitalization reached $96 billion. Sechin "pledged [that] the combined company would be worth $120 billion." Its share prices have not done as poorly as Gazprom's, but in August 2018 its market capitalization, even though buoyed by higher oil prices, had fallen by 30 percent to just $68 billion, while it had paid $55 billion for TNK-BP and Yukos was worth $45 billion in October 2003 before it was confiscated. Even considering today's lower oil prices, if Rosneft had a profit-oriented management, it should be worth four times more, comparing it with other oil majors. Its poor financial performance is indicative of serious financial mismanagement destroying the value of the company.[73]

Overinvestment and excessive asset purchases have caused this poor financial profile. When it bought TNK-BP, Rosneft took on $40 billion of short-term debt, which it had great problems refinancing. In the spring of 2015, Sechin asked Deputy Prime Minister Arkady Dvorkovich to have the government allocate Rosneft $20 billion from the National Welfare Fund (more than a quarter of its total value). But the government stonewalled, attempting to force Rosneft to cut its capital expenditures. Instead, Rosneft issued a huge ruble bond that it had exchanged into dollars in a financial transaction that was blamed for the severe destabilization of the ruble in December 2014.[74]

Unlike Gazprom, Rosneft has successfully closed major deals with foreign oil majors, notably BP and ExxonMobil, but also with Statoil and Total. The most important agreement is probably the continuing Sakhalin I joint venture with ExxonMobil. Sechin concludes such deals personally and usually in or around the Kremlin, involving the president. Conveniently, Rosneft's headquarters are located in the premises of the former USSR Ministry of Oil Industry across the Moscow River from the Kremlin. *Forbes* cites one anonymous Rosneft manager as saying that Sechin sometimes goes to the Kremlin several times in a day because all major deals have to be agreed to by Putin.[75]

Like Gazprom, Rosneft is pursuing foreign policy for the Russian state, though farther ashore. In May 2015, Rosneft and Venezuela announced that Rosneft had committed to a giant investment of $14 billion in Venezuela's oil industry. Given Venezuela's disastrous economic policy, this commitment made little commercial sense, but Sechin appears to be the main Russian emissary to Venezuela. When he visited Venezuela as deputy prime minister in 2009 he concluded arms deals with Venezuela. On April 28, 2014, the US government sanctioned Sechin as part of its Ukraine-related sanctions, and on September 12, Rosneft, too, was sanctioned.[76]

Sechin's appetite is insatiable. After the Bashneft "privatization," the Moscow oil community asked, who's next? Lukoil or Tatneft, the two remaining big private oil companies in Russia that do not belong to a Putin crony? Short of a genuine financial disaster in Rosneft, its ambition seems to be the re-creation of a Soviet Ministry of Oil Industry that can compete with Gazprom in inefficiency.

Vnesheconombank, or VEB, is a strange creation, functioning as Putin's slush fund for big projects and as a generous distributor of state funds. Its predecessor, the Bank for Foreign Economic Affairs of the USSR, was the Soviet foreign debt agency as well as the Soviet foreign trade bank.

When the Russian Federation became independent, it established its own state-owned foreign trade bank, VTB (Vneshtorgbank of Russia), leaving the Bank for Foreign Economic Affairs of the USSR to handle the country's foreign debt and claims. In 2007, the Bank for Foreign Economic Affairs of the USSR was replaced by VEB.

Its website states: "State Corporation 'Bank for Development and Foreign Economic Affairs (Vnesheconombank)' operates to enhance competitiveness of the Russian economy, diversify it and stimulate investment activity. Vnesheconombank is not a commercial bank. . . . VEB does not compete with commercial credit institutions and participates only in those projects that cannot receive funding from private investors." In spite of its name, VEB is not a bank; it has no bank license; and it is not subject to bank regulation. But what is it?[77]

The official VEB history states: "On January 31 [2006], Russian President Vladimir Putin said that it was necessary to establish a National Development Bank with an authorized capital of 2.5 billion US dollars. In December, the Russian Government approved a federal draft law 'On Development Bank.'" It continues: "State Corporation 'Bank for Development and Foreign Economic Affairs (Vnesheconombank)' was established in the Russian Federation. Russian President Vladimir Putin signed a Federal Law 'On Bank for Development' on May 17 2007."[78]

That one special law regulates VEB underlines its official government status: "Vnesheconombank is one of the key instruments of government investment policy. The Bank's activity is aimed at overcoming infrastructure growth restrictions, upgrading and promoting non-raw materials economic sector, high-technology industries, encouraging innovations, exports of high-technology products, implementing projects in special economic zones, environment protection projects and supporting small and medium-sized enterprises." Yet, legally VEB is a nongovernmental organization, and it is exempt from profit tax.[79]

VEB has always been tightly linked to Russia's foreign intelligence (SVR), as is evident from its CEO having been a senior foreign intelligence officer until 2018. VEB's CEO from 2004 to February 2016, Vladimir Dmitriev, served at the Russian embassy in Stockholm in 1992–1993. He was expelled by the Swedish authorities in 1993 after having been identified as the SVR resident in Sweden. Dmitriev's successor as VEB

CEO was Sergei Gorkov, whose official résumé acknowledges that "in 1994, [he] graduated from the Academy of the Federal Security Service of Russia." He was previously also vice president of Sberbank. A recent example of VEB engagement in intelligence is the VEB employee Evgeny Buryakov, who was arrested for spying in the United States in 2015 and sentenced to thirty months in prison. Buryakov was accused of having tried to recruit the former Trump campaign foreign affairs adviser Carter Page. Neither Dmitriev nor Gorkov was considered to be close to Putin. In May 2018, however, longtime first deputy prime minister Igor Shuvalov replaced Gorkov as CEO of VEB. Shuvalov is considered a very able technocrat, but he has been accused of several corruption affairs.[80]

VEB has a supervisory board with nine members, including its CEO. Its chairman is by law the prime minister, while six other members are ministers, and the final member is Putin's economic aide. As is obvious from its main operations, such as the 2008–2009 financial bailout and the Sochi Olympics, discussed below, VEB appears to take orders directly from Putin.[81]

Given its status as an NGO, VEB does not publish an annual report, though it has issued financial statements to raise international bond issues. Neither is VEB subject to public auditing. Its international credit rating equals that of the Russian sovereign, since it is fully covered by state guarantees. Its assets are sizable, amounting to $60.4 billion in October 2017, and its loan portfolio at that time was $44.7 billion. Its central activity is to give loans to giant state investment projects while acting as an agent of the state. It also provides export credits and guarantees, offers government support to large enterprises, and gives some credits to small and medium-sized enterprises. Its export credits tend to be linked to major Russian state corporation export projects, notably those of Rosatom, for example, in Hungary.[82]

In the past decade, VEB has been in charge of two major government operations: the bailout program of Russia's big companies in 2008–2009 and the financing of the Sochi Winter Olympics construction. The Kremlin allocated $50 billion from the National Welfare Fund to VEB for its bailout program to suffering large state-owned and private companies.[83]

Strangely, VEB also financed the Sochi Olympics with another $50 billion from its balance sheet; such public expenditures would normally have been financed from the federal budget. Once again VEB received money from the National Welfare Fund for its capitalization, but only $10 billion. For the rest, Putin's decision to finance the Sochi Olympics from the balance sheet of VEB brought the bank close to bankruptcy, though the big devaluation of 2014 halved this debt in dollar terms. The outcome of the Sochi financing caused the retirement of CEO Dmitriev in February 2016 and the swift ouster of Gorkov. At present, Putin's dilemma is that he seems unable to face up to the fact that VEB is his slush fund and not a development bank.[84]

In the first half of 2010, after Viktor Yanukovych had been elected president of Ukraine, VEB spearheaded a mysterious Russian investment campaign in Ukraine. It bought one big private commercial bank, Prominvestbank, and financed the purchase of half of two large metallurgical companies, the Industrial Union of Donbas and Zaporozhstal. No known owner of the bulk of the Russian shares ever emerged, arousing speculation that Putin was the ultimate Russian owner, but Rinat Akhmetov, Ukraine's leading businessman, stopped the Russian expansion in Ukraine by winning Ukrainian court cases, reportedly enraging Putin. Whatever the VEB design was, it never materialized. Instead, VEB lost about $10 billion in Ukraine. Ironically, it became a victim of the Russian military aggression in eastern Ukraine, which brought both the Industrial Union of Donbas and Prominvestbank to actual bankruptcy.[85]

In 2014, VEB reported a net loss of $4.5 billion, and in late 2015, the need for a capital infusion of $20 billion was discussed, though that figure has gradually been reduced. In the end, the government has had to bail out the nongovernmental organization VEB. Just who benefited from VEB's financing of the Sochi Olympics is a topic pursued in chapter 5.[86]

Through the VEB law of 2007, the president granted himself a vast source of discretionary state funding—in fact, a slush fund. The president can legally disburse vast amounts of funding for any purpose without any accountability. The US government has realized this fact, and on July 16, 2014, it sanctioned VEB as part of its financial sanctions, depriving VEB of its access to international debt markets and thus tightening its financial constraints. Eyebrows were raised when Jared Kushner, the son-in-law of President-Elect Donald Trump, received VEB CEO Gorkov in the middle of December 2016. Yet the US sanctioning is of a mild nature. Like VTB Capital, VEB maintains an office in New York.[87]

Rostec (short for Russian Technologies) is the most mysterious of the state conglomerates discussed here. Putin formed this state corporation in 2007 at the request of Sergei Chemezov, his old KGB friend from Dresden in the 1980s. Chemezov was Rostec's creator and has been its CEO from the outset. He appears to be one of the men closest to Putin, to judge from their many publicized one-on-one meetings.[88]

Commercially, Rostec makes little sense. Its website explains: "The corporation comprises 700 organizations that are currently part of 14 holding companies, nine of which operate in the military-industrial complex, and five in the civilian sectors." But why have these disparate companies been assembled into one enormous conglomerate?[89]

Russia's best military-industrial companies are well known, but they do not belong to Rostec. The aircraft companies belong to United Aircraft Corporation, the rocket companies to Roscosmos, the naval shipyards to United Shipbuilding Corporation, the nuclear assets to Rosatom, and the eminent air defense rockets to Almaz-Antey. The only well-known military-industrial companies pertaining to Rostec are Russian Helicopters and Kalashnikov. Chemezov appears to have collected whatever leftovers he could find in the military-industrial sector to form a state corporation.[90]

Worse, this corporation seems to lack a business idea. Its proclaimed mission is "to support Russian developers and manufacturers of high-tech industrial products in both domestic and foreign markets." More specialized and sophisticated armaments companies do most of that work.[91]

Like other state corporations, Rostec has a supervisory board and a management board, and its members are named on its website until 2017 after which they have disappeared. Its nine-person supervisory board consists of CEO Chemezov and eight top state officials, but curiously it does not name a chairman. Presumably, Chemezov fulfills that function as well. Rostec does not publish any financial reports, annual reports, or other detailed information about its business. This vast business empire of often secret companies is a nontransparent maze. Symptomatically, it abandoned its website in English in 2018 and stopped publishing much of the information offered here.[92]

Rostec makes one thing clear, its dependence on the president: "The Rostec Corporation is governed by its supervisory group, executive board, and general director, who is appointed by the President of the Russian Federation." Chemezov meets with Putin for key Rostec decisions, and these two men decide about this vast nongovernmental organization at will. In the public part of their annual meetings, Chemezov presents the preceding year's operations and discusses new business ventures that win Putin's explicit approval. Rarely does Putin appear as relaxed and chummy in public as when he is with Chemezov. When Dmitri Medvedev was president, by contrast, the meeting reports were minimal, showing the distance between them and that Rostec is subordinate to Putin as a person.[93]

Chemezov offers only information about Rostec that is open to the public in his meetings with Putin. At his presentation to Putin of Rostec's results for 2016, Chemezov claimed that his company "increased earnings [revenues] by 11 percent to over 1.2 trillion rubles" and that Rosoboronexport's exports amounted to $13.1 billion. For 2015, he stated that labor productivity increased by 17 percent and employment "increased slightly (by 1 percent) to 445,000 people." We possess no audited facts about Rostec's finances.[94]

Such a murky conglomerate could not possibly exist in a free market economy. It looks even worse than an old-style Soviet ministry, which had a clear specialization. This impression is reinforced by the names of departments, which include "fulfillment of state programs," "defense of state secrets," and "regional policy." These are not corporate but state functions.

Although Rostec is supposed to be an armaments company, it has branched out into various directions beyond armaments. Its three best-known companies are Russia's biggest civilian car company, Avtovaz, its biggest truck company, Kamaz, and the outstanding titanium producer VSMPO-Avisma. Its real driver seems to be Chemezov's empire-building ambitions.

Rostec has been accused of illicitly taking over other companies through corporate raiding. In 2006, the two dominant owners of VSMPO-Avisma, Russia's main titanium producer, were forced to sell their shares at a price they considered too low to Rosoboronexport, which later became part of Rostec.[95]

During the financial crisis of 2008–2009, many of Rostec's subsidiaries suffered, including Avtovaz and VSMPO-Avisma, but Rostec extracted significant state funds for its subsidiaries. On April 28, 2014, the US government sanctioned Chemezov as a member of the Russian leadership's inner circle, and on September 12, it sanctioned Rostec as part of US sectoral sanctions.[96]

Few companies as large as Rostec have so little to say to justify their mere existence. State secrecy is natural in the military-industrial sphere, but it grows ever greater, and the suspicion lingers that Rostec exists because Putin allows his good friend Chemezov to enjoy a good life. Putin also relies on Chemezov to maintain employment in Russia's many small company towns that the Kremlin fears could breed popular unrest. Rostec looks like a big black hole that should not exist in a normal economy.[97]

The Russian state has regained control of the "commanding heights" of the economy, as Vladimir Lenin's phrase ran. It has recovered control of the main sources of rents and is gobbling up ever more good private enterprises. Yet the state control of these big enterprises is illusory because a small group of men loyal to Putin personally exercises this control. The state enterprises have expanded to the benefit of Putin's cronies.[98]

Formally, these state enterprises have supervisory boards and management boards. As a result of previous reforms, state companies such as Gazprom and Rosneft possess all the formalities of proper corporate governance: annual shareholders' meetings, purportedly independent auditors, published annual reports, independent directors, and policies on corporate governance. The state corporations VEB and Rostec, by contrast, are nongovernmental organizations not subject to any external control or transparency.

The power over state companies and state corporations alike rests in the hands of one man: Vladimir Putin. His closest associates are chief executives. Three state enterprise managers stand out, forming the second circle of Putin's power after the FSB top: Sechin, Chemezov, and Miller. Each of them seems to be allowed to do virtually anything with impunity. All three have engaged in predatory corporate raiding that has undermined property rights in Russia.

A few top state CEOs who were KGB officers and Putin's contemporaries in St. Petersburg have recently been forced to retire. The most important is Vladimir Yakunin, CEO of Russian Railways from 2005 until his retirement in August 2015. He is a contemporary of Putin's and a KGB officer from St. Petersburg, as well as a member of the famous Ozero dacha cooperative. Opinions vary on why Yakunin was ousted. A common view is that Yakunin engaged too aggressively in hardline foreign policy, and he might have been politically too ambitious, mentioned as a possible Putin successor. Yet he has not fallen out of favor altogether; Putin has received him officially following his retirement, and he has set up a well-funded think tank in Berlin pursuing orthodox ideas.[99]

State capitalism is usually associated with long-term state plans of investment and technological development, but Russian state capitalism involves neither. Financial results seem almost irrelevant. The state companies prefer to keep most of their profits to themselves. As the *Financial Times*'s Neil Buckley observed, "It is becoming an annual ritual. Each spring, Russia's government presses its state-controlled companies to pay out more of their profits in dividends. The companies then scurry to find loopholes or lobby for exemptions," and successfully so.[100]

The long tenures of Putin's associates as chief executives indicate that economic efficiency, profits, innovations, and other economic performance criteria barely matter, whereas personal loyalty and the transfer of funds to friends do matter. No CEO of a large company in the world has destroyed more capital than Alexei Miller, who lost market capitalization of $310 billion from 2008 to 2018. The true beneficiaries are not the Russian state but Putin and his friends, and Putin has the legal power to transfer vast state funds to private companies or individuals at will.[101]

Similarly, the Kremlin sees state enterprises as geopolitical tools. Gazprom has obediently cut off gas whenever the Kremlin has requested it to punish a recalcitrant neighbor, even at major commercial cost, as with Ukraine and the European Union in 2009. Rosneft is happy to take over the responsibility for Venezuela, and VEB has thrown vast amounts on every harebrained scheme suggested by the Kremlin.

The law is no restriction; Putin's will appears to be everything. All too obviously, Putin approved of both Sechin's intricate corporate raiding of Yukos and Bashneft and Chemezov's of VSMPO-Avisma. Putin has awarded his lords their fiefdoms, and they are entitled to treat them at their discretion as long as they obey Putin.

The Kremlin considers social peace more important than profits or development. The state enterprises are supposed to pursue government policy inside the country. Gazprom is diligently supplying gas to the whole country regardless of whether people can pay, and the big state companies maintain employment in the many company towns. In his call-in program in June 2017, Putin offered a telling example. When the Kremlin wanted to build a bigger aircraft, "the government did not find the money and I will reprimand them for this. . . . Nevertheless, we found an opportunity and earmarked several dozen billions from Rosneftegaz for the relevant program." A state company was supposed to offer financing for the Kremlin without regard to the private shareholders of Rosneft.[102]

The CEOs of Russian state corporations are very well paid. Standard salaries of the big companies have ranged from $25 million to $50 million. Members of supervisory boards are also well remunerated. As president, Medvedev insisted that these salaries were published, which was done for a few years, but Sechin has made them secret.[103]

Can this system continue as oil rents dry up? The answer is not obvious. Putin has allowed the "systemic liberals" to tighten the budget constraints on the large state companies. Even Rosneft was forced to abandon its most value-destroying investments, such as petrochemicals. Yet if the price of oil stays over $50 per barrel, Russian oil rents will remain substantial.

The Russian model of crony capitalism appears not accidental but deliberate. This is a re-creation of an ancient patrimonial model well described by the dean of Russian history, Richard Pipes. It offers a maximum of freedom to the ruler and far-reaching delegation to the feudal lords. In effect, the state corporations have transformed public property into tsarist ownership. That model lasted for centuries.[104]

The Expansion of Crony Capitalism

I n 2004, a previously unknown group of Putin's friends surfaced, and in an unlikely way. That March, the former oligarch Boris Berezovsky, who had lived in voluntary exile in England since late 2000, sponsored the prominent politician Ivan Rybkin in opposition to Putin in the presidential campaign. Rybkin had been the speaker of the State Duma and was a former national security adviser.

In a mysterious incident, Rybkin disappeared for five days. When he resurfaced in Kiev in Ukraine, he claimed to have been drugged and kidnapped. At an emotional press conference, Rybkin accused four men of being Putin's "cashiers": Roman Abramovich, Gennady Timchenko, and the brothers Mikhail and Yuri Kovalchuk. "I—and not just me— have lots of concrete evidence of Putin's participation in business. Abramovich, as is known, but also Timchenko, the Kovalchuk brothers and others are responsible for Putin's business."[1]

Abramovich was on his way to London, and today he appears to play little role in Putin's circle, though Putin seems to keep him in high regard. The other three, all contemporaries of Putin from St. Petersburg, were completely unknown at the time. The Rybkin affair marked the end of democracy in Russia. The Kremlin reacted sharply: Rybkin's candidacy was not allowed, and he disappeared from public life. But the cat was out of the bag. Information gradually surfaced about these cronies who were becoming billionaires, and a new side of Putin came to light.

The cronies form the third circle around Putin, after the first two circles of security officials and state enterprise managers. Since around 1990, they have been private businessmen, and they have known Putin for a long time. They went into business with him when he was first deputy mayor of St. Petersburg, responsible for foreign economic relations, from 1991 to 1996. Yet their business took off only during Putin's second presidential term.[2]

The three prime cronies are Gennady Timchenko, Arkady Rotenberg, and Yuri Kovalchuk. Timchenko is the most prominent of these businessmen, having made his money in oil trading, gas production, and pipeline construction. Arkady Rotenberg is a major state contractor for roads and pipelines. Yuri Kovalchuk is the chief executive of Bank Rossiya and has made his money by purchasing financial and media assets from Gazprom. Judging from *Forbes*'s published lists of the rich, these three seem to be the most successful businessmen among Putin's cronies.[3]

Other cronies also exist. Nikolai Shamalov was the representative of Siemens and sold its medical equipment to the Russian government. Arkady Rotenberg has a younger brother, Boris, who has lived for many years in Finland, and a son, Igor, who has taken over much of Arkady Rotenberg's business. Yuri Kovalchuk's brother, Mikhail, is director of the Kurchatov Institute in Moscow, Russia's foremost nuclear research institute, but he is hardly a prominent businessman.

Numerous people of lesser significance could be added. Some have taken off commercially, while others have departed, but the stability in Putin's inner circle is striking. In her outstanding book *Putin's Kleptocracy*, Karen Dawisha names them all. So have Yuri Felshtinsky and Vladimir Pribylovsky in their detailed book *The Corporation*. The documentation has been done, and I shall focus on their functions.[4]

Putin's cronies are all men of his age from St. Petersburg. Their education and professions vary, but all have completed higher education. Around 1990, they entered varied businesses, with little expertise. Their accumulation of great wealth did not begin until around 2004.

Andrei Illarionov, a liberal reformer who served as personal economic adviser to Putin from 2000 to 2005, says that he never heard of or saw the cronies as long as he was in the Kremlin. Yet in 2000 a presidential

order arrived in the Kremlin that had not gone through ordinary government channels, ordering the formation of a state alcohol monopoly,
Rosspritprom, with more than one hundred liquor factories. When Illarionov saw this, he called on fellow reformers Economy Minister Herman Gref and Finance Minister Alexei Kudrin. Together they managed to
stop an obvious rent-seeking scheme. Many years later, Illarionov learned
that Arkady Rotenberg had been behind it, which is indicative of how
discreetly the cronies operated.[5]

The cronies never wanted to go public. Timchenko gave his first
interview in 2008, and Arkady Rotenberg in 2010. Putin's close friends
are few, perhaps a score of men (and no women). As mentioned, they
are mostly of Putin's age and from St. Petersburg. Timchenko lived for a
long time in Helsinki and then in Geneva, while Boris Rotenberg appears to have resided in Finland for the past two decades. Both Timchenko and Boris Rotenberg are Finnish citizens.[6]

On March 20, 2014, two days after Russia's annexation of Ukraine's
Crimea, the US Treasury sanctioned "Members of the Inner Circle": Gennady Timchenko, Arkady and Boris Rotenberg, and Yuri Kovalchuk, as
well as Bank Rossiya. They were sanctioned "because each is controlled
by, has acted for or on behalf of, or has provided material or other support to, a senior Russian government official," that is, Vladimir Putin. The
European Union has sanctioned Arkady Rotenberg, Yuri Kovalchuk, and
Nikolai Shamalov, though not Timchenko and Boris Rotenberg because
they are Finnish citizens. It is easier to write about them following the
sanctions, since they can no longer sue for libel with merit.[7]

During the years 1989–1993, Russia's already high murder rate doubled.
Racketeering and gang wars over turf drove this violence. The government's monopoly on violence had broken down during the collapse of
communism, and private entrepreneurs in protection took over. Political scientist Vadim Volkov remarks that "property exists only as long as
it can be protected by the claimant." Gang wars were particularly severe
in St. Petersburg, which earned the nickname "criminal Peter." Russians
drew parallels between St. Petersburg and Chicago at the height of the
Mafia violence during Prohibition in the early 1930s. Contract killers
murdered Mikhail Manevich, the deputy mayor for privatization, in

1997 and the prominent liberal parliamentarian Galina Starovoitova in 1998.[8]

In June 1991, in the midst of this violence, Vladimir Putin became chairman of the Committee for International Relations at the St. Petersburg City Hall, and from 1994 he also became deputy chairman of the St. Petersburg City Government. Putin was the protégé of the newly elected liberal mayor Anatoly Sobchak, a very likable man and a brilliant orator, but a terrible manager. I attended a speech he gave in the St. Petersburg City Hall in 1992. It was outstanding, and he received rapturous applause. Realizing his success, Sobchak repeated the same speech immediately afterwards, to more muted praise. Sobchak was a prominent professor of law, but he constantly improvised and never followed up on his decisions, generating chaos.[9]

Amid this criminal chaos, Putin was in charge of foreign investments, which was suffering from the soaring crime rate. The Swedish consul general in St. Petersburg from 1992 to 1996, Sture Stiernlöf, wrote a devastating picture of Putin, characterizing him as "closed, secretive, and German-oriented" and "an independent operator of power in the shade of Sobchak." Foreign visitors tended to underestimate Putin, who said little, revealed nothing, and was generally unhelpful. The Swedish authorities blamed Putin for ordering the tax police to extort the Swedish company that managed the elegant Grand Hotel Europe, forcing the Swedes out in favor of a German company. Similarly, the European Bank for Reconstruction and Development complained that Putin tried to raid the Astoria, St. Petersburg's other grand hotel.[10]

The first foreign bank office permitted to open an office in St. Petersburg was the German Dresdner Bank, whose local representative was Putin's old friend from the East German Stasi in Dresden Matthias Warnig. He has remained one of Putin's key businesspeople and sits on the supervisory boards of both Rosneft and Nord Stream. Finnish consul generals accused Putin of links to organized crime in Finland in this period. During his five years as deputy mayor, Putin visited Finland sixty to seventy times, nurturing business interests in Turku, where the Finnish authorities asserted that he owned a small hotel.[11]

Several American and German visitors to St. Petersburg in the early 1990s noted that Putin performed services without asking for a bribe, but he appears to have focused on a few big deals. Karen Dawisha tells the story about Putin's engagement in organized crime in St. Petersburg well. My own visits in St. Petersburg in the early 1990s verify many of her points. Yuri Felshtinsky and Vladimir Pribylovsky have also described these events.[12]

One big crime has stuck to Putin. In December 1991, Putin wrote to the Ministry of Economy in Moscow, requesting from state companies some $100 million of commodities, including oil, scrap metal and wood, to be bartered for food because St. Petersburg feared famine during the winter. A prominent liberal St. Petersburg politician, Marina Sal'e, led a city council commission that investigated what happened with these resources. The commission published a substantial report, concluding that "the city did not receive any products and 'lost' about $92 million." Nothing had been delivered, and all the money had been embezzled. Her commission called for Putin's prosecution. Thanks to protection from Sobchak and the Russian government in Moscow, Putin got out of this conundrum. This was presumably Putin's first big money, but he shared it with many.[13]

Putin was tied to another big corruption scandal involving the Tambov group—money laundering via the St. Petersburg Real Estate Holding Co. (SPAG). The Tambov group was the city's leading Mafia group in the early 1990s, and it was headed by Vladimir Kumarin. Putin was a founding member of SPAG's advisory board. Here as in many other cases, Putin appeared both as a representative of the city and as himself, which was often the case in Russia at that time. As Dawisha puts it: "Putin's price for doing real estate deals generally was that 25 percent had to go into the city's coffers for infrastructural and social projects, but there is no evidence of his seeking any commission for this deal." He did not need to because he determined where the money went. In 2001, two of SPAG's founders were indicted in Liechtenstein for money laundering and investment scams.[14]

A third big scandal tying Putin and the Tambov group involved the Petersburg Fuel Company, which Kumarin had set up together with Putin in 1994. The scheme included Putin, his cronies Yuri Kovalchuk and Nikolai Shamalov, and the hard-core organized criminals Vladislav Reznik (later a member of the State Duma), Ilya Traber, Gennady Petrov, and of course Tambov's leader, Vladimir Kumarin. The Tambov group moved to Spain after they had gentrified, and there several of their members were arrested for money laundering in 2008, providing us with ample evidence. In 2007, three hundred police arrested Kumarin, and in 2016 he was sentenced to twenty-three years in prison for attempted contract murder, homicide, extortion, and corporate raiding.[15] Hard-core criminals such as Traber and Petrov, as well as other members of the Tambov gang, are reputed to be fixtures at Putin's highly secretive birthday parties.

No picture of Putin is complete without recognizing his deep involvement in organized crime since at least 1991. Putin is no gentleman but a seasoned street fighter. Few facts reflect his personality more clearly than when he brought his big black Labrador Konni to a meeting with German chancellor Angela Merkel in 2007, knowing that she was scared of dogs.[16]

With his background in organized crime, Putin relies not only on the FSB but also on the Russian Mafia. Mark Galeotti has analyzed how Putin's Kremlin has used criminals for its rule. Chechnya's president Ramzan Kadyrov, whom the United States has sanctioned for human rights violations, has repeatedly given the Kremlin willing soldiers to carry out various lawless acts, such as the murder of opposition leader Boris Nemtsov outside the Kremlin in February 2015. In Crimea and in Eastern Ukraine in 2014, the Kremlin used both Chechen fighters and Russian mercenaries, organized by the Russian businessman Konstantin Malofeev, whom the US government has also sanctioned. The St. Petersburg businessman Evgeny Prigozhin was also involved in recruiting mercenaries for eastern Ukraine as well as for Syria, and he was the organizer of the Internet Research Agency, which organized the Russian manipulation of US voters through Facebook and other social media. Prigozhin, too, has been sanctioned by the United States. This extensive reliance on organized crime has not only criminalized the Russian government but also led to less precision.[17]

Two institutions in St. Petersburg are central to the Putin circle: Bank Rossiya and the Ozero dacha cooperative. Bank Rossiya appears to be the permanent center of the Putin financial network. It is widely known as the "bank of the president's friends."[18]

In June 1990, the Leningrad regional committee of the Communist Party of the Soviet Union established Bank Rossiya. Yuri Kovalchuk was one of its founders and original owners, and he became its permanent chief executive. Putin got involved during his first weeks in office, when his newly formed city committee for foreign liaisons coinvested with Bank Rossiya in July 1991, and the bank was the primary funding vehicle for Putin's city funds.[19]

In December 1991, Putin's close friends—the brothers Andrei and Sergei Fursenko, Nikolai Shamalov, Vladimir Yakunin, and Kovalchuk—became co-owners of Bank Rossiya. Kovalchuk owns one-third of Bank Rossiya, and the other tight friends of Putin own about one-tenth each. In 1997, Timchenko also became a co-owner, and Matthias Warnig has been a board director since 2012. Bank Rossiya was a medium-sized local bank and was virtually unknown in Russia until 2008. At that time, *Moscow Times* published an excellent article detailing its ownership shares, with the telling headline "Bank Rossiya Emerges from Shadows." It was important not as a bank but as the treasury of the Putin group.[20]

In November 1996, an important group of eight friends set up the Ozero dacha cooperative on the leafy outskirts of St. Petersburg. In addition to Putin, members included Yuri Kovalchuk, Vladimir Yakunin, an active KGB officer who later became minister of the Russian Railways, the brothers Andrei and Sergei Fursenko (Andrei was Russian minister of education and science from 2004 to 2012), Shamalov, Viktor Myachin, the head of Bank Rossiya, and Vladimir Smirnov, who became Ozero's head. The local official who assisted them was Viktor Zubkov, Russia's prime minister in 2007–2008. The Ozero cooperative was protected by Kumarin, the head of the Tambov gang.[21]

In March 2014, the US Treasury issued its verdict: "Bank Rossiya . . . is the personal bank for senior officials of the Russian Federation. Bank Rossiya's shareholders include members of Putin's inner circle associated with the Ozero Dacha Cooperative, a housing community in which they live. Bank Rossiya is also controlled by [Yuri] Kovalchuk, designated today. Bank Rossiya is ranked as the 17th largest bank in Russia with assets of approximately $10 billion, and it maintains numerous correspondent relationships with banks in the United States, Europe, and elsewhere. The bank reports providing a wide range of retail and corporate services, many of which relate to the oil, gas, and energy sectors."[22]

Gennady Timchenko has made his fortune as an oil trader, at the independent gas producer Novatek and by building gas pipelines for Gazprom. Among Putin's three main cronies, he appears the most like a real businessman.

Timchenko, born in 1952 like Putin, comes from a military family. He graduated from an engineering institute in Leningrad and worked at a foreign trade organization in the city from 1982 to 1988. Many foreign trade officials belonged to the KGB, but no such evidence is at hand on Timchenko. In the late 1980s, some state enterprises were awarded rights to pursue foreign trade independently of Moscow foreign trade organizations, and Timchenko struck out on his own with two colleagues. They approached the state-owned Kirishi oil refinery in Leningrad and started trading oil for it. Timchenko met Putin in connection with his barter trade in 1991 or earlier.

In 1991, Timchenko started working with a Finnish company and developed oil-trading companies around the Kirishi refinery with three partners. In 1999, he became a Finnish citizen, seemingly living both in Helsinki and in St. Petersburg. In 2001, he moved to Geneva. He did reasonably well, but he was not prominent. The Kirishi refinery became a part of Surgutneftegaz in 1993, when a government decree assigned that company several oil assets. The general presumption has been that Timchenko and Putin received a corresponding share in the notoriously nontransparent Surgutneftegaz.[23]

In the early 2000s, Timchenko's business suddenly took off. Together with the Swedish oil trader Torbjörn Törnqvist, he set up the oil-trading company Gunvor in 2000. Beginning in 2003, Gunvor started trading a large share of the oil and oil products exported from Russia, rapidly becoming the third largest oil trader in the world. Most of this oil came first from Surgutneftegaz and then from the two state-owned companies Rosneft and Gazprom Neft, as well as the privately held TNK-BP. The *Economist* claimed that Gunvor bought oil at a discount from the Russian oil companies. Timchenko sued the magazine for libel, but the case was settled out of court.[24]

After the public became aware of Timchenko's existence in 2004, two suspicions were voiced in the media. One was that there was a third shareholder in Gunvor, namely Putin. Gunvor had a complex owner-ship, with several layers of shell companies, making it impossible to know the actual beneficiary owners. Much later, an unexpected third owner was revealed, a St. Petersburg butcher named Petr Kolbin, who turned out to be a childhood friend of Putin.[25]

In March 2014, the US Department of Treasury sanctioned Tim-chenko because of Russia's annexation of Crimea: "Gennady Timchen-ko is one of the founders of Gunvor, one of the world's largest independent commodity trading companies involved in the oil and en-ergy markets. Timchenko's activities in the energy sector have been di-rectly linked to Putin. Putin has investments in Gunvor and may have access to Gunvor funds." In July 2015, the US Treasury also sanctioned Kolbin.[26]

Gunvor itself was not sanctioned, and Timchenko fortuitously sold his shares in Gunvor to Törnqvist the day before he was designated by the US Treasury. Gunvor continues to trade oil, but it has divested from Russia. Designated by the US Treasury, Timchenko could no lon-ger use Western banks or credit cards, so he was compelled to move from Geneva to Moscow, where he lives in one of the grand old Stalinist Politburo villas on the Sparrow Hills overlooking the capital.

Timchenko has two much bigger investments that have attracted less attention, Novatek and Stroitransgaz. Novatek surged as a highly successful and efficient independent gas producer in Russia under the well-connected entrepreneur Leonid Mikhelson. Unlike other indepen-dent producers in Russia, Novatek succeeded in getting production licenses and was allowed to use Gazprom's pipelines, indicating consid-erable personal leverage. It has even been permitted to export liquefied natural gas.

Novatek took off after Timchenko bought 23.5 percent of its stocks in 2008–2009, and it has benefited through purchases of various gas as-sets from Gazprom. In August 2018, Novatek had a sizable market capi-talization of $47 billion, which means a fortune of $11 billion for Timchenko for this holding alone. The US government has sanctioned Novatek, though mildly, but the EU has not, and Novatek has completed a vast liquefied natural gas plant in Yamal on the Arctic Sea for no less than $27 billion with plenty of Chinese and French financing. Currently, Mikhelson and Timchenko also co-own the large petrochemical company Sibur.[27]

In 2009, Timchenko made another big deal, buying 80 percent of the company Stroitransgaz, which is one of Russia's two biggest builders of gas pipelines, and it remains one of the two biggest suppliers of gas pipelines to Gazprom, thanks to preferential public procurement, with billions of dollars in annual sales.[28]

Timchenko appears to have benefited greatly from his close personal relations with Putin. Gunvor took off from sales from Russian state-related oil companies; Novatek has thrived on unique access to gas field licenses and access to pipelines and now even to exports; Stroitransgaz lives on preferential state orders from Gazprom. These three businesses gained momentum in 2003–2009.

On March 20, 2014, the US Treasury announced: "Arkady Rotenberg and Boris Rotenberg have provided support to Putin's pet projects by receiving and executing high price contracts for the Sochi Olympic Games and state-controlled Gazprom. They have made billions of dollars in contracts for Gazprom and the Sochi Winter Olympics awarded to them by Putin. Both brothers have amassed enormous amounts of wealth during the years of Putin's rule in Russia. The Rotenberg brothers received approximately $7 billion in contracts for the Sochi Olympic Games and their personal wealth has increased by $2.5 billion in the last two years alone."[29]

The brothers Arkady (born in 1951) and Boris Rotenberg (born in 1957) are among Putin's oldest friends. Arkady and Putin did judo together from 1964, when they were twelve. Before 2004, the Rotenberg brothers were unknown to the public, and Russian biographical articles do not discuss their early business. Arkady gave his first interview in 2010 and said virtually nothing.[30]

The brothers Rotenberg were sportsmen and minor businessmen. Arkady did pedagogic studies in sports. Boris emigrated to Finland early on, but he has remained a junior partner to his brother. In the early 1990s, Arkady went into the business of protection, cofounding a St. Petersburg protection company called Shield in 1995. Rotenberg formed the Yavara-Neva Judo Club in 1998 with his brother and Timchenko, and Putin as president. In 2000, Rotenberg joined a company involved in real estate development, gambling, hotels, and restaurants, and in 2001 he set up a small bank with his brother, Boris, which appears to have functioned as their treasury.[31]

In 2008, Arkady Rotenberg struck gold when Gazprom magnanimously sold him five construction subsidiaries for $348 million, out of which Rotenberg formed his company Stroigazmontazh. Only then did his business become significant, focusing on construction of gas pipelines. Stroigazmontazh has been Gazprom's biggest contractor, building gas pipelines. Just after Rotenberg formed the company, Stroigazmontazh won a major tender for the construction of the Nord Stream gas pipeline through the Baltic Sea from Russia to Germany. Without competitive tender, Stroigazmontazh won the contract to build the long pipeline Sakhalin-Khabarovsk-Vladivostok for nearly $7 billion.[32]

In 2010, the Russian media revealed that Arkady Rotenberg had acquired 9 percent of the big Moscow road construction company Mostotrest. Soon, he controlled the whole company, which was building the highway between St. Petersburg and Moscow and many other highways. Mostotrest employs some thirty thousand people.[33]

Rotenberg's great boondoggle was the Sochi Olympics, for which his Stroigazmontazh and Mostotrest were the primary contractors. This was Putin's personal project, and he had set up a special state corporation, Olimpstroi (Olympic Construction), for this purpose in 2007. Rotenberg's companies received projects worth almost $10 billion. Nemtsov and Martynyuk deduce that these nonbid contracts were padded three to four times.[34]

Since 2011, Rotenberg has been the leader in the intricate art of attracting state orders, usually from Gazprom and the road construction agency. In 2015, he hit an all-time record, obtaining state orders of no less than $8.3 billion, of which Gazprom's Power of Siberia pipeline comprised 36 percent. Timchenko usually ranks number three in the state order list. Arkady Rotenberg's son, Igor, and brother, Boris, also rank high on these lists, which are still made public. By and large, big state orders are allocated without open competition at prices that are generally considered to be three times higher than competitive market prices.[35]

When the Blue Stream gas pipeline was built across the Black Sea from Russia to Turkey from 1998 to 2002, the cost per kilometer of pipeline was approximately $3 million; a competitive world market price would have been $1 million–$1.5 million. When Gazprom built Nord Stream through the Baltic Sea from St. Petersburg to Germany, the initial price estimate was $5 billion, but the final cost was $15 billion. As discussed in chapter 4, whenever Gazprom earns more profit than anticipated, capital expenditures are expanded in order to transfer the surplus to the privileged suppliers of major investment projects.[36]

Yuri Kovalchuk has been the chief executive of Bank Rossiya since 1991, but his real role is much bigger. He is the spider in Putin's financial and media empire. He has acquired large financial and media assets from Gazprom, and he manages the financial flows of the whole Putin group as well as some twenty Russian television channels.

The US government designated Kovalchuk as a crony on March 20, 2014. The language was particularly harsh: "Yuri Kovalchuk is the largest single shareholder of Bank Rossiya and is also the personal banker for senior officials of the Russian Federation including Putin. Kovalchuk is a close advisor to President Putin and has been referred to as one of his 'cashiers.'"[37]

Yuri Kovalchuk, born in 1951, was originally a physicist. At his research institute, he worked closely with Putin's friends Andrei Fursenko and Vladimir Yakunin. In 1991, Kovalchuk decided to enter banking without any prior experience, which was common in those days. He became deputy chief executive of the regional Communist Party's Bank Rossiya. Soon St. Petersburg City Hall, under Putin's aegis, took over the bank and made it the financial center for the Putin group.[38]

The ownership of television channels has gradually been concentrated to Kovalchuk. In 2000, when President Putin forced Vladimir Gusinsky to sell his NTV, Gazprom bought it, but in 2004, a subsidiary of Bank Rossiya purchased Gazprom Media Group with five television channels—including NTV, TNT, REN TV, and Petersburg Channel 5—for $166 million. Two years later, First Deputy Prime Minister Dmitri

Medvedev assessed Gazprom Media's value at $7.5 billion. Gazprom Media assists the Kremlin in its propaganda. Kovalchuk has continued gobbling up Russian television channels, buying them at any price. For example, he has purchased the National Media Group with three television channels, whose chairwoman is Alina Kabaeva, widely believed to be Putin's girlfriend.[39]

Bank Rossiya also bought Gazprom's financial assets, notably Gazprombank and its insurance company Sogaz, in a series of complex transactions from 2004 to 2007. In 2004, Sogaz was sold on the Moscow stock exchange MICEX to a few select purchasers in a private deal without competition or transparency. Bank Rossiya claimed that it paid $120 million for Sogaz, which it considered a fair market price. But Sogaz developed rapidly, and *Vedomosti* journalists reported that businesspeople complained about "administrative" pressure to buy their insurances from Sogaz. Nemtsov and Milov assess Sogaz's 2008 market value at $1.5–2 billion and conclude: "The sale of Sogaz became the first example of a transfer of assets from Gazprom to the personal friends of Putin."[40]

In 2006–2007, Bank Rossiya used Sogaz to acquire Gazprom's financial management company Lider, Gazprom's pension fund Gazfond (with more than $6 billion in assets), and the majority of Gazprombank. All these deals were complex, discretionary, and nontransparent. To sum up, during the years 2004–2007, Gazprom transferred vast assets to Bank Rossiya, namely 51 percent of Sogaz, 75 percent of Lider, 50 percent plus one share of Gazprombank, 70 percent of the big chemical company Sibur, and 100 percent of Gazprom Media. Nemtsov and Milov estimate the 2008 market value of Gazprombank at $25 billion, and all its assets were spirited out of Gazprom for virtually nothing. Adding up the market value of the assets that Gazprom transferred to Putin's cronies during the four years 2004–2007, Nemtsov and Milov arrive at the stunning sum of $60 billion. The Kremlin and the Gazprom management supported this asset stripping, for which nobody has been punished. These transactions have continued. They are complex and nontransparent, but their essence is that state companies buy private assets from cronies at very high prices, while the state companies sell vast assets for close to nothing.[41]

As chief executive of the Putin group's bank, Yuri Kovalchuk is the spider in Putin's financial web. His financial performance, however, appears miserable. When Bank Rossiya was sanctioned in 2014, it had just $10 billion in assets, suggesting that it regularly transferred its profits elsewhere.

The best insight into what is going on in the inner Putin commercial circle comes from a combination of three scandals involving Putin's old friend Nikolai Shamalov: a palace being built in Gelendzhik near Sochi, a defecting junior partner, and a Siemens corruption case in the United States.

Shamalov is one of Putin's contemporaries from St. Petersburg, an old friend and both a member of the Ozero dacha cooperative and a long-standing shareholder of Bank Rossiya. He is not in the same financial league as Timchenko, the Rotenbergs, and Kovalchuk, but his wealth is still significant. His primary business was to represent German Siemens in Russia in the sale of medical equipment. He did so quite successfully, but in 2008 Siemens sacked him after sixteen years of loyal service when the US Securities and Exchange Commission and the US Department of Justice fined Siemens $1.34 billion for violating "the Foreign Corrupt Practices Act (FCPA) by engaging in a systematic practice of paying bribes to foreign government officials to obtain business." The SEC named six countries, including Russia. The US authorities assessed the corrupt payments for medical devices in Russia from 2001 to 2007 at $55 million, for which Shamalov was responsible. This verdict had no legal repercussions in Russia.[42]

At the end of 2010, a greater scandal erupted. A junior partner of Shamalov, Sergei Kolesnikov, who had fled Russia, fearing for his life, revealed that $1 billion of public funding for medical equipment had been diverted to build a palace for Putin in Gelendzhik near Sochi. Somebody managed to photograph the palace, which looks like a tasteful Italian palazzo from the late eighteenth century. Kolesnikov presented the global financial crisis of 2008 as a reason for the aggravated corruption. "Today the corrupt civil servants do not reduce their appetite, but on the contrary increase the size of the kickbacks," which he claimed were 35 percent for medical equipment.[43]

Why would a Russian president need a private palace? In a 2012 report, Nemtsov and Leonid Martynyuk detailed Putin's assets. The president of Russia has at his disposal no fewer than twenty official residences, most of them palaces, whereas, according to Felshtinsky and

Pribylovsky, Yeltsin passed only on twelve presidential residences. Admittedly, this was fewer than the twenty-five residences that Joseph Stalin allowed himself, but by any standard it was plenty.[44]

Kolesnikov gave many interviews. The most substantial was with Evgeniya Albats, editor of *Novoe Vremya*, in Washington in February 2012. He described how they channeled diverted state funds through multiple offshore companies. Several layers of shell companies were used in multiple offshore havens. In Kolesnikov's part of the business, there had been more than thirty offshore companies, involving Shamalov and Putin. They were located in places such as the British Virgin Islands and Panama.[45]

A new revelation was that Kolesnikov clarified that Putin personally owned individual shares in each of these companies. Each person involved (including Kolesnikov) had a specific share that varied from company to company, but the general picture seems to be that the principal partner (in this case Shamalov) and Putin together held the overwhelming majority, while the junior partners, who carried out the actual work, obtained a few percent. It seems plausible that Putin held half the ownership, but Kolesnikov stated that the specific shares varied between companies. An additional bit of spice in Kolesnikov's story was that Putin and his cronies used nicknames, as is the custom among Russian gangsters.[46]

Under Putin strong nepotism has developed. In his 2000 interview book, Putin revealed what counted most to him. "I have a lot of friends," he told the interviewers, "but only a few people are really close to me. They have never gone away. They have never betrayed me, and I haven't betrayed them either."[47]

Putin has nationalized Russia's elites. His close friends from St. Petersburg and the Soviet era KGB have educated their sons in Russia, rather than sending them abroad. The children of Russia's previous oligarchs and state officials have largely emigrated, and the children of Putin's cronies have taken their place. As the Russia observer Brian Whitmore put it in 2015, the "children of Vladimir Putin's cronies" are already billionaires, "and most of them are under 40."[48]

Unlike their fathers, most of these oligarchs-in-waiting have no graduate training. After college in Moscow or St. Petersburg, they go straight into career jobs at state-owned banks or companies, such as Gazprom, where, after one or two quick promotions, they usually become a vice president of a big state company. Their sisters, meanwhile, are supposed to marry suitable young men.

Among Putin's golden youth, the sons of his St. Petersburg cronies have done particularly well, usually by working in privatized companies. Nikolai Shamalov's two sons have made splendid careers. In 2005, his older son, Yuri, became the chief executive of Gazfond, Gazprom's large pension fund.[49]

Shamalov's younger son, Kirill, became—at the age of twenty-five—a vice president at Sibur, the large petrochemical company spun off from Gazprom. From 2011 to 2013, Kirill acquired 4.3 percent of Sibur through an executive stock-option program. Then, in 2013, he married Putin's daughter, Ekaterina Tikhonova, in a secret ceremony, after which Putin's wealthiest crony, Timchenko, sold him 17 percent of Sibur at a favorable price. All told, Putin's son-in-law was worth an estimated $1.3 billion by the time he was thirty-four. Incidentally, Russia's National Welfare Fund gave the now-private Sibur a cheap loan of $1.75 billion to help build a new plant in Tobolsk in Siberia. Reuters fine researchers noted that this operation had raised the fortune of Kirill Shamalov to $2.85 billion. Unlike in fairytales, no happiness is eternal, especially not in Russia. Reportedly, Ekaterina divorced Kirill in the spring of 2017, and suddenly he lost most of his wealth in an unclear fashion, being left with "merely" $800 million, according to Bloomberg.[50]

Arkady Rotenberg's sons have also done very well in two companies privatized from Gazprom. His oldest son, Igor, is the majority shareholder in Gazprom Drilling. His second son, Roman, is a vice president at Gazprombank. Similarly, Yuri Kovalchuk's son, Boris, is the CEO of Inter RAO, a state-owned electricity holding company.[51]

The sons of Putin's KGB friends have also ascended quickly in the corporate world, but in state enterprises. Sergei Ivanov, the namesake of Putin's former chief of staff, first became a vice president of Gazprombank at age twenty-five and then was named the president of Alrosa, Russia's state-owned diamond company, at thirty-six. National Security Adviser Nikolai Patrushev's son, Dmitri, became CEO of Rosselkhozbank, the state-owned Russian Agricultural Bank, at thirty-three. In

May 2018, he was appointed minister of agriculture instead, which was interpreted as Rosselkhozbank having serious financial problems. Rosneft CEO Igor Sechin's son, Ivan, became deputy director of a Rosneft department at twenty-five. In this context, FSB Chairman Alexander Bortnikov's son, Denis, was a wise old man of thirty-seven when he joined the VTB Bank management board. Former Russian prime minister (2004–2007) and SVR director Mikhail Fradkov's son, Petr, was more in the generational mold, just twenty-nine when he became a deputy chairman of Vnesheconombank.[52]

Russia's crony capitalism has bred a small class of incredibly wealthy individuals, whose children have been given top state positions, allowing them to become even wealthier. But with fewer career paths to top positions open, resentment among a generation of young, able, and ambitious young Russians bristles. Brian Whitmore notes that a "new nobility is being born in Russia." Opposition leader Alexei Navalny concurs: "Today in Russia, it is absolutely normal that the boards of directors at state banks are headed by children of security service officials, who aren't even 30 years old when they are appointed."[53]

Last, Putin's real family should also be mentioned: his two daughters, Ekaterina and Maria, and their husbands, Putin's friend Alina Kalibaeva, and his cousins. Igor Putin, who appears in the Panama Papers, became vice president of Master Bank, Vera Putina a member of the board of Ganzakombank, Mikhail Putin deputy director of Sogaz, and Mikhail Shelomov, who officially works at a state oil firm but lives on dividends. Putin seems to take good care even of rather distant relatives. Each of these people seems to have a fortune of at least half a billion US dollars.[54]

In June 2017, Putin was asked in his annual call-in program about his children. He responded that his daughters "live here in Moscow . . . involved in science and education and they stay out of the public eye, out of politics and live normal everyday lives." Referring to his grandchildren, he stated, "I do not want them to grow up like some royal princes. I want them to live like ordinary people."[55]

Putin is not widely recognized as a man who stands up for human rights, but when it comes to his close friends—Kovalchuk, the Rotenbergs,

Timchenko—his heart is bleeding. He has defended them repeatedly and passionately in public.

On March 21, 2014, the day after the United States had sanctioned them, Putin solicited the question: "The list includes some names that are difficult to explain, such as Mr. Timchenko, Mr. Rotenberg and Mr. Kovalchuk, for example. Are they being targeted because they are considered to be your friends, or because they are somehow connected to the events in Crimea?" Putin answered sarcastically:

> Well, to be honest, they are those very same "polite people"— the ones in camouflage gear, with semi-automatic rifles strapped to their waists [referring to Russian special forces without insignia]. And their last names are a bit odd too. The names you just mentioned, for example: Kovalchuk, Rotenberg, Timchenko are all typical "moskal" [Ukrainian nickname for Russians] names. I think I'd be wise to keep my distance from them. The sanctions target a bank too. Given that this bank definitely has no connection to the events in Crimea, and it has clients, we will certainly have to give it our protection and do everything we can to make sure that there are no negative consequences for the bank itself or for its clients.[56]

On April 17, in his annual phone-in program with the people, Putin took another question about the Crimean sanctions: "These sanctions hit several major businessmen such as Yury Kovalchuk, Gennady Timchenko and the Rotenberg brothers. They are rumored to be your personal friends and part of your inner circle and that their fortunes were made thanks to that friendship. Now as it happens, they have sanctions imposed on them, also to a large extent due to their friendship with you. Don't you get the feeling that the main target of the EU sanctions is you, personally?" Once again, Putin stood up for his friends:

> It looks as if they are trying to make me the object of these sanctions. As for the people you mentioned, they are indeed my good acquaintances, my friends. But for the most part

they had made their fortunes before we even met. Mr. Timchenko, for example, has been doing business since the 1990s.
... Mr. Timchenko's wife had serious surgery and was unable
to pay for it because her bank account and credit cards were
frozen. This is a flagrant violation of human rights. ... I also
have to tell you that I am not in any way ashamed of my
friends.[57]

In an interview with TASS on November 24, 2014, Putin once again
defended his cronies, claiming that the Americans "proceeded from a
false assumption that I have some personal business interests due to ties
with the people on the list. And by pinching them, they were kind of
hitting me. This absolutely does not correspond to reality. I believe,
we have to a great degree put an end to the so-called oligarchy." He
continued:

We have no oligarchic structures, which substitute state power or influence upon state decisions in their interests. ... All
of them are rich and they made their fortunes a long time
ago. ... They took nothing, they privatized nothing like what
it was done in the 1990s. ... What state property did Timchenko get? Please name at least one asset. Nothing. ... They
are Russian nationals, they consider themselves patriots of
this country and this is true. Someone has decided they
should be punished for this. And it just strengthens the ac-
knowledgement of such their quality. ... This is a direct
violation of human rights.[58]

As discussed above, Timchenko benefited from the privatizations
of Sibur and Stroitransgaz from Gazprom. Timchenko and Boris Rotenberg are Finnish citizens and have lived primarily in Finland and Switzerland since the early 1990s. None of the cronies was particularly
wealthy before 2004. They set up their schemes largely during Putin's
second term, 2004–2008. They made their fortunes from the state,
though Putin might be right that this is not a new oligarchy but an
aristocracy.

As a consequence of the European sanctions against Rotenberg, Italy froze luxury properties belonging to Arkady Rotenberg in September 2014. These assets included the Berg Luxury Hotel in Rome and properties in Sardinia, which together were valued at $36 million. The Duma responded by authorizing the Kremlin to seize foreign assets in Russia and use them as compensation for individuals and businesses being hurt by Western sanctions over the Ukraine crisis. This bill was called the Rotenberg Law. In the end, however, the Kremlin changed its mind, and Putin never signed this into law, presumably because doing so would scare away foreign investors. In 2017, Putin signed an alternative Rotenberg Law. The Russian state itself would offer compensation out of the state coffers to Russian individuals who had suffered from Western sanctions. Because of the sanctions Arkady Rotenberg transferred much of his ownership to his son Igor, who was subsequently sanctioned by the United States.[59]

Putin's loyalty to his friends extends also to their families. He lives by the old authoritarian motto: "For my friends everything, for my enemies the law." On November 15, 2015, the Russian government introduced a new road tax, strangely called Platon, which provoked large-scale protests among independent long-haul truckers. A road toll monopoly was given to an operating company half-owned by Arkady Rotenberg's son Igor.[60]

Putin defended Platon and Igor Rotenberg during his annual press conference in December 2015. A questioner claimed, "Rotenberg Jr . . . has received the country's long-haul truckers as a present." Putin brushed off her concerns as being "of secondary importance." He continued, "Take young Rotenberg, whom you mentioned: his father does not hold any government posts, as far as I know." According to Putin, revenues from the tax "do not go into somebody's pocket but into the Road Fund of the Russian Federation, down to the last cent." He also claimed, it "is spent on road construction in Russian regions." In fact, Igor Rotenberg's company, which received the contract without competition, was guaranteed a payment of $150 million a year until 2027. Despite Putin's reassurances, massive protests have continued, but so has the flow of money into Igor Rotenberg's pocket. On April 15, 2017, the Platon tariff was doubled, arousing mass protests among thirty thousand truckers in at least sixty cities around Russia.[61]

Putin reacted particularly sharply against the 2016 revelation of the Panama Papers, leaked documents from Panamanian law firm Mossack Fonseca. He clearly saw it as a US provocation against him personally, lashing out sharply and claiming that the Panama Papers investigation was "an attempt to destabilize the situation" in Russia. He insisted that this investigation did not show corruption but was an attempt to "make Russia more yielding," carried out by US officials, "as Wikileaks has shown."[62]

Why has Putin gone to such lengths to protect his dubious friends? He has built his career on trust, but it is difficult to escape the suspicion that his adamant support for his friends and his fury over the US sanctions against his close friends reflect his own financial interests.

Many still talk about Russia as an oligarchy, but Putin's Russia—as he rightly claims—is not an oligarchy. It is something much worse, an authoritarian kleptocracy. An oligarchy implies some balance between different forces based on wealth. In Putin's Russia, the central state rules, and there is no balance of power because Putin rules supreme. With this concentration of political power, wealth also appears to have been more concentrated, while transparency has declined, so that we now know less than in the happy years of openness before 2003 when Khodorkovsky was arrested.

This book does not discuss the old oligarchs of the 1990s, but many people ask about them, so here's a quick review. By and large, they have lost out both politically and in business, while most of them remain very rich. Many, perhaps most, have emigrated to the West, mainly London, but also Monaco, southern France, and the United States. Predominantly, their outstanding skill was to adjust rapidly to a new and quite different situation. They were skillful opportunists rather than innovators. Some were good managers, while most of them were clever private equity investors.

Most of the oligarchic banks went bankrupt in the financial crash of 1998. The foremost among the oligarchs, Alexander Smolensky of SBS-Agro Bank, disappeared from public view. The two big media oligarchs, Vladimir Gusinsky and Boris Berezovsky, were dispossessed and chased out of the country by Putin in 2000. Gusinsky lives quietly in exile in New York and Israel, while Berezovsky and two of his closest associates died under mysterious circumstances in London. In 2003, Khodorkovsky was arrested, and his impressive group of associates and Yukos managers fled Russia.

Many others have disappeared less dramatically. The enigmatic Roman Abramovich sold Sibneft and moved to London. The late Kakha Bendukidze, who became minister of economy in Georgia under President Mikheil Saakashvili, had little choice but to sell his heavy machine-building company OMZ to Gazprom at a low price. An even wealthier Georgian, Bidzina Ivanishvili, left for Georgia slightly later and became prime minister there in 2012. The only female billionaire, Elena Baturina, left the country when her husband, Moscow mayor Yuri Luzhkov, was ousted. Russia's leading high-tech investor, Yuri Milner, decided to move to Silicon Valley. The top producer of fertilizers, Dmitri Rybolovlev, was more or less compelled to sell his company Uralkali after it suffered a major ecological disaster. Instead he bought a house from Donald Trump in Palm Beach, while settling in Monaco. Yevgeny Chichvarkin developed the extraordinary Euroset chain of five thousand mobile phone outlets, which became too much for others, so he had to escape to London after having been forced to sell for too low a price. Russia's top Internet geek, Pavel Durov, beat Facebook in Russia with his vKontakte, but since he refused to give his database to the FSB, he hastily fled the country for Dubai. The list could be made much longer.

Of the original seven oligarchs from the mid-1990s, only three hold up. Vladimir Potanin still owns and controls the giant company Norilsk Nickel that he acquired in the loans-for-shares auction in 1995. Mikhail Fridman and Petr Aven have turned their Alfa Group into the biggest private corporation in Russia, with a bank, a mobile phone company, and a big retail company, although they were forced to sell their quarter of TNK-BP in 2012. In general, the big metallurgical businessmen hang on and seem to do the best at present.

However wealthy these men may be, they are not running the show. Unfortunately, the most criminal of the survivors seem to be the most successful, but they must not be mentioned here. The state has come back and taken over, but it has not become legal.

How Large Is Russian Wealth, and Why Is It Held Offshore?

N obody who studies modern Russia can avoid being stunned by the large concentrated wealth. Although the owners of these riches prefer to shroud their fortunes and live in secrecy, substantial knowledge is nonetheless available. This chapter is devoted to decoding this wealth.

What can we know about the enrichment of the Russian top elite? We can tell a lot about what the top individuals earn and own in Russia, and we have a reasonable idea of how much the collective elite takes out of their country each year, but we know far less about what happens to their money when it leaves Russia.

The fundamental source for our understanding of the enrichment of Putin's cronies is the excellent work of the opposition activists Boris Nemtsov and Vladimir Milov. In their pioneering study of Putin and Gazprom, they establish four sources of crony enrichment: privileged public procurement, stock manipulation, asset stripping, and privileged trade. Adding up the market value of the assets that Gazprom transferred to Putin's cronies during the four years 2004–2007, Nemtsov and Milov arrive at the stunning sum of $60 billion.[1]

Amazingly, Russia still publishes total public procurement in a database, which makes it possible to see who gets how much. The Rotenbergs and Gennady Timchenko are the steady kings of public procurement. Because literally all their contracts are no-bid for big infrastructure projects, their rent is tremendous. Half of the contracts in sheer rent would make sense. The other elements are much more difficult to assess.

Stock manipulation is often published in the Russian business press, since purchase prices are often given in specific transactions, but that requires great labor, though excellent investigative Russian journalists often do that job.

The same is true of asset stripping, though it is often so blatant that it appears in the media. For an analyst, asset stripping is complicated because it occurs ad hoc and irregularly. Moreover, the same asset is often subject to many confusing transactions.

Privileged trade—when someone buys at one low price and resells as a monopolist at a much higher price—used to be blatant, as with Dmytro Firtash's gas trade between Russian and Ukraine, but often a variety of markets are simply monopolized, making it less apparent.

As Russia has grown more kleptocratic and authoritarian, another form of elite enrichment has become more important—namely, extortion by the Kremlin and law enforcement of the truly rich. Bill Browder argues that after Mikhail Khodorkovsky's conviction in 2005, Putin demanded 50 percent of the wealth of the other oligarchs. "He wasn't saying 50 percent for the Russian government or the presidential administration, but 50 percent for Vladimir Putin personally. From that moment on, Putin became the biggest oligarch in Russia and the richest man in the world." This is possible, but not proven. What we do know from many interviews is that Kremlin extortion is a standard procedure, and it is at least in the tens of millions of dollars in donations to "charity" from each individual oligarch. Visits to the Kremlin are costly, so most oligarchs stay abroad most of the time. Much of the wealth officially belonging to Russian oligarchs may be owned or at least controlled by Putin. President Viktor Yanukovych's family acted in that way in Ukraine, which was one reason why the Ukrainian oligarchs turned against him.[2]

There are also important sporadic sources. Sergei Kolesnikov, the junior partner of Putin and Nikolai Shamalov who fled to the West in 2010, has offered substantial evidence. The Panama Papers, which were publicized in April 2016 to Putin's great chagrin, are a rich source. Currently they have all been overtaken by the anticorruption investigations by Alexei Navalny and his Anti-Corruption Foundation.

Since the early 2000s, Russian *Forbes* has maintained a standard rich list of the wealthiest Russians. Russia has about a hundred official billionaires, which is a lot, but the real numbers are probably even higher. *Forbes* can presumably capture the wealth of the old Yeltsin oligarchs from the 1990s rather well, since it is publicly displayed, but hardly the hidden wealth of the later Putin cronies.

Evgeniya Albats, editor of the independent weekly *Novoe Vremya*, told me that the best sources are divorced wives and dismissed commercial lawyers. Both groups tend to have valuable documents and a personal interest in harming their personal nemeses. Business competitors are another good source, especially those that have been forced to leave Russia.

The Central Bank of Russia maintains excellent statistics on Russia's international transactions on the web, showing a steady and large current account surplus, which is accompanied with an also large but smaller capital outflow.

Thus, we know a surprising lot about the situation in Russia, though we must avoid disinformation. The most striking example of misinformation is the official declaration of incomes and assets that senior Russian officials must submit. Only the foolish tell the truth, since only the honest can fear punishment. Official statistics have little to tell about individuals.

All the wealthy in Russia transfer their liquid assets abroad. The reasons for capital outflows from Russia are many, but they have varied. These large capital flows started as illegal transfers in 1988, when the Soviet Union started its first liberalization. In the late 1980s, no private holdings of capital in Russia were legal, so they had to be safeguarded abroad (in Cyprus). Throughout the 1990s, Russian banks kept collapsing, so wealthy Russians sought secure banks abroad. Until the tax reforms around 2000, Russian taxation was confiscatory, which was another reason for the wealthy to keep their money abroad.

Since 2006, capital outflows have largely been legal. Still, substantial illicit flows have continued even during the best of times as managers have defrauded the owners of both private and state-owned companies through transfer pricing and underinvoicing to embezzle money from other enterprise owners and evade taxes. As Putin has reinforced his control over law enforcement, businesspeople prefer to keep their money abroad, where property rights are more secure. With the start of Putin's "deoffshoreization," capital controls have tightened.[3]

The basic reason for capital flight is that money is not safe in Russia. Tax or law enforcement agencies can seize any assets at any time, as Bill Browder has shown so eloquently in the case of his company, Hermitage Capital Management, and the Sergei Magnitsky case. Banks abroad are used even for short-term cash holdings, since most funds that have been transferred abroad return to Russia, whether for purchases of assets, investment, or simple transactions.[4]

Russian businesspeople overwhelmingly move abroad when they retire. Business life in Russia is tough. On any given day, a couple of hundred thousand Russian businesspeople sit in pretrial detention. Why take that risk? Russians need to consider that they risk months of arrest by pursuing their trade. Moreover, life in Moscow is expensive, traffic is cumbersome, and the weather is cold.[5]

A common assumption has been that the newly wealthy businesspeople would demand judicial reforms to achieve secure property rights when they had enriched themselves, but this has not happened. The old oligarchs no longer matter. They have lost their political clout. They have no voice, while they can still exit, as Albert Hirschman put it, and take their cash with them. Therefore, the old oligarchs, sometimes called the "white oligarchs," in distinction from Putin's "black oligarchs," are no threat to the regime. They are too far from the real power and too well surveyed to intimidate it.[6]

If they demand secure property rights, they may lose what they own in Russia and be forced to leave the country, as happened with Yevgeny Chichvarkin, who was mentioned in chapter 5. He was an outstanding entrepreneur who set up the company Euroset with five thousand outlets all over Russia selling mobile phones. When he objected to being expropriated in 2008, he opted for political protest and was forced to emigrate within forty-eight hours. Instead, the truly wealthy remaining in Russia have become ever more cautious and obedient to Putin.[7]

The rulers, by contrast, benefit from weak property rights as long as they are in power, because the weak property rights of others allow them to acquire assets in Russia at low prices through corporate raiding. Strong courts in Russia would hinder their wealth accumulation. The wealth of the rulers, however, is secure only as long as they stay in power. Whenever anybody falls out of favor with the Kremlin, his or her property is in danger. No one feels safe until they have all political power and own everything, which explains the rulers' rapacious lust for both wealth and political control. In Russia power is wealth, and wealth is power. To defend their political power, the rulers aspire to a maximum of wealth, and they transfer their profits abroad, where they enjoy secure property rights guaranteed by British or US law.

Putin's authoritarian kleptocracy of three circles is not complete without a fourth circle, the Anglo-American offshore. In the late 1980s, the amassing of vast holdings of money of dubious origin in anonymous companies started in offshore havens. The start was the "big bang" financial liberalization in the United Kingdom in 1986. Dozens of British or former British overseas territories developed into financial centers, ranging from the Channel Islands and Isle of Man to Cyprus and Malta, Bermuda, the many Caribbean territories, some Pacific islands, Dubai, Singapore, and Hong Kong. From 1988, these financial services encountered new demand from private operators in the former Soviet republics, as new smart operators made instant fortunes on commodity trading, buying oil for $1 a ton in Russia and selling it abroad for $100 a ton.[8]

Other emerging markets moved along. The first solid study of this topic is Raymond Baker's *Capitalism's Achilles Heel: Dirty Money and How to Renew the Free-Market System,* published in 2005. At that time, he considered that "$1 to $2 trillion annually can be taken as a rough estimate of global dirty money."[9]

Throughout the 1990s, most of the money flowing from Russia seems to have gone through Cyprus because the Soviet Union and Cyprus had concluded a uniquely favorable double-taxation agreement in 1982 that relieved Russians of taxation when they took out their money that way. It was succeeded by a similar agreement between Russia and

Cyprus in 1998. As a consequence, Russian commodity traders set up plenty of small trading companies in Cyprus, which had excellent financial services and good rule of law but minimal transparency.

The Russian money has not stayed in Cyprus. Typically, it just passes through Cyprus to other offshore havens. These havens have varied over time, but the current dominant pattern is first to the British Virgin Islands and then to the Cayman Islands. The money usually passes through several offshore havens, because each haven adds several layers of shell companies. For seriously dirty money, a layer of twenty to thirty shell companies is common. Of these havens, only the Cayman Islands has a large banking sector. Malta is a smaller parallel channel to Cyprus. During the global financial crisis of 2008–2009, several alternative Caribbean islands, such as Antigua and Turks and Caicos, lost out because they ended up in financial crisis and scandals, which led to further concentration in the British Virgin Islands and the Cayman Islands.

In the end, the money tends to flow to the United States, mainly Delaware, and the United Kingdom. Vladimir Milov, who has an eminent understanding of Russian wealth, observes that since the Western sanctions were imposed in 2014, Russians have increasingly channeled their funds to Dubai, Singapore, and Hong Kong, but these havens have much less financial depth than the United States and the United Kingdom.[10]

In 2013, Cyprus went through a severe banking crisis, which was caused by the Greek government writing off much of its bonds. The IMF took this opportunity to investigate Russian investment there. It established that Russian foreign direct investment in Cyprus was 150 percent of its GDP in 2013, or $36 billion, of which $22 billion pertained to "special purpose enterprises," registered there but invested elsewhere. Thus, Russian direct investment in Cyprus itself was only $14 billion, and the Russian losses in the bank bail-in must have amounted to several billion dollars.[11]

The common feature of all these jurisdictions is that they are current or former British territories with good rule of law and extensive usage of anonymous ownership. Unfortunately, these territories offer little relevant statistics. The renowned Organized Crime and Corruption Reporting Project broke the story about the "Russian Laundromat" in 2014, and together with reporters from the indefatigably independent

Novaya Gazeta, they detailed how 19 Russian banks laundered $20.8 billion to 5,140 companies with accounts at 732 banks in 96 countries from January 2011 to October 2014.[12]

Money laundering, which is usually defined as the concealment of illegally obtained money, has long been a concern of Western governments. It is a derivative crime difficult to combat, because the initial crime has been committed in another country, usually lacking good rule of law or even being pervasively corrupt, convicting honest people, while letting true culprits go free. Russia is such a country.

Therefore, the West has adopted new laws and formed new institutions against money laundering. As early as 1989, Western members of the Organization of Economic Cooperation and Development (OECD) set up the Financial Action Task Force (FATF) to stop such dirty monetary flows. FATF is the international police force for money laundering. Its standard advice to bank regulators is "follow the money!" and know your customer (KYC)! It has compelled small island havens to clean up their act. Even Switzerland has had to give up its cherished centuries-old bank secrecy. In order to be able to investigate dirty money, the US Treasury Department established the Financial Crimes Enforcement Network (FinCEN) in 1990, which remains the main US institution for this task.

After the terrorist attacks on the World Trade Center in New York and the Pentagon on 9/11, 2001, the United States became serious about fighting money laundering in order to stop terrorist financing. Congress adopted the Patriot Act, which contains strict rules against money laundering. It prohibits the activities of shell banks in the United States and imposes the KYC rule not only on US banks but on all banks that operate within the United States. Whoever violates these rules is subject to large fines.

But the two biggest offshore havens with a vast capacity to receive anonymous investment are the United States and the United Kingdom, and they remain intact. Although no serious statistics are available, these two countries are undoubtedly the dominant offshore havens in the world, hosting most of Russian anonymous offshore investment. The *Financial Times* has quoted Alex Cobham, chief executive of Tax Justice Network, a campaign group, stating that the United States is "the elephant in the room." "If you were going to produce a tax haven blacklist with only one member, it wouldn't be a small Caribbean island—it would be tax haven USA."[13]

In the early 1990s, the United States opened its floodgates for dubious foreign funds, allowing not only anonymous ownership but also anonymous money transfers. In 2015, the US Treasury assessed that no less than some $300 billion a year was laundered into the country, but the US lack of transparency leads to a dearth of relevant statistics. The United Kingdom is hardly better. The UK National Crime Agency claims that $125 billion is being laundered in that country each year. These are enormous amounts.[14]

In the United States, there are four major reasons for this vast inflow of dark money. The most important is the extensive usage of companies with anonymous owners. Second, although real estate was included in the Patriot Act of 2001, after half a year, the US Treasury granted real estate a temporary exemption, which remains in force. A third venue for dark money is that law firms are permitted to take in dirty money under the attorney-client privilege. Last, the US government capacity to investigate dirty money, through FinCEN, is minimal. In 2013, it employed only 350 people.[15]

In London, post-Soviet oligarchs have become so conspicuous that "kleptocracy" tours have been organized to display their splendid mansions with price tags of up to $200 million. A few outstanding British journalists have courageously cleaned up the public record. Edward Lucas of the *Economist* pursued Timchenko, who responded with a vicious libel case. In 2011, Luke Harding was expelled from Russia for his hard-hitting anticorruption reporting, the same year as his Russia book *Mafia State* was published. Ben Judah has scourged the UK policy, complaining that the Russians "know that London is a center of Russian corruption, that their loot plunges into Britain's empire of tax havens—from Gibraltar to Jersey, from the Cayman Islands to the British Virgin Islands—on which the sun never sets." The Russian offshore in London has driven up real estate prices.[16]

The ways to transfer money into countries with Anglo-American law are many and shift over time. The most important method, though, is the extensive usage of anonymous companies. The four main US states that produce anonymous limited liability companies (LLCs) are Delaware, Nevada, Wyoming, and South Dakota. Ben Judah and Belinda Li note that the United States "produces more than 2 million corporate entities per year, pumping out 10 times more such shell companies than the world's other 41 tax havens combined."[17]

Michael Findley, Daniel Nielson, and Jason Sharman have established through a broad survey that with regard to compliance to international transparency rules, "on nearly every count, tax havens outperform the OECD countries." Their main conclusion is that it "is more than three times more difficult to obtain an anonymous shell company in tax havens than in OECD countries."[18]

The Russian arms trader Viktor Bout, renowned as the "Merchant of Death," had used "at least a dozen shell companies in Delaware." In 2012, the *New York Times* reported that one single building in Wilmington, Delaware, harbored as many as 285,000 legal entities, but nothing has been done to rein in this dubious practice. By comparison, "only" 18,857 companies are registered in the main building for the registration of companies in the Cayman Islands.[19]

Money launderers use all kinds of peculiar enterprises that offer anonymity. Through the Panama Papers, Transparency International UK and Bellingcat found that Scottish limited partnerships had become major vehicles of Russian money laundering after a legal amendment in 2008. They reported that 113 such companies had laundered $20 billion–$80 billion from Russia into the United Kingdom in just four years. In 2016, 3,677 Scottish limited partnerships were registered in secrecy jurisdictions including the British Virgin Islands, Belize, and the Seychelles.[20]

The embarrassment of all these revelations in the Panama Papers became just too great for the British government. In May 2016, Prime Minister David Cameron organized an international conference to oppose anonymous ownership. Twenty-nine countries already demand full disclosure of beneficiary owners, and at that conference eleven countries agreed to prohibit anonymous ownership. One was the United Kingdom, but in June 2016, Cameron lost the Brexit referendum and was forced to resign, and the political momentum was lost. The United States did not, claiming that the federal government could not decide such a state issue. Even Ukraine has successfully done so with all its banks.[21]

The dominant destination of anonymous investment is real estate, which has both great capacity and desired secrecy. Every year, more than $100 billion of foreign funds flow into US real estate, more than half of it in cash.[22]

The investigative journalist Oliver Bullough found that "almost one-third of top-end property purchases in America's biggest cities are suspect, according to the Financial Crimes Enforcement Network, the body at the Treasury Department." While "China was the leading investor in real estate in the United States by the end of 2015, with $350 billion in related investments and holdings," Russia is high up on the list, but the United States has no numbers.[23]

Dirty Russian investment in real estate appears to abound in New York and Florida. One Reuters investigative report found that "at least 703—or about one-third—of the owners of the 2044 units in the seven Trump buildings [in Sunny Beach Isles in Florida] are limited liability companies, or LLCs, which have the ability to hide the identity of a property's true owner. And the nationality of many buyers could not be determined." But the "zip code that includes the Sunny Isles buildings has an estimated 1,200 Russian-born residents ... U.S. Census data show." The project generated $2 billion in initial sales, of which at least sixty-three individuals with Russian passports or addresses had bought at least $98.4 million worth of property, while the more dubious Russians are to be found in the LLCs.[24]

The situation is similar in the United Kingdom. James Nickerson of the *New Statesman* cited the assessment that anonymous offshore companies own thirty-six thousand properties in London at an estimated value of $156 billion. Russians own a large share of this real estate. In May 2016, David Cameron lamented that ninety-nine thousand buildings in the United Kingdom had anonymous owners.[25]

A third major entry point for tainted funds into the United States is law firms. The legal excuse is attorney-client privilege, which is supposed to keep communication between an attorney and his or her client secret, but the United States has extended this secrecy to unlimited money flows. In December 2016 the *Wall Street Journal* revealed, in an analysis of the looting of the Malaysian sovereign wealth fund 1MBD, that "tens of billions of dollars every year move through opaque law-firm bank accounts that create a gap in U.S. money-laundering defenses." Companies controlled by the two culprits "sent a total of $489 million into Shearman & Sterling's pooled account from overseas." The journalists Rachel Louise Ensign and Serena Ng assess these anonymous flows at $40 billion–$400 billion a year. When these journalists asked the American Bar Association president Linda A. Klein about these practices, she replied that the ABA supported the legal profession's efforts to prevent misconduct involving client money, but "additional financial reporting requirements would be unnecessary and burdensome because there are few examples of client trust accounts being misused." Well, without transparency, no evidence would be available.[26]

Remarkably, we know far less about Russian financial and real estate investment in the United States than we know about them in Russia. We can assess Russian capital outflows on the basis of Russian statistics, Russian official publications of public procurement, and the Russian *Forbes* assessments of fortunes of wealthy Russians. In the United States, by contrast, we have no other sources than serious investigative journalism.[27]

Money laundering is a complex and often incomplete procedure. Seriously dirty money goes through many countries, and in each country several layers of shell companies are often added. The dirty funds tend to stay in anonymous shell companies, which may be allowed to purchase real estate but little else. When the real estate is being sold, the unexplained wealth remains. Anonymous companies cannot hold money in banks or purchase listed stocks, while they may buy some hedge funds and private equity funds in offshore havens. The many transactions in the process of money laundering easily lead to multiple counting of the laundered volumes, so we focus on the stocks, not on the flows.

If the United States wishes to alter the behavior of Russian and other kleptocrats, its first measure should be to investigate the assets of those Russian individuals and enterprises already sanctioned and supposed to be subject to asset freezes. Second, it should carry out legislative changes to force all beneficial owners of property in the country to reveal themselves, as is standard in most European countries. Third, all currency transfers into the United States should be subject to elementary bank regulation, which is the case in most European nations. Fourth, large cash payments should never be allowed. Fifth, FinCEN should be greatly reinforced, having its staff multiplied.

In May 2018, the *Berliner Zeitung* revealed that a dozen companies belonging to Arkady Rotenberg, who is also sanctioned in the EU, owned major public and office buildings in Berlin, Frankfurt, Hamburg, and Munich worth about €1 billion ($1.2 billion) through complex layers of shell companies. This shows that the problem with hidden ownership also exists in other countries.[28]

Since 1989, Russia has seen steady and large capital outflows, although the Russian government made the ruble fully convertible and liberalized capital flows only in July 2006.

Russia has thus experienced large and persistent capital outflows. For the period 1994–2010, the International Monetary Fund estimates that the average capital outflows were $30 billion a year. In a fine analysis, Global Financial Integrity assesses that the total legal and illegal outflows averaged $43 billion a year from 1994 to 2011. The big peak occurred during the global crisis of 2008, when capital outflows surged to $203 billion (table 6.1).

The authors of the Global Financial Integrity report note that their estimates are close to the IMF numbers for the period 2000–2005, while the difference is greater for the period 2006–2011 because of increased misinvoicing, which is not included in the IMF estimates. Factoring in the size of the enterprises of the Putin cronies, whose businesses took off around 2006, can explain the increased misinvoicing. If we multiply the alternative annual assessments with twenty-six post-Soviet years, 1992–2017, the total capital outflows from Russia would be $780 billion, according to the IMF, or $1,118 billion, according to Global Financial Integrity.[29]

Table 6.2 offers the IMF numbers for capital and financial account, a broader measure also including public financial flows. Comparable numbers in current US dollars are available from 2001 to 2016. The annual average is $35.8 billion a year, a bit more than in table 6.1, but the contrasts between different years are more striking. From 2001 to 2006, Russia seems

Table 6.1: Estimated capital outflows from
Russia, 1994–2011 (billion current US$)

Year	Global Financial Integrity: Licit and illicit	IMF: Capital flight
1994	20	16.7
1995	0	4
1996	20.3	25
1997	0.9	22.3
1998	57.2	26.8
1999	21.4	22
2000	15.6	21.9
2001	37.7	18.3
2002	12.5	21.6
2003	38.2	24.4
2004	51.5	30.1
2005	66.4	42.3
2006	4.6	20.7
2007	48.6	57.7
2008	203.3	118.5
2009	14.9	17.5
2010	69.8	24.5
2011	99.5	n/a
Total	782.4	514.3

Source: Kar and Freitas 2013, 13, 16

to have stabilized, while 2007 appears to have been a wild boom. The boom was followed by a sharp capital outflow in 2008 of $131 billion. The capital outflows stayed high, with a minor peak in 2011 and a massive peak of $173 billion in 2014. Looking at the numbers, it appears as if investors lost their confidence in Russia in 2008, and they never recovered it. That was the year when Russia went from boom to stagnation.

Professor James S. Henry of Columbia University has assessed for the Tax Justice Network that by the end of 2014 no less than $1.3 trillion

Table 6.2: Capital and financial
account, 2001–2016

Year	Billion US$
2001	−13.9
2002	−10.9
2003	−0.9
2004	−6.4
2005	−11.7
2006	6.9
2007	85.7
2008	−131
2009	45.1
2010	−26.9
2011	−86.2
2012	−30.9
2013	−45.4
2014	−173.1
2015	−70.3
2016	−13.9
Total	−483.8

Source: IMF Article IV Reviews, various years

of assets from Russia were sitting offshore. He formulated this figure on the basis of data from global international institutions, approximately as Global Financial Integrity has done. This number appears too high as an assessment of Russian funds abroad, because it includes outflows that returned to Russia. His aim and the goal of Global Financial Integrity is to assess tax evasion through total misinvoicing in both capital outflows and inflows, whereas the focus in this book is total net private assets held by Russians abroad.[30]

These assessments refer only to capital outflows from Russia. Filip Novokmet, Thomas Piketty, and Gabriel Zucman have analyzed Russian offshore wealth to analyze inequality, offering a different perspective on the same facts. They argue that Russia is the country in the world where offshore wealth is most significant. They estimate "offshore wealth at about $800 billion or 75 percent of national income in 2015, with 100 percent as a maximum and 55 percent as a minimum." This assessment of $800 billion of net private Russian offshore wealth contrasts with the *Forbes* assessment of the total wealth of the Russian billionaires of $400 billion.[31]

These authors assume low returns for Russian assets abroad, but high returns for foreign investments in Russia. Considering all the efforts Russians make to hide their offshore wealth, their return is likely to be small or negative, since the investors opt for secrecy, security, and stability rather than maximum return. Money laundering is usually a misnomer, because the money is rarely completely cleansed. Some regulator or other can usually ask about the money's origin. This is one reason why much of the dirty money is hidden in anonymous real estate that does not move fast. Stocks and banks are quite transparent. Many of the holders of this capital, moreover, are not professional investors but corrupt state officials.

The Piketty group arrives at several important conclusions. They assess that Russia's total national wealth was 400 percent of national income in 1990 (which is a European average for the last century) and still only 450 percent of national income in 2015. This reflects that savings of about one-tenth of GDP are taken out of Russia each year and not invested in the Russian economy, depressing growth. They calculate further that aggregate national wealth surged from about 300 percent of GDP in 1999 to 550 percent of GDP in 2008. This occurred during the oil boom, when private enterprise still dominated, but they do not even mention the renationalization and new Putin oligarchy.[32]

The Piketty group also notes that the offshore wealth, which is private, grossly changes the proportions of private and public shares of Russian wealth. They assess the private share of Russia's national wealth at almost 80 percent, which includes the real estate sector, and is predominantly private. The offshore wealth also raises the concentration of wealth. They assess the share of Russian wealth owned by the top 1 percent at 43 percent in 2015, even slightly more than in the United States.

The top 1 percent earned 20 percent of all incomes, approximately the same as in the United States.[33]

In May 2001, Putin seized management control of Gazprom, but until 2004, the remaining independent members of the Russian government, such as Prime Minister Mikhail Kasyanov and Presidential Chief of Staff Alexander Voloshin, raised many barriers, hindering the Putin group from acquiring absolute control over Gazprom's cash flow.

Thanks to the Yukos affair, which erupted in the winter of 2003–2004, Putin could consolidate his political power, sweeping away the remaining barriers. No big Russian businessmen dared to stand up against Putin after Khodorkovsky's arrest. In December 2003, Putin gained full control over the State Duma. Voloshin and Kasyanov, who had checked Putin's power and opposed the Yukos confiscation, were forced out, leaving Putin in charge of the state, its powers, and its assets. It was only during Putin's second term, starting in 2004, that Putin and his friends became truly wealthy. The main source of their wealth was Gazprom. It is difficult to comprehend what floodgates of wealth they opened for themselves.[34]

In principle, Russian law requires open competition for public contracts, but as the journalist Joshua Yaffa notes, "Although Russian law requires that state procurement contracts be awarded through open bidding, it also allows them to get granted in a closed, no-bid process if the projects are deemed strategically important." A 2015 report prepared for the Russian government showed that 95 percent of state purchases were noncompetitive and 40 percent went to one supplier. The letter of the law was observed even as the spirit was violated.[35]

Sergei Kolesnikov has testified that the rents in the medical equipment procurement were 35 percent, but that was early on, and rents have clearly risen as the share of competitive purchases has declined. The Gazprom pipelines seem to cost three times too much. Some is waste, but a net rent of 50 percent appears likely. From what we know from Kolesnikov, we may assume that half of these rents goes to Putin and half to his chief partners—Timchenko, the Rotenbergs, Kovalchuk, and Shamalov—with tiny shares of a few percent for junior partners.[36]

Russian *Forbes* has published regular assessments of the wealth of top Russian businessmen since the early 2000s and comparable assessments in

Table 6.3: Russian Forbes assessment of the wealth of the cronies,
2011–2017 (billion current US$)

	2011	2012	2013	2014	2015	2016	2017
Gennady Timchenko	5.5	9.1	14.1	15.3	10.7	11.4	16
Arkady Rotenberg	1.1	1	3.3	4	1.4	1	2.6
Igor Rotenberg	—	—	—	—	0.5	0.4	0.7
Boris Rotenberg	0.55	0.5	1.4	1.7	0.95	1	1
Rotenberg family	1.65	1.5	4.7	5.7	2.85	2.4	4.3
Yuri Kovalchuk	1.5	1.2	1.1	1.4	0.65	0.5	1
Total crony wealth	8.65	11.8	19.9	22.4	14.2	14.3	21.3

Source: Russian Forbes 2017

current US dollars from 2011 to 2017. These numbers are compiled in table 6.3. Presumably they include only assets in Russia, not financial assets in offshore havens, which are impossible to assess. Although their wealth is considerable, some developments are peculiar.

Gennady Timchenko's wealth rose sharply from $5.5 billion in 2011 to $15 billion in 2014, when he was hit by Western sanctions and low oil prices in 2015–2016. In 2017, Timchenko apparently figured out how to solve his problems, and his fortune surged again. His wealth has developed as one would expect from a successful businessman.

The Rotenbergs have acted as a family, and Arkady Rotenberg has transferred considerable wealth to his son Igor, so Arkady, Boris, Igor, and Roman Rotenberg are best understood as one holding company. Until 2013, the Rotenbergs were not very wealthy by Russian standards, but they struck gold with the Sochi Olympics. Like Timchenko, they were hit by sanctions in 2015–2016, but in 2017 they came back because of the construction of the bridge over the Kerch Straits to Crimea and some other compensatory business contracts. Theirs looks like a thoroughly crony, not very efficient, business. Yet, considering that Rotenbergs have been the kings of state contracts for a decade, the *Forbes* assessment of their fortunes looks far too low.[37]

Kovalchuk's wealth numbers make no sense. Although he is the spider in the Putin financial web, his fortune plummeted from $1.9 billion in 2008 to $500 million in 2016. Admittedly, television advertising and banking revenues plunged with the price of oil and depreciation of the ruble, as well as with Western sanctions, though few enjoy more privileges than Kovalchuk. But his aim was probably not profit maximization. He is more of a political operator, as the chief distributor of political funds and the top media overseer.[38]

The *Forbes* assessed fortunes of the cronies of $21 billion in 2017 are great by any standard except contemporary Russian norms. The most plausible explanation is that most of the crony wealth is being transferred to anonymous shell companies in offshore havens. Clearly, *Forbes* did not know that Arkady Rotenberg owned real estate in Germany worth $1.2 billion. The *Forbes* wealth assessments seem strangely unrelated to the amounts transferred from state enterprises to the cronies' companies. Nemtsov and Milov set the looting of Gazprom through public procurement, asset stripping, and stock manipulation from 2004 to 2007 at a total of $60 billion, or $15 billion a year. Their assessment might be a bit high, and not all was transferred out of the country. Yet Vladimir Milov thinks that the amount can only have increased, given that the cronies have expanded their ownership so much. The rents from Gazprom and other state procurement would suggest a transfer to this group of at least $10–15 billion annually from 2006 to the present. These funds have in all probability been transferred to offshore havens.[39]

The cronies enjoyed many other flows, as the Panama Papers show. Asset stripping is not a one-way street. State companies tend to sell and buy the same companies, such as Gazprombank and Sogaz, over and over again, making it hard to keep up with current ownership. Stock manipulation is another permanent game. Extortion of private businesses should be added.

Without probing deeper into the numbers, it would be reasonable to assume that Putin and his cronies made slightly less than twice as much each year as they made on Gazprom alone, that is, $15–25 billion a year since 2006. The newly minted Putin aristocracy has seized control over the Russian state and the state corporations, letting their fortunes slip into their crony companies. Both the state companies and the crony companies enjoy monopoly rents. The crucial last fourth circle of the Putin system is the offshore havens. At home, Putin has facilitated capital outflows through minimal taxation and loose currency regulations. The old Soviet Cyprus-Russia double-taxation agreement allows him and his cronies to transfer any funds through Cyprus without any hassle.

In June 2013, the retiring long-time chairman of the Central Bank Sergei Ignatiev made a remarkable statement to the State Duma. He declared that the Central Bank had revealed a network of fly-by-night firms that had illegally transferred at least $25 billion out of Russia in violation of currency and tax laws in 2010–2012. Ignatiev stated: "I have the impression that this whole net of one-day firms is controlled by one group of people."[40]

The same day the Central Bank posted a memorandum on its website claiming that about $15 billion had been transferred illegally through Belarus and $10 billion through Kazakhstan through fictitious import invoices in 2012. This is $25 billion in one year. Neither piece of information had been publicized before. Russian insiders interpreted Ignatiev's dramatic statement in the Duma as a daring exposure of Putin's crony group. No other group possessed such amounts of cash, but nothing more was heard about this. It appears that Ignatiev meant to say that the Putin group illegally transferred $25 billion in 2012 and that this was their pattern.[41]

How large is Putin's personal fortune? We know that Putin lives a life of extraordinary luxury and that he appreciates every comfort, not least multiple watches worth tens of thousands of dollars. Anybody who is under the illusion that Putin is an honest citizen should read Boris Nemtsov and Leonid Martynyuk's booklet *The Life of a Galley Slave*. They conclude that Putin has at his disposal twenty palaces, four yachts, fifty-eight aircraft, and a collection of watches worth $600,000.[42]

For ordinary people it is difficult to fathom why anybody would need that much money, but former Kremlin adviser Stanislav Belkovsky has a good answer: "This is the principle of plutocracy (*monetokratiya*), the power of money, which exists in Russia today." Because property rights are not safe in Russia, you need political power or strong political connections to maintain property, which requires a lot of money. In today's Russia, money is power, and power is money. If you lose one, you may lose big. Ask Khodorkovsky! Therefore, the Putin group tries to keep both.[43]

In 2007, Belkovsky claimed in several interviews that Putin had acquired $40 billion through his cronies during his eight years in power. Until then, it had been presumed that his cronies held "his" wealth in their names, but Belkovsky stated that Putin owned shares of companies outright, which was later borne out by Sergei Kolesnikov's detailed testimony in 2011. Belkovsky claimed that Putin owned a 37 percent stake of the big oil company Surgutneftegaz, 4.5 percent of Gazprom, and at least half of Timchenko's Gunvor.[44]

The ownership of Surgutneftegaz has been notoriously opaque, and together with Putin Timchenko seems to have swapped his investment in the Kirishi oil refinery for shares in Surgutneftegaz. Nemtsov and Milov set Putin's share in Gazprom higher, at 6.4 percent of the shares, issued to him during the restructuring of Gazprom's ownership in 2006. Gunvor has strongly disputed that Putin is an owner, but it has long acknowledged a third secret owner, holding 10 percent. More recently, the secret owner was revealed to be Putin's childhood friend, the butcher Petr Kolbin.[45]

Belkovsky, who is currently an independent intellectual, has been asked repeatedly about Putin's wealth. In 2012, he assessed it at $70 billion. His most recent statement appears to be from 2013, when he claimed that Putin's wealth had reached some $100 billion and that Putin held his wealth in stocks, still in Surgutneftegaz and Gazprom as well as in a third unnamed company.[46]

The numbers appear reasonable, but it is implausible that Putin kept his Gazprom shares. The collapse of its stock price and the notoriously low stock price of Surgutneftegaz indicate that Putin does not care about their price. Instead, the large capital outflows suggest that he has put his money in more reliable assets abroad. A plausible interpretation is that Belkovsky had real inside information in the mid-2000s, when he was close to the Kremlin, whereas his later numbers and their lack of detail are the result of extrapolation or guesswork.

In 2015, Bill Browder entered the stage, claiming that Putin possessed a personal wealth of $200 billion. In July 2017, Browder stated in testimony before Congress: "I estimate that [Putin] has accumulated $200 billion of ill-gotten gains from these types of operations over his 17 years in power. He keeps his money in the West and all of his money in the West is potentially exposed to asset freezes and confiscation. Therefore, he has a significant and very personal interest in finding a way to get rid of the Magnitsky sanctions." Browder's argument is that Putin has demanded half of the wealth of the Russian oligarchs, which is about $400 billion. This is a vast sum. If Russia's total capital outflows since 1991 have totaled $780 billion, Putin himself would have appropriated more than one-fourth. This makes a lot of sense. The biggest gift identified in the Panama Papers is $259 million from the private businessman Suleiman Kerimov. We do not know whether Kerimov was a business partner of Putin or was simply extorted. Both are possible, but in any case, Putin and his friends would have received a lot of money.[47] Kerimov was sanctioned by the US government on April 6, 2018.

An alternative method of assessing Putin's wealth is to assess capital flows in which Putin may have played a part. To judge from the examples in Kolesnikov's testimony, the share reserved for Putin from all the crony business was nearly half. My guesstimate of the Putin crony group's capital outflow above is $15 billion–$25 billion a year since 2006, or some $195 billion–$325 billion. Assuming that Putin's share is half, he would have transferred $100 billion–$160 billion to offshore havens. These numbers are higher than those suggested by Belkovsky, though lower than those offered by Browder.[48]

I arrive at five conclusions:

1. Putin personally holds tens of billions of dollars of assets abroad, probably in the range of $100 billion to $160 billion;
2. These assets are held secretly, deeply concealed in anonymous offshore companies;
3. Even the ruler keeps his money abroad, because he knows that it is not safe in Russia;
4. His vast wealth abroad makes it possible for Putin to buy politics in Russia and many other countries; but
5. Because his fortune is held abroad, Putin is highly vulnerable to transparency and effective Western financial sanctions.

The Russian *Forbes* rich list includes not only the by-now well-known cronies (Timchenko, three Rotenbergs, Kovalchuk, and Shamalov) but also four old friends of Putin in the Putin circle: Petr Kolbin, Sergei Roldugin, Vladimir Litvinenko, and Il'gam Ragimov. These four all knew Putin early on in St. Petersburg and have become fantastically wealthy for no other apparent reason.[49]

Putin's childhood friend Petr Kolbin was a butcher and later a professional gunner in St. Petersburg. In 2005, he became a shareholder in Gunvor, but as mentioned earlier, his stock ownership was kept secret for many years. In 2009, he bought stocks in the Yamal liquefied natural gas plant from Gazprombank very cheaply for $90 million, and a few months later he sold them at the normal market price of $526 million. A government commission chaired by Putin, who was then prime minister, made that decision. Since 2012, Russian *Forbes* has assessed Kolbin's wealth at $550 million.[50]

The publication of the Panama Papers in the spring of 2016 revealed that a publicly known childhood friend of Putin, the cellist Sergei Roldugin, had received more than $2 billion in offshore wealth from Russian oligarchs and the Russian state without having had any possibility of earning it. He is understood to hold money for Putin. The Organized Crime and Corruption Reporting Project has published an insightful analysis of Roldugin's income. Much of the money comes from the stock and contract manipulation of Russian state companies. In 2010, a company linked to Roldugin bought shares of Bank Rossiya and sold them just days later to an unknown investor for thirty-two times the price. Another source is "donations" from big private Russian businessmen, which should be called extortion. A third source is bank loans. VTB's subsidiary in Cyprus gave Roldugin's company a credit line of $650 million. As with VEB, VTB has suffered massive losses on loans like this that have never been paid back. Seemingly to cover its tracks, VTB sold this subsidiary to Bank Otkritie, which went under in 2017.[51]

A third private friend of Putin is Vladimir Litvinenko, the alleged author of Putin's doctoral dissertation and president of St. Petersburg Mining Institute, where in 1996 Putin defended his doctoral dissertation. Russian *Forbes* assesses Litvinenko's wealth in 2017 at $850 million, and he has made this fortune on Apatity, the company that the Russian prosecutors accused Khodorkovsky of having bought too cheaply in a privatization.[52]

A fourth, until recently unknown, personal friend of Putin is Il'gam Ragimov, who was a classmate of Putin and Bastrykin, the head of the Investigative Committee, at the law faculty at Leningrad State University. Russian *Forbes* assesses Ragimov's wealth at $500 million.[53]

None of these four men seems to be a businessman. *New York Times* correspondent Steven Lee Myers visited Roldugin and concluded that he was not even aware of the immense wealth held in his name and that he seemed to live quite humbly. The only plausible explanation is that these four men are caretakers, holding parts of Putin's wealth in their own names.[54]

The whole phenomenon is intriguing. Is Putin so insecure that he feels compelled to engage his trusted childhood friends to hold his wealth? The same is true of his cousins, who have benefited greatly from his power and wealth.

Most of Putin's and his cronies' wealth is undoubtedly held in the West because of the lack of real property rights in the former Soviet Union, but a new awareness has arisen in the West of the hazards of anonymous companies.

The reasons for the reaction against anonymous companies are many. Governments remain concerned about terrorist financing and large-scale tax evasion, but the threat to national security is a far greater concern. Russian hybrid warfare through corruption and election interference has created a new scare, especially in the United States. Special Counsel Robert S. Mueller III is investigating Russian interference in the US presidential election of 2016. One of his indictments accuses the Russian military intelligence agency, GRU, of financing its hacking of the Democratic National Committee through anonymous transfers via cryptocurrencies.

For years, numerous nongovernmental organizations, notably Transparency International, Global Witness, and Global Financial Integrity, have campaigned against corruption and anonymous companies. In the United States, forty NGOs have formed the Financial

Accountability and Corporate Transparency (FACT) Coalition to coordinate these efforts.

Western concerns with Russian actions through anonymous companies grew intense after Russia's surprise attack on Ukraine in 2014, which seems to have been a catalyst of similar effect as the 9/11 terrorist attacks in New York and Washington in 2001, which engendered the Patriot Act, which in turn cleaned up the global banking system. Legislative efforts to open up and disarm anonymous companies have been pursued mainly along three geographical lines—through the European Union, in the United Kingdom, and in the United States.

The European Union has taken the lead. On May 20, 2015, the European Parliament and the European Council adopted the Fourth Anti-Money Laundering Directive. It requires all enterprises and entities in the twenty-eight countries of the European Union and the European Free Trade Association (Iceland, Liechtenstein, Norway, and Switzerland) to reveal their ultimate beneficiary owners. They must be registered in a centrally held registry in each member state. This obligation also applies to business owners residing outside the region who operate within it. A beneficiary owner is defined as the owner of 25 percent plus one share of an entity.[55]

An EU directive has no direct legal impact but calls on all member states to adopt appropriate national legislation within two years. Most countries usually delay action, and in this case only Germany, the United Kingdom, and Denmark complied with the two-year deadline. Yet however slowly the European Union acts, it does act. Most member countries have legislation under way. The directive calls on countries to make their central registries available to relevant authorities, such as financial intelligence and tax authorities, but many countries plan to make their registries available to the public, namely Denmark, Estonia, Finland, Lithuania, the Netherlands, Poland, Portugal, Slovakia, Slovenia, and Sweden.[56]

The United Kingdom has made great strides in its anti-money-laundering legislation, but UK transparency is actually less, because British legislation allows so many peculiar forms of legal entities. Furthermore, the many overseas British territories operate independently, and London is the dominant financial center in Europe. Of course, Britain's vast sector of anonymous companies has many well-paid legal and financial helpers. On paper, the British legislation should lead to the revelation of all beneficiary owners, but so far it has not happened.[57]

In 2018, the United Kingdom introduced a new legal tool, "unexplained wealth orders," which allows British authorities to claim property in a civil recovery process if the legal authorities can prove that the wealth cannot have been earned honestly. It remains to be seen whether this tool will be used. In a controversial move in May 2018, Parliament legislated that fourteen British overseas territories, including the key financial centers the British Virgin Islands and the Cayman Islands, must introduce public ownership registries by the end of 2020.[58]

In the United States, important measures have been undertaken within the current legal framework. On August 22, 2017, the US Treasury FinCEN required "U.S. title insurance companies to identify the natural persons behind shell companies used to pay for high-end residential real estate in seven metropolitan areas," including Miami-Dade, Broward, Palm Beach, New York, and Los Angeles, all favored destinations for Russians. They start at different price levels, such as at $1 million in south Florida. These checks focus on cash and wire transfer payments. As a consequence, anonymous purchases of real estate have fallen sharply in the whole country.[59]

As this is being written, several legislative initiatives are under way in Congress to prohibit anonymous companies. The basic idea is that FinCEN should be entitled to collect information on all beneficiary owners of corporations or limited liability companies from states that do not collect this information themselves.[60]

To sum up, a reasonable assessment is that private Russian assets held anonymously abroad are about $800 billion. This is private wealth, not belonging to the state, but much of it belongs to public officials. The owners' prime objective is to keep the assets safe, which is not possible in Russia or other countries that lack the rule of law. Second, the owners want to hide their ownership, which they typically do through multiple layers of shell companies. Third, big undercover investors need countries that have great financial depth. Only two countries comply with these three prerequisites: the United States and the United Kingdom.

The Russian holders of large offshore wealth can be divided roughly into those who made their money before Putin and those who have
benefited from Putin's assistance. These two groups should receive completely different treatment. A big question is how much of the Russian
offshore wealth belongs to Putin and his cronies versus other Russians.
Browder has given a clear answer: Putin and cronies have taken over
half of it. That would be $400 billion, which sounds like a reasonable
estimate.

These vast holdings of anonymous Russian wealth in the West
amount to a major national security concern. After the recent Russian
interference in the US and other Western elections, people are exasper-
ated by the ruthlessness and imagination of Kremlin actions. But the
opposite point is that Kremlin operators can do little if they do not have
access to the US financial system, and the US government can easily cut
them off if it imposes one simple condition: Tell us who you are! Both
the United States and the United Kingdom need to prohibit anonymous
ownership for the sake of national security, as most EU countries have
already done. Even more obviously, the United States must no longer
allow money laundering through real estate or law firms. The simple
rule should be that all international financial flows must be subject to
ordinary bank regulation.

From International Economic Integration to Deglobalization

Postcommunist Russia has found it difficult to find its place on the international stage. Two opposing trends have coexisted. The Russian intellectual and commercial elite has embraced globalization, whereas security interests have become anti-Western. Since 2012, the beginning of Putin's third term, the protectionist tendencies have gained the upper hand. Chief economist at the European Bank of Reconstruction and Development Sergei Guriev has summed up Russia's situation: "The real cost of Russia's current isolation will be felt in the long term: the country will miss opportunities for growth and will continue to stagnate."[1]

In the early 1990s, no clear idea of Russia's role in the world existed. The Soviet Union was gone. Trade policy was not an urgent concern, since Russia mainly exported oil, unhampered by trade barriers. Years of disinterested trial and error ensued, but the Russian government has been unable to find a satisfactory solution. Politics have further complicated Russia's trade conundrum. Moscow has been all too keen to impose unilateral trade sanctions on neighboring countries, and in 2014, the West imposed sanctions on Russia because of Russia's annexation of Crimea and invasion of eastern Ukraine. The outcome has been growing alienation between Russia and the West, even though the Russian elite and Russian capital are deeply integrated into the Western financial system.

Russia's geography—a big continental power with high transportation costs and few ports—adds to the complications. When oil prices were high, oil and gas accounted for two-thirds of Russia's exports. Metals comprised another 20 percent, and arms 4 percent. These exports encountered few trade barriers, limiting Russian interest in trade policy.

The Soviet Union imploded suddenly and dramatically in December 1991. Dissolution seemed inevitable. The dominant concern was that the collapse be peaceful, and the Soviet Union managed to avoid the bloody civil war that befell Yugoslavia.

The former Soviet republics needed an organization to manage their mutual relations. Eleven of them signed onto a loose association, the Commonwealth of Independent States (CIS), which Georgia later joined. Turkmenistan and Ukraine never ratified the CIS treaty and were thus not formal members. Ukraine tended to participate in summits, whereas Turkmenistan kept a neutral distance.

The function of the CIS was left undetermined for years. The two chief models were the British Commonwealth and the European Union. Almost every year, Russia attempted to set up a new organization with some CIS countries, but nothing seemed to work. Apart from Russia, the most interested countries were Belarus and Kazakhstan. These two republics were highly dependent on Russia for geographical reasons, and they preferred to deal with Russia in a multilateral framework rather than being left one-on-one with the Kremlin. The most successful cooperation effort was probably the multilateral CIS free trade agreement of 1994. Although it was never ratified, it formed the basis for similar bilateral free trade agreements among the CIS countries.[2]

The worst economic costs of the collapse of the Soviet Union were caused by the tardy breakup of the ruble zone, which lasted until September 1993. Fifteen central banks competed in issuing the largest volume of ruble credits in order to extract the largest share of the common GDP. This competition generated hyperinflation in all the Soviet successor countries. In 1992–1994, state trade with prices far below the market level prevailed between these countries, which resulted in a massive decline in mutual trade of some 70 percent. The very system forced Russia to give large involuntary credits to all the other post-Soviet countries. Great arbitrage opportunities in energy benefited old state enterprises and a few budding oligarchs. Russia's imperial past and its continued economic and political dominance rendered the other former Soviet republics suspicious of Russian initiatives for cooperation.[3]

Yeltsin and Putin held opposite views of the Soviet Union. In his 1994 memoirs, Yeltsin concluded: "In signing this agreement [on the dissolution of the Soviet Union], Russia was choosing a different path, a path of internal development rather than an imperial one." Yet Yeltsin enjoyed the annual CIS summits and the company of the presidents of other CIS countries, who had similar backgrounds, spoke Russian, and understood one another. Sometimes Yeltsin went along with the Russian state administration dealings with the CIS, which was Soviet in its outlook, for example, in forming a new union state between Russia and Belarus, but eventually he abandoned such initiatives or put them on the back burner. Though inconsistent, Yeltsin was an anti-imperialist with no real designs on the CIS.[4]

In 2000, Putin entered the presidency with the opposite attitude. He expressed sympathy with the communist putschists in August 1991: "In principle, their goal—preserving the Soviet Union from collapse— was noble." In his annual address in April 2005, Putin made his most famous statement along these lines: "The collapse of the Soviet Union was the greatest geopolitical disaster of the century. . . . Tens of millions of our co-citizens and compatriots found themselves outside Russian territory. . . . Old ideals [were] destroyed." But initially Putin lacked any clear idea of what to do with the CIS. He devoted less attention to the CIS summits than Yeltsin and did not enjoy the company of the other CIS presidents. Thus, neither Yeltsin nor Putin knew how to work with the former Soviet republics.[5]

In January 1991, President George H. W. Bush made a visionary State of the Union speech: "What is at stake is . . . a big idea: a new world order, where diverse nations are drawn together in common cause to achieve the universal aspirations of mankind—peace and security, freedom, and the rule of law. Such is a world worthy of our struggle and worthy of our children's future." Unfortunately, little followed.[6]

Later that year, as a newly independent country, Russia jeopardized its old empire, but where did it belong? Where should it go? President Boris Yeltsin wanted Russia to join the new world order, the West, and its economic institutions, notably the International Monetary Fund and the World Bank, to build a normal market economy.[7]

Russia had abandoned communist prejudices against these institutions and swiftly acceded to both the IMF and the World Bank in June 1992, becoming a permanent member of their executive boards. The European Bank for Reconstruction and Development was formed to manage the transformation of the former Soviet Bloc. These three organizations have played major roles in Russia's economic development and spearheaded most of its economic reforms.

The World Trade Organization, by contrast, offered far greater challenges and less support. Russia joined only in 2012. Russia has still not acceded to the Organization for Economic Cooperation and Development, which is the guardian of legal standards.

Russian democrats looked at the European Union with great sympathy, but the European Union turned its back on them. In 1991, the European Union had only twelve members, but it was about to expand to fifteen and soon to accept the East European members of the former Soviet Bloc. President Yeltsin aspired to join the European Union, but German chancellor Helmut Kohl rebuked him that Russia was too big and powerful ever to do so. The European Union offered Russia and other former Soviet republics a rudimentary Partnership and Cooperation Agreement with minimal market access, providing miserly technical assistance of €1.2 billion from 1991 to 1999.[8]

The eleven other former Soviet republics were Russia's obvious partners, but the breakup of the Soviet Union destroyed their relationship. The recent memory of the Soviet Union, Moscow's dominance, and attempts at integration and Russification aroused resistance among the other newly independent countries against renewed integration with Russia. They all looked to the outside world, whereas the Russian officials who took charge of economic cooperation with their neighbors tended to come from old Soviet institutions and maintained a Great Russian perspective.

The former Soviet republics fell into two groups in their relationship with Russia. One group, comprising Belarus, Kazakhstan,

Kyrgyzstan, Armenia, and Tajikistan, desired close cooperation with Russia. Belarus and Kazakhstan were so dependent on Russia that they had little choice, while Kyrgyzstan, Tajikistan, and Armenia were small countries far from Russia that needed its support for their security. The other six—Ukraine, Moldova, Georgia, Azerbaijan, Turkmenistan, and Uzbekistan—by contrast, wished to minimize their contacts with Russia as soon as they could afford to.

The Soviet Union's great pride had been that it was one of the two superpowers, the only nuclear power that could match the United States, but economically it was a dwarf. The Soviet Union was always swinging between megalomania and an inferiority complex, and Russia has not yet been healed from this tendency.[9]

Both Yeltsin and Putin cherished grand international events with pomp and gravitas over tedious but economically useful organizations. They had an unfortunate infatuation with the Group of Seven (G-7) biggest industrial democracies. Soviet President Mikhail Gorbachev first met with the G-7 leaders on the sidelines of their summit in London in 1991. Beginning in 1992, President Boris Yeltsin participated, but he was allowed to attend only half the summit. In Denver in 1997, President Bill Clinton invited Yeltsin to attend the whole summit, which he called G-8. Yet Russia was never invited to the full meetings of the G-7 ministers of finance and central bank governors.[10]

This integration process unraveled in 2014 when the other G-7 members suspended Russia's participation in protest of its annexation of Crimea and the G-7 itself became the main coordinating body for Western sanctions. Since the G-7 is a club of the big and powerful rather than an international organization, Russia's participation in the G-8 hardly contributed to its economic development. In 2008, the United States invited Russia to be a full-fledged member of the newly constituted G-20 of the twenty biggest economies in the world, which was a better fit for Russia.

In June 2009 in Yekaterinburg, Russia hosted the first summit of BRICS, consisting of Brazil, Russia, India, China, and later South Africa, the community of large, fast-growing emerging economies. None of the BRICS nations had good governance, but even so they were growing faster than the Western countries. Apparently, Putin drew the conclusion that corruption and state ownership do not harm growth. As oil production and oil prices rose, the Kremlin toyed with the concept of Russia becoming an energy superpower, but Russia did not perceive the oil-producing countries as its peers.[11]

Several regional initiatives involving some post-Soviet states and various other countries have offered Russia high-level contacts but minimal institutional integration. In 1998, Russia joined the Asia-Pacific Economic Cooperation (APEC), which organizes grand annual summits. Russia hosted its lavish summit in Vladivostok in 2012.[12]

In 2001, six countries—Russia, China, Kazakhstan, Kyrgyzstan, Tajikistan, and Uzbekistan—formed the Shanghai Cooperation Organisation (SCO) as a permanent intergovernmental international organization, focusing on Central Asia. China initiated this organization with an agenda involving both security and economic cooperation. One of China's main aims appears to be to support its economic integration into Central Asia with its One Belt One Road infrastructure initiative.[13]

However Russia tried, it remained an odd fit in international contexts. It was too big for its neighborhood and the EU, and it had no obvious peer. The two organizations that have attracted the most Russian policy attention have been the WTO and the Eurasian Economic Union (EAEU).

In August 2012, after nineteen long years as an applicant, Russia joined the WTO, but its integration was aborted by international conflicts. Russia's WTO accession illustrates its evolving thinking about trade policy. In June 1993, Russia applied to join the General Agreement on Tariffs and Trade (GATT), which soon became the WTO. A large GATT Working Party on Russia's accession was formed, but it worked at a leisurely pace and the Russian government devoted little attention to it.[14]

In 2000, Putin made Russia's accession to the WTO a priority for his first term. His chief reformer, Minister of Economic Development and Trade Herman Gref, pursued this task energetically. It was a key element in the Gref reform program and Putin's extensive institutional reforms from 2000 to 2003.[15]

In his annual address in April 2002, Putin advocated Russia's membership in the WTO at length: "The WTO is a tool. Those who know how to use it become stronger. . . . Membership in the WTO should become a tool to protect Russia's national interests on the world market." But for

Putin, the WTO was probably most interesting because it would raise Russia's international standing, and China had entered the organization in 2001. Russia was the only G-8 member that was not a WTO member, and Russia's long-standing foreign policy ambition was to have a seat at every worthy international table.[16]

The WTO enhances access to export markets, which is important for exporters of goods sensitive to protectionist measures, but not for an oil and gas exporter, such as Russia. Liberal Russian economists had long advocated WTO membership to open up their economy to more competition to spearhead modernization and diversification. The World Bank and the Russian Ministry of Economic Development and Trade commissioned several studies of the potential effects of WTO entry on the Russian economy. The estimated impact was limited, boosting Russia's economic growth by 0.5 percent to 1 percent a year in the medium term. The gains would come mainly from the improvements in Russia's domestic economy through the liberalization of foreign direct investment in the service sector, and not from improved market access for Russian exports.[17]

Russia's comparative advantage is overwhelmingly in hydrocarbons, other crude materials, and chemicals. British researcher Julian Cooper finds that Russia had a "revealed comparative advantage" (defined as a country's share of world exports of a particular good divided by its share of total world exports) in seventy product groups. Of these, only four were manufactured goods—namely, nuclear reactors, condensers for steam boilers, rail freight wagons, and steam turbines. All were traditional Soviet products exported primarily to former Soviet republics. Russia was not ready to break into new export markets of manufactures. It has comparatively high wages because of its ample raw material exports.[18]

In substance, it was much easier for Russia than for China to fulfill the conditions for entering the WTO, because Russia has a far more open market economy. But Russia was much less motivated to comply with WTO demands than China, for which market access for its manufactures was vital. Nor did Russia have the same need as China for WTO guidance for its reforms.[19]

After having promoted Russia's accession to the WTO for three years, Putin reversed course to become its biggest obstacle. In 2003, he lost interest in WTO accession and instead launched the idea of a Common Economic Space among Russia, Ukraine, Kazakhstan, and Belarus. In 2009, Russia's WTO accession became one of the goals of the Barack Obama–Dmitri Medvedev "reset." Possibly for that reason, in June 2009, Putin repeated his trick of 2003, proposing a customs union between Belarus, Kazakhstan, and Russia, which yet again delayed Russia's WTO accession.

In August 2012, Russia finally became the 156th member of the WTO, but its practical impact became limited, as Putin focused on his new Eurasian Economic Union instead. The United States could not recognize Russia's WTO membership unless it granted Russia permanent normal trading rights, which it did in December 2012, but it did so together with the Sergei Magnitsky Rule of Law Accountability Act, which sanctioned a number of Russian officials responsible for the murder of this lawyer. As of 2018, the United States has sanctioned forty-nine Russians for related human rights violations, including Alexander Bastrykin, the chairman of the Investigative Committee and Putin's law school friend from St. Petersburg. At least six more countries have adopted similar Magnitsky Acts.[20]

While Washington saw the adoption of permanent normal trading relations with Russia as the essential legislation, Putin got greatly upset over the accompanying Magnitsky Rule Act. Although its aim was to punish looters of the Russian state, the Kremlin saw it as a hostile act, seemingly acknowledging complicity in the crime. The Kremlin took revenge with a law prohibiting the adoption of Russian children by Americans in early 2013, named the Dima Yakovlev Act for a Russian adopted child who died in the United States.

In 2016, the US Congress adopted the Global Magnitsky Human Rights Accountability Act, which sanctions violators of human rights throughout the world. In December 2017, the first designations were made. It sanctioned one Russian, Artem Chaika, the son of Russia's prosecutor general, who had been vilified by Alexei Navalny. The US Treasury stated that Chaika had "leveraged his father's position and ability to award his subordinates to unfairly win state-owned assets and contracts and put pressure on business competitors."[21]

As discussed in chapter 2, Putin became increasingly disenchanted with the West, starting with the US withdrawal from the Anti-Ballistic Missile Treaty in July 2002. In trade, a new strife started in March 2003, when

Putin initiated a Common Economic Space between Russia, Ukraine, Kazakhstan, and Belarus. It was supposed to be a free trade area, a customs zone, and eventually a currency union. These countries already had a free trade zone but because of the absence of an agreed arbitration mechanism it did not work. They needed the WTO's well-functioning arbitration rather than more far-reaching integration proposals that could not be implemented. Yet Putin insisted.

In September 2003, a four-nation agreement on the Common Economic Space was adopted, and it was ratified by all four parliaments. In parallel, the European Union launched its low-key European Neighborhood Policy, which aimed at some integration of the European post-Soviet countries. Putin had planted a new seed of geopolitical competition.[22]

Putin's priority since 2003 was to integrate Ukraine together with Kazakhstan and Belarus, and he wanted to do so before Ukraine's presidential elections in the fall of 2004. Putin met with Ukraine's president Leonid Kuchma once a month that year, even campaigning for the presidential candidate Viktor Yanukovych, although Putin did not think much of him. Instead, the Orange Revolution upset Putin. After Yanukovych lost the 2004 presidential elections, the Common Economic Space was forgotten, though it had delayed Russia's accession to the WTO.[23]

Putin hardly said so in public, but he clearly favored an East Slavic, or Russian, alliance of Russia, Belarus, Ukraine, and Kazakhstan in line with Alexander Solzhenitsyn's famous 1990 essay "Rebuilding Russia," advocating a "Russian Union" encompassing Ukraine, Belarus, Russia, and the ethnic Russian parts of Kazakhstan, and he wanted to use trade policy for this purpose.[24]

Instead, Putin faced a new Ukrainian crisis. In the summer of 2013, Russia started sanctioning Ukrainian companies that were pro-European. Russia opposed Ukraine's intention to conclude a Free Trade Agreement with the European Union. The tension between Russia and the West escalated with the Russian annexation of Crimea and further military aggression in eastern Ukraine. In March 2014, the West started imposing sanctions on Russia because of its aggression in Ukraine.

In June 2009, Prime Minister Putin surprised everybody, including his cabinet, by declaring that Russia, Belarus, and Kazakhstan would form a customs union. This time Putin's endeavor was serious. In 2010, these three countries created a Customs Union. In a next step in 2012, they constituted a Single Economic Space, and finally in January 2015, they formed the Eurasian Economic Union. Armenia decided to join in September 2013, and Kyrgyzstan did so in May 2015.[25]

The Eurasian Economic Union mimics the European Union. Its declared purpose is economic integration and freer trade. When the Customs Union came into existence in 2010, common customs tariffs and a joint customs code were established. In January 2012, border controls were abolished. A joint secretariat, the Eurasian Economic Commission, designed like the European Commission, was set up in Moscow that year with a staff of more than a thousand well-paid international civil servants. The Eurasian Development Bank in Almaty, Kazakhstan, and an arbitration court in Minsk were also established.[26]

The Treaty of the Eurasian Economic Union is a massive tract that runs to 855 pages in English. Its structure and content are reminiscent of the Treaty of the European Union, which is its obvious model. Russia wanted to drop "Economic" and call it the Eurasian Union, but Kazakh president Nursultan Nazarbayev prevailed, insisting that the EAEU be entirely economic.[27]

This is the first attempt at a supranational institution among post-Soviet countries. The commission is balanced by the absence of any weighted voting that would favor Russia, so decisions are supposed to be made by consensus. However, national governments nominate all commission members, in practice controlling them. Its secretariat is located in Moscow and chaired by a longtime Russian minister, Viktor Khristenko. The highest body of the EAEU is its Supreme Council, which consists of the presidents of the member states. Neither the Eurasian Commission nor the Eurasian court has any power of enforcement. Therefore, the Eurasian Commission is intergovernmental rather than supranational. This is a Russian initiative, dominated by Russia. The eminent German Russia scholar Hannes Adomeit observes: "The ostensible purpose of [the Eurasian Economic Union] is economic. Its primary objectives, however, are geopolitical, and these are to be achieved in large part by economic means."[28]

The EAEU offers less than meets the eye economically. Its proclaimed customs union is not even a free-trade area. Not all tariffs have actually been unified. Many agricultural goods are not permitted into Russia because of its national sanitary regulations (seemingly inspired by protectionist agricultural producers), blocking Russian consumers from the benefit of cheaper food. Kazakh officials complain bitterly that they are not allowed to transit oil or gas through Gazprom or Transneft's pipelines. Export tariffs persist and have not been harmonized but are negotiated bilaterally. The free movement of services is unlikely to be realized anytime soon.[29]

The economic interests of the member states vary greatly. Russia and Kazakhstan are raw material exporters, while Belarus exports Soviet-style manufactured goods. To improve competitiveness, ordinary trade theory teaches that economies should open up to competition, but the EAEU has done the opposite. Russia is comparatively protectionist, and it has forced the other member countries to raise their tariffs to its level. Kazakhstan produces no cars, but it had to adopt Russia's higher car tariffs. Russia and Belarus have gained captive markets, which will ultimately hurt their competitiveness. Belarus remains a highly regulated economy and does not qualify as a market economy.

Even if the EAEU were an open market, its members would not necessarily benefit. The union is small—only 2 percent of global GDP at current exchange rates, less than one-tenth of the European Union. The EU countries have benefited from common, modern EU standards, whereas the EAEU has reinforced obsolete Soviet standards through an intergovernmental treaty, though many businesspeople praise the unification of standards. Nor has the Customs Union brought about any direct benefit—the members already pursued tariff-free trade. One advantage of the Customs Union is the abolition of border controls between member countries. Yet in the spring of 2017, Russia restored border controls with Belarus, not least because Belarus has been a major conduit in transit trade of sanctioned goods to Russia.[30]

Kazakhstan is highly dependent on Russia because of its geography, and President Nazarbayev has consistently favored multilateral relations, preferring not to be left alone with Russia. He claims to have been the first to voice the idea of a Eurasian Union in 1994. Yet Kazakhstan has gained almost nothing economically from the EAEU. The World Bank assessed the cost to Kazakhstan of joining the Customs Union in its baseline scenario at 0.2 percent of GDP.[31]

Belarus's president Alexander Lukashenko has skillfully extracted large subsidies from Russia through cheap oil and gas supplies, and Russia offers a vast market for its not very competitive manufactures. From 2009 to 2013, Armenia worked on concluding an Association Agreement with the European Union, but suddenly on September 3, 2013, Putin met with President Serzh Sargsyan and persuaded him to switch to the EAEU, presumably threatening a Russian withdrawal or reduction of its vital military support for Armenia against Azerbaijan. Kyrgyzstan thrived on transit trade from China to Russia and Kazakhstan, which the Customs Union interrupted with a tall customs wall, so Kyrgyzstan was financially pressured to join the EAEU. In 2013, the Kremlin imposed great political pressure and economic sanctions on Ukraine to persuade it to join the EAEU, but Ukraine resisted.[32]

The two greatest enthusiasts of Eurasian integration are Putin and his economic adviser for Eurasia, Sergei Glaziev. Putin often cites dubious numbers on EAEU benefits. In December 2012, he praised the Customs Union: "Trade with these countries grew by 10 percent [in 2012]—that is not bad at all. Most importantly, . . . we have a very good structure of trade with the Customs Union countries. Machinery and equipment make up 20 percent of [Russian exports]. That is very good, because machinery and equipment make up only 2 percent in our [exports to] the rest of the world." In other words, Belarus and Kazakhstan were forced to raise their import tariffs for cars to buy cars from Russia rather than from South Korea and Japan.[33]

When Ukraine discussed whether to conclude an Association Agreement with the European Union or join the EAEU, many econometric studies were produced using standard gravity and general equilibrium models. All but those of the Eurasian Development Bank obtained comparable results. Veronika Movchan and Ricardo Giucci made the most complete mainstream study of the effects on Ukraine of both the Deep and Comprehensive Free Trade Area with the European Union and the Customs Union. They concluded that in the long term, the Association Agreement would add 11.8 percent to Ukraine's GDP, while the Customs Union would reduce it by 3.7 percent because of trade diversion. The Association Agreement would substantially increase trade (both exports and imports), whereas the Customs Union would reduce trade.[34]

A group of economists affiliated with the Eurasian Development Bank presented a counter study that was based not on calculations but on "scenarios" with peculiar assumptions. Because of a reduction in exports to the EAEU countries, Ukraine would lose up to 1.5 percent of its GDP. Another Eurasian Development Bank study reached a similar conclusion: if Ukraine embraced the Customs Union, its GDP could be boosted by 6–7 percent by 2030. Glaziev stated that Ukraine would gain $9 billion a year if it joined the Customs Union, because Ukraine would be allowed to buy Russian oil and gas at the same low prices as Belarus. None of these studies reveals any solid quantitative methodology, leaving the impression that they are little but propaganda and assumptions about Russian subsidies or sanctions.[35]

Some scholars in the West believe that the EAEU deserves to be taken seriously as a Russian attempt at economic integration for the benefit of economic efficiency. They emphasize the formal steps taken, such as the many treaties, but real integration has not developed correspondingly. Since their arguments are largely based on public statements rather than economic statistics, they fail to convince.[36]

The EAEU isolates Russia from the rest of the world, limits competition at home, prevents its economy from modernizing, and aggravates its relations with its closest neighbors, while costing Russia billions of dollars every year in lost customs revenues and subsidies to other members. In December 2016, Belarus boycotted the annual summit of the EAEU in protest against the draft customs code to be adopted. The EAEU has been tried, but it has not worked. Russia and the other EAEU members would be better off without this geopolitical project but with the previously existing free trade area, which should have been reinforced with functioning arbitration.

The big blow to Russia's foreign economic policy has been the Western sanctions after Russia's military aggression in Ukraine in 2014. In the night of February 27, 2014, Russian special forces without insignia seized the regional parliament in Simferopol in Ukrainian Crimea. Within days, they had occupied the whole peninsula. On March 18, Russia annexed Crimea, swiftly integrating it into Russia.

Russia's occupation of Crimea came as a complete surprise to the West. Military support for Ukraine was never considered an option, but the West felt that it had to do something. Immediately in March 2014, the European Union and the United States announced Crimea-related sanctions with visa bans and assets freezes on individuals and companies accused of undermining democracy, misappropriating Ukrainian property, and violating human rights. Gradually both the United States and the EU have expanded their sanctions to people responsible for Russian policy on Crimea and enterprises operating there. Ukraine has cut off almost everything—electricity, water, trade, and transportation—isolating Crimea from the outside world.[37]

A novelty in the US sanctions was that four of Putin's cronies were sanctioned, namely Yuri Kovalchuk, Arkady and Boris Rotenberg, and Gennady Timchenko, as well as their Bank Rossiya (as discussed in chapter 5). The European Union has also sanctioned Kovalchuk, Arkady Rotenberg, and another crony, Nikolai Shamalov, but it has not sanctioned Boris Rotenberg and Gennady Timchenko because they are Finnish citizens.

The West had multiple aims with its sanctions: to punish the culprits, to isolate Crimea, to stop Russia's aggression, and to deter Russia from further aggression. The Russian advance in Ukraine has been stopped, and Crimea is utterly isolated, but Russia has not withdrawn on either front, and no solution is in sight.

In April 2014, anonymous Russian special forces tried to stir up unrest among ethnic Russians in eastern and southern Ukraine, but with limited results. Unrest took root only in parts of Ukraine's two easternmost regions, Donetsk and Luhansk. In the summer of 2014, the military situation was fluid. With amazing speed, the Ukrainian military caught up and advanced against the Russian-backed volunteers, many of whom were Russian citizens. The war heated up in July. Russia reacted by sending in regular troops.

In response to the regular Russian forces entering Ukraine, on July 16, the United States imposed serious sectoral sanctions on Russia. The next day, a Russian Buk missile shot down a Malaysian airplane, flight MH17, from occupied Ukrainian territory, killing all 298 people on board, which convinced hesitant Europeans to impose similar sectoral sanctions. Most Western countries joined the US-EU sanctions, including Japan, Canada, Australia, New Zealand, and Switzerland, but no developing nation did. The sanctions differed slightly but were quite similar.

The July 2014 sanctions went much further than the Crimea sanctions. They covered three sectors: finance, oil, and defense technology, focusing on large state companies. Individuals responsible for Russian policy in the occupied territories and enterprises involved were also sanctioned. These sanctions have been gradually expanded, but the same principles have applied.

The financial sanctions have been quite effective. They prohibit lending to the sanctioned state banks and companies for terms of thirty days or more. The European Bank for Reconstruction and Development was blocked from offering new financing in Russia. Almost all international lending to Russia ceased, and the country nearly faced a liquidity freeze. Both the government and private firms had to pay off their foreign debt obligations as they came due, with minimal possibilities to refinance them. Western banks were afraid of being trapped if the sanctions were to change. Even the four big Chinese state banks obeyed the US financial sanctions, because they all have activities in the United States and all dollars pass through New York, thus being subject to US jurisdiction, and the US authorities can impose severe fines that are not subject to judicial appeals.

The impact of the financial sanctions was the greatest in 2014, when Russia faced large foreign debt repayments. The IMF assessed the impact: "Model-based estimates suggest that sanctions and counter-sanctions could initially reduce real GDP by 1 to 1½ percent. Prolonged sanctions may compound already declining productivity growth. The cumulative output loss could lead to a cumulative output loss over the medium term of up to 9 percent of GDP, as lower capital accumulation and technological transfers weakens already declining productivity growth." Over time, the effect has diminished as Russia has paid down much of its foreign debt.[38]

Russian corporations had no choice but to pay off their debt service as it fell due, and they had scarcely any possibilities of refinancing. Russia's total foreign debt declined from $732 billion in June 2014 to $519 billion in December 2015, and it has stayed at about that level. Meanwhile, Russia's international currency reserves declined from $510 billion at the end of 2013 to a low of $356 billion in March 2015.[39]

The energy sanctions were limited to three kinds of oil development: deep offshore drilling, arctic offshore, and tight oil. They did not harm production in the short term but damaged it in the long term. The European Union insisted that gas must not be subject to sanctions because of its great dependence on Russian gas.

The sanctions on Russia were not severe in comparison with those imposed on Iran, though no such large country had been subject to such severe Western sanctions before. The Russian government itself was excepted, being allowed to sell bonds. Nor were the Central Bank of Russia and its reserves abroad subject to any restrictions, and Russia could continue using the international bank clearing system SWIFT. Even assets abroad of most sanctioned companies were not frozen. The West was reticent to cause itself harm while also wanting to have opportunities to escalate.

Because the Russian economy is so much smaller than the Western economy, Russia cannot respond effectively without hurting itself more. It sanctioned some Western officials, which was of little consequence. In August 2014, Russia introduced "countersanctions" against food imports from the countries that had imposed sanctions on Russia. These sanctions raised eyebrows because they hurt Russian consumers, with worse and fewer supplies of many foods and higher inflation, and the Russian customs office destroyed large volumes of food that had been smuggled into the country. Russia's agricultural producers vocally supported this protectionism. In June 2017, Putin extended Russia's embargo on food products from the West until the end of 2018. Many other kinds of sanctions were discussed, such as the prohibition of flights over Russian territory, but they were never adopted. The Kremlin realized that Russia was the underdog.[40]

The cost to the West of the Western sanctions and the Russian countersanctions has been minimal. Russian imports fell sharply in 2014 and 2015, but that was because of the falling price of oil, and the European Union has maintained its large market share in Russia of about 45 percent.

Plausibly, Daniel Gros and Mattia Di Salvo have concluded that "the position of European exporters in the Russian market has not been infringed" because of the EU sanctions. "The impact of the Russian counter-sanctions on agro-food imports from the EU has been minimal. Russian imports of these goods have fallen by about €400 million," which is less than 0.3 percent of EU GDP, while overall EU exports of these goods have increased because of increased sales to other markets.[41]

With regard to direct investments, Russia and the West have grown apart with the sanctions. In July 2017, Siemens announced that it would sell its 46 percent stake in a turbine factory in St. Petersburg because its partner, the state corporation Rostec, had delivered turbines to Crimea, contrary to its agreement with Siemens. Rostec had not been the original partner of Siemens, but it had purchased the dominant share of the company from a private investor, who had exited. A spokesperson for Germany's foreign minister reminded Russia that it had been assured that sanctions would not be broken and lamented "that such a massive violation of sanctions would place new burdens on German-Russian relations."[42]

The Russian company Kaspersky Lab has become one of the largest global security software companies. During the 2016 presidential elections, the United States accused Russia of cybercrime, and the General Services Administration has instructed federal agencies not to purchase software from Kaspersky Lab.[43]

The sanctions are like a squirrel's wheel. Each measure provokes countermeasures, and both sides protect themselves, resulting in stricter security efforts, less foreign investment, and isolation. Businesspeople face sanction risks, because sanctions can change on short notice and are difficult to interpret, which then aggravates credit risks, and Russia's hostile relationship with the West exposes foreign investors to reputational risks. Although Putin's cronies and state corporations have been singled out for Western sanctions, the sanctions seem to have reinforced the role of both the state and the cronies in the economy, since they are being given even more privileges, as is usually the case and many bona fide private businesspeople flee abroad.

Since the sanctions were imposed and the price of oil collapsed in 2014, Western investment in Russia has been tiny. The sanctions have aggravated Russia's already low credit rating and rendered capital scarcer and more expensive. In defense, the Central Bank of Russia has maintained a very high real interest rate, which also depresses investment.

The US sanctions were imposed through presidential executive orders, that is, by decree, which meant that they could be modified at any time, aggravating the sanctions risk. Because of the fear that President Donald Trump would abolish the Russia sanctions, Congress codified these sanctions into law in the Combating America's Adversaries through Sanctions Act (CAATSA), which President Trump signed into law on August 2, 2017. As a consequence, the president can no longer alter the Russia sanctions without congressional consent.

In April 2018, the US Treasury issued its first sanctions based on CAATSA, sanctioning twenty-four people and fourteen enterprises. The far-reaching nature of the sanctions caused shockwaves. For one thing, most of the people sanctioned are really close to Putin, including his former son-in-law, Kirill Shamalov. Several major oligarchs were sanctioned, notably Oleg Deripaska, as were no fewer than eight of his companies, including Rusal, which accounted for 6 percent of global aluminum production. The widened sanctions caused havoc in the global aluminum industry, forcing the US Treasury to backtrack several steps. Unlike the Obama administration, the Trump administration neither consulted nor forewarned its European allies, who were hit hard by the sanctions against Rusal.[44]

Putin has used public means to compensate his sanctioned cronies, which reinforces state and crony capitalism. One of the nationalized banks that collapsed in the fall of 2017, Promsvyazbank, was singled out to finance sanctioned companies. The sanctions and countersanctions might have helped Putin's endeavors to isolate Russia from the West with his "deoffshoreization" and import substitution. Major Russian businesspeople face the choice of staying in Russia and reducing their links to the West or selling their assets in Russia and moving to the West. By and large, the elite from the 1990s has made the latter choice.

In parallel, direct Russian investment in the United States has plummeted as Russian businesspeople find it increasingly difficult to satisfy the contradictory demands of the US and Russian governments.

The consequence is growing alienation between Russian and Western businesses. The general assumption is that the sanctions will likely last a long time. No solution of the Ukrainian conflict is in sight, and because the conflicts that caused them are not resolved, the sanctions tend to be inert, and, moreover, Congress codified them in July 2017. The outcome is deglobalization.[45]

Through his many public statements, Putin has made clear what he thinks of the sanctions. He reacted strongly against the Magnitsky Act and the Western sanctions of March 2014 against his close friends, which blocked them from visas, cut them out of the Western financial system, and potentially froze their assets in the West. By contrast, he played down the impact of the sectoral sanctions and imposed the countersanctions on food for the Russian people himself.[46]

Putin reacted most strongly against the release on April 3, 2016, of the Panama Papers, which revealed his offshore holdings of at least $2 billion through his cellist friend Sergei Roldugin. Andrei Soldatov and Irina Borogan have chronicled the Kremlin response. Putin's spokesman Dmitri Peskov commented on them immediately. On April 7, Putin himself attacked the journalists who had released the Panama Papers: "What did they do? They manufactured an information product. They found some of my friends and acquaintances. . . . There are many, many people in the background—it is impossible to understand who they are, and there is a close-up photo of your humble servant in the foreground." Putin continued: "Besides, we now know from Wikileaks that officials and state agencies in the United States are behind all this!" The next day, Putin convened the Security Council. On April 14, Putin again brought up the Panama Papers to defend his friend Roldugin in public. "Who is engaged in these provocations? We know that there are employees of official US agencies." Putin saw the release of the Panama Papers as a US attack against him personally.[47]

Putin tried to belittle the sectoral sanctions, but he has said comparatively little about them in public. The countersanctions on food imports, by contrast, have received great media attention and been presented as successful import substitutions, even though they have hit the Russian population the hardest. The April 2018 sanctions clearly shook the Kremlin. Sanctions were no longer seen as a joke, and they hit the stock market hard. A view might have developed that Trump was Russia's and that he would not permit additional sanctions against Russia. The Kremlin might also have been scared by an obvious popular approval of the US sanctioning of both billionaires and people close to Putin.

Putin has pursued a vicious economic war against Ukraine. His approach to Ukraine has been far more severe than his tactics with the West; as a smaller economy, Ukraine is highly vulnerable, and Russia was by far its largest trading partner. These two countries have hit each other with one sanction after the other in a steady escalation after Russia started blocking imports from certain pro-European Ukrainian businesses in August 2013. In January 2016, the EU and Ukraine provisionally applied their Deep and Comprehensive Free Trade Agreement. Russia responded by suspending the existing multilateral free-trade agreement among the members of the Commonwealth of Independent States with regard to Ukraine, thus imposing import tariffs on Ukraine, and Ukraine responded by leaving the CIS.[48]

The two countries have gradually intensified their many trade sanctions, and mutual trade plummeted by 80 percent from 2012 to 2016, though it recovered substantially in 2017. This cruel trade war has hurt Ukraine the most, but Russia has lost a significant market and important military supplies. Russia's share of Ukraine's trade fell from 29 percent in 2012 to 11.5 percent in 2016. These trade disruptions have caused great damage to Ukraine's economy, and 2016 marked the nadir. Ukraine's trade expanded sharply in 2017, although the Russian sanctions did not ease.[49]

As discussed in chapter 4, Gazprom is Russia's favorite geopolitical tool, manipulating both prices and supplies for political aims. In the first quarter of 2014, Gazprom charged Ukraine $268.50 per 1,000 cubic meters (mcm) in accordance with an agreement between Presidents Putin and Yanukovych on December 17, 2013. On April 1, however, Gazprom hiked the price to $385 per mcm, announcing that it would no longer give any special Yanukovych discount. Two days later, Gazprom raised the price again, by another $100 per mcm, to $485 per mcm, arguing that since Russia had annexed Crimea, it was no longer obligated to offer any discount for Russia's lease of the Sevastopol naval base, as Putin had agreed with Yanukovych in Kharkiv in April 2010. Kyiv responded by not paying, and on June 16, 2014, Gazprom stopped supplying gas to Ukraine.[50]

Gazprom and Ukraine's Naftogaz sued each other in the Stockholm Arbitration Institute, and in June 2017, Naftogaz won an extraordinary victory, relieving it from Gazprom claims valued of as much as $75 billion. Since November 2015, Ukraine has not imported any gas from Russia. Naftogaz also won a great victory over Gazprom over gas transit through Ukraine. The Stockholm Arbitration Court obliged Gazprom to pay Naftogaz $2.56 billion. However, Gazprom refused to pay, prompting Naftogaz to state that it would go after Gazprom assets abroad to cover its award.[51]

Ukraine has banned its previously substantial military supplies to Russia, and it has stopped trade with Crimea and, in March 2017, also with occupied Donbas. Russia has restricted transit of Ukrainian goods through Russia, while Ukraine has banned Russian flights over its territory. To add insult to injury, Russia also imposed transit restrictions on Ukrainian exports to Kazakhstan and Kyrgyzstan, which eliminated 0.4 percent of Ukraine's total exports.[52]

What about China? After the collapse of the Soviet Union, Russia and China drifted apart. The Chinese leadership was appalled by the Soviet demise, and the Kremlin looked to the West, while Russia's economic crisis led to a sharp decline in the two countries' mutual trade. Gradually, Russia and China have restored and expanded their political and economic relations. In 2009, China became Russia's biggest trading partner, and its lead has continued to rise, even if Russia's trade with the European Union as a whole is much larger.[53]

As the West closed to Putin, he attempted a pivot to China, but the Russia-China economic relationship is quite unbalanced. Russia exports raw materials, primarily oil, and arms to China, while China supplies Russia, and the rest of the world, with manufactures. Chinese investment in Russia has been remarkably small, because the Kremlin has hardly allowed Chinese state companies to invest in Russian raw material extraction, and mutual suspicions prevail. The ultimate Russian fear is that millions of Chinese will invade its depopulated Far East and exploit its vast natural resources. These worries have impeded commercial integration.[54]

Russia has been most comfortable with China in high-level politics. Russia and China tend to act together in the United Nations Security Council. In 1998, Russia joined the Asia-Pacific Economic Cooperation forum. The Shanghai Cooperation Organisation, created in 2001, was a big step forward. In 2009, Russia convened the first summit of the BRICS, but most important are bilateral summits.

After its annexation of Crimea, the Kremlin attempted a pivot to China. This was a textbook case of realpolitik, or how not to pursue foreign policy. Russia was cornered, whereas China could choose among Russia, the United States, and the European Union, and it has several times more trade with the two latter markets. In May 2014, Putin traveled to China and he was all in. His prime ambition was to conclude an agreement with China on Russian delivery of gas to China. He did so, but on Chinese conditions. Russia wanted to use gas from Western Siberia, but China insisted on the development of new gas fields in the Far East, which would be exclusively for China. The Kremlin wanted to deliver that gas to a new liquefied natural gas plant in Vladivostok, which would give Russia the flexibility to sell to other countries as well, whereas China preferred a pipeline going only to China. After having won on these two accounts, China had gained a monopoly on this future gas production and could do nothing but win on the last issue, the price.[55]

It would get worse. Within two months, Russia suffered two major blows, the collapse of oil prices and Western financial sanctions. The agreement on gas deliveries to China had not been final, and ample energy supplies cooled China's interest. The Chinese government had promised to provide $25 billion in credits toward building the large Russian gas pipeline the Power of Siberia in the summer of 2014, but after the US financial sanctions were imposed, the Chinese state banks with substantial exposure to the United States refused to provide the credit, fearing US fines for violating its Russia sanctions. Neither was China helpful to Russia on Ukraine. In the IMF board, China has persistently voted for IMF funding of Ukraine since 2014, leaving Russia as the lone dissenter. Ukraine had become China's biggest supplier of corn and its second biggest provider of arms after Russia.[56]

Many years ago, former first deputy minister for foreign affairs Anatoly Adamishin told me that Russia had refused to become a junior partner to the United States. Instead, it had become a junior partner to China. Although Russia-China relations are arguably better than ever, Russia is the weaker partner.

Independent Russia is an odd fit in the global order, and it has been unable to find its place. The Kremlin sees only the United States and China as its equals, but neither returns the compliment. Although the European Union accounts for almost half of Russia's trade, the Kremlin continues to treat the member countries as separate entities. Its foreign economic policy can be summarized as an odd combination of increasing protectionism in trade and remarkably liberal capital flows.

In substance Russia might not have changed its policies much, but its ambitions have switched from increased international integration to isolation and protectionism. Sergei Guriev puts it succinctly: "The Ukraine crisis changed everything. Russia's March 2014 annexation of Crimea and the resulting Western sanctions brought about a clear division in Russia between 'us' and 'them.'" Putin's foreign economic policy must be seen in the light of Ukraine, which Putin perceives as the elusive geopolitical jewel in his crown.[57]

Other economic developments have not contributed to international integration. The strongest force is the global price of oil. When the price of oil was high in 2011–2013, oil and gas accounted for two-thirds of Russia's exports. When it was low, as in 2016, their share fell to half of the exports. Thus, lower oil prices drive diversification, but other exports have not increased in absolute terms. The main beneficiary has been agriculture, while poor investment conditions have hampered manufacturing. The government has consistently blamed the poor economic results on the West, which makes a lot of political sense, but it might not be quite correct.

The Russian leaders seem most comfortable with the G-20 and BRICS, which are exclusive and treat Russia as an equal. The G-8 was always a misfit, because the other countries were wealthier, more democratic, and less corrupt than Russia. These constellations, however, are clubs rather than institutions, having minimal impact on the real economy. The WTO is the most important organization for world trade. Although Russia became a member in 2012, the WTO has not influenced the Russian economy much, as the government has not attempted to use it for diversification or modernization. On the contrary, Russia has turned more protectionist since it joined the WTO.

Instead of using the WTO to reform its economy, the Kremlin has focused on the EAEU and cooperation with China. The EAEU is currently Putin's main focus, but it is difficult to see what good it can bring. For all the five countries involved, it amounts to trade diversion rather than trade creation. To Russia it is costly, since it tempted the other members with material incentives. The unequal rules of the EAEU arouse hostilities rather than affinity among the member states. And it contributes to Russia's increasing isolation. Even the Kremlin seems to have lost interest in the EAEU.

Import substitution is currently the leading Russian slogan, and protectionism appears to have increased in the Russian economy, though these tendencies should not be exaggerated. In comparison with the high customs tariffs of other BRICS countries, the Russian economy remains quite open. The Soviet Union cherished the Latin American arguments of the need for infant industry support through protectionism, but such protectionism nurtures state enterprises that pursue selective procurement.[58]

Increasingly, the Kremlin has become preoccupied with national security. In 2008, Russia enacted the Strategic Sectors Law, which restricted foreign investment. Originally, this law specified forty-two sectors of strategic significance, in which foreign investment required special government permission. Most of these sectors are of obvious importance for national security, but not all, notably broadcasting and publishing. The law has repeatedly been amended and expanded to forty-five activities that require government approval for significant foreign investment. The October 2014 law "On Mass Media" restricted foreign ownership of any Russian media company to 20 percent. Large sectors, such as energy, telecommunications, and media, are closing up to foreign business, depressing the market prices of such assets.[59]

Internet companies face particular problems in Russia. The FSB has two important demands. It insists on having access to all data, including ciphered information, and it wants all computer servers used in Russia to be stored in the country. This nationalizes the Internet and separates Russian from international Internet companies, harming such Russian companies as the excellent search engine Yandex, which had outcompeted Google in Russia, but now it has been barred from Ukraine. Before the Russian elections in March 2018, Russia adopted two laws ending Internet anonymity. Admittedly, in all these regards, Russia appears quite liberal in comparison with China.[60]

In contrast to the increasing protectionism for trade in both goods and services, Russia has maintained free capital flows since 2006. The official tolerance to capital outflows is remarkable, given the great and sharp capital outflows in 2008 and 2014. The best explanation is that the main beneficiaries of these capital outflows are the rulers themselves, as discussed in chapter 5.

The policy conclusion for the West is that it makes more sense to go after the money of the cronies, sanctioning them and their capital flows and freezing their assets abroad, while trade sanctions hurt the population as a whole. This is in line with the selective sanctions of cronies and their companies, but those assets need to be uncovered and frozen.

Liberalism versus Statism, or Reform versus Corruption?

To divine where Russia's economic policy may be moving, we need to examine the public debate. In comparison with discussions about politics and law, the economic debate is quite open, even if it has become less so in the past decade. The economists are divided into two big ideological camps, classical liberals versus statists and nationalists. A new strand focuses on combating corruption.

In this chapter I shall assess the current state of economic thinking. A first bout of economic policy debate occurred in 2012–2013, when a new chair of the Central Bank of Russia was about to be appointed. In May 2016, Putin invited a new round of economic debate in preparation for the presidential elections scheduled for March 2018.

In the early 1990s, the Russian economic debate was intensely ideological. The liberal market reform program was driven by three men: President Boris Yeltsin, First Deputy Prime Minister Yegor Gaidar, and Deputy Prime Minister and Minister of Privatization Anatoly Chubais. They embraced the ideas of the Washington Consensus and the Polish Leszek Balcerowicz program, which both embraced a normal market economy with reasonably stable prices, a free exchange of goods and services, dominant private ownership, free trade, and the rule of law. In this economy, taxes would be low and stable and public expenditures limited, while the state would provide a reasonable social safety net. The state would set the rules for the market rather than interfere directly in the market.[1]

Yeltsin, Gaidar, and Chubais carried out a first reform wave in the years 1991–1994, building the essentials of a market economy with private enterprise, but they failed to stabilize the economy, build the rule of law, or carry out social reform.

The financial crash of August 1998 brought about a second reform wave, 1998–2002. The crisis made it politically possible to eliminate the large Russian budget deficit, and a wave of second-generation reforms ensued. These included reform of the tax system and the judicial system, deregulation of small enterprises, land reform, and pension reform.

Throughout these years, a few important liberals held key positions in the Russian government. Although the specific individuals varied, they were all friends and formed a tight group of like-minded thinkers, whether inside or outside government. Gaidar and Chubais remained the informal leaders of this group.[2]

After Putin became president in 2000, the two most important liberal ministers were Finance Minister Alexei Kudrin and Minister of Economic Development and Trade Herman Gref. Prime Minister Mikhail Kasyanov (2000–2004) and presidential chief of staff Alexander Voloshin (1999–2003) were perceived as close to big business, but they supported the liberals most of the time. In 2007, Gref left the government to become CEO of Sberbank, the former Soviet savings bank, leaving Kudrin as the leading economic liberal, which he still is. In September 2011, Kudrin resigned from the government in protest against Dmitri Medvedev's becoming prime minister and against increasing military expenditures. Unlike most of his colleagues, Kudrin has not departed for big business but stays involved in the policy discussion as head of a nongovernmental organization, the Civil Initiative, and since May 2018 as chair of Russia's Auditing Chamber.

The Russian liberals have always faced severe opposition. Although communism as an ideology died with the Soviet Union, its ideas have lingered in various remnants. From 1992, old-style communists and Russian nationalists formed a so-called red-brown coalition in the Russian parliament. They embraced a statist ideology, combining ideas of dominant state ownership, extensive state intervention, protectionism, and macroeconomic stimulus.

Throughout this period Gennady Zyuganov has led the Communist Party of the Russian Federation. He has maintained old Soviet ideas, lauding Stalin, the Russian Orthodox Church, and Russian nationalism simultaneously. The Communist Party even displays icons with Stalin as a saint. It operates as a trade union for retirees, constantly demanding higher pensions. It favors maximum public expenditures and a very loose fiscal and monetary policy, evincing no interest in balancing the books.

The leading nationalists have varied. Vladimir Zhirinovsky emerged as the nationalist leader in the Duma elections in December 1993, but soon he turned out to be a political jester, happy to support the government for suitable returns. In the early 2000s, the hard-core nationalist Dmitri Rogozin formed the nationalist party Motherland (Rodina). From 2011 until 2018, he was deputy prime minister for the military-industrial complex, and he is now CEO of Roscosmos, the State Corporation for Space Activities.

The communists and nationalists had only one credible economic policy advocate, Sergei Glaziev, who paradoxically gained his authority as a "young reformer" as first deputy minister for external economic relations in November 1991 at age thirty-one. However, he was more young than reformist. In December 1992, Glaziev advanced to become minister for external economic relations, but he resigned in September 1993 in protest against Yeltsin's dissolution of the predemocratic parliament. Initially, he joined the communists and became their chief economist, but soon he jumped ship to the nationalists, and, like Rogozin, he eventually joined Putin.[3]

Kudrin and Glaziev stand out as the most prominent spokesmen of the liberals and the Russian statists, respectively. There are many others, but for the sake of focus and relevance, I shall concentrate on these two men. Kudrin's position largely coincides with the Western economic mainstream, though he is more conservative on fiscal policy. He has many eloquent companions. Glaziev is more exotic, representing statist and nationalist positions. He is a prolific author, and his ideological outlook has changed little over time.[4]

Putin incorporated the strife between liberalism and statism in his administration by appointing Sergei Glaziev as his adviser (*sovetnik*) in

July 2012, responsible for economic affairs in Eurasia. At the same time, Glaziev became a member of the board of the Central Bank of Russia.[5]

In 2004, Glaziev ran as an independent nationalist presidential candidate against Putin, coming in third, with 4.1 percent of the votes. In his campaign, he attacked Putin sharply for being a liberal. Afterward, he gradually moved toward Putin, though ideologically it was Putin who increasingly adopted Glaziev's views. Starting in 2010, Glaziev was deputy general secretary of the Eurasian Economic Commission.[6]

As Putin's official adviser, Glaziev has remained a free-wheeling radical. He advocates state capitalism, protectionism, and loose monetary and fiscal policy. In January 2013, he presented a big economic program written under the auspices of the Russian Academy of Sciences. He argued that monetary policy had constrained the supply of money and financed commercial banks' international speculation rather than domestic production. Russia had become too dependent on international credits. Glaziev favored cheap credits for business and support for small and medium-sized businesses with subsidized, long-term credits. Inflation, he argued, should be controlled through a more effective antimonopoly policy, and not through tight monetary policy.[7]

Glaziev complained that "our tax and budget system holds back economic development, although right now it is necessary to pour enormous resources into the modernization of infrastructure and the development of new technologies." In particular, Glaziev opposed the budget rule transferring a share of oil and gas revenues to the Reserve Fund, one of the two national wealth funds. He wanted to abolish the value-added tax and introduce a progressive income tax as well as a progressive ecological tax, and he wished to stimulate investment and research and development with generous depreciation rules.[8]

Under his leadership, the Institute of Economic Forecasting of the Russian Academy of Sciences, one of the Soviet-oriented institutes, formulated a development strategy to achieve and exceed Putin's goals with an annual GDP growth rate of 8 percent, industrial production growth rate of 10 percent, fixed investment growing annually by 15 percent, and research and development by 20 percent.[9]

Glaziev condemns the structural reforms of the 1990s as a "catastrophe." He attacks privatization as harmful, complaining about the criminalization of property relations, the destruction of Russia's scientific and technical potential, and the impoverishment of the people. The privatization hampered the formation of large, competitive companies, while it benefited foreign investors.[10]

His salient idea is that a militarization of the economy and a stronger role of the state will lead to technological leap-frogging and higher economic growth. He claims that Ronald Reagan's Strategic Defense Initiative catapulted the information technology revolution in the United States. Increased military expenditures would stimulate the demand for new technological products. He calls for more nationalization of large enterprises as well as state planning: "To achieve the necessary investments and innovation activity state participation in the development of the economy must sharply expand both in volume and quality." He favors industrial policy: "It would make sense to work out a five-year program for the modernization of the economy."[11]

This sounds like the Soviet past, which probably explains its popularity among old Russian academics. Yet Glaziev carefully avoids Soviet references, and his language is modern and technological, without socialist or Marxist terms. His militarized state capitalism rings like President Putin's actual policy. He emphasizes that Putin salvaged Russian corporations from bankruptcy with large credits during the global financial crisis and that only the state can provide long-term financing for investment today.[12]

As Putin's main prophet of Eurasian integration, Glaziev rules supreme on this favorite topic of Putin's. Glaziev cites fantastic and implausible numbers about the positive effects of the Eurasian Economic Union, which he claims will add up to $900 billion to the GDP of the three member countries Russia, Kazakhstan, and Belarus. Born in Ukrainian Zaporizhe, Glaziev played a leading role in designing the Russian military aggression against Ukraine and has been sanctioned by both the United States and the European Union for that reason. Surprisingly, he mentions the World Trade Organization positively, although his industrial policy involves considerable protectionism. He saves his scorn for the International Monetary Fund and the Washington Consensus.[13]

Putin has repeatedly cited Glaziev, especially on the positive economic effects of the Eurasian Economic Union, but as a skillful politician, Putin has a habit of appealing to contradictory constituencies. During a meeting with his Economic Council in 2012 just before Glaziev's appointment as his adviser, Putin mentioned the liberal former minister of economy Yevgeny Yasin and Glaziev as counterpoints, suggesting that they should work together.[14]

In late 2012 and early 2013, Moscow's large liberal economic establishment had a field day attacking Glaziev during the battle over the chairmanship of the Central Bank. Leading critiques were Yasin, Kudrin, and Vladimir Mau, Gaidar's former adviser and president of the Russian Academy of the National Economy and State Administration.

The liberals agreed with Glaziev on the poor state of the economy and shared many of his concerns: decelerating economic growth, deteriorating demographics, technological backwardness, low labor productivity, and the absence of structural modernization. The outflow of capital also disturbed them. However, they sought the opposite solution, a conservative fiscal and monetary policy and more market reforms, especially in the social sphere.[15]

The liberal economists knew they were on the safest ground on macroeconomics, with Kudrin as Russia's leading fiscal conservative. Yasin put it succinctly: "Glaziev's option is absolutely unacceptable: He proposes an increase of money supply in excess of demand, which inevitably raises inflation, excludes private investments and leads to reliance on state investments, which are considerably less efficient." Kudrin recommended that a substantial share of the oil and gas rents continue to be set aside in a stabilization fund, which was anathema to Glaziev. Kudrin also insisted on controlling inflation with a flexible exchange rate, that is, inflation targeting.[16]

Mau delivered his most stinging attack on Glaziev's program, though he carefully avoided mentioning him by name. Instead, he attacked the Soviet Union and its backward economy as a deterrent. "In the present Russian situation the main macroeconomic indicators are reminiscent of the situation of the USSR at the end of 1970s and the beginning of the 1980s." In the late Brezhnev years, the Moscow leadership overestimated the "crisis of capitalism" while underestimating the West's successful reforms. Now the Kremlin exaggerated the Western crisis and did not realize the significance of Western developments. Russia's "key problem is poor capacity of the economy to generate innovations and modernization."[17]

The old division between backward and progressive industries no longer held true, Mau argued. "In the contemporary world, any industry can be high-tech or outdated," the technological revolution in energy being a prime example. Economic growth must derive from increased productivity, which requires far more creative destruction. Even Mau, who favored privatization, said little about it, understanding how unpopular privatization had become.[18]

Mau and other liberals emphasized the need for real democracy for the sake of economic modernization, again drawing parallels with the Soviet system. "The political system of the USSR was exceedingly rigid, unable to react flexibly to arising new global challenges." Russia needed "political modernization, meaning qualitatively broadening of political and economic freedoms, which must correspond to contemporary international standards."[19]

Mau carefully avoided contradicting Putin or Glaziev on the need for Eurasian economic integration and the Customs Union, but he emphasized the WTO and economic integration with the European Union and the United States. His positive view of the European Union contrasted with Putin's dismissive attitude.

The disagreement between the liberals and Glaziev was almost total. First of all, the liberals criticized Glaziev's haphazard macroeconomic policies, arguing that fiscal and monetary stimulus would not generate much growth because Russia no longer had an output gap. Second, they advocated substantial deregulation and opposed state capitalism while remaining understated about the need for privatization. Third, the liberals aspired to international economic integration primarily with the most developed economies rather than the Customs Union. Last, they spoke up for real democracy, though rather softly.

In May 2012, Putin returned as president, and the official mood turned less liberal. Clearly, he had been taken aback by the large-scale public protests against fraud in the December 2011 Duma elections. He accused the US State Department and Secretary of State Hillary Clinton of having instigated the unrest. He claimed that opposition leaders had "heard the signal and with the support of the US state department began active work." In response, he unleashed repression of the opposition and an anti-American campaign.[20]

This change of mood influenced economic thinking. Vladimir Yakunin, then CEO of the Russian Railways and one of Putin's close associates from the KGB in St. Petersburg, remarked on the new official attitude: "The neo-liberal paradigm was exhausted by the 2008 crisis and never recovered."[21]

Russia's liberals feared that Putin would dismiss them and replace them with Glaziev and others of his ilk. Glaziev's appointment as Putin's counselor in July 2012 appeared to be a first step. In 2013, the longtime liberal chairman of the Central Bank, Sergei Ignatiev, was set to retire. Glaziev declared himself a candidate in competition with several bankers and liberal economic officials. The Moscow rumor mill reported that Putin wanted Glaziev, but all Putin's senior economic policy makers united against him. Unexpectedly, Putin selected his close economic aide (*pomoshchnik*) Elvira Nabiullina, who had been minister of economy. Though Nabiullina had not dealt much with macroeconomics, she was the liberal closest to Putin. As her successor, Putin appointed Andrei Belousov, a statist, and Glaziev was ousted from the Central Bank board.

Even so, both Glaziev and the liberals suspected that the president would adopt Glaziev's policies. The key issues were fiscal and monetary policies. However, with Nabiullina as Central Bank governor and Kudrin's former deputy Anton Siluanov as minister of finance, Putin has remained committed to conservative macroeconomic policies.

For the rest, Glaziev won. He praised Putin's policy of state capitalism, discretionary state intervention, enterprise concentration, and militarization, telling him to proceed even more daringly on that anti-liberal road. In doing so, he also appealed to Putin's power base of state corporations, the armaments industry, and the old Soviet industries. Putin usually refuses to acknowledge shortcomings in Russian structural policies, blaming the West instead. In December 2012, for example, he faulted the eurozone and the bad harvest: "What were the causes of the slowdown this year? . . . The general slowdown in global economic growth and even a recession in the Eurozone, one of the leading global centers. The second reason is our domestic problem, which is primarily crop failure."[22]

Only rarely has Putin expressed worries about the slowing growth. In April 2013, he stated: "The Economic Development Ministry has revised its economic growth forecast for 2013 downwards to 2.4 percent, but this is with energy prices still high. Let me bring to your attention that a growth rate of 2.4 percent is lower than the global economy's growth rate. It's been a long time since we were last in this situation ... we need to do everything we can to ensure our economy's stable development. We need a package of measures to stimulate economic growth." As the economic growth disappeared, Putin glossed over the bad news.[23]

In his December 2012 annual address to the Federal Assembly, Putin embraced state capitalism explicitly: "Russia is characterized by a tradition of a strong state." He adopted Glaziev's view of the "damned 1990s": "You know that the anarchy of the 1990s discredited both the market economy and democracy." He moderated his statement slightly: "Poor government efficiency and corruption are major problems that everyone can see." From time to time, Putin complains about corruption, but less and less, and his tone has changed. Early on, it was a problem to be resolved. Now he emphasizes that corruption exists everywhere and that Russia is no worse than other countries.[24]

Putin's choice of economic policies is firmly set. He favors macroeconomic stability, as proposed by the liberals. He insists on propping up international currency reserves, secured with a current account surplus, thanks to a competitive floating exchange rate. In his view, the budget should be reasonably close to balanced and public debt minimal. These policies aim at securing Russia's sovereignty. He also desires low inflation and limited unemployment to keep the public satisfied.

For the rest, Putin has opted for statism and protectionism. His code word has become a "strong state," which implicitly means that state companies are allowed to expand and that the power of the state agencies is more important than the rule of law. In foreign trade policy, his favorite topic is the Eurasian Economic Union, whereas he scarcely mentions the World Trade Organization.

Though they remain in high government positions, the remaining liberals cannot defend democracy, the rule of law, or structural reforms.

They have therefore been nicknamed "systemic liberals," prior liberals who have remained within the system but do little for any liberal cause.

In the spring of 2016, Putin encouraged a new discussion about economic policy. His initial signal was to appoint Kudrin, who had been out of government since the fall of 2011, vice chairman of his Economic Council. Kudrin also became president of the Center for Strategic Research, a think tank, which was formerly called the Gref Center when it prepared his reform program in 2000.

Putin convened a first meeting of the Presidium of the Economic Council on May 25, 2016. His obvious but unstated purpose was to prepare for the presidential elections on March 18, 2018. He proposed "that the Economic Council Presidium serves as the platform for holding a whole series of discussions, including on the transformations that will take place in our social sector, in healthcare, education, and the housing and utilities system, technological modernization of our country's economy, improving the business climate, and enhancing our state management system." He encouraged "a broader and more open discussion," continuing "that the Presidium's membership includes people with a range of different views. In some cases, they hold diametrically opposed views." Yet he also told the participants "to put aside as much as possible ideological preferences and not stay locked within particular theoretical constructs and concepts, but to take a pragmatic approach and concentrate on coming up with realistic and objective decisions."[25]

Putin returned to the need for higher economic growth. He lamented that if "we do not find new growth sources, we will see GDP growth of around zero. ... We must simultaneously ensure higher growth rates in the economy and carry out structural reforms to make it more efficient. At the same time, it is very important to preserve macroeconomic stability and not allow the budget deficit to grow and inflation to pick up speed." He called on the participants to "start with the growth sources for Russia's economy over the next decade."[26]

Whereas Putin mentioned the magical phrase "structural reforms," photos of the Economic Council meeting that showed Kudrin sitting far down the table clarified that his standing was not great. This looked more like a trial balloon than a policy declaration.

A year later, answering a question about Kudrin's coming program, Putin said that "the Government is drafting a program too. I have agreed with Prime Minister Dmitry Medvedev that he will present it very soon. We also have other groups working on programs, the Stolypin Club, for example. These are different approaches and often different visions."[27] He could hardly have been more noncommittal, and no program was actually presented. Putin acknowledged that Russia's economy was likely to stay stagnant. Yet he warned against undesired ideological views, and censorship had tightened. Clearly, he did not want much change, and the sophisticated participants understood that.

Both the Center for Strategic Research and the Stolypin Club have published studies numbering thousands of pages about the details in their proposed reforms. Although the number of pages is intimidating, these studies have attracted little public attention, for good reason. With the publication of his empty program decree in May 2018, Putin made it clear that he did not wish to pursue reform of any kind. Glaziev remained as his adviser for Eurasian affairs, and Kudrin became chair of the not very powerful Auditing Chamber.

Each January, Mau's Academy of the National Economy and State Administration organizes the giant Gaidar Forum in memory of Russia's great reformer. For three days, thousands of Russia's social scientists and hundreds of foreigners gather to discuss economic policy. Moscow's economics professors hope to hear something radical and liberal, but they show no interest in challenging the ruling elite. The ministers on the panels are relaxed and open, appearing highly competent, but carefully avoiding stark pronouncements. Russia's large economic establishment is too well off to want to rock the boat, and the conservative elite is sufficiently confident to allow a reasonably open economic discussion.

At the meeting in January 2017, which I attended, the main event was Kudrin's speech. He called for reining in law enforcement agencies, judicial reform, releasing private initiatives, and checking state companies, but quietly and briefly. He did not even mention democracy.[28]

Kudrin and Yevsei Gurvich offered the best presentation of the liberal camp's agenda in an article published in 2014. Having taken a victory lap around macroeconomic stability, they now focused on productivity, which stopped growing after 2009, and they saw no reason for anything but stagnation unless Russia adopted a new growth model. "The problems of our economy are of a chronic character and cannot be resolved with singular measures, such as a softening of the monetary or budget policy. The roots of these problems lie in the weakness of the market, which have been caused by the dominance of state and quasi-state companies, which have distorted objectives . . . and informal relations with the state." They recommended "a radical reduction of the burden of state regulation and defense of property rights."[29]

The expansion of the state and quasi-state sector has emasculated the market forces, and state enterprise managers act like government officials rather than trying to achieve profits. Kudrin and Gurvich called for more competition, stronger property rights, less state regulation, and harder budget constraints to provoke creative destruction. The larger the share of state employment in a region is, the worse its economic performance. Most of all, they emphasized the poor defense of property rights and the excessive regulatory burden on business.

Although their critique was hard in substance, they did not criticize anyone specifically for this unfortunate development. With great political caution, they merely recommended that the government implement numerous existing laws and decrees, such as abandoned privatization plans, reduce political and noncommercial commands to state companies, restore local self-government, establish a stronger antimonopoly policy, and publicly audit state companies. They concluded that it is necessary "to radically weaken the burden of state regulation and defend property rights."[30]

Kudrin has always favored judicial reform and decriminalization of the legal system, and the eminent scholar Vadim Volkov is responsible for his judicial reform proposals. Kudrin has also opposed increased military expenditures and has desired the restoration of good relations with the West. In his public posture, however, he has become more cautious over time.[31]

A typical example of how Kudrin's technocratic Center for Strategic Research operates is a two-hundred-page report of December 2016 evaluating the fulfillment of the official 2008 program known as Strategy 2020 and Putin's eleven decrees of May 2012. The study concludes that only 30 percent of Strategy 2020 has been accomplished, in comparison with 39 percent of the far larger and more ambitious Gref program, or Strategy 2010. This bureaucratic product resulted in one article in the business newspaper *Vedomosti*, but little else. It refrained from the obvious conclusion that Putin is not interested in reforms. Even as economic problems have increased, official political debate has become more cautious.[32]

During a trip to Moscow in October 2017, I met Kudrin and several of his collaborators. Although they were all positive on their program and their freedom to elaborate it, the prospects did not sound very plausible. Kudrin had forty people working full-time on his program and five hundred people altogether engaged in various working groups. To this outsider, the program seemed more like official therapy to keep reformers away from real opposition than any serious effort toward reform.

In 2016, the Stolypin Club was formed as a counterweight to Kudrin and his Center for Strategic Research. The club was named for Petr Stolypin, the authoritarian tsarist reformer and prime minister from 1906 until his assassination in Kiev in 1911. Its leader was Boris Titov, the president's business ombudsman and cochairman of the association for small enterprises Delovaya Rossiya, which the Kremlin had promoted to take the wind out of more independent and liberal business associations.

The Presidium of the Stolypin Club has twenty-one members, all men. They are slightly younger than Kudrin's group, and several are businessmen. They are allowed to participate in public television debates. Several are token liberals, and no outright communist has been included, though the club's most prominent member is Glaziev. The Stolypin Club has taken a big step toward mainstream economics. It calls for a looser monetary policy, but only moderately so, advocating "quantitative easing" and using modern economic discourse. Members present themselves as "market-oriented realists and market-oriented pragmatists."[33]

At Putin's request, the Stolypin Club's economic institute elaborated a growth strategy for Russia to 2025. Its analysis of Russia's economic problems is confusingly similar to that of Kudrin's center. The club regrets that market competition and the role of the private sector have dwindled and that investment projects in most sectors are unprofitable. It points out that in purchasing power parities, Russia ranks fifty-second in the world in GDP per capita. The number of jobs fell by 6.8 million from 2011 to 2015. Western sanctions have restricted Russia's access to capital, and the country suffers from technological backwardness. Entrepreneurs and qualified specialists have emigrated en masse. The quality of institutions and governance is poor.[34]

Yet, with astounding optimism, the Stolypin Club expects Russia's GDP growth to rise to 5–6 percent a year by 2025 by diversifying the economy and developing an innovative business environment. These grand forecasts have not been substantiated by credible policy proposals. The Stolypin Club claims to propose an alternative model of development, stimulating real competition, the growth of a multitude of private enterprises, an inflow of investment, accelerated industrial modernization, and effective social policy. It wants to stimulate investment, consumer demand, and import substitution through a low exchange rate. It favors entrepreneurial initiative, competition between all forms of property, and more private production without stating how. For the rest, the Stolypin Club offers no concrete policy proposals but moves on to "determine a group of first-priority growth projects," as if it has a sound methodology for doing so. The club also calls for a "cardinal reduction of the administrative pressure on business, judicial reform, and reform of the criminal economic legislation." In short, the Stolypin Club wants all good and nothing bad, but it cannot say exactly how.[35]

Both groups agree on the need for a larger private sector, but neither has a credible prescription for this outcome. Kudrin has called for privatization of the entire oil sector within seven to eight years, whereas the Stolypin Club hopes for the emergence of new private enterprises.[36]

Corruption and democracy are the key issues, but both of these insider groups leave such battles to others. Sometimes Kudrin discreetly expresses his preference for freedom and democracy, while the Stolypin Club ignores these themes. Both groups call for judicial reform and the reform of law enforcement, but they downplay the details. The Center for Strategic Research has serious proposals on how to fight corruption, but it does not emphasize them. Titov responded to Kudrin's demands for institutional reforms that "maybe somewhere, some day, when the conditions are right, the 'institutions' will improve, but here and now, everyone will just keep on stealing and taking the riches abroad." Instead, Titov called for a partial rollback of the flexible exchange rate, a looser monetary policy, and subsidized corporate loans.[37]

In one area, they agree, namely on the need for a streamlining and simplification of administrative controls of enterprises, and here Russia has been successful. In his decree on economic policy of May 7, 2012, Putin called for an improvement of "Russia's ranking in the World Bank's ease of doing business index from 120th place in 2011 to 50th place in 2015 and 20th place in 2018." Russia has performed quite well in this regard, rising to the rank of 36 in 2015. This was a measurable variable that did not intrude on the interests of Putin or his cronies but in fact facilitated their enrichment.[38]

The range of discussion has narrowed. Titov's moderate calls for quantitative easing have replaced Glaziev's massive monetary expansion, hard-core nationalism, and statism, while the liberals have become more cautious in their advocacy of democracy and the freedom of political discourse. The murder of Boris Nemtsov on February 27, 2015, taught everyone the danger of criticizing Putin outright. His political preference for the Stolypin Club was made obvious when Titov and his Party of Growth were allowed to participate in the Duma elections in September 2016; Kudrin scarcely dared to ask for such a favor.

Putin has gone through the motions of opening up a public debate, but this discussion has been of little interest to the public. The differences are too small, and the caution is too great. Nobody has stood up against the corruption and for democracy, the two fundamental concerns. This debate has not appeared serious. Presumably Putin wished to render the government policy more credible. He might also have wanted to keep an updated reform program and reform team ready in case the economic situation turned really bad.

Corruption has been a constant concern, but its nature has changed. In the early 1990s, Russia suffered from what Andrei Shleifer and Robert Vishny call disorganized corruption. Anyone anywhere could demand bribes but did not necessarily deliver the services the bribe payer had purchased.[39]

Over time, the number of bribes has declined while the size of the average bribe has increased and the total volume of bribes has grown, as Transparency International and Georgy Satarov's INDEM Foundation have shown in multiple surveys. Corruption has become concentrated among ever fewer people at the top of the Russian society.[40]

Although surveys have been many and are publicly available, for a surprisingly long time corruption did not catch on as a political theme. No major political figures focused on corruption as their main political plank. The Russian elite is so permeated with corruption that few want to throw stones because they are painfully aware of living in glass houses. Putin has responded by accusing opposition activists, such as Khodorkovsky and former prime minister Mikhail Kasyanov, of corruption. In addition, honest people have corrupt friends, whom they do not wish to embarrass. Nor do they want to irritate their funders. Many liberals, moreover, consider it populist to criticize corruption, fearing that it may result in arrests of the innocent and Soviet-style repression. Last, many anticorruption activists and journalists have been murdered, showing the dangers of public criticism of corruption.

In 2008, the booklet *Putin and Gazprom,* by the opposition activists Boris Nemtsov and Vladimir Milov, broke the mold. It showed in considerable detail how Putin and his friends enriched themselves. It attained an extraordinary circulation. Nemtsov told me that it was downloaded 1.5 million times. Nemtsov and Milov followed up with other devastating booklets about corruption in Putin's inner circle. They led street protests, but society was not ready, and in February 2015, Nemtsov was brazenly murdered outside the Kremlin wall.[41]

Around 2010, a new opposition star emerged, the anticorruption lawyer and blogger Alexei Navalny. He made corruption the main argument against Putin and his regime. Navalny bought shares in state companies to receive information, targeting their corrupt practices. His big breakthrough was the revelation that the management of Transneft, the state oil pipeline company, had stolen $4 billion while building the Eastern Siberia–Pacific Ocean oil pipeline. Transneft's former CEO Semen Vainshtok, who had been sacked and emigrated to Israel, was blamed. Putin's friend from the KGB in Dresden Nikolai Tokarev took over, but the case was never brought to court.[42]

During the popular protests against election fraud from November 2011 to May 2012, Navalny surged as Russia's foremost opposition leader and was arrested repeatedly. He called the ruling United Russia party the "Party of Swindlers and Thieves," a label that stuck in the public conscience. In September 2013, Navalny cemented his position as opposition leader by gathering an official vote count of 27 percent in the mayoral election in Moscow despite a media blockade and massive harassment.

To eliminate Navalny, the Russian authorities convicted him and his brother in December 2014 of money laundering and defrauding their business partners. Navalny received a suspended sentence of three and a half years, while his brother, Oleg, got a real prison sentence of the same length. This was a pure kangaroo court. The brothers Navalny complained to the European Court of Human Rights (ECHR) and won against the Russian Federation in October 2017. The court declared the verdict against the Navalny brothers "arbitrary and manifestly unreasonable" and ordered the Russian government to pay them compensation, which the government did. Even so, the government kept Oleg Navalny in prison for his full sentence of three and a half years.[43]

In another case, a Russian court found Navalny guilty of embezzlement in a timber firm called Kirovles and gave him a five-year suspended jail sentence. The ECHR had already rejected that verdict and ordered a retrial. Navalny considered that the aim of this trial was to block his participation in the presidential election in March 2018.[44]

After the authorities quelled the popular unrest, Navalny continued to focus on corruption. He founded a small nongovernmental organization, the Anti-Corruption Foundation (*Fond bor'by s korruptsiei*, FBK), which has developed great skill with social media. Navalny produces weekly programs on Google-owned YouTube, exposing high-level corruption. He concludes each program with the refrain: "Here we tell the truth."[45]

Two of Navalny's investigative documentaries have attracted extraordinary popular attention. In December 2015, Navalny aired the film *Chaika*, about Russia's prosecutor general Yuri Chaika's two sons, whom he revealed as filthy-rich organized criminals, the older son even being a billionaire. No fewer than seven million people have viewed this film on YouTube, and the authorities did nothing to block it. Chaika himself dismissed the film as garbage. Curiously, nothing happened either to him or to Navalny. In his annual big press conference on December 17, 2015, Putin responded lamely to a question about Chaika's sons that if they had done something wrong, the relevant authorities would investigate them.[46]

In December 2016, the United States adopted the Global Magnitsky Human Rights Accountability Act. It envisioned sanctions for people all over the world responsible for "extrajudicial killings, torture, or other gross violations of internationally recognized human rights" or complicit in "acts of significant corruption." The elder son, Artem Chaika, was one of the first people to be sanctioned on the Global Magnitsky list.[47]

On March 2, 2017, Navalny launched an even more outstanding documentary, "Do Not Call Him Dimon" (diminutive for Dmitry) about the alleged corruption of Prime Minister Dmitri Medvedev. It suggests that the seemingly powerless and diminutive prime minister is a major crook. Twenty-five million have seen this video on YouTube, as have a few million on the Russian social network Odnoklassniki. With meticulous documentation, Navalny shows six estates, two vineyards (one in Tuscany), and two yachts, all belonging to Medvedev, through nongovernmental organizations set up for the sole purpose of benefiting Medvedev and his wife. These NGOs have boards and managers who are friends of Medvedev.[48]

Navalny states that Medvedev's fortune has been financed through $1.2 billion of bribes, with the two biggest contributors being the Russian multibillionaires Alisher Usmanov and Leonid Mikhelson. Usmanov made his fortune by privatizing Gazprom's steelworks in the 1990s, whereas Mikhelson is the leading partner with Timchenko in Novatek and has also made his fortune on Gazprom. Both are among the wealthiest men in Russia.

The official resistance against the Navalny film about Medvedev was surprisingly timid. Not all too convincingly, Medvedev defended himself that Navalny was "a sentenced criminal" who had "political ambitions." He asked: "Who benefits from this?" After one month, Usmanov started attacking Navalny on the Internet quite viciously but not very convincingly. He sued Navalny in a Moscow court for libel, which he of course won.[49]

On March 26, 2017, Navalny called for national protests against corruption and attracted an estimated sixty thousand protesters, many of them teenagers, in more than eighty cities all over Russia. The main slogans targeted Medvedev, but a second prominent slogan was "Putin is a thief" (*Putin vor*). Navalny repeated these protests on an even larger scale in almost two hundred cities on June 12. These protests were the largest since May 2012, and the size of the March protest came as a general surprise.

Navalny is currently the most interesting political leader in Russia, although he barely registers in the opinion polls. After a political trial-and-error process, he has concentrated on top-level corruption, pursuing investigative reporting at its best. He hangs out one top culprit after another in well-documented films. He uses drones to film the properties of the affluent and retrieves documents from official registers, showing the nature and scale of Russia's corruption, though he does not discuss the cure. Navalny uses crowdsourcing, avoiding funding from rich Russian businessmen or foreigners. He works skillfully with social media, targeting the young and the provinces. Navalny long avoided attacking Putin himself for larceny, but now he also scourges Putin for major corruption. Navalny has been arrested many times, seriously harassed, injured, and sentenced to prison, but he has proven his courage. Given the political situation in Russia, it is remarkable that he is alive and can operate there.

Two objections are being raised against Navalny. One is that he has been toying with Russian nationalism with his earlier slogan, "Stop feeding the Caucasus!" (*Khvatit' kormit' Kavkaz!*), but Putin's support for Chechnya's ruthless dictator Kadyrov through massive state subsidies has been a mainstay of his power. Moreover, most European center-right parties combine a mixture of three elements: economic liberalism, mild nationalism, and some religious values.

The other criticism of Navalny is that he does not have a full economic policy program, but the Russian democratic opposition is nowhere near achieving political power. It needs to concentrate on a few key questions to gain cohesion and popular support rather than splintering because of policy details. Navalny wisely tries to keep a broad front together by focusing on corruption.

The official economic debate in Russia is stuck. It remains ideologically frozen with a division between liberalism and statism. Even the combatants remain the same as in the 1990s, though they are twenty years older. The public discourse is repetitive and timid, since the freedom of expression has been reduced, and the participants know that the probability of implementing serious reform is minimal. It appears as an imitation of a debate, like a reshuffling of the deck chairs on the *Titanic*.

Alexei Kudrin's Center for Strategic Research stands against Boris Titov's Stolypin Club. Both groups agree that Russia suffers from near stagnation because of minimal growth in productivity, which is further depressed by the declining workforce. Kudrin wants to resolve this problem through structural reforms to stimulate supply, whereas Titov wants to jumpstart the economy with fiscal and monetary stimulus, which he alleges will somehow also stimulate productivity.

Kudrin and his systemic liberals have won Putin's support when it comes to macroeconomic stability because Russia's financial crash of August 1998 taught Putin that financial destabilization also means political destabilization. For the rest, the statists have won. The state sector expands steadily in spite of miserable economic and innovative performance, becoming more secretive and monopolistic. To the limited extent that Putin cares about technical progress, he expects it to come from the state-owned military-industrial complex. In foreign trade, he has chosen import substitution, protectionism, and the Eurasian Economic Union, taking his cue from Glaziev. Putin shows no credible interest in the reform of law enforcement or the judiciary.

This official economic discussion is stale because the economists do not really want to discuss the main problems—corruption and weak property rights. None of these problems can be solved without democratization. Both liberals and statists seem to agree on this, without saying so too loudly, but as a result, they have all lost touch with the real popular concerns.

Rather than improving technicalities, the economic debate needs to focus on Russia's essential problem, the capture of the state by a small ruling elite. Navalny has done this by focusing on corruption and has thus risen to be the central political opponent of the current policy, as the undisputed opposition leader. He has transformed the Russian economic debate. It is no longer liberalism versus socialism that is the relevant paradigm but reform versus corruption.

The new Russian government in May 2018 showed that Putin was not interested in any reform or change. Many ministers changed, but most could be described as technocrats, lacking particular views and political platforms. Their main property is loyalty to Putin. Kudrin did not get a government job but was appointed head of the apolitical Auditing Chamber, which has not had any impact under Putin.

Conclusion

Where Is Russia Going, and What
Should the West Do?

We must not have any illusions. My aim in this book is to establish what regime Vladimir Putin has built, where it is going, how it is likely to act, and how the West can influence it. Putin has constructed an iron quadrangle of four circles of power. The first circle is the vertical state power; the second circle consists of the big state enterprises; the third circle comprises his cronies; and the fourth circle is the Anglo-American offshore havens, where he and the cronies can safely keep their money.

This system can deliver macroeconomic stability but only minimal economic growth: it is so petrified that it is more likely to collapse than reform. Its minimal economic growth may not suffice for political stability. Russia's assets are unbalanced in favor of military, not economic, power, which naturally tempts the Kremlin to opt for armed aggression, which can mobilize the nation to give Putin some legitimacy.

The West needs to safeguard its military defenses to avoid being drawn into war, but its main approach to Russia should be transparency at home. Hundreds of billions of dollars of ill-gotten Russian wealth is hidden in Western offshore havens, primarily in the United States and the United Kingdom. All Western countries should demand the revelation of all beneficiary owners. All monetary flows should be subject to ordinary bank regulation, and Western governments should devote sufficient resources to investigate tainted funds in the West. Then they can break up the fourth circle of the Anglo-American offshore havens.

With the help of his loyal friends, Putin has built three circles of power—the state, the state enterprises, and the cronies' companies. Putin's first term appears to be a masterpiece of consolidation of power by a budding authoritarian. He was everything to everyone. In the eyes of liberals, he pursued excellent market economic reforms and seemed to build the rule of law. The giveaway was his immediate clampdown on independent television, which was well understood by human rights activists, but he pursued an elaborate salami tactic, cutting off one television channel after the other, accusing each one of poor finances or specific crimes.

State power comprises Putin's first circle. As chairman of the FSB in 1998–1999, he seized control over the secret police. In the summer of 2000, he took charge of television. Next, he established his "vertical of power" over the federal and regional administrations. His "dictatorship of law" over the judicial system ensued. In the elections in December 2003, Putin gained solid control over the State Duma and the Federation Council. At the Security Council, the pinnacle of power, his top men are three contemporary KGB generals from St. Petersburg, his successors as FSB chairs—Sergei Ivanov, Nikolai Patrushev, and Alexander Bortnikov.

Putin's second circle consists of the big state enterprises. He seized control of them one by one, starting with Gazprom in May 2001. He appointed his loyalists as chief executives and chairmen of their supervisory boards and rounded off his victory lap with the formation of the state corporations in 2007. The state enterprises have been allowed to expand with cheap state funding, often monopolizing their sector. They have been buttressed with protectionist measures, and the only governance that matters is obedience to Putin. Russian state capitalism is peculiarly disinterested in competition, investment, technological development, entrepreneurship, and productivity. The state sector is treated as a source of power and rents instead of an object of economic growth. The three top state managers are Igor Sechin of Rosneft, Alexei Miller of Gazprom, and Sergei Chemezov of Rostec.[1]

The third circle is more idiosyncratic. It comprises Putin's top private cronies and their companies. The four top cronies appear to be

Gennady Timchenko, Arkady and Boris Rotenberg, and Yuri Kovalchuk. Their activity usually appears not only corrupt but kleptocratic. Yet because he controls Russian legislation, Putin has legalized many of their dubious activities. The cronies are entitled to buy assets from state companies at basement prices and provide state procurement at high prices without competition. Since 2006, the ruble has been fully convertible and Russia maintains liberal currency regulations. The cronies can thus transfer their palpable gains to offshore havens.

International offshore havens form the fourth circle. The two biggest offshore havens are the United States and the United Kingdom. The United States even allows law firms to circumvent bank regulations on a massive scale. The US and UK acceptance of secrecy of ownership and anonymous currency inflows is critical for the sustenance of the Putin regime.[2]

The Putin economic system is based on monopolies and cartels. The most important economic sectors are divided among a few companies, which in turn are each dominated by one person. Oil and gas production belongs to five companies—Gazprom, Rosneft, Novatek, Surgut, and Lukoil. Pipelines are built by the companies belonging to either the Rotenbergs or Timchenko. The crony company Sogaz is the leading insurance company. Rotenberg's Mostotrest is responsible for big road construction projects. Mergers are allowed, but antitrust is not. Creative destruction appears to be declining, as is new enterprise formation. Competition is dissuaded or worse, allowing the incumbent companies to reap monopoly rents. Outstanding new entrepreneurs tend to emigrate. The South Korean chaebols (family-owned conglomerates) are quite an inspiration. This system is the opposite of a competitive market economy.[3]

These four circles comply with the German fascist thinker Robert Michels's idea of the iron law of oligarchy, with various circles of power reinforcing one another and, eventually, all organizations controlled by a leadership class. In 1993, Daniel Yergin and Thane Gustafson published a book offering various future scenarios for Russia in 2010. One scenario, the "two-headed eagle," is remarkably similar to contemporary Russia. It "is based on a coalition of three groups, managers of large industries (with the defense industries at their core); the central bureaucracies in Moscow; and military, police, and state-security officers." The only elements missing are the cronies and the financial offshore havens.[4]

The countries that are most comparable to Russia are China and Brazil, which are both big countries with a system of crony capitalism that are at a similar level of economic development, but they are very different. China is fast-growing and innovative, still ruled by the Communist Party. The Chinese state sector is far smaller than the Russian, and shrinking, and China is more decentralized. But Russia has a freer market than China and has long been recognized as a market economy by both the European Union and the United States.[5]

Brazil appears to be a more relevant comparison for Russia, but its disparities are also great. However imperfect, Brazil is a democracy, and it has a surprisingly strong judicial system that, in sharp contrast to Russia, has sentenced its past three presidents to prison. Brazil's private sector is far larger than Russia's, but so are its income and education differentials.

In a BRICS context, Russia stands out as having particularly centralized authoritarian politics, a large monopolistic state sector without interest in development or profits, and an elaborate crony system, while it performs well in terms of economic level, education, and openness.

The behavior of Russia's super-rich raises many eyebrows. Why do multibillionaires want to make so much more money? Why are they so short-sighted and invest so little? Why do they transfer billions abroad, investing in real estate or large yachts they rarely use? Why do they waste so much money on lavish consumption? Why don't they stand up to Putin?

The main answer to all these questions is that property rights are very weak in Russia. Everybody adjusts their behavior accordingly. Tragically, Russia has reverted to what Richard Pipes has termed the patrimonial state, a state with weaker property rights than a feudal state and in which everything depends on the whims of the tsar.[6]

In the absence of a reliable judiciary, trust and obedience become the basic values. In *First Person*, Putin repeatedly returned to the topic of trust. When pressed by KGB colleagues to betray St. Petersburg mayor Sobchak in the early 1990s, Putin rebuked them: "Can't you see that this man trusts me?" When asked about his later longtime close collaborators Sergei Ivanov and Alexei Kudrin, Putin answered "trust." He did not specify, but he appeared to mean absolute loyalty. In his choice of early partners, Putin did not differ from the early oligarchic groups, such as Menatep (Yukos) or the Alfa Group, which were formed by men who had been college pals. All these groups were based on trust, based on friendship among young men.[7]

In the early 2000s, leading Russian private companies, such as Yukos and Lukoil, opted for transparency and good corporate governance. They formalized and publicized their ownership. They published audited financial results, appointed independent directors, listed on international stock markets, and attracted minority shareholders. The erstwhile oligarchs were gentrifying at an amazing speed, and the public trading of their stocks enhanced their fortunes. If this process had continued, Russia might have been able to become a normal capitalist country with transferable ownership and democracy.

But Putin ended this process abruptly with the lawless confiscation of Yukos in 2004–2005. In Putin's eyes, Khodorkovsky had committed many sins, such as opposing him, setting up his own political block in the Duma, and pursuing his own foreign policy, but Putin's main objective seemed to be to defeat the oligarchs as a class by taking out the wealthiest and most daring of them.

The jailing of Khodorkovsky and the confiscation of Yukos had many consequences. Once again, ownership became concealed, anchored in offshore havens, and property rights became less safe. Russia's big businessmen know that they can keep their assets only if they prove their obedience to the ruler and pay him the required tribute. In medieval fashion, political opposition can be punished through the confiscation of all property. After the seizure of Yukos, Russia's oligarchs started talking about their property as something temporary they had borrowed from the state.

Human beings are fragile, and the men of Putin's generation have reached retirement age, necessitating a mechanism for transfer of their wealth. Putin faced three choices. One was to democratize and modernize. Another option was to build a fascist police state, a Sparta. A third possibility was to establish a new aristocracy, drawing on Russia's tsarist tradition, which appears to be Putin's choice. Political scientist Francis Fukuyama notes that "the natural human propensity to favor family and friends— . . . patrimonialism—constantly reasserts itself in the absence of strong countervailing incentives."[8]

Russia is developing a new tsarist aristocratic system, a hereditary plutocracy. The princes are immensely rich, but they are all dependent on the tsar. They are building themselves eighteenth-century palaces either in the late baroque manner of the Italian architect Francesco Bartolomeo Rastrelli or in the neoclassical style of Catherine II's favorite architect, Scotsman Charles Cameron. Such conspicuous luxury is characteristic of people who know that their gains are ill gotten and easily lost.

Stalinism severely disrupted the family, but today it has recovered at the expense of the Soviet collective. Family has taken over from political and judicial institutions, and it rules Russia through a vertical state apparatus confusingly similar to tsarist Russia. It is distinct from the Soviet regime with its Marxist-Leninist ideology and Communist Party, though all three regimes share a tradition of a strong secret police and military. The new dominance of the family testifies to the deinstitutionalization of the state. The outstanding Russian political analyst Lilia Shevtsova noticed this pattern as early as 2005.[9]

Wealthy businessmen outside the immediate Putin circle are left without secure property rights. They have little choice but to pay tribute to the rulers in the Kremlin, the single political authority. During Putin's first term, two oligarchs told me that when they were called to the Kremlin, they were asked to put up $10 million or $20 million in "donations," either for Putin's reelection campaign or for some other charitable purpose. . . . Putin attracted $300 million in "donations" for the reconstruction of the Konstantinov Palace in St. Petersburg, which became the president's official residence there.[10]

The Panama Papers show how private big Russian businessmen have paid large "donations" to Putin's cellist friend Sergei Roldugin, who seems to hold funds for Putin. The eloped junior Putin partner Sergei Kolesnikov named two major donors to the Putin funds, the big businessmen Roman Abramovich and Alexei Mordashov. At the end of 2003, just after Khodorkovsky's arrest, Mordashov's steel and mining company Severstal bought 9 percent of Bank Rossiya for $20 million, which was later written down. The Panama Papers record that companies close to Mordashov had paid Roldugin $30 million for "consulting services."[11]

The oligarchs from the 1990s who have not fallen out with Putin have gradually sold off their holdings in Russia and transferred their fortunes to safer places abroad. Prominent examples are Roman Abramovich, who sold Sibneft to Gazprom and the television company ORT to the Russian government; the four owners of Alfa Group, Viktor Vekselberg, and Len Blavatnik, who sold TNK-BP to Rosneft; and Dmitry Rybolovlev, who sold Uralkali to other Russian businessmen. Although they still own substantial assets in Russia, these and other wealthy businessmen are no longer leading forces in the country but tread softly, and they appear to spend most of their time abroad.[12]

In the early 2000s, the ideas of peace and free markets had conquered the world, but that time has passed. In 2005, Berkeley professor Steven Fish assessed that democracy had been derailed in Russia. The Freedom House has documented that for the past decade democracy has not gained but lost ground worldwide. Thomas Wright concludes that the convergence myth is over, and so is the transition to democracy. Samuel Huntington's famous third wave of democratization, which started with the Carnation Revolution in Portugal in 1974 and went through Southern Europe, Latin America, and Eastern Europe, is long over.[13]

Russia is no longer pursuing democratic or market economic reforms. The current regime is a personal authoritarian rule that aims to maintain and enrich its ruling elite. The nation and its people do not really matter to these rulers as long as they "hang in there," as Prime Minister Dmitri Medvedev so vividly put it in a conversation with pensioners in Crimea in 2016. Unless energy prices skyrocket or Russia seizes large foreign assets, its economy cannot generate significant growth, while macroeconomic stability is likely to hold. As political scientist Ivan Krastev states: "Russia is not an illiberal democracy by default: it is an illiberal democracy by design."[14]

Putin has been one of the global leaders of the reversal of democracy, building a neofeudal, patrimonial, and plutocratic system. He has meticulously annihilated the budding institutions of capitalism, democracy, and the rule of law that emerged in Russia in the 1990s. In their place, he has formed a strong vertical of power controlled by his cronies, who oppose the rule of law, favoring their own unlimited powers over the state. The current Russian rulers, who have destroyed all beneficial institutions, will not start rebuilding them.

This ruling group has proscribed civil society with discretionary laws. The Soviet prohibition against "speculation" impeded the emergence of a normal market economy. Now trade is allowed, but similar laws against "extremism" hinder the evolution of a normal civil society. An undesired view can send a culprit to prison for up to six years. Independent nongovernmental organizations can be prohibited as "undesired" or as "foreign agents." With political control of the judiciary, anybody can be sentenced to prison for some obscure economic crime not committed; Alexei Navalny is the prime example.[15]

Russia is not alone. The Corruption Perceptions Index of Transparency International depicts vast corruption in the region. Ten of the twelve post-Soviet countries are among the worst ranked, ranging from 107th to 167th (out of 180 countries ranked in 2017), and the situation has not improved but deteriorated slightly in the past decade. Russia ranks 135th. Only Georgia has managed to get corruption under control, rising to 46th place, and Belarus ranks 68th.[16]

Authoritarianism and corruption go together. The postcommunist countries fall into three distinct groups. The eleven countries in Central and Eastern Europe that have joined the European Union are all full democracies, as defined by Freedom House, and have corruption under control, according to Transparency International. They represent a positive, stable equilibrium. Their opposites are seven post-Soviet countries led by Russia that are both highly corrupt and authoritarian, forming a negative stable equilibrium. Both equilibriums are strong and not easily shaken. The fundamental insight is that corruption is not an accident but cherished by the ruling elite (fig. 9.1).[17]

The most interesting country is Ukraine because it is a complete outlier (together with Moldova). It is as corrupt as Russia but is almost a full democracy, reflecting an extreme disequilibrium. Either Ukraine moves toward authoritarianism, as under President Viktor Yanukovych, or Ukraine's democrats gain control over the state and establish real democracy with the rule of law. Ukraine is therefore the natural battleground between the Kremlin and the European Union, which Putin seems to understand better than most. This is a battle of unmitigated

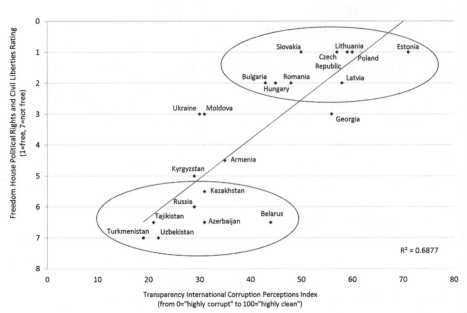

Fig. 9.1 Democracy and corruption, 2017. *Sources: Freedom House (2018);*
Transparency International (2018)

enrichment of the elite versus democracy and the rule of law, and not
a fight over the reestablishment of the Russian Empire. Putin might
be right in seeing this struggle as the greatest threat to his regime in
Russia.[18]

Russia has experienced nine years of stagnation since 2009. Its GDP
per capita approaches $10,000 at current exchange rates. Is this a mid-
dle-income trap? An IMF paper defines "middle-income trap" as "the
phenomenon of hitherto rapidly growing economies stagnating at middle-income levels and failing to graduate into the ranks of high-income
countries." This growth slowdown usually occurs around $10,000 per
capita.[19]

The concept of middle-income trap is statistically controversial,
but Russia appears to have gotten stuck in such a trap at a typical middle-
income level. Its public and external finances are stable, but it does not
generate much innovation or increased productivity. In 1976, Soviet leader Leonid Brezhnev talked about the need to move from extensive to in-

tensive growth at the Twenty-Fifth Congress of the Communist Party of the Soviet Union in a similar fashion. Naturally, it never happened. Although Russia currently has a market economy, competition is restricted, and its institutions do not appear to allow much economic growth.

The critical feature is probably Russia's institutional transformation. Distinguishing between the enforcement of property rights and contractual obligations, the economists Daron Acemoglu and Simon Johnson find that "property rights institutions have a major influence on long-run economic growth, investment and financial development, while contracting institutions . . . have a more limited impact on growth."[20]

This Russian model of combined corruption and authoritarianism matches the idea of Daron Acemoglu and James Robinson of regimes as either inclusive or extractive, entering vicious or virtuous cycles of governance. Russia's model is extractive, and the country is firmly stuck in a vicious equilibrium. Market economic reform is unlikely under Russia's current administration, because it requires judicial and political reforms, which are anathema to this regime. Periodic reports that Putin is preparing serious market reforms can be dismissed as propaganda or disinformation. Only a new regime collapse is likely to initiate reforms aiming at the building of the rule of law and democracy, though nobody can guarantee that a new government will succeed.[21]

An additional observation by Acemoglu is that property rights and the rule of law are more important for economic growth at a higher level of economic development. He argues that oligarchic property rights might deliver faster growth at an early stage of development with large economies of scale and limited technological demands, when the dominant obstacles are administrative barriers, which big business can break more easily. An intermediary industry, such as steelworks, has done well under oligarchic rule in Russia. At a higher stage of economic development, the rule of law and the reinforcement of intellectual property rights are more important for economic growth because they boost small and medium-sized enterprises, innovations, and creative destruction.[22]

Economic growth is determined by capital (investment), technology, human capital, and institutions. Because of the capital flight, Russia loses 3–4 percent of GDP in investment each year, and about as much does not arrive as foreign direct investment because of poor property rights and Western sanctions. Russia's labor force is projected to decrease by slightly less than 1 percent a year for the next decade, and Russia's expenditures on education are miserly. Russia is suffering from a steady deinstitutionalization. The only plausible positive influence would come from imported technology, rising commodity prices, and foreign demand.

Russia is thus caught in an antireform trap, maintained by both political and institutional forces. The ruling elite of top state officials, law enforcement, state corporations, and cronies holds power, and this elite would be the chief victim of reform. The rich and powerful would suffer a loss of rents if property rights and the rule of law were enforced at home, whereas they enjoy excellent legal protection abroad. Meanwhile, the opposition is weak, and its freedom and resources are shrinking. The deinstitutionalization and personalization of Russian state power have gone far. Therefore, no institutional preconditions appear to exist for Russia to break out of the middle-income trap short of regime collapse.[23]

Russia is a classical declining power, but its powers wane at different speeds. The disparity between its current military and economic powers is great and potentially explosive, and Russia's economic regression aggravates this tension.

The first dimension of power is demographic. Russia's population has been roughly stagnant at 143 million since the dissolution of the Soviet Union in 1991. If 2 million Crimeans are included, the population increases to the current official number of 145 million. Many have forecast a drastic contraction of Russia's population, but high immigration from poorer former Soviet republics has balanced low Russian birth rates and high death rates, leaving Russia's population stagnant. At present, Russia is the ninth most populous country in the world after Bangladesh but before Mexico. Several countries, including Ethiopia and the Democratic Republic of Congo, are set to soon overtake Russia, squeezing it out of the top ten.[24]

The second dimension is economic. GDP is measured either at current exchange rate or at purchasing power parities (PPP), which is considered more relevant for the comparative economic strength of a country. The International Monetary Fund, which publishes the authoritative statistics, ranked Russia sixth in the world in terms of GDP at PPP in 2017, accounting for no less than 3.2 percent of global GDP, superseded only by China, the United States, India, Japan, and Germany, though the Russian numbers look strangely high. Russia's GDP in current US dollars, by contrast, was merely $1.53 billion, leaving Russia as the twelfth largest economy in the world after South Korea and just before Australia and Spain. Similarly, by export volume Russia ranks eleventh in the world.[25]

The level of economic development is illustrated best by GDP per capita. In 2017, Russia's GDP per capita at current exchange rates was merely $10,608, according to the IMF, leaving it in the sixtieth place in the world, after all EU countries except Bulgaria and after Argentina, but just before the BRICS partners China and Brazil. Whereas Russia's GDP at current exchange rates swings with the price of oil, it is essentially an upper-middle-income country with a GDP per capita of about $10,000.[26]

A third dimension is military power, where Russia excels. According to the authoritative Stockholm International Peace Research Institute (SIPRI), Russia has the third largest military expenditures in the world at $69 billion in 2016, though US military expenditures were nine times larger at $611 billion, and the Chinese spent $215 billion. Whereas most other countries have been disarming since 1991, Russia has been arming since 2008. Carrying out a major rearmament and modernization of its forces, it boosted its military expenditures from 3.3 percent of GDP in 2008 to 5.3 percent in 2016, according to SIPRI (fig. 9.2). Meanwhile, the United States reduced its military expenditures from a peak of 4.7 percent of GDP in 2010 to 3.3 percent in 2016. Russia cannot rival the United States or China militarily, but it is far stronger than any other military power in Europe. It remains a superpower in one single area, nuclear arms, with the United States as its only peer.[27]

Russia could have other dimensions of power. Starting in 2006, after oil prices had surged, Russian leaders began to talk about Russia as an "energy superpower." In recent years, Russia, Saudi Arabia, and the United States have rivaled one another as the largest energy producer in the world, but after the halving of energy prices in 2014, energy has lost much of its allure. Russia had the preconditions to excel in research and technology, but since it has not developed these favorable conditions, numerous outstanding Russian researchers and high-tech entrepreneurs have emigrated to the United States.[28]

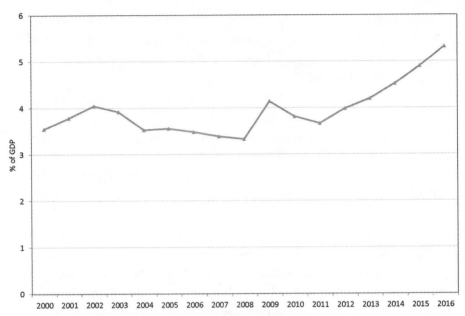

Fig. 9.2 Russian military expenditure as percentage of GDP, 2000–2016.
Source: SIPRI Military Expenditure Database

Russia's assets lack balance. With the world's ninth largest but stagnant population, Russia is set to decline economically and militarily. In
economic strength, it ranks from sixth to twelfth depending on the measure, and it will fall further. Its military still ranks number three, but its
military strength will dwindle with the weakening economy. Only in
nuclear arms can Russia spar with the United States. Such a combination of assets is scary and characteristic of a declining power. For the
Kremlin, the temptation might be overwhelming to exploit its military
strength while it still can. Quite logically, it has pursued three wars since
2014—the annexation of Crimea, the incursion into eastern Ukraine,
and the military intervention in Syria.

Putin's understanding of the sources of his regime's legitimacy appears
impressive. His first two terms, 2000–2008, can be summarized as political stability and a rising standard of living. Russians were tired of the
unruly 1990s. They desired political stability, democratic or not. Initially,
Putin spoke favorably of democracy. He denied that Russia would need

a special path, claiming that it had "already been found. It's the path of democratic development," though he gradually played down democracy's benefits. In 2012, Putin exclaimed, "The anarchy of the 1990s led to the discrediting of the market economy and democracy as such." But he explained, "Democracy is first of all the implementation of laws."[29]

In February 2008, Putin made a triumphant speech before the State Council, summarizing his accomplishments. "Russia has returned to the global stage as a strong state," and "the main thing we achieved is stability." The decade 1999–2008 delivered the greatest growth in Russia's history. The average annual real GDP growth was 7 percent, and the standard of living rose even faster. At current exchange rates, Russia's GDP skyrocketed from $200 billion in 1999 to $1.9 billion in 2008. Lev Gudkov, head of the Levada Center, an independent polling organization, notes that "popular support for Putin is based primarily on consumption growth."[30]

Since 2009, by contrast, the Russian economy has almost stagnated, and a broad consensus expects the growth rate to linger at 1.5–2 percent a year for the foreseeable future. The Russian people have not yet expressed much discontent, but this figure cannot arouse much enthusiasm. As discussed in chapter 3, Putin focuses successfully on macroeconomic stability, with low inflation and minimal unemployment, but his policies are barely raising the standard of living. The Russian popular reaction to the global financial crisis was a grateful remembrance of the good decade: "It was too good. It could not last forever." But for how long will that satisfaction last?

Political stability has gradually turned into political repression and manipulation. In the 1990s, Russia's television, led by Vladimir Gusinsky's NTV, was outstanding, but with increasing Kremlin control it has become so propagandistic that it is losing credibility. Most Russians still rely on television for their news, but eventually the discrepancy between official television and reality is likely to become too blatant.

By standard definitions, Putin's regime is a personal authoritarian system. Such regimes usually end with the death or ouster of the incumbent. The regime has no spiritual source of legitimacy, such as monarchy, ideology, party, nationalism, or religion. As Lilia Shevtsova wrote before Putin's departure as president in 2008: "There is a growing fear that with his departure [as president in 2008] Putin's pyramid will begin to crumble, since it was created for a particular individual." It did survive, because Putin did not leave, but if he ever does, the legitimacy of his regime would crumble.[31]

Putin seems acutely aware of his need for another source of legitimacy besides stability. The Kremlin keeps itself well informed with several alternative opinion polls to understand what is going on among the population, and the FSB is focused more on gathering intelligence than on repression. Putin sees popular uprisings in Russia's global neighborhood as a threat to his power in Russia but also as an opportunity to enhance his legitimacy by rallying the nation against an external enemy.

An oft-quoted line in official Russian discourse is: "We need a small victorious war." The tsarist minister of interior Vyacheslav von Plehve uttered these words in early 1904 before the disastrous Russo-Japanese War, which became neither small nor victorious, but the Russian foreign policy elite continues to cherish this idea, just as the Roman emperors offered the people bread and circus. With less bread available, the demand for circus increases, and today circus equals war.

Putin knows how to boost his legitimacy through small, victorious wars. He rose to popularity and the presidency on the back of the housing bombings in the fall of 1999 and the ensuing second Chechen war. In 2003, his arrest of Khodorkovsky amounted to a war on the oligarchs. It won him the Duma elections in December 2003 and the presidential elections in March 2004.[32]

After President Mikheil Saakashvili had quashed organized crime and corruption in Georgia, Putin pursued a five-day war in Georgia, August 8–12, 2008. It was an ideal small, victorious war. It was a real war, but brief and not very costly. It raised Putin's popularity to a new height, according to the Levada Center.[33]

In the winter of 2013, a new democratic outbreak occurred in Ukraine, but this time Putin was prepared. In February 2014, he instigated the swift occupation of Crimea, and on March 18 he annexed it before the new Ukrainian government could organize any resistance. This action was approved by no less than 88 percent of Russians, according to the Levada Center, taking Putin's popularity to the highest point ever.[34]

The Crimean success encouraged the Kremlin to proceed. It attempted uprisings in the half of Ukraine with a predominantly Russian-speaking population in April–May 2014, but it failed except in parts of the two easternmost regions of Donetsk and Luhansk, where troops backed, equipped, and commanded by Russian military have been bogged down in a low-intensity war without evident solution. The war in the Donbas has been neither small nor victorious, though the Russian government has shown great financial restraint, limiting its costs.

The Russian war in the Donbas indicates a major Russian weakness. The Kremlin tries by all means to hide the human losses of Russian soldiers, volunteers, and locals. Independent activists have reported hundreds of concealed deaths, but they have been subject to uncommonly severe repression and censorship, showing that the Kremlin does not want to let these numbers out. By contrast, the Ukrainian government publishes its losses daily; more than ten thousand people have been killed on the Ukrainian side. Presumably, the losses on the Russian side are of a similar nature, but we have no summarized data. The body bags coming home from Afghanistan are widely considered a major reason for the late Soviet aversion to war, and their number was limited to fifteen thousand, so the large secret human losses in the Donbas might be a dangerous destabilizing factor for the regime.[35]

In September 2015, Putin opted for a new military endeavor, a limited military intervention in Syria. His action turned the civil war in Syria to the advantage of the incumbent regime of Bashar al-Assad. It has not been very costly, but it has not aroused any enthusiasm among ordinary Russians, while it greatly raised Russia's international standing.

Putin's actions are reminiscent of Tsar Nicholas I, who functioned as the gendarme of Europe during the liberal European revolutions of 1848–1849, quashing democratic uprisings from Poland to Hungary. In a similar fashion, Putin sees the so-called colored revolutions as his main enemy, whether they occur in post-Soviet or Arab countries.

The Kremlin's increasing inclination to pursue small wars to mobilize the Russian nation may be rational, but this tactic is becoming increasingly risky as others start understanding what is going on. The power base of the regime appears to be narrowing to the state administration, the secret police, and other militarized branches of government.

Wars are expensive. Russia's fiscal statistics remain surprisingly open. They show that Crimea costs the Russian federal budget about $2 billion a year. No public numbers seem to be available for the Donbas, but a fair guess is that it costs about as much. That would mean 0.3 percent of Russia's GDP a year. In the discussion of the cost of Western sanctions, the IMF has suggested 1–1.5 percent of Russia's GDP each year. Finally, the SIPRI numbers on Russia's military expenditures show a rise by 2 percent of GDP from 2008 to 2016 (fig. 9.2). This is 3–4 percent of GDP each year, which is a lot for a country whose economy grows by merely 1.5 percent a year. It is not clear whether Russia can manage such a large military cost politically.

In the summer of 2018, the Russian government raised the retirement age for men from sixty to sixty-five and for women from fifty-five to sixty, which aroused great popular unrest, arguably the greatest since Putin's attempt at a social-benefit reform in January 2005. At the same time, the government raised the value-added tax by two percentage points from 18 to 20 percent. The political implication is that Putin has violated the implicit social contract, that he delivers a growing standard of living while the people stay out of politics. Real disposable income fell by 17 percent from 2014 to 2017, and now government policy is eroding the standard of living.

It is difficult to see any opportunity for closer relations between Russia and the West unless the Kremlin decides to return the Donbas to Ukraine. The sanctions have marginalized Russia's importance to Western economies, and a broad consensus is that they are likely to last. A problem for the West is that Russia has so little to benefit from cooperation with the West that it may abandon all international rules.

Putin's regime is not likely to reform, but is it sustainable? Many stagnant and backward regimes have survived for decades. Fidel Castro's Cuba and Robert Mugabe's Zimbabwe are illustrative examples. In 1919, the liberal economist Ludwig von Mises concluded that the Soviet economic system without private property rights was not sustainable. He was right, but the Soviet Union persisted until 1991. Immense natural wealth, war, and repression did the trick. Moreover, changes usually require a catalyst that might be absent for years.[36]

Portugal offers another challenging example. The authoritarian António Salazar ruled as prime minister for thirty-six years until 1968 and died of old age in 1970. He was a nationalist who pursued corporatist authoritarianism and opposed democracy, communism, socialism, and liberalism. His economic policies can be summarized as fiscal responsibility and protectionism, leaving Portugal as the poorest and least educated country in Western Europe. Salazar pursued three colonial wars in Africa but managed to survive politically. Only in 1974, four years after his death, did the Carnation Revolution take place. Today Portugal is twice as wealthy as Russia in terms of GDP per capita at current exchange rates.[37]

Putin's regime possesses considerable sources of sustenance. It appears rational and well informed. The Kremlin understands its current budgetary constraints and its military inferiority in a big war. Few democratic governments can boast a corresponding coordination of policies. The risk of accidents in economic policy seems uncommonly small. Nor does the regime proffer any definite goal against which it could be measured, such as the restoration of the Russian Empire or any specific economic goal, which could lead to exaggerated expectations. Whatever happens, Putin may with some credibility say that the result was his aim.

Still, the reasons for the unsustainability of the Putin regime appear stronger. The regime's power base seems to be shrinking, and serious economic reforms are out of the question. Russian sociologist Natalia Zubarevich remarks that "the general direction of the Putin regime is clear: antimodernization and isolationism." Lev Gudkov of the Levada Center concurs that "Putin has lost the support of the urban middle class of larger cities, and he does not expect to win it back." The elite abandoned Putin in 2011, and he decided to cultivate the working class, the old, the poorly educated, and the provincial population, pursuing an antimodern electoral strategy similar to that of President Alexander Lukashenko in Belarus.[38]

The greatest risk may be that Putin is tempted to take greater risks than he can manage. So far, he has been cautious, but as the range of his options is shrinking, he seems increasingly prone to take greater risks. As the common cake is not growing, the competition for the pickings among different vested interests within the ruling elite is intensifying.

The disastrous Russo-Japanese War of 1904–1905, which unleashed the Russian revolution of 1905, is the outstanding example of excessive

Kremlin risk-taking. Another example is the Crimean War of 1853–1856, which ended the reign of Nicholas I, and allowed his successor Tsar Alexander II to launch imperial Russia's greatest reforms. A third case is the Soviet war in Afghanistan from 1979 to 1988, which contributed greatly to the collapse of the Soviet Union and the Yeltsin reforms of the 1990s. A severe tremor would be needed to break this seemingly solid system. Such shocks are usually surprising and can lead either to disaster or to fortuitous reforms.

The Russian liberal veteran politician Leonid Gozman summarizes the essence of the Putin regime: "To judge from the statements of our propagandists, the Russian state is very valuable and at the same time a very fragile construct that can be destroyed by anything: the fight against corruption, independent monitoring of elections, protest meetings with demands for the ouster of stealing or incompetent officials." The state's decisions are "often not beneficial to the citizens, but to the state itself, or to those state capitalists and special services that actually say: 'The state is us.'" As a consequence, the state budget is increasingly militarized at the expense of science, education, and health care. In order to justify such an allocation of state financing, the Russian "government talks about external threats (NATO and terrorists), while it is actually preparing for an attack from its people, which it perceives as a terminal danger."[39]

The big question is what strategy the Kremlin may choose. In his thoughtful book *Destined for War*, the eminent strategic thinker Graham Allison focuses on the risk of war between the world's two leading powers, the United States and China, because China is currently overtaking the United States in economic strength, and such shifts usually lead to war.

A subtheme in Allison's book is Austria-Hungary, which was a declining power at the beginning of World War I. The empire started the war after having been dissatisfied with Serbia's response to its ultimatum, and the Russian Empire, then a rising power, defended Serbia. Today Russia looks like a dangerous declining power reminiscent of Austria-Hungary in 1914, with its stagnant economy and impressive military might set to decrease. Its natural inclination is to be a spoiler in international affairs rather than a constructive player. Logic encourages the Kremlin to act while it still has the third largest military budget in the world and nuclear arms that are matched only by the United States. That means that we should expect Moscow to be ever less cooperative and more prone to risk-taking until the Kremlin realizes that the chips are down.[40]

The United States has become Russia's prime enemy. Both sides have been guilty in this gradual drift. Political scientist James Goldgeier and former US ambassador to Russia Michael McFaul determine that in the 1990s the "pro-American lobby in Russia, including Yeltsin, often felt cheated by their American partners. Disappointed expectations … eventually produced disillusion."[41]

Since 2007, anti-Americanism has been a dominant feature of Putin's foreign policy, even if the Barack Obama–Dmitri Medvedev reset in 2009 brought about a pause until Putin returned to the presidency in 2012. The Kremlin needs a credible external enemy to mobilize the nation around the flag, and the United States is the only suitable candidate. Europe is too wobbly, and China too dangerous. Russian popular sentiment toward the United States fluctuates considerably, but usually about 60 percent of the Russians express a negative attitude to the United States, and the Kremlin can raise Russian negativity.[42]

As an old imperial power, Russia possesses great strategic thinking and considerable diplomatic skills. It wants to be represented at each important international table, and it knows how to make its presence felt. The official propaganda uses foreign policy to strengthen the domestic standing of the Russian leaders. Its foremost aims are to detach the United States from the European Union, to divide the European Union, and to isolate former Soviet republics—notably Ukraine, Georgia, and Moldova—from the West.[43]

After the warfare in Ukraine began, an article published one year earlier by Russia's powerful chief of the general staff, Army General Valery Gerasimov, attracted great attention. It has become known as the Gerasimov Doctrine. Gerasimov noted that the line between war and peace had been blurred, because nobody declared war any longer. Focusing on the Ukrainian Orange Revolution and the Arab Spring, his salient line was that "the role of nonmilitary means of achieving political and strategic goals has grown, and, in many cases, they have exceeded the power of weapons in their efficacy."[44]

The essence of the Gerasimov Doctrine is that Russia's economic resources are limited, and military hardware is expensive. Therefore, Russian warfare must rely more on unconventional military components, such as cyber, disinformation, economic warfare, and subversion. The Prussian general and military theorist Carl von Clausewitz famously claimed: "War is . . . the continuation of politics by different means." This statement frames Russia's new hybrid warfare. Cyber especially has dissolved the dividing line between war and politics.[45]

Now that Putin has engaged in four wars in the past decade, he appears hungry for another "small victorious war" when he feels it would be beneficial for national mobilization and his domestic political standing. Hardly anyone predicted the Russian annexation of Crimea or the Russian military engagement in Syria, rendering it foolhardy to try to foresee what comes next.

Putin is no chess player, but he pursues judo, of which he has said, "Judo is not just a sport. . . . It's a philosophy. It's respect for your elders and for your opponents. It's not for weaklings." Judo favors surprises. We should expect the unexpected. So far, Putin's actions can be characterized as intelligent and rational, but his appetite is clearly increasing with his eating, and so is his appetite for risk as his domestic situation becomes more embattled.[46]

Mark Galeotti offers an interesting assessment of Russian intelligence services. There "can be little question about the aggressiveness of the Russian intelligence community." In the Ukrainian conflict, "the Russians often displayed extremely good intelligence on a tactical [military] level," but there was "a startling dearth of effective political and strategic intelligence." The problem lies with Putin, who possesses all this intelligence but is caught in "his dreams of Russia as a renewed great power." Overall, the cruder and more aggressive FSB is expanding at the expense of the more sophisticated SVR or GRU. Increasingly, the Kremlin is outsourcing subversion, disinformation, and cyber warfare to private contractors and outright organized crime, which offers the Kremlin deniability but also undermines its control and professionalism.[47]

Because the Kremlin no longer can build its legitimacy on rising standards of living, or bread, it needs more circus, which means war. The Kremlin has jeopardized its old ideas of international law. Russia used to be legalistic but not necessarily legal. Now the Kremlin is increasingly appearing as a rogue actor. It has thrown aside all international conventions concluded from the end of World War II, including the Founding Charter of the United Nations, the Helsinki Act of 1975 and all its consecutive agreements, the Russia-Ukraine Friendship Treaty of 1997, and so on. Why should anybody even try to conclude an agreement with such an actor? Therefore, we should expect the Kremlin to attempt more small victorious wars, as in Georgia and Crimea. This implies that the likelihood is increasing that the Kremlin takes on excessive risks and gets bogged down in wars that are too costly.

Everything came to a head in the US presidential elections of 2016, when the Kremlin did whatever it could to influence the outcome of the elections to the benefit of Donald Trump. Two Russian intelligence services, the FSB and the GRU, hacked the Democratic National Committee. They distributed the leaks through the social networks, skillfully dominating the dumbfounded US media. The Kremlin interacted in an unprecedented fashion with many members of the Trump campaign. It instigated massive social network interference and, in all probability, assisted with financing. It remains to see what was illegal and how effective it was, but the Russian interference was massive and multipronged. The Kremlin has made it a habit to interfere in elections all over the West with anonymous slander on social networks and on the web, hacking of a political nature, financing of both right-wing and left-wing extremists, and many other things.[48]

The Kremlin has also become blatant with murders in the West. It has been accused of sixteen suspicious deaths connected with Russia in the United Kingdom since the murder of the former FSB officer Alexander Litvinenko in November 2006, which the British government neglected to investigate for years. Similarly, the former Russian information minister Mikhail Lesin, who had fallen out with Putin's media tsar Yuri Kovalchuk, seems to have been murdered in a Washington hotel in November 2015. The biggest shock was the attempted murder of the former Russian intelligence agent Sergei Skripal with a nerve agent in the United Kingdom in March 2018.[49]

The Kremlin appears to have abandoned all the old rules of the game, but this also means that it has boxed Russia into a corner. The

United States and Europe have united against its aggression toward Ukraine and will likely remain unified on this issue. The neighboring former Soviet republics are dead scared. Few observers see any hope for the economic reforms necessary for significant economic growth.

In many ways, the Kremlin has returned to the 1980s. Former ambassador Daniel Fried summarizes the situation: "Moscow now, like then, has been going down a dark road of confrontation with the United States and aggression elsewhere. As with the Soviets and reactionary tsars, external confrontation coincides with, and may be compensation for, stagnation at home. Putin's tactics, like the demonization of the United States in Russian official media, appear recycled from the Cold War." This is a risky tactic, and the Kremlin appears more prone to risk today than in the 1980s.[50]

The West must no longer harbor any illusions about Putin. In the past decade, Putin has played a weak economic, political, and military hand with remarkable skill, and for its part, the West has reacted poorly. The West needs to get serious to counter Russian foreign policy better. The postcommunist transition is over, and no systemic convergence is under way. The Kremlin no longer sees democracy building as desirable but views it as a hostile, subversive act. It no longer aspires to join the West, which must face up to this new reality.

The West needs to maintain a credible military defense and military solidarity so that Russia dares not launch a small war against any NATO member. NATO is the best deterrent against Russian military adventures and thus the best framework for preserving the peace. The West needs to stay united and shore up support for both NATO and the European Union. If NATO splinters, Europe would lack the US nuclear umbrella and the security guarantee of mutual assured destruction. My late friend Boris Nemtsov always said that Putin respects NATO's article 5, which states the principle of one for all, all for one. So far, this has held true. As long as that holds, all the NATO countries seem to be out of bounds for outright Russian aggression. Subversion is another matter.

Although Western military strength is overwhelming, its credibility is weak. When Soviet leader Nikita Khrushchev took the measure of John F. Kennedy in Vienna in June 1961, he found Kennedy lacking. His assessment provoked the Cuban missile crisis. Putin might have drawn similar conclusions from his meetings with President Trump in Hamburg on July 7, 2017, and in Helsinki on July 16, 2018. The West must reinforce its unity and credibility for the sake of peace.[51]

The basic Western demand is that Russia end its military aggression in Ukraine. Short of credible security guarantees or constructive negotiations, sanctions are the West's tool of political choice. However, sanctions are always a second best, because they reduce interaction and aggravate alienation, and yet they are preferable to doing nothing in the face of aggression or violations of international law. The four main categories of sanctions at play are: trade, financial, technological, and personal.

Trade sanctions are a double-edged sword. They impose certain costs on the nation sanctioned, but they offer such regimes great opportunities to seize control over private trade and companies. In Serbia, Iraq, and Iran, international trade sanctions greatly strengthened the regime's control over the economy. They also aggravated organized crime's collusion with the regime. Trade sanctions hurt ordinary citizens, who naturally turn against the countries that have imposed the sanctions, rendering their political benefit dubious. Putin regularly praises trade sanctions for supporting import substitution, and the Kremlin has imposed its own countersanctions on Western food.

Financial sanctions have proven quite effective on Russia. The US dollar rules the world of finance, and every dollar passes through one of the three biggest banks in New York and is thus subject to US jurisdiction. Financial sanctions have reduced investment and output in Russia, though to a limited extent. A potential danger is that the United States overexploits financial sanctions, undermining the international role of the dollar. Moreover, the impact of financial sanctions declines over time as the sanctioned country reduces its financial dependence on the West, as Russia has done through its conservative financial policy.

As discussed in chapter 5, Putin has protested most of all against personal sanctions, the Sergei Magnitsky Act of 2012, and the sanctions of his friends, indicating that they have had considerable effect. Of all the types of sanctions, personal sanctions against people close to Putin appear to be the most effective.[52]

The United States and the rest of the West need to reformulate the task. It is not Russia or Russians but Putin's crony capitalism that should be contained. The sanctioned Putin cronies hold tens of billions of dollars in the West. Most of the ill-gotten Russian wealth is presumably in the United States and the United Kingdom, which have frozen few assets. The West can reveal and freeze this wealth if it unites and adopts this as its goal. The United States needs to take five steps:

1. First, the intelligence community should be asked to assess how much laundered Russian money is held in the United States and how much of that is held by designated individuals and entities.

2. Congress should adopt legislation prohibiting the formation of new anonymous companies in the United States, and existing anonymous companies should be required to provide their beneficiary owners within a limited time, such as two years. The Financial Crimes Enforcement Network could be charged with assembling this information.[53]

3. The temporary exemption granted to real estate in the Patriot Act should be ended through an executive decision by the Treasury. All financial flows into the United States should go through regulated financial institutions.[54]

4. Similarly, international money transfers should no longer be considered as subject to attorney-client privilege but should have to go through regulated financial institutions.[55]

5. With its expanded tasks, FinCEN should be given far greater resources to implement stricter anti-money laundering regulations. The United States has actually cut the funding of such investigations in recent decades, minimizing the risk of detection.[56]

Transparency is the greatest and most important weapon the West possesses. It must deploy it with full force. The European Union has already adopted relevant legislation, but it has to implement it. For the United States, the prohibition of anonymous companies stands as the top item on the legislative agenda. If the West takes these steps, tens of billions of dollars of hidden wealth of Russian criminals would be revealed, which would benefit both Russia and the West. Without its fourth circle of secure offshore wealth, Russia's crony capitalism could collapse.[57]

Today's Russian crony capitalism is unlikely to persist. It is too petrified and brittle to stand the challenges of our time. The current official Russian mentality is reminiscent of the late Brezhnev period in the early 1980s before Gorbachev's perestroika. Sooner or later, the Russian people are likely to stop the extraordinary looting by the Putin circles. Then, the populace can start contemplating the establishment of an orderly state based on the rule of law. The people will need to rebuild elementary state institutions, especially the judiciary and law enforcement.

In spite of the deinstitutionalization under Putin, Russia has progressed immensely since communism. It has gone through a far-reaching modernization in the past quarter-century. Russia has a relatively well functioning and open market economy, even if cartels are a concern. It enjoys macroeconomic balance, and it has a well-functioning state administration, a decent infrastructure, and a vast number of well-educated citizens.

As one of the founders of modernization theory, Seymour Martin Lipset, would see it, Russia is too wealthy, too well educated, and too open to be so authoritarian. A strong authoritarian tradition and imperial legacy can delay democratization but hardly block it forever. The curse of oil is a more serious obstacle, but low oil prices reduce it. The essence of the oil curse is that rents were concentrated in the hands of the ruling few. The Russian economy can be diversified through lower oil prices or more economic growth. Political scientist Larry Diamond observes that there is good hope that the current "democratic recession" will eventually end.[58]

This is a propitious time to consider the many mistakes and mishaps in the late 1980s and early 1990s that aborted the postcommunist transition so that it did not lead to democracy and rule of law with convergence with Western democracies as in the new EU members. The next generation of Russian reformers needs to learn from the mistakes of the past to get it right. In the early 1990s, Russia's economic collapse was the primary concern. Russia did not have time or ability to build institutions at that time. Whenever a new democratic breakthrough comes, the focus must be on creating new political and state institutions.[59]

To begin with, Yeltsin did not dissolve the KGB; he only split and weakened it. Second, Russia had no early founding election of its parliament. Third, the Soviet constitution was only amended, leaving a poison pill that was not discarded in time. Fourth, no early judicial reform occurred. Fifth, the reformers failed to gain control over the Central Bank and break up the ruble zone, so they could not stop monetary emissions. Sixth, the West played only a minor role, since it did not offer any material support for reform early on. Seventh, deregulation was too slow and limited, allowing considerable monopolization and rent seeking. Eighth, privatization was not adjusted to political demands.

Today Russia's main problem is that the state has been captured by a small group of top officials. Technical competence is no longer a problem. Many senior officials are highly competent, but they have the wrong objectives, namely their own enrichment at the expense of the state and society. Russia needs to surgically cut out this cancer, the three ruling circles of the Putin system, and establish checks and balances that can maintain a new system.

A new political elite needs to be elected. A new Russian transformation should start with a democratic breakthrough, leading to early elections of president, parliament, and regional authorities, under a sound electoral system. Instead of a constitution with strong presidential powers, Russia should opt for a parliamentary system that has proven conducive to democracy throughout the European Union.[60]

The ensuing step should be the abolition of the secret police, the FSB. Normal countries do not have a secret police that check their populations, whereas they have foreign intelligence and domestic counter-intelligence. Russia should finally carry out a proper decommunization, condemn Stalin's terror, and topple all the monuments of terrorists.

The third step should be to build a new judicial system with new people. Both the institutions and their officeholders need to be replaced simultaneously. East Germany, Estonia, and Georgia did so successfully, abolishing the old prosecutors' offices and courts, building up new institutions with outsiders. Given the small numbers of officeholders required, this is perfectly feasible with lawyers from the private sector and newly minted lawyers plus returning émigrés.[61]

After these three critical political and judicial tasks, the ordinary slog of economic reforms could start. The best means to fight corruption are transparency and democracy, embodying good governance. A democratic Russia should opt for maximum transparency, especially of ownership of banks, real estate, and enterprises. The big state enterprises need to be disassembled once again, and the state enterprises should be privatized in a transparent fashion through open auctions. It would be much easier now when markets and market prices exist. Markets need to be deregulated and opened up for normal competition. Public procurement must be exposed to real competition.

The Russian public is greatly concerned about the privatization of large enterprises in the 1990s, which many see as the "original sin." The eventual owners became very wealthy. Yet this must not be the policy focus. All of these enterprises, with the single exception of Norilsk Nickel, have been renationalized and their former owners have emigrated. They became so wealthy because they managed to turn their companies around. Because Russia never had strong property rights, corporate governance was poor, and an enterprise could be successful only if ownership was concentrated, which by necessity means that the owners become very rich. Today, Russia needs to focus on strengthening property rights first through a sound judicial reform. Then it should split up the state companies and demonopolize all markets, exposing them to normal competition. At this time, Russia should privatize using standard Western techniques; the nation will have time for this unless it suffers a new financial collapse, which is not on the horizon as yet.

Last, the West needs to engage. This is likely to be primarily the European Union, which has proven in eleven postcommunist accession countries that it knows how to build democracy and the rule of law. The European Union should engage with the same agenda in Russia after the end of cronyism. Article 49 of the European Union's Lisbon Treaty states: "Any European State which respects the values referred to in Article 2 and is committed to promoting them may apply to become a member of the Union."

By every definition, Russia is a European country. Its level of GDP is slightly higher than in the poorest EU country, Bulgaria. The European Union should engage fully with Russia, as well as with Ukraine, Belarus, Moldova, the Caucasian countries, and, of course, with the Western Balkans.

Notes

Introduction

1. On oil and gas, see Sachs and Warner 1997; Gaddy and Ickes 2005, 2009; Goldman 2008; Gustafson 2012; and Dabrowski 2015.

2. On Putin's respect for the KGB, see Felshtinsky and Pribylovsky 2008; and Baker and Glasser 2005; as a free marketer and fiscal conservative, see Goldman 2008; and Hill and Gaddy 2015; as an advocate of state capitalism, see Åslund 2007a; and Sutela 2012; as a kleptocrat, see Nemtsov and Milov 2010a; Gessen 2012; and Dawisha 2014; Lee Myers 2015 might offer the most balanced view in competition with Hill and Gaddy 2015.

3. Chris Miller's 2018 book is titled *Putinomics.*

4. Åslund 1989, 194.

5. Brzezinski 1983; Pipes 1984, 49–51.

6. Judah 2013, 325.

7. Dawisha 2014, 350.

8. Zygar 2016, 346.

9. For Putin as the new tsar, see, e.g., Steven Lee Myers 2015.

10. On ideology, see Laqueur 2015; and Clover 2016.

11. Pomeranz 2017; Barber 2017.

12. On the 1990s, my main contributions are Åslund 1995 and Åslund 2007a. Michael Alexeev and Shlomo Weber 2013 edited the giant *Oxford Handbook of the Russian Economy,* which covers everything. Like-minded contributions are Gaidar 1999, 2007, 2012; Shleifer 2005; Shleifer and Treisman 2000; and Treisman 2011. Opposing views include Reddaway and Glinsky 2001; and Goldman 2003, 2008.

On the economy since 2000, the most substantial contributions are Miller 2017 and Sutela 2012, but Sutela discusses only up to 2009.

13. Felshtinsky and Pribylovsky 2008; Nemtsov and Milov 2008, 2010a, 2010b; Dawisha 2014.

ONE The Origins of Putin's Economic Model

1. Ostrovsky 2015; Mau and Starodubrovskaya 2001; McFaul 2001.

2. Pipes 1974; Pipes 2005, 1.

3. For Uvarov, see Pipes 2005, 100; and Laqueur 2015, 214; for Ivanov, see Ivanov 2006; on nationalisms, see Smith 2010; for Eurasianism, see Clover 2016.

4. Malia 1999.

5. Ibid.

6. Raikin quoted in *Izvestiya*, October 12, 1986.

7. Kornai 1992, 360–365; the preceding classic was Nove 1977.

8. The story is eminently told by Dobbs 1997 and Ash 1983.

9. This section draws on my books Åslund 1995, 102–136; and Åslund 2013, 19–35. My preferred source on the demise of communism and the Soviet Union is Dobbs 1997; see also Dunlop 1993 and Remnick 1994 for lively, detailed accounts of the Soviet collapse.

10. Gaidar 2007.

11. Nove 1989 details how glasnost proceeded with one revelation after the other. Kolakowski quoted in Murphy, Shleifer, and Vishny 1992.

12. Åslund 1990.

13. Gorbachev 1987a, 86.

14. On the Brezhnev doctrine, see Brown 1996, 240; Gorbachev quoted in ibid., 225.

15. Putin 2000a, 81.

16. Gorbachev 1987b, 118.

17. On the financial crisis, see Åslund 1991; for the budget deficit, see EBRD 1994.

18. Lieven 2000.

19. Aron 2000, 459.

20. Putin 2000a, 79.

21. Ostrovsky 2015 describes the 1990s well.

22. For opinion polls, see Levada Center 2017.

23. There are two excellent biographies of Yeltsin: Aron 2000 and Colton 2008. The two last of Yeltsin's three memoirs are very substantial, even if they are considered to be ghost-written to a large extent (Yeltsin 1994, 2000). My fondest memory of Yeltsin is a meeting in the Moscow White House on December 11, 1991. The last time I saw him was at a dinner in London in July 2004.

24. Remington 2005, 235.

25. On the dissolution of the tsarist imperial service, see Pipes 1990, 298–300. Yeltsin 1994, 129. When I last saw Yeltsin in July 2004, he said that he spent most of his time reading one history book a day.

26. Yeltsin 1994, 115.

27. Both Gaidar and Chubais were my friends at the time and Chubais still is, though Gaidar passed away far too early in 2009, deeply unhappy about where Putin had taken Russia. Their views are well represented by Gaidar and Chubais 2012. Yeltsin quoted in Yeltsin 1991.

28. Gaidar 1999, 114.

29. Yeltsin 1991.

30. The main programmatic document was the academic book Boycko, Shleifer, and Vishny 1995. For 1995 statistics, see Blasi, Kroumova, and Kruse 1997, 189, 192–193.

31. On the drop in Russian GDP, see Åslund 2002, 113–158.

32. On Yeltsin's attempt to rule by decree, see Remington, Smith, and Haspel 1998.

33. Dunlop 1998; Lieven 1998.

34. Russian organized crime has attracted a huge literature, some of it serious, some fiction. The main sources for this section are Volkov 2002; Gilinskiy 2000; Handelman 1995; and Dixelius and Konstantinov 1998. Organized crime has been a dominant theme in Russian fiction, films, and TV programs. Vadim Volkov 2002 has analyzed the evolution of crime and protection in Russia in line with Gambetta's analysis. For the comparison with Chicago, see ibid., 19.

35. On "powerful" oligarchs, see Klebnikov 2000, 44. The two outstanding books on the oligarchs are Freeland 2000 and Hoffman 2002. Fortescue 2006 offers a refreshing positive view of the economic role of the oligarchs, while Klebnikov 2000 focuses on the criminal sides of the oligarchy.

36. For the seven oligarchs, see Freeland, Thornhill, and Gowers 1996. On the demise of Russia's democracy, see Freeland 2000.

37. Chubais 1999; Kokh 1998, 115–130; Freeland 2000; Hoffman 2002; Klebnikov 2000, 135.

38. Shleifer and Treisman 2004; Shleifer 2005, 167.

39. Åslund 2007a, 205–206.

40. This section draws on Åslund 2007a, 189–232; Sutela 2012; and Baker and Glasser 2005.

41. EBRD 2003.

42. McKinsey Global Institute 1999.

43. Osnovnye 2000.

44. Putin quoted in Baker and Glasser 2005, 86–87.

45. On Russian taxes, see Shleifer and Treisman 2000; for reforms, see Owen and Robinson 2003; and Gaidar 2003.

46. On legalization of the sale of agricultural land, see Remington 2002; and Kirchik 2004; for other reforms, see CEFIR 2003; and Yakovlev and Zhuravskaya 2007.

47. Shevtsova 2005, 262.

48. On rising oil prices, see Åslund 2007a, 235–236.

49. On Yukos, see ibid., 234–241.

50. On Igor Sechin, see Gustafson 2012, 340; on Gazprom, see Åslund 2007, 253.

51. Åslund 2007a, 251–254.

52. Ibid., 264–267.

53. Putin 2006b.

54. Strategiya-2020 2008.

55. Guriev and Tsyvinski 2010, 13–14.

56. Sergei Ivanov speaks excellent Swedish, and we speak Swedish together.

57. Medvedev 2009d.

58. Yuri Kovalchuk's brother Mikhail Kovalchuk is the director of the famous Kurchatov nuclear research institute in Moscow. Arkady Rotenberg's younger brother Boris Rotenberg is also involved in business, living in Finland as a Finnish citizen. A fourth major crony is Nikolai Shamalov, whose son, Kirill, was married to Putin's daughter Ekaterina. See Dawisha 2014, 115. On Bank Rossiya, see Felshtinsky and Pribylovsky 2008; Nemtsov and Milov 2010a, 2010b; and Dawisha 2014.

59. Nemtsov and Milov 2010a, 2010b; for Gazprom stock price, see symbol OGZD:LI.

60. Quoted in Lee Myers 2015, 384–385.

61. I attended one of his campaign events at a business conference.

62. Zubarevich 2015.

63. Putin 2018b.

64. Putin 2016c.

65. Minxin Pei 2016.

TWO Putin's Consolidation of Power

1. Hill and Gaddy 2015, 386.

2. Nemtsov and Milov 2008; Felshtinsky and Pribylovsky 2008; Dawisha 2014.

3. On Putin's views, see Stent 2014; on the Orange Revolution, see Åslund and McFaul 2006; Hill and Gaddy 2015, 385.

4. On plagiarism, see Hill and Gaddy 2015, 197; on Litvinenko, see Dawisha 2014, 101; on the dissertation, see Gaddy and Danchenko 2006; and Hill and Gaddy 2015, 198–199.

5. Baker and Glasser 2005, 47; Felshtinsky and Pribylovsky 2008; Dawisha 2014; Åslund 2007a, 201.

6. On Putin quoting Ilyin, see Laruelle 2017; and Clover 2016.

7. Laqueur 2015, 180, 181.

8. Snyder 2016; Laruelle 2017.

9. On Putin's avoidance of attachment, see Barbashin and Thoburn 2015; on his praise of Gumilev, see Clover 2016; and Putin 2012c.

10. Åslund 2007a, 275.

11. Putin 2017d; Putin 2017h; Putin 2017d.

12. Of the two Swedish diplomats, one is dead, and the other one is alive. Hill and Gaddy 2015, 153.

13. Putin 2000a, 41.

14. Ibid., 77.

15. Ibid., 53, 85.

16. Putin 2001, quoted in Hill and Gaddy 2015, 167.

17. Personal information from former official in Putin's cabinet; Judah 2014a.

18. Putin 2001, quoted in Hill and Gaddy 2015, 167.

19. Kryshtanovskaya and White 2003, 2009; Werning Rivera and Rivera 2006, 2017.

20. On Rotenberg, see Lee Myers 2015; on Roldugin, see Harding 2016b; on Kolbin, see US Department of the Treasury 2015b.

21. Dawisha 2014, 39–59.

22. Putin 2000a, 65–81; Dawisha 2014, 39–59.

23. Dawisha 2014, 63–70.

24. Ibid., 80–91.

25. Cherkezov 2007.

26. On Yeltsin, see Breslauer 1982, 2002; on *ponyatie,* see Dawisha 2014, 38.

27. On deoffshoreization, see Putin 2013c; on the division of the elite, see Devitt 2017.

28. For the contrarian view, see Satter 2003; and Dunlop 2014. Politkovskaya 2001.

29. Pomerantsev 2014.

30. Putin 2000a, 186, 129.

31. On *gosudarstvenost',* see Laqueur 2015, 139.

32. On state administration improvements, see Mereu 2006; for the business index, see World Bank and International Finance Corporation 2017.

33. McFaul 2001, 356, 355.

34. For an empirical study of the deinstitutionalization and personalization of the state, see Baturo and Elkink 2016. For an analysis of this process, see Shevtsova 2005.

35. Åslund 2013, 283–300.

36. Gans-Morse 2017, 74; Hendley 1997, 236.

37. Putin 2000a, 179, 187.

38. Putin 2000b.

39. Solomon 2002; Supreme Court of the Russian Federation n.d.

40. Buchanan 2003; Solomon 2002, 121.

41. Taylor 2006; Gans-Morse 2017, 191.

42. Yasin 2004.

43. Gans-Morse 2017, 9, 86.

44. On the economic courts until 2014, see Hendley 2002; and Hendley et al. 2013; on the merger, see Reevell 2014.

45. Frye 2010, 94.

46. Putin 2015c.

47. Putin 2017e.

48. US Department of the Treasury 2017b.

49. Transparency International 2017.

50. Putin 2000a, 177.

51. Talbott 2002, 412.

52. Bush 2001.

53. Putin 2018a.

54. Putin 2003e, 2017g.

55. Bush 2003; Putin 2004b.

56. Putin 2006a. The Orange Revolution explains why Putin was so hostile to Michael McFaul, US ambassador to Moscow, 2012–2014. McFaul is one of the foremost authorities on revolutions. Why would the State Department send such a specialist to Moscow?! McFaul's case was hardly helped by his having coedited a book with me about the Orange Revolution (Åslund and McFaul 2006).

57. Quoted in Stent 2014, 147; Putin 2007.

58. NATO 2008.

59. Putin 2008b.

60. Ibid.

61. Levada Center 2017.

62. Putin 2014b.

63. Ibid.

64. On corporate raiding, the best evidence is Alexei Navalny's long documentary film *Chaika* of December 2015 (Anti-Corruption Fund 2015), which documents the activities of the sons of Prosecutor General Yuri Chaika, involving many senior prosecutors. The oldest son, Artem Chaika, was one of the first people to be sanctioned by the US government on the Global Magnitsky list (US Department of the Treasury 2017a). On the Investigative Committee, see Dawisha 2014, 91.

65. BBC 2016; Luzin 2017.

66. Lally 2011.

67. Browder 2015; US Department of the Treasury 2017b, 2017c; Navalny 2015.

68. Putin 2015d.

69. Bazanova et al. 2016.

70. Gans-Morse 2017, 189.

71. Aptekar' and Sinitsyn 2016.

72. Nazarov 2014.

73. For the survey, see Yeremenko 2017; on Medvedev's laws, see Lally 2011; for 2016, see Prime 2016.

74. A telling example is Putin 2017e. For the decree see Nielsen 2017; and Putin 2017c. On Ivan the Terrible's *oprichnina,* see Pipes 1974.

75. *Euroactive* 2015.

76. McFaul 2006; Galeotti 2016.

77. Galeotti 2016.

78. Nechepurenko 2017.

79. Minchenko 2012.

80. President of Russia, en.kremlin.ru.

81. Putin 2017f.

82. Ibid.

83. Bensinger, Elder, and Schoofs 2017. In the absence of other better information, the Steele dossier is worth taking seriously.

84. Zygar 2016.

THREE Conservative Fiscal and Monetary Policy

1. The share of GDP depends greatly on how transportation and trade are counted (Dabrowski 2015); Guriev and Tsyvinski 2010, 18–20.

2. Gaddy and Ickes 2005.

3. Illarionov 1998a, 1998b.

4. Alesina and Drazen 1991; Drazen and Grilli 1993.

5. Mau and Starodubrovskaya 2001; Gaidar 2004; McKinsey 1999 makes the same argument.

6. The seminal report on the crash of 1998 is Aleksashenko 1999.

7. RECEP 1999.

8. Åslund 2007a, 177.

9. Åslund 1998; Åslund 2007a, 178.

10. *CNN Money* 1998.

11. Johnson 2000.

12. Lloyd 1998.

13. Åslund 2007a, 179.

14. Schumpeter [1943] 1976.

15. Åslund 2007a, 179.

16. Ibid., 183.

17. Yukos is an oil company, Sibneft is the Siberian oil company, Rusal is Russian Aluminum, and SUEK is Russia's biggest coal company.

18. Commander and Mumssen 1998; *Russian Economic Barometer* 2004; Gaddy and Ickes 2002.

19. Gudkov 2015, 54.

20. As stated at the Political Panel at the Gaidar Forum in Moscow, January 14, in which I participated.

21. Putin 2004b.

22. EBRD 2003, 187.

23. Pinto, Drebentsov, and Morozov 1999; Gaddy and Ickes 1998 explain how barter and nonpayments became subsidies; *Russian Economic Barometer* 2004.

24. BOFIT 2004.

25. Papernaya 2004; Diamond 2002.

26. Fedorov 1999; Shleifer and Treisman 2000.

27. Owen and Robinson 2003, 82–84.

28. Ibid.; Gaidar 2003.

29. On the flat tax, see Ivanova, Keen, and Klemm 2005; and Keen, Kim, and Varsano 2006; on Estonia, see Laar 2002; and Åslund 2002, 228; for the increase in revenues, see Gaidar 2003, 193; quotation in Gorodnichenko, Martinez-Vazquez, and Peter 2009, 1.

30. Federal Tax Service of Russia n.d.; quotation in Gaidar 2003, 197.

31. Owen and Robinson 2003, 34–39; Klerk 2004.

32. Decree of the President of the Russian Federation 2016.

33. Criminal Code of the Russian Federation 2003.

34. Central Bank of the Russian Federation 2018b.

35. Statistically, the Stabilization Fund was still considered part of the international currency and gold reserves of the Central Bank of Russia.

36. Ministry of Finance of the Russian Federation 2018b.

37. Ministry of Finance of the Russian Federation 2018a.

38. Russian Direct Investment Fund n.d.; US Department of the Treasury 2015b.

39. BOFIT 2018.

40. Ministry of Finance of the Russian Federation 2018b; Guriev and Tsyvinski 2010, 20–22.

41. Kar and Freitas 2013, 16.

42. Sokolov and Davydova 2012.

43. Central Bank of the Russian Federation 2018a.

44. Putin 2014b, 2014e.

45. Putin 2015a.

46. Putin 2015b.

47. Central Bank of the Russian Federation 2018b.

48. Bershidsky 2017.

49. Rosstat 2017, 6.

50. Miller 2018.

51. Bank of Finland Institute for Economies in Transition 2017.

52. On increasing drinking, see Shapiro 1995; Brainerd 1998; and Shkolnikov, Andreev, and Maleva 2000; for life expectancy, see World Bank 2018.

53. Guriev and Tsyvinski 2010, 38.

FOUR The Rise of State Capitalism

1. The other major armaments holdings are Rosatom, United Aircraft Corporation, United Shipbuilding Corporation, and Almaz-Antey that produces antiaircraft defense systems. An alternative group would be the transportation giants the Russian Railways, Transneft the oil pipeline company, and Rosseti the Russian Grid.

2. EBRD 2003.

3. Mereminskaya 2016. FAS, "Doklad o sostoyanii konkurentsii v Rossiiskoi Federatsii za 2015 god" [Report on the State of Competition in the Russian Federation in 2015], Moscow: Federal Antimonopoly Service, 2016, cited in Radygin 2018, 12.

4. Own calculations from Westman and Krivoshapko 2017 and United Nations Statistics Division 2017. The Rosstat statistics vary greatly from the UN statistics, especially when it comes to the energy sector.

5. Radygin 2018, 13.

6. Kurlantzick 2016, 42.

7. Radygin 2018, 13; on corporate governance, see Gans-Morse 2017, 189.

8. Nemtsov and Milov 2008, 2010a, 2010b; Nemtsov and Martynyuk 2014; Karen Dawisha 2014; OCCRP 2017.

9. Malkova 2013.

10. Gustafson 2012, 320.

11. Putin 2003c.

12. Personal interview with Khodorkovsky, Washington, DC, October 9, 2003.

13. Baker and Glasser 2005, 282; Lee Myers 2015, 220–221; Putin 2003b; Khodorkovsky interview.

14. Fortescue 2006, 121–148.

15. Ibid, 148.

16. Gustafson 2012, 345.

17. Arvelund 2004; Putin quoted in Gustafson 2012, 346.

18. Putin 2003a.

19. Putin 2003d; Interfax, Tashkent, June 17, 2004; Belton 2004.

20. Personal conversations with investment bankers and fund managers.

21. Blasi, Kroumova, and Kruse 1997; Chubais 1999, chap. 1.

22. Vernikov 2012.

23. Putin 2006b.

24. On Ivanov, see Putin 2000a, 200–201; on Chemezov, see Dawisha 2014, 52, 54.

25. Volkov 2008.

26. On state corporations as nongovernmental organizations, see Solov'ev 2009; as benefiting the president, see *Kommersant*, 2008; Volkov 2008.

27. Volkov 2008.

28. Ibid.

29. Medvedev 2009b, 2009a.

30. On Medvedev's actions in 2011, see Meyer 2011.

31. On Abramovich acquiring a majority in Sibneft, see Kokh 1998, 121, 123, 126; Freeland 2000; and Hoffman 2002. On Gazprom's purchase, see Ostrovsky 2005; on the price, see Belton 2005: "While Sibneft's price tag appears cheap compared to valuations of Western majors, the deal looks like an expensive buy for the state. . . . BP paid $1.80 per barrel for half of Tyumen Oil, said Chris Weafer, chief strategist at Alfa Bank." On Abramovich as one of five, see Åslund 2007a, 200.

32. Fortescue 2006, 146.

33. Gazprom 2017a; Troika Dialog 2012, 5.

34. Åslund 1995, 159; Stern 2005.

35. Åslund 2007a, 140–142; Klebnikov 2000, 134–135.

36. Hoffman 2000; Goldman 2008, 104–105.

37. Private conversation with Chernomyrdin in the Russian Embassy in Kyiv, May 2006.

38. On Putin's appointments in 2001, see Gustafson 2012, 267. Federov was a member of Gazprom's board as an independent director; Gazprom 2017c. Quotation in *Economist* 2013.

39. On the board, see Gazprom 2017b. In January 1992, Zubkov became Putin's deputy when Putin was chairman of the Committee for Foreign Relations of the Mayor's Office in St. Petersburg. Zubkov was also a founding member of Putin's exclusive *Ozero dacha* cooperative in St. Petersburg. He was involved in two of Putin's major corruption scandals in St. Petersburg in the early 1990s: the food import scandal and the takeover of the prime hotel in St. Petersburg, Grand Hotel Europe (Dawisha 2014, 81, 83–84; Felshtinsky and Pribylovsky 2008, 255). On Bergmann, see Gazprom 2011.

40. For natural gas figures, see Gazprom 2017d; for 2017 figures, see TASS 2018; on LNG, see Panin 2014.

41. Gazprom 2017e.

42. On free trade of Gazprom stocks, see Putin 2005b; for recent prices, see symbol OGZD:LI.

43. As of August 3, 2018 (OGZD:LI); JP Morgan Cazenove 2015, 5, 29.

44. Nemtsov and Milov 2008.

45. Balmaceda 1998; Nemtsov and Milov 2008.

46. Troika Dialog 2012, 26–27.

47. *Russia Market Daily* 2012; Gazprom 2014; personal conversation, London, 2012.

48. Latynina 2017; Kleiner 2005, 40–41.

49. Podobedova 2015; *Novaya Gazeta* 2009b.

50. Novikov 2015.

51. For perceptions of Miller, see Farchy 2015; for *Forbes* quotation, see Malkova 2013; *Economist* 2013, 59.

52. Hedenskog and Larsson 2007, 46.

53. Grey et al. 2014.

54. European Commission 2015c.

55. Ibid.; Hedenskog and Larsson 2007, 46.

56. European Commission 2015a, 2017.

57. European Commission 2018.

58. Balmaceda 2004, 2013; on Russia's raising of gas price, see Burmistrova and Zinets 2014.

59. Naftogaz Ukrainy 2017; Olearchyk and Foy 2018.

60. US Department of the Treasury 2014b; *Financial Times* 2015.

61. Gustafson 2012, 195.

62. Ibid., 272–318; Putin 2010a, 202; on Sechin in GRU, see Kramer 2014b; on Sechin at Rosneft, see Malkova 2013.

63. BP 2013.

64. Putin 2012e.

65. On Yevtushenkov's arrest, see Weaver 2014; on the purchase of Bashneft, see Kobzeva and Korsynskaya 2016.

66. On Sistema's stock plunge, see Reuters 2017b; for *Forbes* quotation, see Foy 2017; investor quoted in Rudnitsky 2017.

67. Peskov quoted in TASS 2016; Sechin and Putin quoted in Putin 2016e.

68. On financing, see RBC 2016; on Bank Otkritie, see Devitt and Korsunskaya 2016; and Bershidsky 2017; on the Order of Friendship, see Zhigalkin 2017.

69. On shell companies, see Latynina 2017; and Stanovaya 2017; on Rosneft's announcement, see McFarlane and Said 2017.

70. On the sale, see Foy and Hume 2017; on the cancellation, see Guo, Mazneva, and Chen 2018.

71. On Sechin's access to Putin, see Dawisha 2014, 84; Rosneft n.d., "Board of Directors."

72. CEIC 2013; for Exxon stock, see symbol XOM:US; Rosneft 2017.

73. For $96 billion and Sechin's remark, see Galouchko and Bierman 2014; market capitalization as of May 11, 2018, stock symbol ROSN:LI; for Yukos's worth, see Åslund 2007b.

74. For $40 billion, see Galouchko and Bierman 2014; for Sechin's request, see Zakvasin 2015.

75. Rosneft's *Annual Report 2014* makes the deal-signing process clear: "Rosneft and Pirelli Expand Cooperation in Sales and Marketing: the companies signed a Memorandum of understanding denoting the spheres of cooperation within joint marketing projects in the Rosneft retail network. The signature ceremony was led by the President of the Russian Federation Vladimir Putin" (Rosneft 2014, 8); "The long-term development program is developed in accordance with the assignment given by the President of the Russian Federation V.V. Putin on 27.12.2013 No. Пр-3086" (ibid., 22); "August 9, 2014, the world's most northern exploration well Universitetskaya-1 began to be drilled in the Vostochno-Prinovozemelskiy-1 License Block of the Kara Sea. The go-ahead to the operations was given by President Vladimir Putin during the teleconference with the Company Management Board Chairman Igor Sechin" (ibid., 68). For *Forbes*'s claim, see Malkova 2013; in order to be able to do so, Sechin insists on using official blue lights, although they are supposed to be reserved for top state officials.

76. On the Rosneft deal with Venezuela, see Reuters 2015; on arms deals, see Amsterdam 2009; on sanctions, see US Department of the Treasury 2014c.

77. VEB 2017b.

78. Ibid.

79. Ibid.

80. Bloomberg 2017; for Gorkov, see VEB 2017b; on Buryakov, see Radio Free Europe/Radio Liberty 2015; on recruiting Page, see Zavadski 2017.

81. VEB 2018.

82. VEB 2017a.

83. On the two projects, see Kramer 2008; on the National Welfare Fund bailout, see Sokolov and Davydova 2012; and *Novaya Gazeta* 2009c.

84. On Sochi Olympics funding, see Nemtsov and Martynyuk 2014; on National Welfare Fund money, see Birman 2015.

85. On Akhmetov, see Kuzio 2010. In the first half of 2017, VEB's subsidiary Prominvestbank made a net loss of $1.8 billion; Kolesnichenko 2017.

86. On the discussion of a capital infusion, see Bush 2015; on the reduction, see Papchenkova, Korsunskaya, and Kobzeva 2016.

87. For sanctions, see US Department of the Treasury 2014c; on Kushner, see Filipov et al. 2017.

88. For Putin forming Rostec at the request of Chemezov, see Felshtinsky and Pribylovsky 2008, 221; Dawisha 2014, 54; and Lee Myers 2015, 260. On their many meetings, see Putin 2015e, 2016d, 2016b, 2017a.

89. Rostec 2017b.

90. Rostec 2017c.

91. Rostec 2017a.

92. Ibid.

93. Rostec 2017d; on annual meetings with Putin, see Putin 2014d, 2015e, 2016b; on meetings with Medvedev, see Medvedev 2010, 2011.

94. Putin 2017a, 2016b.

95. Buckley and Ostrovsky 2006.

96. US Department of the Treasury 2014b, 2014d.

97. Primakov and Lazareva 2013, 10.

98. Yergin and Stanislaw 1998.

99. Yakunin was sanctioned by the United States on March 20, 2014, as one of Putin's cronies. US Department of the Treasury 2014a.

100. Buckley 2017.

101. As evidenced by Nemtsov and Milov 2008, 2010a, 2010b; and Dawisha 2014.

102. Putin 2017b. Rosneftegaz is the government holding company of Rosneft.

103. In 2013, Gazprom CEO Miller officially earned $25 million (RBC 2015); on secret salaries, see Sharkov 2015.

104. Pipes 1974.

FIVE The Expansion of Crony Capitalism

1. On Rybkin's disappearance, see Lee Myers 2004; for the press conference, see Lee Myers, Becker, and Yardley 2014; quotation in Dawisha 2015, 115.

2. Detailed by Felshtinsky and Pribylovsky 2008 and Dawisha 2014.

3. Nemtsov and Milov 2010a, 2010b.

4. Dawisha 2014, 63–80, 94–99; Felshtinsky and Pribylovsky 2008.

5. Interview with Illarionov, July 17, 2017; on Rosspritprom, see Yaffa 2017.

6. On Putin's close friends, see Albats 2012. For Timchenko and Rotenberg, see Nemtsov and Milov 2010a, 2010b; Dawisha 2014; and Felshtinsky and Pribylovsky 2008.

7. US Department of the Treasury 2014a; European Union 2018.

8. On the murder rate, see Mikhailovskaya 1994; on racketeering, see Gilinskiy 2000, 89–94; quotation in Volkov 2002, xi. I knew both Starovoitova and Manevich, Starovoitova well.

9. Putin n.d.; Gessen 2012 is highly accurate in her assessment of Putin, but she is too negative on Sobchak.

10. Stiernlöf 2000; on the Astoria: conversation with my late friend Boris Fedorov at the time.

11. On Warnig, see Felshtinsky and Pribylovsky 2008, 61–62; on Putin's trips to Finland: personal conversations with four senior Finnish diplomats on various occasions.

12. Dixelius and Konstantinov 1998; Felshtinsky and Pribylovsky 2008.

13. The sums vary significantly with the time, as exchange rates changed swiftly, from $92 million to $122 million; the commission's report of 101 pages is widely available on the Internet, e.g., Compromat 2007. On Putin receiving protection, see Felshtinsky and Pribylovsky 2008, 71–82; and Dawisha 2014, 106–125.

14. Kumarin adopted his mother's name, Barsukov. Dawisha 2014, 132–141, quotation on 137.

15. For the Petersburg Fuel Company scandal, see Volkov 2002, 114; on the arrest for money laundering, see Dawisha 2014, 141–145; for the sentencing, see *Kommersant* 2016; and *Vedomosti* 2016.

16. *Business Insider* 2017.

17. Galeotti 2018.

18. Anin, Shmagun, and Velikovskiy 2016.

19. Dawisha 2014, 63–64.

20. On Bank Rossiya, see Dawisha 2014, 64–66; on Kovalchuk, see Milov et al. 2011; on Timchenko, see Reznik and Petrova 2008; on Warnig, see Dawisha 2014, 63–70; and Nemtsov and Milov 2008, 33; on the *Moscow Times,* see Stewart 2008.

21. Felshtinsky and Pribylovsky 2008, 107–108, 257.

22. US Department of the Treasury 2014a.

23. On Timchenko, see Melnikov 2012; and Dawisha 2014, 111–112; on Surgutneftegaz, see Gustafson 2012, 125.

24. Gunvor was apparently the first name of Törnqvist's grandmother; Melnikov 2012.

25. Badanin 2016.

26. US Department of the Treasury 2014a.

27. Melnikov 2012; for stock prices, see stock symbol NVTK:LI.

28. Melnikov 2012.

29. US Department of the Treasury 2014a.

30. Yarosh and Bulavinov 2010.

31. Biografiya Arkady Rotenberg, www.peoples.ru.

32. Yaffa 2017; *Forbes* Russia 2018c; on the contract, see Milov et al. 2011.

33. *Vedomosti* 2010; Mostotrest n.d.

34. Nemtsov and Martynyuk 2014, 8, 11–12.

35. Levinsky 2016; Schreck 2016.

36. Nemtsov and Milov 2008, 34–36.

37. US Department of the Treasury 2014a.

38. Reznik and Petrova 2008.

39. Nemtsov and Milov 2008, 27; Lee Myers, Becker, and Yardley 2014; Polman 2016.

40. Nemtsov and Milov 2008; Reznik and Petrova 2008; quotation in Nemtsov and Milov 2008, 24–25.

41. Nemtsov and Milov 2008, 27, 32–33.

42. On Shamalov, see *Novaya Gazeta* 2009a; quotation in Lichtblau Dougherty 2008; US Securities and Exchange Commission 2008; Albats 2012.

43. On the palace, see Shleinov 2010; quotation in Anin 2011.

44. Nemtsov and Martynyuk 2012; Felshtinsky and Pribylovsky 2008, 108; Sebag Montefiori 2005.

45. Albats 2012.

46. Albats 2012; Anin 2011.

47. An earlier version of this section was published in Åslund 2017a; Putin 2000a, quoted in Yaffa 2017.

48. Whitmore 2015.

49. Reznik and Petrova 2008; Nemtsov and Milov 2008, 24–28.

50. On Kirill Shamalov, see Milov et al. 2011; on his marriage, see Stubbs et al. 2015; on his wealth, see Savchuk 2016; on Tobolsk, see Kuzmin, Zavyalova, and Grey 2016; and on his divorce, see Reznik, Arkhipov, and Sazonov 2018.

51. Grey, Kuzmin, and Piper 2015; Whitmore 2015.

52. On Ivanov, see Alrosa 2017; on Patrushev, see Bloomberg, "Russian Agricultural Bank Atle Staalesen 2015 Patrushev Junior in charge of Prirazlomnaya," Barents Observer, April 8, 2015; on Sechin, see *Moscow Times* 2015; on Bortnikov, see VTB 2017; on Fradkov, see VEB 2015.

53. Whitmore 2015.

54. Dawisha 2014, 337; International Consortium of Investigative Journalists n.d.; *Moscow Times* 2017.

55. Putin 2017b.

56. Putin 2014a; Kovalchuk and Timchenko are Ukrainian names, while Rotenberg is a Jewish name.

57. Putin 2014b. In fact, only the United States had sanctioned Putin's cronies, not the European Union.

58. Putin 2014e.

59. On Italy's freezing of assets, see Rudnitsky and Sirletti 2014; on the Rotenberg Law, see Kramer 2014a; on the transfer of ownership, see Chellanova, Filatov, and Fedorov 2014.

60. The motto is ascribed to Óscar Raymundo Benavides Larrea, who was president of Peru in the 1930s, though many people have ruled along these lines; *Economist* 2012. On Platon, see *Moscow Times* 2016a.

61. Putin 2015c; on the payment, see Yaffa 2017; on the protests, see Filipov 2017; and Bovt 2017.

62. *Moscow Times* 2016b.

SIX How Large Is Russian Wealth, and Why Is It Held Offshore?

1. Nemtsov and Milov 2008, 32–33, 2010a, 2010b.

2. Quotation in Browder 2017; Åslund 2015, 88–90.

3. Gans-Morse 2017; Medvedeva 2018.

4. Browder 2015; Kar and Freitas 2013.

5. Lally 2011.

6. Hirschman 1978.

7. Gentleman 2013.

8. Åslund 1995.

9. Baker 2005, 163.

10. Interview with Vladimir Milov on April 18, 2018.

11. IMF 2015b, 20, GDP values in current USD from IMF 2017.

12. OCCRP 2017.

13. On offshore havens, see Houlder 2017; and Casey 2017; Elgot 2016; quotation in Houlder 2017.

14. US Department of Treasury 2015a, 2; Hodge 2018.

15. Ensign and Ng 2016; Judah and Sibley 2018.

16. Quotation in Judah 2014b.

17. Casey 2017; Judah and Li 2017, 19–20.

18. Findley, Nielson, and Sharman 2014, 72, 74.

19. Browning 2009; Wayne 2012; FACTCoalition 2017.

20. Transparency International UK and Bellingcat 2017

21. Michel 2017; Mance and Houlder 2016.

22. Judah and Li 2017, 22, 24.

23. Bullough 2017.

24. Layne et al. 2017.

25. Nickerson 2016; Mance and Houlder 2016.

26. Ensign and Ng 2016.

27. Three that are particularly laudable are Wayne 2012; Ensign and Ng 2016; and Layne et al. 2017.

28. *Berliner Zeitung* 2018.

29. Kar and Freitas 2013, j.

30. Stewart 2016.

31. Novokmet, Piketty, and Zucman 2017, 8, 21, 23.

32. Piketty 2013, 165; Novokmet, Piketty, and Zucman 2017, 16.

33. Novokmet, Piketty, and Zucman 2017, 16, figs. 12b, 11b.

34. Nemtsov and Milov 2008, 32–33.

35. Yaffa 2017.

36. Anin 2011; Albats 2012.

37. Yaffa 2017.

38. Stewart 2008.

39. Nemtsov and Milov 2008; interview with Vladimir Milov, May 18, 2018.

40. Ignatiev quoted in Voronova and Nikol'sky 2013.

41. Biyanova 2013.

42. Nemtsov and Martynyuk 2012.

43. Belkovsky 2013.

44. Albats 2012; Blomfield 2007; Belkovsky 2006.

45. Nemtsov and Milov 2008, 20–21; Balmforth 2016.

46. Wile 2017; Belkovsky 2013.

47. On Browder's claim, see Taylor 2015; quotation in Browder 2017; on the Panama Papers, see Anin, Shmagun, and Velikovskiy 2016.

48. Anin 2011; Albats 2012. After having discussed with people of real insight into these matters, I have gradually increased the numbers.

49. Kozyrev 2017; Shleynov 2017.

50. Badanin 2017; *Forbes* Russia 2018b.

51. Harding 2016a; Anin 2016; Anin, Shmagun, and Velikovskiy 2016.

52. Gaddy and Danchenko 2006; *Forbes* Russia 2018d.

53. *Forbes* Russia 2018a.

54. Interview with Steven Lee Myers, July 2016; Lee Myers 2015.

55. European Commission 2015b; NataDutilh 2017, 4–5.

56. NataDutilh 2017, 5.

57. Transparency International UK 2017; NataDutilh 2017, 106–121.

58. Davies 2017; Sabbagh 2018.

59. FinCEN 2017; Nehamas and Rodriguez 2017.

60. Interview with Gary Kalman and Clark Gascoigne of the FACTCoalition, April 5, 2018.

SEVEN From International Economic Integration to Deglobalization

1. Guriev 2015.

2. Åslund 2010, 224–228.

3. On hyperinflation, see Granville 1995; on 1992–1994 prices, see Michalopoulos and Tarr 1997; and Michalopoulos and Drebentsov 1997; on suspicions of Russian initiatives, see Olcott, Åslund, and Garnett 1999.

4. Yeltsin 1994, 113; Olcott, Åslund, and Garnett 1999.

5. Putin 2000a, 93; Putin 2005a.

6. Bush 1991.

7. Yeltsin 1991.

8. Åslund 2002, 421. This amount includes only EU grants, not commodity credits.

9. Brzezinski 1983.

10. Åslund 2006.

11. The concept of BRICS had been invented by Jim O'Neill of Goldman Sachs in 2001 as a marketing device (Wilson and Purushothaman 2003); Medvedev 2009a.

12. Asia-Pacific Economic Cooperation n.d.

13. The Shanghai Cooperation Organisation. http://eng.sectsco.org/about_sco/.

14. This section draws on Åslund 2010 and Åslund and Hufbauer 2012, 55–58.

15. Osnovnye 2000.

16. Putin 2002.

17. On the estimated impact, see Jensen, Rutherford, and Tarr 2004; on gains, see Yudaeva et al. 2002.

18. Cooper 2006a, 2006b; Oomes and Kalcheva 2007.

19. Connolly and Hanson 2012.

20. WTO 2012; Browder 2015.

21. US Congress 2016; US Treasury Department 2017c.

22. Åslund and McFaul 2006.

23. Tarr 2007.

24. Coalson 2014.

25. Roberts and Moshes 2016.

26. Movchan and Giucci 2011.

27. United Nations 2014.

28. Roberts and Moshes 2016, 548–549; Adomeit 2012; Krickovic 2014 expresses a similar analysis.

29. Åslund 2013b.

30. Carneiro 2013.

31. On Nazarbayev's claim, see Roberts and Moshes 2016, 543; World Bank 2012.

32. Garbert 2013; Åslund 2013b.

33. Putin 2012e.

34. Movchan and Giucci 2011, 11. For a list of other studies, see Åslund 2013b.

35. Ivanter et al. 2012, 40; Eurasian Development Bank 2012, 29 (cf. Putin 2013a); Moshes 2013.

36. Libman and Vinokurov 2012; Dutkiewicz and Sakwa 2015. Roberts and Moshes 2016 do a nice job taking them apart.

37. Aleksashenko 2016 offers an excellent and detailed analysis.

38. IMF 2015c.

39. Central Bank of Russia n.d.

40. Radio Free Europe/Radio Liberty 2017; Kramer 2014a.

41. Gros and Di Salvo 2017.

42. Deutsche Welle 2017; Reuters 2017a.

43. Gillum and Davis 2017.

44. Heavey and Devitt 2018.

45. Hufbauer et al. 2009.

46. As discussed in chapter 5.

47. Soldatov and Borogan 2017, 314–319.

48. Agence France-Presse 2015.

49. IMF 2018, data for 2017.

50. Åslund 2015, 215.

51. Reuters 2018a, 2018b.

52. Movchan, Saha, and Kirchner 2018.

53. Alexander Gabuev 2015 offers an excellent overview of China-Russia relations.

54. Ibid.

55. On realpolitik, see Walt 1987; on Putin's visit to China, see Putin 2014c.

56. Gabuev 2015.

57. Guriev 2012.

58. Åslund and Hufbauer 2012.

59. US Department of Commerce 2016.

60. Soldatov and Borogan 2017; Meduza 2017.

EIGHT Liberalism versus Statism, or Reform versus Corruption?

1. On the Washington Consensus, see Williamson 1990. On the Leszek Balcerowicz program, see Balcerowicz 1992; Gaidar, a prolific writer, expounded his ideas at length (Gaidar 1993, 1999, 2007, and 2012), while Chubais has done so more sparsely (Chubais 1999; Gaidar and Chubais 2012).

2. At the Gaidar Forum in Moscow in January 2017, Chubais sat in the first row in an audience of a thousand people. Although he did not say one word, the panel referred to him incessantly, showing his authority.

3. I first met Glaziev in 1990, and I was surprised how socialist his views were. We kept in touch until the Ukrainian conflict in 2013.

4. I have known Kudrin since 1990 and have maintained friendly and regular contacts with him; Glaziev 1996, 2005.

5. This section draws on Åslund 2013c.

6. See especially Glaziev 2005, 22–23, where Glaziev summarizes in fifteen points his differences with Putin.

7. Glaziev 2013a.

8. Glaziev 2013b, 2013a, 24.

9. Glaziev 2013a, 2.

10. Glaziev 2013c.

11. Glaziev 2013a, 18, 23.

12. Glaziev 2013b.

13. Glaziev 2013a, 45–48.

14. Putin 2012b.

15. E.g., Mau 2013b; Tsentr Strategitcheskikh rasrabotok 2017.

16. Yasin 2013; Kudrin 2013.

17. Mau 2013a, 16–17.

18. Ibid., 6.

19. Ibid., 17, 9.

20. Elder 2011.

21. Clover 2013.

22. Putin 2012e.

23. Putin 2013b.

24. Putin 2012e, 2012d.

25. Putin 2016a.

26. Ibid.

27. Putin 2017b.

28. Kudrin 2017.

29. Kudrin and Gurvich 2014, quotation on 33. I checked this with Gurvich in June 2017.

30. Ibid., 33.

31. Kudrin 2016.

32. Dmitriev 2016; Prokopenko 2016.

33. Stolypinsky Klub 2016.

34. Institute of Economic Growth P.A. Stolypin 2017.

35. Ibid.; Stolypinsky Klub 2016.

36. Hille and Foy 2017.

37. Hille 2017.

38. Putin 2012a; Trading Economics 2018.

39. Shleifer and Vishny 1993.

40. Transparency International Russia n.d.; INDEM 2001.

41. Nemtsov and Milov 2008, 2010a, 2010b.

42. BBC 2010.

43. Reilhac 2017.

44. Ibid.

45. Anti-Corruption Foundation n.d.

46. Anti-Corruption Foundation 2015; "Chaika" means Seagull and is the name of one of Anton Chekhov's most famous plays. Putin 2015f.

47. US Congress 2016; US Department of the Treasury 2017a.

48. The title refers to a widely ridiculed statement by Medvedev's press secretary Natalia Timakova, complaining that people were talking too casually about the president. Pal'veleva 2013. Anti-Corruption Foundation 2017.

49. *Novaya Gazeta* 2017.

Conclusion

1. On Russian state capitalism, see Kurlantzick 2016, 42.

2. Houlder 2017; Ensign and Ng 2016.

3. This is inspired by a conversation with Vladimir Milov, May 17, 2018.

4. Michels 1911; Yergin and Gustafson 1993, 136.

5. On China, see Lardy 2014; on Russia, see Pei 2016; and Shambaugh 2016.

6. Pipes 1974.

7. Putin 2000a, 91, 200, 202; Freeland 2000; Hoffman 2002. Note that the same was true of the coteries of both Leonid Brezhnev and Mikhail Gorbachev, though not of Boris Yeltsin; Breslauer 1982, 2002.

8. Fukuyama 2011, 17.

9. Shevtsova 2005.

10. Åslund 2007a, 228.

11. Anin 2011; Stewart 2008; Anin, Shmagun, and Velikovskiy 2016.

12. Mandelbaum 2005.

13. Fish 2005; Freedom House 2016; Wright 2017; Shevtsova 2007; Huntington 1991.

14. Krastev 2006.

15. Library of Congress n.d.

16. Transparency International 2017.

17. Åslund 2017b.

18. Ibid.

19. Eichengreen, Park, and Shin 2013; Aiyar et al. 2013.

20. Acemoglu and Johnson 2005.

21. Acemoglu and Robinson 2006; Linz 1978.

22. Acemoglu 2003.

23. For an empirical study of the deinstitutionalization and personalization of the state, see Baturo and Elkink 2016. For an analysis of this process, see Shevtsova 2005.

24. United Nations 2015.

25. IMF 2018; Arkhipov, Martin, and Colitt 2017.

26. IMF 2018.

27. The SIPRI numbers are significantly larger than the Russian numbers for the Ministry of Defense, because many military expenditures in Russia are paid for by other ministries, for example, the Ministry of Interior finances the substantial internal troops. SIPRI 2017.

28. Rutland 2008.

29. Putin 2000a, 169; 2012f.

30. Putin 2008a; Gudkov 2015, 58.

31. McFaul and Stoner-Weiss 2008; Shevtsova 2007, 83.

32. Dunlop 2014; Satter 2003; Treisman 2011.

33. Levada Center 2017.

34. Ibid.

35. Zoria 2018.

36. Von Mises 1920.

37. De Meneses 2009; IMF 2018.

38. Zubarevich 2015, 31; Gudkov 2015, 56.

39. Gozman 2017.

40. Allison 2017, 82.

41. Goldgeier and McFaul 2003, 356.

42. Levada Center 2017.

43. Stent 2014.

44. Gerasimov 2013.

45. Galeotti 2016; Bartles 2016; Gerasimov 2013.

46. Putin 2000a, 19.

47. Galeotti 2016.

48. On social network interference, see Harding 2017; and Isikoff and Corn 2018. On Kremlin interference in elections, see Soldatov and Borogan 2017.

49. Blake et al. 2017; Leopold et al. 2018.

50. Fried 2017.

51. Aron 2017.

52. *Moscow Times* 2012.

53. Michel 2017.

54. I owe this point to Gary Kalman of the FACTCoalition.

55. Ensign and Ng 2016.

56. Judah and Li 2017, 28.

57. Michel 2017.

58. Lipset 1959; Diamond 2008.

59. I have done so repeatedly, notably in Åslund 2007a.

60. Ibid., 239–282.

61. I discuss that in Åslund 2015, 138–146.

References

Acemoglu, Daron. 2003. "The Form of Property Rights: Oligarchic vs. Democratic Societies." NBER Working Paper 10037. Cambridge, MA: National Bureau of Economic Research.

Acemoglu, Daron, and Simon Johnson. 2005. "Unbundling Institutions." *Journal of Political Economy* 113: 949–995.

Acemoglu, Daron, and James A. Robinson. 2006. *Economic Origins of Dictatorship and Democracy*. New York: Cambridge University Press.

Adomeit, Hannes. 2012. "Putin's 'Eurasian Union': Russia's Integration Project and Policies on Post-Soviet Space." Neighborhood Policy Paper 4. Istanbul: Kadir Has University.

Agence France-Presse. 2015. "Russia Suspends Free-Trade Deal with Ukraine from 2016." December 16.

Aiyar, Shekhar, Romain Duval, Damien Puy, Yiqun Wu, and Longmei Zhang. 2013. "Growth Slowdowns and the Middle-Income Trap." IMF Working Paper 71. Washington, DC: International Monetary Fund.

Albats, Evgeniya. 2012. "Chisto konkretny kandidat" [Simply a concrete candidate]. Interview with Sergei Kolesnikov. *Novoe Vremya,* February 27.

Aleksashenko, Sergey. 1999. *Bitva za rubl'* [The battle for the ruble]. Moscow: AlmaMater.

———. 2016. "Evaluating Western Sanctions on Russia." Washington, DC: Atlantic Council.

Alesina, Alberto, and Allen Drazen. 1991. "Why Are Stabilizations Delayed?" *American Economic Review* 81, no. 5: 1170–1188.

Alexeev, Michael, and Shlomo Weber, eds. 2013. *The Oxford Handbook of the Russian Economy*. New York: Oxford University Press.

Allison, Graham. 2017. *Destined for War: Can America and China Escape Thucydides's Trap?* New York: HMH.

Alrosa. 2017. "Sergey Ivanov elected as president of ALROSA." March 14. http://eng.alrosa.
    ru/sergey-ivanov-elected-as-president-of-alrosa/.

Amsterdam, Robert. 2009. "Are Russia's Arms Deals to Venezuela Destabilizing Central
    America?" *Huffington Post*, July 28.

Anin, Roman. 2011. "Tainy 'Proekta Yug'" [The secrets of "Project South"]. *Novaya gaze-
    ta*, January 11.

———. 2016. "Russia: Banking on Influence." *Organized Crime and Corruption Report-
    ing Project*, June 9.

Anin, Roman, Olesya Shmagun, and Dmitry Velikovskiy. 2016. "The Secret Caretaker."
    Organized Crime and Corruption Reporting Project, April 3.

Anti-Corruption Foundation. n.d. "Corruption Today Is the Main Problem in Russia."
    https://fbk.info/about/.

———. 2015. *Chaika*. Documentary film. https://www.youtube.com/watch?v=3eO8Z
    HfV4fk&t=.

———. 2017. *Do Not Call Him Dimon*. Documentary film. https://www.youtube.com/
    watch?v=qrwlk7_GF9g.

Aptekar', Pavel, and Andrei Sinitsyn. 2016. "Prezident poobeshchal biznesu pryamoi dia-
    log s silovikami" [The president promised business a direct dialogue with the law
    enforcers]. *Vedomosti*, February 17.

Arkhipov, Ilya, Peter Martin, and Raymond Colitt. 2017. "China Blasts G-20 over Trade
    as Trump and Putin Shake Hands." Bloomberg, July 7.

Aron, Leon. 2000. *Yeltsin: A Revolutionary Life*. New York: St. Martin's Press.

———. 2017. "Trump Admires Putin, but He Does Not Understand Him." *Politico*, July 10.

Arvelund, Erin. "Russia Moves to Auction Crucial Unit of Yukos." *New York Times*, No-
    vember 20.

Ash, Timothy Garton. 1983. *The Polish Revolution: Solidarity, 1980–82*. London: Jonathan
    Cape.

Asia-Pacific Economic Cooperation. n.d. "History." http://www.apec.org/About-Us/
    About-APEC/History.

Åslund, Anders. 1989. *Gorbachev's Struggle for Economic Reform*. Ithaca, NY: Cornell
    University Press.

———. 1990. "How Small Is the Soviet National Income?" In *The Impoverished Super-
    power: Perestroika and the Soviet Military Burden*, ed. Henry S. Rowen and Charles
    Wolf Jr., 13–61, 288–305. San Francisco: Institute for Contemporary Studies.

———. 1995. *How Russia Became a Market Economy*. Washington, DC: Brookings Insti-
    tution.

———. 1998. "Russia's Financial Crisis: Causes and Possible Remedies." *Post-Soviet Ge-
    ography and Economics* 39, no. 6: 309–328.

———. 2000. "Russia and the International Financial Institutions." Paper presented to
    the International Financial Institution Advisory Commission, January 18, Wash-
    ington, DC.

———. 2002. *Building Capitalism: The Transformation of the Former Soviet Bloc*. New
    York: Cambridge University Press.

———. 2006. "Russia's Challenges as Chair of the G-8." *Policy Briefs in International Economics*. Washington, DC: Peterson Institute for International Economics, March.

———. 2007a. *Russia's Capitalist Revolution: Why Market Reform Succeeded and Democracy Failed*. Washington, DC: Peterson Institute for International Economics.

———. 2007b. "US-Russia Economic Relationship: Implications of the Yukos Affair." Testimony before the Committee on Financial Services, Subcommittee on Domestic and International Monetary Policy, Trade, and Technology, US House of Representatives, US Congress, October 17.

———. 2010a. "Why Doesn't Russia Join the WTO?" *Washington Quarterly*, April, 49–63.

———. 2010b. "The Post-Soviet Space: An Obituary." In Åslund, Guriev, and Kuchins 2010, 223–240.

———. 2013a. *How Capitalism Was Built: The Transformation of Central and Eastern Europe, Russia, the Caucasus, and Central Asia*. 2nd ed. New York: Cambridge University Press.

———. 2013b. "Ukraine's Choice: European Association Agreement or Eurasian Union?" *Policy Brief*, 12–17. Washington, DC: Peterson Institute for International Economics, September.

———. 2013c. "Sergey Glazyev and the Revival of Soviet Economics." *Post-Soviet Affairs* 29, no. 5: 375–386.

———. 2015. *Ukraine: What Went Wrong and How to Fix It*. Washington, DC: Peterson Institute for International Economics.

———. 2017a. "Russia's Oligarchs-in-Waiting." *Project Syndicate*, June 28.

———. 2017b. "The Three Regions of the Former Soviet Bloc." *Journal of Democracy* 28, no. 1: 89–101.

Åslund, Anders, and Gary Clyde Hufbauer. 2012. *The United States Should Establish Permanent Normal Trade Relations with Russia*. Washington, DC: Peterson Institute for International Economics, April.

Åslund, Anders, and Michael McFaul, eds. 2006. *Revolution in Orange: The Origins of Ukraine's Democratic Breakthrough*. Washington, DC: Carnegie Endowment for International Peace.

Åslund, Anders, Sergei Guriev, and Andrew Kuchins, eds. 2010. *Russia after the Global Economic Crisis*. Washington, DC: Peterson Institute for International Economics.

Badanin, Roman. 2016. "Kto on—drug detstva Putina iz Pustomerzhi i reitinga Forbes" [Who is he? Putin's childhood friend from Pustomerzha and from the Forbes rating]. *Dozhd'*, September 26.

Baker, Peter, and Susan Glasser. 2005. *Kremlin Rising: Vladimir Putin's Russia and the End of Revolution*. New York: Scribner.

Baker, Raymond W. 2005. *Capitalism's Achilles Heel: Dirty Money and How to Renew the Free-Market System*. Hoboken, NJ: Wiley.

Balcerowicz, Leszek. 1992. *800 dni skontrolowanego szoku* [800 days of controlled shock]. Warsaw: Polska Oficyna Wydawnicza "BGW."

Balmaceda, Margarita Mercedes. 1998. "Gas, Oil and the Linkages between Domestic and Foreign Policies: The Case of Ukraine." *Europe-Asia Studies* 50, no. 2: 257–286.

———. 2004. "Ukraine's Persistent Energy Crisis." *Problems of Post-Communism* 51, no. 4: 40–50.

———. 2013. *The Politics of Energy Dependency: Ukraine, Belarus, and Lithuania between Domestic Oligarchs and Russian Pressure.* Toronto: University of Toronto Press.

Balmforth, Tom. 2016. "Childhood Friend of Putin's Strikes It Rich, Report Says." Radio Free Europe/Radio Liberty, September 27.

Bank of Finland Institute for Economies in Transition (BOFIT). 2004. "Russia Statistics."

———. 2017. "Number of Employed All-Time High in Russia." Weekly Report, August 4.

———. 2018. "Russia Statistics."

Barbashin, Anton, and Hannah Thoburn. 2015. "Putin's Philosopher: Ivan Ilyin and the Ideology of Moscow's Rule." *Foreign Affairs*, September 20.

Barber, Tony. 2017. "Why Putin Would Rather Forget 1917." *Financial Times*, August 4.

Bartles, Charles K. 2016. "Getting Gerasimov Right." *Military Review* January–February, 30–38.

Baturo, Alexander, and Johan A. Elkink. 2016. "Dynamics of Regime Personalization and Patron-Client Networks in Russia, 1999–2014." *Post-Soviet Affairs* 32, no. 1: 75–98.

Bazanova, Elizaveta, et al. 2016. "Vladimir Putin vnov' poobeshchal biznesu zashchitu ot pravookhranitelei" [Vladimir Putin once again promised business defense against law enforcers]. *Vedomosti*, June 20.

BBC. 2010. "Russia Checks Claims of $4bn Oil Pipeline Scam." November 17.

———. 2016. "Putin Creates New National Guard in Russia 'to Fight Terrorism.'" April 6.

Belkovsky, Stanislav. 2006. "How Do Ordinary Officials and Politicians Make Billions?" *Argumenty i Fakty*, May 17.

———. 2013. "Osoboe Mnenie" [Personal view]. *Ekho Moskvy*, February 15.

Belton, Catherine. 2004. "Putin: Tell Me Who Wants Yukos Broke." *Moscow Times*, September 9.

———. 2005. "Gazprom Scoops Up Sibneft for $13 Billion." *Moscow Times*, September 29.

Bensinger, Ken, Miriam Elder, and Mark Schoofs. 2017. "These Reports Allege Trump Has Deep Ties to Russia." *Buzzfeed*, January 10.

Berliner Zeitung. 2018. "Der Kudamm-Komplex im TV." May 18.

Bershidsky, Leonid. 2017. "A Big Russian Bank Just Couldn't Stay Private." *Bloomberg*, August 30.

Birman, Alexander. 2015. "Pylesos razvitiya: Pochemu Vneshekonombank reshil vytashchit' iz ekonomiki trillion rubley" [Vacuum of development: Why did Vnesheconombank decide to pull a trillion rubles out of the economy?]. Lenta. ru, May 29.

Biyanova, Nataliya. 2013. "TsB: 40% ottoka kapitala iz Rossii obespechil Tamozhenny soyuz CB" [The Customs Union facilitated 40% of the capital outflow from Russia]. *Vedomosti*, June 20.

Blake, Heidi, et al. 2017. "From Russia with Blood." *Buzzfeed*, June 15.

Blasi, Joseph R., Maya Kroumova, and Douglas Kruse. 1997. *Kremlin Capitalism: Privatizing the Russian Economy*. Ithaca, NY: Cornell University Press.

Blomfield, Adrian. 2007. "$40bn Putin 'Is Now Europe's Richest Man.'" *Telegraph*, December 21.

Bloomberg. 2017. "Vladimir Alexandrovich Dmitriev." http://www.bloomberg.com/research/stocks/private/person.asp?personId=9876082&privcapId=9284392.

Bovt, Georgy. 2017. "The Hushed Up Story of Russia's Trucker Revolt." Intersection Project, April 14.

Boycko, Maxim, Andrei Shleifer, and Robert W. Vishny. 1995. *Privatizing Russia*. Cambridge, MA: MIT Press.

BP. 2013. "Rosneft and BP Complete TNK-BP Sale and Purchase Transaction." Press Release, March 20. www.bp.com.

———. 2017. "Statistical Review of World Energy 2017: Historical Data." www.bp.com.

Brainerd, Elizabeth. 1998. "Market Reform and Mortality in Transition Economies." *World Development* 26, no. 11: 2013–2027.

Bremmer, Ian, and Nouriel Roubini. 2011. "A G-Zero World." *Foreign Affairs*, March–April.

Breslauer, George W. 1982. *Khrushchev and Brezhnev as Leaders*. London: George Allen and Unwin.

———. 2002. *Gorbachev and Yeltsin as Leaders*. New York: Cambridge University Press.

Browder, Bill. 2015. *Red Notice: A True Story of High Finance, Murder, and One Man's Fight for Justice*. New York: Simon and Schuster.

———. 2017. "Testimony to the Senate Judiciary Committee." *Atlantic*, July 25.

Brown, Archie. 1996. *The Gorbachev Factor*. Oxford: Oxford University Press.

Browning, Lynnley. 2009. "Delaware Laws, Helpful to Arms Trafficker, to Be Scrutinized." *New York Times*, November 4.

Brzezinski, Zbigniew. 1983. "The Tragic Dilemma of Soviet World Power: The Limits of a New-Type Empire." *Encounter* 61, no. 4: 10–16.

Buchanan, Elizabeth. 2003. "Start with a Level Playing Field: How CEELI Helped Bring about a New Criminal Procedure Code That Gives Russia's Defendants a Voice." American Bar Association, February. www.abanet.org.

Buckley, Neil. 2017. "Russia State Businesses with Clout Benefit from Relaxed Dividend Rules." *Financial Times*, June 1.

Buckley, Neil, and Arkady Ostrovsky. 2006. "Putin's Allies Turn Russia into a Corporate State." *Financial Times*, June 18.

Bullough, Oliver. 2017. "Offshore Money, Bane of Democracy." *New York Times*, April 7.

Burmistrova, Svetlana, and Natalia Zinets. 2014. "Russia Raises Gas Price for Ukraine by 80 Percent." Reuters, April 3.

Bush, George H. W. 1991. "Address before a Joint Session of the Congress on the State of the Union." January 29. http://www.presidency.ucsb.edu/ws/?pid=19253.

Bush, George W. 2001. "Press Conference by President Bush and Russian Federation President Putin." June 16. georgewbush-whitehouse.archives.gov.

———. 2003. "President Bush Meets with Russian President Putin at Camp David." September 27. georgewbush-whitehouse.archives.gov.

Bush, Jason. 2015. "VEB's $20 Bln Bailout Request Casts Harsh Light on Development Bank's Operations." Reuters, November 27.

Business Insider. 2017. "That Time Putin Brought His Dog to a Meeting to Scare Angela Merkel." July 7.

Carneiro, Francisco G. 2013. "What Promises Does the Eurasian Customs Union Hold for the Future?" Economic Premise 108. Washington, DC: World Bank.

CEIC. 2013. "Trend towards Centralisation in the Russian Oil Market as Rosneft Acquires TNK-BP." May 10. www.ceicdata.com.

Centre for Economic and Financial Research (CEFIR) and World Bank. 2003. "Monitoring administrativnykh bar'erov na puti razvitiia malogo biznesa v Rossii: Rezul'taty vtorogo raunda" [Monitoring the administrative impediments to the development of small business in Russia: The results of the second round]. www. worldbank.org.ru.

Central Bank of the Russian Federation. 2018a. "External Debt of the Russian Federation." http://www.cbr.ru/eng/statistics/print.aspx?file=credit_statistics/debt_an_ det_new_e.htm&pid=svs&sid=itm_272.

———. 2018b. "International Reserves of the Russian Federation." http://www.cbr.ru/ eng/hd_base/mrrf/mrrf_m/.

Chellanova, Milana, Anton Filatov, and Yevgeny Fedorov. 2014. "Biznes—na detakh" [Business to the children]. *Vedomosti*, October 13.

Cherkezov, Viktor. 2007. "We Must Not Allow Warriors to Become Merchants." *Kommersant*, October 9.

Chubais, Anatoly B., ed. 1999. *Privatizatsiya po-rossiiski* [Privatization in a Russian way]. Moscow: Vagrius.

Clover, Charles. 2013. "Slowdown in Russia Challenges Liberal Wing." *Financial Times,* April 18.

———. 2016. *Black Wind, White Snow: The Rise of Russia's New Nationalism.* New Haven: Yale University Press.

CNN.com. 2001. "Transcript: Bush, Putin News Conference." June 18. http://www.cnn. com/2001/WORLD/europe/06/18/bush.putin.transcript/index.html.

CNN Money. 1998. "Russia's 'Black Thursday.'" August 13.

Coalson, Robert. 2014. "Is Putin 'Rebuilding Russia' according to Solzhenitsyn's Design?" Radio Free Europe/Radio Liberty, September 1.

Colton, Timothy J. 2008. *Yeltsin: A Life.* New York: Basic Books.

Compromat. 2007. "Doklad Mariny Sal'e i Yuriya Gladkova o deyatel'nosti V.V. Putina na postu komiteta po vneshnim svyazam merii Sankt-Peterburga" [Report of Marina Sal'e and Yuri Gladkov on the activities of V.V. Putin as head of the Committee on External Relations of the City Hall of St. Petersburg]. Compromat.ru, November 28. http://www.compromat.ru/page_21848.htm.

Commander, Simon, and C. Mumssen. 1998. "Understanding Barter in Russia." EBRD Working Paper 37.

Connolly, Richard, and Philip Hanson. 2012. "Russia's Accession to the World Trade Organization." *Eurasian Geography and Economics* 53, no. 4: 479–501.

Cooper, Julian. 2006a. "Of BRICs and Brains: Comparing Russia with China, India and Other Populous Emerging Economies." *Eurasian Geography and Economics* 47, no. 3: 255–284.

———. 2006b. "Can Russia Compete in the Global Economy?" *Eurasian Geography and Economics* 47, no. 4: 407–425.

Criminal Code of the Russian Federation. 2003. Stat'ia 199: Uklonenie ot uplaty nalogov i ili sborov s organizatsii [Article 199: Evasion of payment of a corporate tax and/ or toll], "Federal'nyi zakon N 162-FZ: O vnesenii izmenenii i dopolnenii v Ugolovnyy kodeks Rossiiskoi Federatsii" [Federal Law No. 162-FZ: On introducing changes and amendments to the criminal code of the Russian Federation]. https://www.legislationline.org/documents/id/4188.

Dabrowski, Marek. 2015. "The Impact of the Oil-Price Shock on Net Oil Exporters." Bruegel, November 24.

Davies, Rachel. 2017. "Unexplained Wealth Orders: A Brief Guide." *Transparency International UK.* May 30.

Dawisha, Karen. 2014. *Putin's Kleptocracy: Who Owns Russia?* New York: Simon and Schuster.

Decree of the President of the Russian Federation. 2016. "No. 306: Voprosy sovershenstvovania gosudarstvennogo upravleniia v Rossiiskoi Federatsii" [No. 306: Issues concerning the improvement of state management in the Russian Federation]. June 30.

De Meneses, Filipe. 2009. *Salazar: A Political Biography.* New York: Enigma.

Deutsche Welle. 2017. "Siemens Sells Stake in Russian Firm after Crimea Turbine Scandal." July 21.

Devitt, Polina. 2017. "Declare Offshore Wealth? Russia Tycoons Would Rather Ship Themselves Off Shore." Reuters, June 6.

Devitt, Polina, and Darya Korsunskaya. 2016. "Kremlin Says Glencore, Qatari Fund to Buy 19.5 Pct Stake in Rosneft." Reuters, December 7.

Diamond, Jack. 2002. "The New Russian Budget System: A Critical Assessment and Future Reform Agenda." IMF Working Paper 02/21. Washington, DC: International Monetary Fund.

Diamond, Larry. 2008. *The Sprit of Democracy.* New York: Times Books.

Dixelius, Malcolm, and Andrej Konstantinov. 1998. *Maffians Ryssland* [The mafia's Russia]. Stockholm: Kommentus.

Dmitriev, Mikhail E., ed. 2016. "Analiz faktorov realizatsii dokumentov strategicheskogo planirovaniya verkhnego urovnya" [Analysis of the realization of documents of strategic planning]. St. Petersburg: Center for Strategic Research, December.

Dobbs, Michael. 1997. *Down with Big Brother: The End of the Soviet Empire.* New York: Knopf.

Drazen, Allen, and Vittorio Grilli. 1993. "The Benefit of Crises for Economic Reforms." *American Economic Review* 83, no. 3: 598–607.

Dunlop, John. 1993. *The Rise of Russia and the Fall of the Soviet Empire*. Princeton, NJ: Princeton University Press.

———. 1998. *Russia Confronts Chechnya: Roots of a Separatist Conflict*. New York: Cambridge University Press.

———. 2014. *The Moscow Bombings of September 1999: Examinations of Russian Terrorist Attacks at the Onset of Vladimir Putin's Rule*. 2nd ed. Stuttgart: Ibidem Press.

Dutkiewicz, Piotr, and Richard Sakwa, eds. 2015. *Eurasian Integration—The View from Within*. Oxford: Routledge.

EBRD. 1994. *Transition Report, 1994*. London: European Bank for Reconstruction and Development.

———. 2003. *Transition Report, 2003*. London: European Bank for Reconstruction and Development.

———. 2004. *Transition Report, 2004*. London: European Bank for Reconstruction and Development.

Economist. 2012. "Knock, Knock." July 21.

———. 2013. "Russia's Wounded Giant." March 23.

Eichengreen, Barry, Donghyun Park, and Kwanho Shin. 2013. "Growth Slowdowns Redux: New Evidence on the Middle-Income Trap." NBER Working Paper 18673. Cambridge, MA: National Bureau of Economic Research.

Elder, Miriam. 2011. "Vladimir Putin Accuses Hillary Clinton of Encouraging Russian Protests." *Guardian*, December 8.

Elgot, Jessica. 2016. "World Leaders Pledge to Tackle Corruption at London Summit—as It Happened." *Guardian*. May 12.

Ensign, Rachel Louise, and Serena Ng. 2016. "Law Firms' Accounts Pose Money-Laundering Risk." *Wall Street Journal*, December 26.

Eurasian Development Bank. 2012. "Ukraine and the Customs Union. Report 1." www.eabr.org/general//upload/reports/Ukraina_ doklad_eng.pdf.

Euroactive. 2015. "Russia Overrules the European Court of Human Rights." July 14.

European Commission. 2015a. "Antitrust: Commission Sends Statement of Objections to Gazprom for Alleged Abuse of Dominance on Central and Eastern European Gas Supply Markets." Press Release, Brussels, April 22.

———. 2015b. "Directive EU 2015/849 of the European Parliament and of the Council, on the Prevention of the Use of the Financial System for the Purposes of Money Laundering or Terrorist Financing." May 20.

———. 2015c. "Energy Union: Secure, Sustainable, Competitive, Affordable Energy for Every European." Press Release, Brussels, February 25.

———. 2017. "Antitrust: Commission Invites Comments on Gazprom Commitments concerning Central and Eastern European Gas Markets. Press Release, Brussels, March 13.

———. 2018. "Antitrust: Commission Imposes Binding Obligations on Gazprom to Enable Free Flow of Gas at Competitive Prices in Central and Eastern European Gas Markets." Press Release, Brussels, May 24.

European Union. 2018. "EU Sanctions against Russia over Ukraine Crisis." August 5. https://europa.eu/newsroom/highlights/special-coverage/eu-sanctions-against-russia-over-ukraine-crisis_en.

FACTCoalition. 2017. "FACT Sheet." Washington, DC: FACTCoalition. November.

Farchy, Jack. 2015. "Gazprom Gas Output for 2015 Set to Be Lowest since Soviet Era." *Financial Times,* July 29.

Federal Tax Service of Russia. n.d. "Profit Tax."

Fedorov, Boris G. 1999. *10 Bezumnykh let* [10 mad years]. Moscow: Sovershenno Sekretno.

Felshtinsky, Yuri, and Vladimir Pribylovsky. 2008. *The Corporation: Russia and the KGB in the Age of President Putin.* New York: Encounter.

Filipov, David. 2017. "In Russia, Truckers Strike against Increased Road Tax." *Washington Post,* April 23.

Filipov, David, et al. 2017. "Explanations for Kushner's Meeting with Head of Kremlin-Linked Bank Don't Match Up." *Washington Post,* June 1.

Financial Crimes Enforcement Network (FinCEN). 2017. "FinCEN Targets Shell Companies Purchasing Luxury Properties in Seven Major Metropolitan Areas." US Treasury, August 22.

Financial Times. 2015. "Vestager Takes a Tough Stance on Gazprom." Editorial. April 21.

Findley, Michael, Daniel Nielson, and Jason Sharman. 2014. *Global Shell Games.* New York: Cambridge University Press.

Fish, Steven. 2005. *Democracy Derailed in Russia: The Failure of Open Politics.* New York: Cambridge University Press.

Forbes Russia. 2018a. "Il'gam Ragimov." *Forbes,* http://www.forbes.ru/profile/255059-ragimov.

———. 2018b. "Petr Kolbin." http://www.forbes.ru/profile/petr-kolbin.

———. 2018c. "Stroigazmontazh." http://www.forbes.ru/profile/stroigazmontazh.

———. 2018d. "Vladimir Litvinenko." http://www.forbes.ru/profile/237255-litvinenko.

Fortescue, Stephen. 2006. *Russia's Oil Barons and Metal Magnates.* New York: Palgrave McMillan.

Foy, Henry. 2017. "Rosneft-Sistema Case Poses Threat to Russia's Investment Climate." *Financial Times,* July 27.

Foy, Henry, and Neil Hume. 2017. "CEFC China Energy Buys $9bn Stake in Rosneft." *Financial Times,* September 8.

Freedom House. 2016. "Freedom in the World, 2016." www.freedomhouse.org.

Freeland, Chrystia. 2000. *Sale of the Century: Russia's Wild Ride from Communism to Capitalism.* New York: Crown Business.

Freeland, Chrystia, John Thornhill, and Andrew Gowers. 1996. "Moscow's Group of Seven." *Financial Times,* November 1.

Fried, Daniel. 2017. "Russia's Back-to-the-80s Foreign Policy." *Atlantic,* August 2.

Frye, Timothy. 2010. "Corruption and the Rule of Law." In Åslund, Guriev, and Kuchins 2010, 79–94.

Fukuyama, Francis. 2011. *The Origins of Political Order.* New York: Farrar, Straus and Giroux.

Gabuev, Alexander. 2015. "A 'Soft Alliance'? Russia-China Relations after the Ukraine Crisis." Policy Brief. London: European Council on Foreign Relations, February.

Gaddy, Clifford G., and Igor Danchenko. 2006. "The Mystery of Vladimir Putin's Dissertation." Washington, DC: Brookings Institution, March.

Gaddy, Clifford G., and Barry W. Ickes. 2002. *Russia's Virtual Economy*. Washington, DC: Brookings Institution.

———. 2005. "Resource Rents and the Russian Economy." *Eurasian Geography and Economics* 46, no. 8: 559–583.

———. 2009. "Russia's Declining Oil Production: Managing Price Risk and Rent Addiction." *Eurasian Geography and Economics* 50, no. 1: 1–13.

Gaidar, Yegor T. 1993. "Inflationary Pressures and Economic Reform in the Soviet Union." In *Economic Transition in Eastern Europe*, ed. P. H. Admiraal. Oxford: Blackwell.

———. 1999. *Days of Defeat and Victory*. Seattle: University of Washington Press.

———. 2004. Public presentation at the World Bank, January 26, Washington, DC.

———. 2007. *Collapse of the Empire: Lessons for Modern Russia*. Washington, DC: Brookings Institution.

———. 2012. *Russia: A Long View*. Cambridge, MA: MIT Press.

Gaidar, Yegor T., and Anatoly Chubais. 2012. *Ekonomicheskie zapiski* [Economic notes]. Moscow: Rosspen.

Gaidar, Yegor T., et al., eds. 2003. *Ekonomika perekhodnogo perioda: Ocherki ekonomicheskoi politiki postkommunisticheskoi Rossii, 1998–2002* [Transition economics: Essays on the economic policies of post-Communist Russia, 1998–2002]. Moscow: Delo.

Galeotti, Mark. 2014a. "The 'Gerasimov Doctrine' and Russian Non-Linear War." In Moscow's Shadows (blog), July 6.

———. 2014b. "Putin and His Judo Cronies." *Foreign Policy*, May 14.

———. 2016. "Putin's Hydra: Inside Russia's Intelligence Services." Policy Brief. London: European Council on Foreign Relations, May.

———. 2018. *The Vory: Russia's Super Mafia*. New Haven: Yale University Press.

Galouchko, Ksenia, and Stephen Bierman. 2014. "Russia's Oil Giant Battles Debt after $55 Billion Deal." Bloomberg, November 27.

Gambetta, Diego. 1993. *The Sicilian Mafia*. Cambridge, MA: Harvard University Press.

Gans-Morse, Jordan. 2012. "Threats to Property Rights in Russia: From Private Coercion to State Aggression." *Post-Soviet Affairs* 28, no. 3: 263–295.

———. 2017. *Property Rights in Post-Soviet Russia: Violence, Corruption, and the Demand for Law*. New York: Cambridge University Press.

Garbert, Folkert. 2013. "Belarus und die Zollunion—Eine Bestandsaufnahme" [Belarus and the Customs Union: An assessment]. German Economic Team Belarus, Newsletter 22, March–April.

Gazprom. 2011. "Alexey Miller Appoints Burckhard Bergmann as His Advisor." Press Release, June 30. http://www.gazprom.com/press/news/2011/june/article114559/.

———. 2014. "Investor Day 2014." Brochure. http://www.gazprom.com/f/posts/28/866895/gazprom_investor_day_2014_slides.pdf.

———. 2017a. "About Gazprom." http://www.gazprom.com/about/.

———. 2017b. "Board of Directors." http://www.gazprom.com/about/management/directors/.

———. 2017c. "Boris Fedorov." http://www.gazprom.com/about/history/people/fedorov/.

———. 2017d. "Gas and Oil Production." http://www.gazprom.com/about/production/extraction/.

———. 2017e. "Sakhalin II." http://www.gazprom.com/about/production/projects/lng/sakhalin2/.

Gentleman, Amelia. 2013. "Exile in Mayfair: Millionaire Yevgeny Chichvarkin's New Life in London." *Guardian*, December 27.

Gerasimov, Valery. 2013. "Tsennost' nauki v predvidenii" [The value of science in prediction]. *Voenno-promyshlenny kur'er*, February 27.

Gessen, Masha. 2012. *The Man without a Face: The Unlikely Rise of Vladimir Putin*. New York: Riverhead Books.

Gilauri, Nika. 2017. *Practical Economics: Economic Transformation and Government Reform in Georgia, 2004–2012*. New York: Palgrave MacMillan.

Gilinskiy, Yakov. 2000. *Crime and Deviance: Stare from Russia*. St. Petersburg: St. Petersburg Branch of the Institute of Sociology of the Russian Academy of Sciences.

Gillum, Jack, and Aaron C. Davis. 2017. "Local Governments Still Use Russian Brand of Software." *Washington Post*, July 24.

Glaziev, Sergei. 1996. "Ob otkrytosti i razumnoi zashchite rossiiskoi ekonomiki" [On openness and sensible protection of the Russian economy]. In Oleg Bogomolov, ed., *Reformy glazami amerikanskikh i rossiiskikh uchenykh* [The reforms through the eyes of American and Russian scholars]. Moscow: Rossiiskii ekonomicheskii zhurnal.

———. 2005. *Vybor Budushchego* [Choice for the future]. Moscow: Algoritm.

———. 2013a. "O tselyakh, problemakh i merakh gosudarstvennoi politiki razvitiya i integratsii" [On the goals, problems and measures of state policy for development and integration]. Russian Academy of Sciences, Moscow, January 29.

———. 2013b. "Parusnik bez rulya" [Boat without rudder]. Lenta.ru.

———. 2013c. "Sergei Glaziev i uchenye RAN dali sovety otnositel'no privatizatsii" [Sergei Glaziev and scholars at the Russian Academy of Sciences gave advice on privatization]. *Vedomosti*, February 28.

Goldgeier, James M., and Michael McFaul. 2003. *Power and Purpose: U.S. Policy Toward Russia after the Cold War*. Washington, DC: Brookings Institution.

Goldman, Marshall I. 1991. *What Went Wrong with Perestroika*. New York: Norton.

———. 2003. *The Piratization of Russia: Russian Reform Goes Awry*. London: Routledge.

———. 2008. *Petrostate: Putin, Power, and the New Russia*. New York: Oxford University Press.

Gorbachev, Mikhail S. 1987a. *Izbrannye rechi i stati* [Selected speeches and articles]. Vol. 3. Moscow: Politizdat.

———. 1987b. *Perestroika: New Thinking for Our Country and the World*. New York: Harper and Row.

Gorodnichenko, Yuriy, Jorge Martinez-Vazquez, and Klara Sabirianova Peter. 2009. "Myth and Reality of Flat Tax Reform: Micro Estimates of Tax Evasion Response and Welfare Effects in Russia." *Journal of Political Economy* 117, no. 3: 504–554.

Gozman, Leonid. 2017. "Chto okhranyaem?" [What are we protecting?]. *Novaya Gazeta*, July 2.

Granville, Brigitte. 1995. "So Farewell Then Rouble Zone." In *Russian Economic Reform at Risk*, ed. Anders Åslund. New York: St. Martin's Press.

Grey, Stephen, Andrey Kuzmin, and Elizabeth Piper. 2015. "Putin's Daughter, a Young Billionaire, and the President's Friends." Reuters, November 10.

Grey, Stephen, Tom Bergin, Sevgil Musaieva, and Roman Anin. 2014. "Putin's Allies Channeled Billions to Oligarch Who Backed Pro-Russian President of Ukraine." Reuters, November 26.

Gros, Daniel, and Mattia Di Salvo. 2017. "Revisiting Sanctions on Russia and Counter-Sanctions on the EU: The Economic Impact Three Years Later." Brussels: Center for European Policy Studies.

Gudkov, Lev. 2015. "Resources of Putin's Conservatism." In *Putin's Russia*, ed. Leon Aron, 52–72. Washington, DC: American Enterprise Institute.

Guo, Aibing, Elena Mazneva, and Judy Chen. 2018. "China's Russian Oil Marriage Nixed amid Fall of Suitor CEFC." Bloomberg, May 6.

Guriev, Sergei. 2015. "Deglobalizing Russia." Carnegie Moscow Center, December 16.

Guriev, Sergei, and Aleh Tsyvinski. 2010. "Challenges Facing the Russian Economy after the Crisis." In Åslund, Guriev, and Kuchins 2010, 9–38.

Gustafson, Thane. 2012. *Wheel of Fortune: The Battle for Oil and Power in Russia*. Cambridge, MA: Belknap Press of Harvard University Press.

Handelman, Stephen. 1995. *Comrade Criminal: Russia's New Mafiya*. New Haven: Yale University Press.

Harding, Luke. 2011. *Mafia State*. London: Guardian.

———. 2016a. "Revealed, the $2 Billion Offshore Trail That Leads to Vladimir Putin." *Guardian*, April 3.

———. 2016b. "Sergei Roldugin, the Cellist Who Holds the Key to Tracing Putin's Hidden Fortune." *Guardian*, April 3.

———. 2017. *Collusion: Secret Meetings, Dirty Money, and How Russia Helped Donald Trump Win*. New York: Vintage.

Harding, Luke, and Nick Hopkins. 2017. "How 'Dirty Money' from Russia Flooded into the UK and Where It Went." *Guardian*, March 20.

Heavey, Susan, and Polina Devitt. 2018. "U.S. Extends Deadline for Rusal Sanctions, Aluminum Prices Dive." Reuters, April 23.

Hedenskog, Jacob, and Robert L. Larsson. 2007. *Russian Leverage on the CIS and the Baltic States*. Stockholm: Swedish Defence Research Agency.

Hendley, Kathryn. 1997. "Legal Development in Post-Soviet Russia." *Post-Soviet Affairs* 13, no. 3: 228–251.

———. 2002. "Suing the State in Russia." *Post-Soviet Affairs* 18, no. 2: 122–147.

Hendley, Kathryn, Barry W. Ickes, Peter Murrell, and Randi Ryterman. 2013. "Observations on the Use of Law by Russian Enterprises." *Post-Soviet Affairs* 13, no. 1: 19–41.

Hill, Fiona, and Clifford G. Gaddy. 2015. *Mr. Putin*. 2nd ed. Washington, DC: Brookings.

Hille, Kathrin. 2017. "Kremlin Enters Economists into Beauty Contest to Find Answers to Anaemic Growth." *Financial Times*, May 31.

Hille, Kathrin, and Henry Foy. 2017. "Kremlin Aide Urges Oil Industry Privatization." *Financial Times*, June 2.

Hirschman, Albert O. 1965. *Journeys toward Progress: Studies of Economic Policy-Making in Latin America*. Garden City, NY: Doubleday.

———. 1978. "Exit, Voice, and the State." *World Politics* 31, no. 1: 90–107.

Hodge, Margaret. 2018. "This Is How to Curb Putin: Stop Welcoming Russian Kleptocrats." *Guardian*, March 16.

Hoffman, David. 2000. "Foreign Investors Criticize Deals by Russian Gas Giant." *Washington Post*, December 24.

———. 2002. *The Oligarchs: Wealth and Power in the New Russia*. New York: Public Affairs.

Houlder, Vanessa. 2017. "Trinidad and Tobago Left as the Last Blacklisted Tax Haven." *Financial Times*, June 28.

Hufbauer, Gary Clyde, Jeffrey J. Schott, Kimberly Ann Elliott, and Barbara Oegg. 2009. *Economic Sanctions Re-Considered*. Washington, DC: Peterson Institute for International Economics.

Huntington, Samuel. 1991. *The Third Wave: Democratization in the Late Twentieth Century*. Norman: University of Oklahoma Press.

Illarionov, Andrei N. 1998a. "Kak byl organizovan rossiisky finansovy krizis (1)" [How the Russian economic crisis was organized (1)]. *Voprosy Ekonomiki* 70, no. 11: 20–35.

———. 1998b. "Kak byl organizovan rossiisky finansovy krizis (2)" [How the Russian economic crisis was organized (2)]. *Voprosy Ekonomiki* 70, no. 12: 12–31.

IMF (International Monetary Fund, www.imf.org). 2015a. "Russian Federation: 2015 Article IV Consultation." Country Report 15/211.

———. 2015b. "Cyprus: Fifth, Sixth, and Seventh Reviews under the Extended Arrangement under the Extended Fund Facility." June 4.

———. 2015c. "IMF Survey: Cheaper Oil and Sanctions Weigh on Russia's Growth Outlook." August 3.

———. 2017. "Direction of Trade Statistics (DOTS)."

———. 2018. IMF World Economic Outlook database, April.

INDEM Foundation. 2001. "Praktika delovoi korruptsii" [The practice of business corruption]. In *Diagnostika rossiiskoi korruptsii: Sotsiologicheskii analiz* [Diagnostics of Russian corruption: A sociological analysis]. December. http://www.anti-corr.ru/awbreport/index.htm.

Institute for the Economy of Growth, Stolypin, P.A. 2017. "Strategiya rosta" [Growth strategy]. February 28.

The International Consortium of Investigative Journalists. n.d. "Igor Putin." https://offshoreleaks.icij.org/nodes/12136740.

Isikoff, Michael, and David Corn. 2018. *Russian Roulette: The Inside Story of Putin's War on America and the Election of Donald Trump*. New York: Twelve.

Ivanov, Sergei. 2006. "Triada natsional'nykh Tsennostei" [Triad of national values]. *Izvestiya*, July 13.

Ivanova, Anna, Michael Keen, and Alexander Klemm. 2005. "The Russian Flat Tax Reform." IMF Working Paper 05/16. Washington, DC: International Monetary Fund.

Ivanter, Viktor, et al. 2012. "The Economic Effects of the Creation of the Single Economic Space and Potential Accession of Ukraine." In *Eurasian Integration Yearbook, 2012.* Almaty, Kazakhstan: Eurasian Development Bank.

Jensen, Jesper, Thomas Rutherford, and David Tarr. 2004. "Economy-Wide and Sector Effects of Russia's Accession to the WTO." Washington, DC: World Bank, May 26.

Johnson, Juliet. 2000. *A Fistful of Rubles: The Rise and Fall of the Russian Banking System.* Ithaca, NY: Cornell University Press.

JP Morgan Cazenove. 2015. *Russian Oil and Gas.* JP Morgan, July 23.

Judah, Ben. 2013. *Fragile Empire: How Russia Fell in and out of Love with Vladimir Putin.* New Haven: Yale University Press.

———. 2014a. "A Day in the Life of Vladimir Putin: The Dictator in His Labyrinth." *Independent,* July 25.

———. 2014b. "London's Laundry Business." *New York Times,* March 14.

Judah, Ben, and Belinda Li. 2017. "Money Laundering for 21st Century Authoritarianism: Western Enablement of Kleptocracy." Briefing Paper. Washington, DC: Hudson Institute, Kleptocracy Initiative, December.

Judah, Ben, and Nate Sibley. 2018. "Countering Russian Kleptocracy." Briefing Paper. Washington, DC: Hudson Institute, Kleptocracy Initiative, April.

Kar, Dev, and Sarah Freitas. 2013. "Russia: Illicit Financial Flows and the Role of the Underground Economy." Washington, DC: Global Financial Integrity, February.

Keen, Michael, Yitae Kim, and Ricardo Varsano. 2006. "The 'Flat Tax(es)': Principles and Evidence." IMF Working Paper 218. Washington, DC: International Monetary Fund.

Kharas, Homi, Brian Pinto, and Sergei Ulatov. 2001. "An Analysis of Russia's 1998 Meltdown: Fundamentals and Market Signals." *Brookings Papers on Economic Activity* 1: 1–50.

Kirchik, Olesia. 2004. "Zemel'naia reforma: 1990–2002" [Land reform: 1990–2002]. *Otechestvennye Zapiski* [Notes from the fatherland], no. 1: 16.

Klebnikov, Paul. 2000. *Godfather of the Kremlin: The Decline of Russia in the Age of Gangster Capitalism.* Orlando, FL: Harcourt.

Kleiner, Vadim. 2005. "How Should Gazprom Be Managed in Russia's National Interests and the Interests of Its Shareholders?" Moscow: Hermitage Capital Management, June.

Klerk. 2004. "Zakonoproekt po snizheniu ESN priniat vo vtorom chtenii" [A bill to reduce the single social tax passes its second reading]. Klerk.ru, June 11, https://www.klerk.ru/buh/news/10009/.

Kobzeva, Oksana, and Darya Korsynskaya. 2016. "Putin Says Rosneft Buy of Bashneft Gives Impetus to Privatization." Reuters, October 12.

Kokh, Alfred. 1998. *The Selling of the Soviet Empire.* New York: Liberty Publishing House.

Kolesnichenko, Aleksandr. 2017. "Reiting pribilnosti TOP ukrainskikh bankov" [The profitability rating of the TOP Ukrainian banks]. *Ekonomicheskaya prada,* August 5.

Kommersant. 2008. "Aleksei Kudrin raskryl skrytuyu privatizatsiyu" [Aleksei Kudrin revealed hidden privatization]. June 10.

———. 2016. "Vladimira Barsukova zhdut FSB" [They wait for Vladimir Barsukov at FSB]. August 19.

Kornai, János. 1992. *The Socialist System: The Political Economy of Communism.* Princeton, NJ: Princeton University Press.

Kozyrev, Mikhail. 2017. "Vosem' chelovek i \$24 milliardov: Predprinimateli 'putinskogo prizyva' v reitinge Forbes" [Eight men and \$24 billion: The entrepreneurs of the "Putin calling" in the Forbes rating]. *Forbes,* April 26.

Kramer, Andrew E. 2008. "A \$50 Billion Bailout in Russia Favors the Rich and Connected." *New York Times,* October 30.

———. 2014a. "Russia Seeks Sanctions Tit for Tat." *New York Times,* October 8.

———. 2014b. "Sanctions over Ukraine Cause Headaches in the Energy Sector." *New York Times,* April 28.

Krastev, Ivan. 2006. "Democracy's Doubles." *Journal of Democracy* 17, no. 2: 52–62.

Krickovic, Andrej. 2014. "Imperial Nostalgia or Prudent Geopolitics? Russia's Efforts to Reintegrate the Post-Soviet Space in Geopolitical Perspective." *Post-Soviet Affairs* 30, no. 6: 503–528.

Kryshtanovskaya, Olga, and Stephen White. 2003. "Putin's Militocracy." *Post-Soviet Affairs* 19, no. 4: 289–306.

———. 2009. "The Sovietization of Russian Politics." *Post-Soviet Affairs* 25, no. 4: 283–309.

Kudrin, Aleksei. 2013. "Vliyanie dokhodov ot eksporta neftegazovykh resursov na denezhno-kreditnuyu politiky Rossii" [The impact of oil and gas export revenues on Russia's monetary policy]. *Voprosy Ekonomiki,* March, 4–19.

———. 2016. "Stavka na goskompanii ne sygrala" [The option of state companies did not work]. *Vedomosti,* December 7.

———. 2017. "Ustoichivy ekonomicheskii rost" [Sustainable economic growth]. Aleksei Kudrin official site, January 13.

Kudrin, Aleksei, and Yevsei Gurvich. 2014. "Novaya model' rosta dlya rossiiskoi ekonomiki" [A new growth model for the Russian economy]. *Voprosy Ekonomiki,* December, 4–36.

Kurlantzick, Joshua. 2016. *State Capitalism: How the Return of Statism Is Transforming the World.* New York: Oxford University Press.

Kuzio, Taras. 2010. "Will Russia Buy Up Ukraine?" *Eurasia Daily Monitor,* July 26.

Kuzmin, Andrey, Kira Zavyalova, and Stephen Grey. 2016. "Corrected—Putin's Son-in-Law Boosted by \$1.75 Billion Russian State Loan." Reuters, January 28.

Laar, Mart. 2002. *Little Country That Could.* London: Centre for Research into Post-Communist Economies.

Lally, Kathy. 2011. "Laws to Rein in Russia's Pretrial Detention System Are Ignored." *Washington Post,* November 25.

Laqueur, Walter. 2015. *Putinism: Russia and Its Future in the West*. New York: St. Martin's Press.

Lardy, Nicholas R. 2014. *Markets over Mao: The Rise of Private Business in China*. Washington, DC: Peterson Institute for International Economics.

Laruelle, Marlene. 2017. "In Search of Putin's Philosopher." Intersection Project, March 3.

Latynina, Yulia. 2017. "Zachem 'Gazprom' i 'Rosneft' zalezayut v gromadnye dolgi?" [Why are Gazprom and Rosneft accumulating enormous debts?]. *Novaya Gazeta*, February 27.

Layne, Nathan, et al. 2017. "Moscow on the Beach: Russian Elite Invested nearly $100 Million in Trump Buildings." Reuters, March 17.

Lee Myers, Steven. 2004. "A Candidate from Russia Is in London with New Tale." *New York Times*, February 14.

———. 2015. *The New Tsar: The Rise and Reign of Vladimir Putin*. New York: Knopf.

Lee Myers, Steven, Jo Becker, and Jim Yardley. 2014. "Private Bank Fuels Fortunes of Putin's Inner Circle." *New York Times*, September 27.

Leopold, Jason, et al. 2018. "Christopher Steele's Other Report: A Murder in Washington." *Buzzfeed*, March 27.

Levada Center. 2017. Obshchestvennoe Mnenie: Sbornik [Public opinion: Collection]. Moscow: Levada Analytical Center.

Levinsky, Aleksandr. 2016. "Master Boevich iskusstv" [The master of martial arts]. *Forbes*, February 25.

Libman, Alexander, and Evgeny Vinokurov. 2012. *Holding-Together Regionalism: Twenty Years of Post-Soviet Integration*. Hampshire, UK: Palgrave Macmillan.

Library of Congress. n.d. "Legal Provisions on Fighting Extremism: Russia." https://www.loc.gov/law/help/fighting-extremism/russia.php#skip_menu.

Lichtblau, Eric, and Carter Dougherty. 2008. "Siemens to Pay $1.34 Billion in Fines." *New York Times*, December 15.

Lieven, Anatol. 1998. *Chechnya: Tombstone of Russian Power*. New Haven: Yale University Press.

Lieven, Dominic. 2000. *Empire: The Russian Empire and Its Rivals*. New Haven: Yale University Press.

Linz, Juan J. 1978. *The Breakdown of Democratic Regimes: Crisis, Breakdown, and Reequilibration*. Baltimore: Johns Hopkins University Press.

Lipset, Seymour Martin. 1959. "Some Social Requisites of Democracy: Economic Development and Political Legitimacy." *American Political Science Review* 53, no. 1: 69–105.

Lloyd, John. 1998. "Who Lost Russia?" *New York Times*, August 15.

Lucas, Edward. 2008. *The New Cold War: Putin's Russia and the Threat to the West*. New York: Palgrave MacMillan.

Luzin, Pavel. 2017. "The Ominous Rise of Russian National Guard." Intersection Project, July 21.

Malia, Martin. 1999. *Russia under Western Eyes*. Cambridge, MA: Harvard University Press.

Malkova, Irina. 2013. "Poslednii konkvistador: kak Igor' Sechin vedet bor'bu za neftya-noe gospodstvo" [The last conquistador: How Igor Sechin pursues his struggle for oil rule]. *Forbes* Russia, December 20.

Mance, Henry, and Vanessa Houlder. 2016. "Cameron Targets Offshore Owners of UK Property." *Financial Times,* May 11.

Mandelbaum, Michael. 2005. *The Ideas That Conquered the World.* New York: Public Affairs.

———. 2016. *Mission Failure: America and the World in the Post–Cold War Era.* New York: Oxford University Press.

Mau, Vladimir. 2013a. Mezhdu modernizatsiei i zastoem: Ekonomicheskaya politika 2012 goda [Between modernization and stagnation: Economic policy in 2012]. *Voprosy ekonomiki* 2 (February): 4–23.

———. 2013b. "Chetyre dolgosrochnye problemy razvitiya" [Four long-term problems of development]. *Vedomosti,* February 20.

Mau, Vladimir, and Irina Starodubrovskaya. 2001. *The Challenge of Revolution: Contemporary Russia in Historical Perspective.* Oxford: Oxford University Press.

McFarlane, Sarah, and Summer Said. 2017. "Russia's Rosneft State Sale with a Twist: Moscow Always Wanted It Back." *Wall Street Journal,* June 7.

McFaul, Michael. 2001. *Russia's Unfinished Revolution: Political Change from Gorbachev to Putin.* Ithaca, NY: Cornell University Press.

———. 2006. "Conclusion: The Orange Revolution in a Comparative Perspective." In Åslund and McFaul 2006. Washington, DC: Carnegie Endowment for International Peace.

———. 2010. *Advancing Democracy Abroad: Why We Should and How We Can.* New York: Rowman and Littlefield.

McFaul, Michael, and Kathryn Stoner-Weiss. 2008. "The Myth of the Authoritarian Model." *Foreign Affairs* 87, no. 1: 68–84.

McKinsey Global Institute. 1999. *Unlocking Economic Growth in Russia.* Moscow: McKinsey.

Meduza. 2017. "Russia's Senate Adopts New Legislation Cracking Down on Internet Anonymity." July 25.

Medvedev, Dmitri A. 2009a. "Dmitry Medvedev Instructed Prime Minister Vladimir Putin to Present Proposals on Reform of State Corporations by March 1, 2010." November 13. en.kremlin.ru.

———. 2009b. "Dmitry Medvedev Instructed Prosecutor General Yury Chaika and Presidential Aide and Director of the Presidential Control Directorate Konstantin Chuychenko to Carry Out Comprehensive Checks into the Activities of State Corporations." August 7. en.kremlin.ru.

———. 2009c. "First BRIC Summit Took Place in Yekaterinburg." June 16. en.kremlin. ru.

———. 2009d. "Forwards Russia!" September 10. www.kremlin.ru.

———. 2010. "Working Meeting with the General Director of the State Corporation 'Rostechnologies' Sergei Chemezov." September 13.

————. 2011. "Meeting with CEO of Russian Technologies (Rostekhnologii) State Corporation Sergei Chemezov." May 19.

Medvedeva, Elena. 2018. "Eksperty TsSR predlagayut otmenit' valyutny kontrol'" [The experts of the Center for Strategic Research proposes to abolish currency control]. *Vedomosti*, March 14.

Melnikov, Aleksandr. 2012. "Gennady Timchenko, Biografiya." July 29. http://vspro.info.

Mereminskaya, Yekaterina. 2016. "Gosudarstvo i goskompanii kontroliruyut 70% rossiiskoi ekonomiki" [The state and state companies control 70% of the Russian economy]. *Vedomosti*, September 29.

Mereu, Francesca. 2006. "Bureaucrat Numbers Booming under Putin." *Moscow Times*, April 13.

Meyer, Henry. 2011. "Medvedev Shakes Up the Kremlin." *Bloomberg*, April 7.

Michalopoulos, Constantine, and Vladimir Drebentsov. 1997. "Observations on State Trading in the Russian Economy." *Post-Soviet Geography and Economics* 38, no. 5: 264–275.

Michalopoulos, Constantine, and David G. Tarr. 1997. "The Economics of Customs Union in the Commonwealth of Independent States." *Post-Soviet Geography and Economics* 38, no. 3: 125–143.

Michel, Casey. 2017. "The United States of Anonymity." Briefing Paper. Washington, DC: Hudson Institute, Kleptocracy Initiative, November.

Michels, Robert. 1911. *Zur Soziologie des Parteiwesens in der modern Demokratie* [The sociology of the party system in the modern democracy]. Leipzig: Werner Klinkhardt.

Mikhailovskaya, Inga B. 1994. "Crime and Statistics: Do the Figures Reflect the Real Situation?" *Demokratizatsiya* 2, no. 3: 412–425.

Miller, Chris. 2018. *Putinomics: Power and Money in Resurgent Russia*. Chapel Hill: University of North Carolina Press.

Milov, V., B. Nemtsov, V. Ryzhkov, and O. Shorina. 2011. "Putin. Corruption. An Independent White Paper." Translated by Dave Essel. https://www.putin-itogi.ru/putin-corruption-an-independent-white-paper/.

Minchenko, Yevgeny. 2012. "Vladimir Putin's Big Government and the 'Politburo 2.0.'" Moscow: Minchenko Consulting. www.minchenko.ru.

Ministry of Finance of the Russian Federation. 2018a. "Volume of the National Wealth Fund." http://old.minfin.ru/en/nationalwealthfund/statistics/volume/index.php?id_4=5830.

————. 2018b. "Volume of the Reserve Fund." http://old.minfin.ru/en/reservefund/statistics/volume/index.php?id_4=5817.

Moscow Times. 2012. "Obama Signs Magnitsky Bill." December 16.

————. 2015. "Rosneft Defends Medal for 'Grown Man' Ivan Sechin." January 23.

————. 2016a. "Moscow Court Orders Rotenberg Company to Reveal Platon Tax System Deal." January 28.

————. 2016b. "Putin Responds to Panama Papers after 4 Days of Keeping Silent." April 7.

————. 2017. "Putin's Cousin Earned $95,000 Every Day in 2016." November 2.

Moshes, Arkady. 2013. "Will Ukraine Join (and Save) the Eurasian Customs Union?" PONARS Eurasia Policy Memo 247. Washington, DC: PONARS Eurasia.

Mostotrest. n.d. Mostotrest vkratse [Mostotrest in short]. http://ir.mostotrest.ru/ru/o-kompanii.html.

Movchan, Veronika, and Ricardo Giucci. 2011. "Quantitative Assessment of Ukraine's Regional Integration Options: DCFTA with European Union vs. Customs Union with Russia, Belarus and Kazakhstan." Policy Paper PP/05/2011. Kiev: Institute for Economic Research and Policy Consulting.

Movchan, Veronika, David Saha, and Robert Kirchner. 2018. "The Impact of Russia's Transit Restrictions on Ukraine's Exports to Kazakhstan and Kyrgyzstan." Policy Briefing Series, February. Berlin: German Advisory Group.

Murphy, Kevin A., Andrei Shleifer, and Robert W. Vishny. 1992. "The Transition to a Market Economy: Pitfalls of Partial Reform." *Quarterly Journal of Economics* 57, no. 3: 889–903.

Naftogaz Ukrainy. 2017. "The Stockholm Arbitration Tribunal Rejects Gazprom's 'Take-or-Pay' Claim regarding the Gas Sales Contract," May 31. www.naftogaz.com.

NataDutilh. 2017. "Status Overview UBO Register Europe." August 31. www.nautadutilh.com.

NATO (North Atlantic Treaty Organization). 2008. "Bucharest Summit Declaration." Bucharest, April 3. www.nato.int.

Nazarov, Andrei. 2014. "Bezopasnost': Glavnaya problema—ugolovnoe presledovanie" [Security: The main problem of criminal investigation]. *Vedomosti,* January 30.

Nechepurenko, Ivan. 2017. "5 Who Killed Boris Nemtsov, Putin Foe, Sentenced in Russia." *New York Times,* July 13.

Nehamas, Nicholas, and Rene Rodriguez. 2017. "Feds Widen Hunt for Dirty Money in Miami Real Estate." *Miami Herald,* August 23.

Nemtsov, Boris, and Leonid Martynyuk. 2012. *Zhizn' raba na galerakh* [The life of a galley slave]. Moscow. www.putin-itogi.ru.

———. 2014. *Winter Olympics in the Sub-Tropics: Corruption and Abuse in Sochi.* Moscow. https://www.putin-itogi.ru/cp/wp-content/uploads/2013/05/Report_ENG_SOCHI-2014_preview.pdf.

Nemtsov, Boris, and Vladimir Milov. 2008. *Putin i Gazprom* [Putin and Gazprom]. Moscow: Novaya Gazeta.

———. 2010a. *Putin: Itogi. 10 let* [Putin: What 10 years of Putin have brought]. Moscow: Novaya Gazeta.

———. 2010b. *Putin: Korruptsiya 2* [Putin: Corruption 2]. Moscow: Novaya Gazeta.

Nickerson, James. 2016. "I Took a 'Kleptocracy Tour' around London and Discovered the Corruption Capital." *New Statesman,* March 7.

Nielsen, Thomas. 2017. "FSB Gets Right to Confiscate Land from People." *Barents Observer,* May 16.

North, Douglass C. 1994. *Structure and Change in Economic History.* New York: Norton.

Novaya Gazeta. 2009a. "13 druzei Putina" [13 friends of Putin]. December 29.

———. 2009b. "Pokhozhy na Millera, stroit dachu pokhozhuyu na dvorets v Petergofe" [A person similar to Miller builds a palace similar to Peterhof]. June 9.

————. 2009c. "Vse Goskorporatsii Rossii" [All state corporations of Russia]. July 24.

————. 2017. "Medvedev otvetil no obvineniya Navalnogo" [Medvedev responded to Navalny's accusations]. April 4.

Nove, Alec. 1977. *The Soviet Economic System*. London: George Allen and Unwin.

————. 1989. *Glasnost' in Action: Cultural Renaissance in Russia*. Boston: Unwin Hyman.

Novikov, Alexey. 2015. "Gazprom Picks Russian Auditor over PwC." Interfax, March 30.

Novokmet, Filip, Thomas Piketty, and Gabriel Zucman. 2017. "From Soviets to Oligarchs: Inequality and Property in Russia, 1905–2016." NBER Working Paper 23712. Cambridge, MA: National Bureau of Economic Research.

Olcott, Martha Brill, Anders Åslund, and Sherman Garnett. 1999. *Getting It Wrong*. Washington, DC: Carnegie Endowment for International Peace.

Olearchyk, Roman, and Henry Foy. 2018. "Ukraine's Naftogaz Claims $2.5 Billion Win over Russia's Gazprom." *Financial Times*, March 1.

Oomes, Nienke, and Katerina Kalcheva. 2007. "Diagnosing Dutch Disease: Does Russia Have the Symptoms?" IMF Working Paper 07/102. Washington, DC: International Monetary Fund.

OCCRP. 2017. "The Russian Laundromat Exposed," March 20. Organized Crime and Corruption Reporting Project. www.occrp.org.

"Osnovnye napravleniya sotsial'no-ekonomicheskoi politiki pravitel'stva Rossiiskoi Federatsii na dolgosrochnuiu perspektivy" [Basic directions of the social-economic policy of the government of the Russian Federation in the long-term perspective]. 2000. Mimeo. Moscow: "Gref Program."

Ostrovsky, Arkady. 2005. "Gazprom Buys Sibneft Stake for $13.1bn." *Financial Times*, September 28.

————. 2015. *The Invention of Russia: The Journey from Gorbachev's Freedom to Putin's War*. London: Atlantic Books.

Owen, David, and David O. Robinson, eds. 2003. *Russia Rebounds*. Washington, DC: International Monetary Fund.

Pal'veleva, Lilya. 2013. "On vam ni Dimon" [He is not Dimon]. Radio Liberty, April 1. https://www.svoboda.org/a/24942521.html.

Panin, Alexander. 2014. "Gazprom's Grip on Russian Gas Exports Weakens as Novatek Gets Export License." *Moscow Times*, September 7.

Papchenkova, Margarita, Darya Korsunskaya, and Oksana Kobzeva. 2016. "Putin Removes Head of VEB State Development Bank as Crisis Bites." Reuters, February 18.

Papernaya, Inessa. 2004. "Regiony zagoniat v Federal'noie kaznacheistvo" [The regions will be herded into the Federal Treasury]. *Finans*, March 29–April 4. http://www.finansmag.ru/offline/num53/banki/5906.

Pei, Minxin. 2016. *China's Crony Capitalism: The Dynamics of Regime Decay*. Cambridge, MA: Harvard University Press.

Piketty, Thomas. 2013. *Capital in the Twenty-First Century*. Cambridge, MA: Belknap Press of Harvard University Press.

Pinto, Brian, Vladimir Drebentsov, and Alexander Morozov. 1999. "Dismantling Russia's Nonpayments System: Creating Conditions for Growth." Report. Moscow: World Bank, September.

Pipes, Richard. 1974. *Russia under the Old Regime*. London: Weidenfeld and Nicolson.

———. 1984. "Can the Soviet Union Reform?" *Foreign Affairs* 63, no. 1: 47–61.

———. 1990. *The Russian Revolution*. New York: Vintage Books.

———. 2005. *Russian Conservatism and Its Critics: A Study in Political Culture*. New Haven: Yale University Press.

Podobedova, Liudmila. 2015. "Big Earners: What Are Gazprom's Top Executives Paid For?" *Russia behind the Headlines*, October 16.

Politkovskaya, Anna. 2001. *A Dirty War: A Russian Reporter in Chechnya*. London: Harvill.

Polman, Mitchell. 2016. "The American Corporations Advertising with a Racist Russian TV Channel." *Daily Beast*, March 3.

Pomerantsev, Peter. 2014. *Nothing Is True and Everything Is Possible: The Surreal Heart of the New Russia*. New York: PublicAffairs.

Pomeranz, William. 2017. "Why Putin Will Be Skipping the 100th Anniversary of the Russian Revolution." Washington, DC: Kennan Institute, The Russia File, February 22.

Primakov, Denis, and Elena Lazareva. 2013. "Reyting otkrytosti zakupok goskorporatsiy: Monitoring korporativnoy otkrytosti gosudarstvennykh korporatsiy i soblyudeniya komplayens" [Rating of the transparency of procurement of state corporations: Monitoring of corporate openness of state corporations and their compliance]. Moscow: The Center for Anti-Corruption Studies and Initiatives of Transparency International—Russia.

Prime. 2016. "Verkhovny sud Rossii predlagaet zapretit' aresty biznesmenov" [The Supreme Court of Russia proposes to prohibit the arrest of businessmen]. November 3.

Prokopenko, Aleksandra. 2016. "TsSR nashel prichiny provala prezhnikh strategii Rossii" [CSR found the reasons for the failure of previous Russian strategies]. *Vedomosti*, December 27.

Putin, Vladimir V. n.d. "Vladimir V. Putin." Personal website. http://eng.putin.kremlin.ru/bio.

———. 2000a. *First Person*. New York: Public Affairs.

———. 2000b. "Annual Address to the Federal Assembly of the Russian Federation." July 8. en.kremlin.ru.

———. 2001. "Conversation with Heads of Local Bureaus of Leading U.S. Media Outlets." June 18. en.kremlin.ru.

———. 2002. "Annual Address of the President of the Russian Federation V.V. Putin to the Federal Assembly of the Russian Federation." April 18. en.kremlin.ru.

———. 2003a. "Remarks by President Vladimir Putin on Yukos Affair at Government Meeting." RTR Vesti Program, October 27, Federal News Service. en.kremlin.ru.

———. 2003b. "Introductory Words and Answers to Questions from Journalists at Press Conference about the Results of the Russia-EU Summit." Rome, November 6. en.kremlin.ru.

———. 2003c. "Introductory Remarks at the Meeting with Representatives of the Russian Union of Industrialists and Entrepreneurs." February 19. en.kremlin.ru.

———. 2003d. "Interview with the ANSA Italian News Agency, *Corriere della Sera* Newspaper and the RAI Television Company." November 3. en.kremlin.ru.

———. 2003e. "Interview Granted to Bulgarian National Television and the Newspaper *Trud*." February 28. en.kremlin.ru.

———. 2004a. "Remarks by President Vladimir Putin at a Meeting in the Ministry of Finance." RTR Vesti Program, March 19, Federal News Service. en.kremlin.ru.

———. 2004b. "Address by President Vladimir Putin." September 4. en.kremlin.ru.

———. 2005a. "Annual Address to the Federal Assembly of the Russian Federation." April 25. en.kremlin.ru.

———. 2005b. "The President Signed Laws on the Liberalization of Gazprom's Shares." December 23. en.kremlin.ru.

———. 2006a. "Transcript of Meeting with Participants in the Third Meeting of the Valdai Discussion Club." September 9. en.kremlin.ru.

———. 2006b. "Transcript of the Hot Line with President of Russia Vladimir Putin." October 25. en.kremlin.ru.

———. 2007. "Speech and the Following Discussion at the Munich Conference on Security Policy." February 10. en.kremlin.ru.

———. 2008a. "Speech to Widened Meeting of the State Council 'on Russia's Strategic Development until 2020.'" February 8. en.kremlin.ru.

———. 2008b. "What Precisely Vladimir Putin Said at Bucharest." *Zerkalo nedeli*, April 19.

———. 2012a. "Executive Order on Long-Term State Economic Policy." May 7. en.kremlin.ru.

———. 2012b. "Economic Council Meeting." July 20. en.kremlin.ru.

———. 2012c. "Greetings to International Academic Congress Honouring the Legacy of Lev Gumilev." October 1. en.kremlin.ru.

———. 2012d. "Address to the Federal Assembly." December 12. en.kremlin.ru.

———. 2012e. "News Conference of Vladimir Putin." December 20. en.kremlin.ru.

———. 2013a. "Meeting with President of Ukraine Viktor Yanukovych." March 4. en.kremlin.ru.

———. 2013b. "Meeting on Economic Issues." April 22. en.kremlin.ru.

———. 2013c. "Address to the Federal Assembly. December 12. en.kremlin.ru.

———. 2014a. "Comments regarding US Sanctions against Russia, Effective from March 20, 2014." March 21. en.kremlin.ru.

———. 2014b. "Direct Line with Vladimir Putin." April 17. en.kremlin.ru.

———. 2014c. "Replies to Journalists' Questions Following a Visit to China." May 21. en.kremlin.ru.

———. 2014d. "Meeting with CEO of Rostec State Corporation Sergei Chemezov." June 19. en.kremlin.ru.

———. 2014e. "Interview with TASS." November 24. en.kremlin.ru.

———. 2014f. "Annual Address to the Federal Assembly of the Russian Federation." December 4. en.kremlin.ru.

———. 2014g. "Transcript of Press Conference with the Russian and Foreign Media." December 18. en.kremlin.ru.

———. 2015a. "Meeting with Government Members." January 21. en.kremlin.ru.

———. 2015b. "Meeting with Economic Experts." February 13. en.kremlin.ru.

———. 2015c. "Expanded Session of the Interior Ministry Board." March 4. en.kremlin.ru.

———. 2015d. "Presidential Address to the Federal Assembly." December 3. en.kremlin.ru.

———. 2015e. "Meeting with CEO of Rostec State Corporation Sergei Chemezov." December 4. en.kremlin.ru.

———. 2015f. "Annual Press Conference." December 17. en.kremlin.ru.

———. 2016a. "Meeting of the Economic Council Presidium." May 25. en.kremlin.ru.

———. 2016b. "Meeting with Rostec State Corporation CEO Sergei Chemezov." August 2. en.kremlin.ru.

———. 2016c. "Russia Calling." Investment Forum, Moscow, October 12. en.kremlin.ru.

———. 2016d. "Meeting with Mikhail Fradkov and Sergei Chemezov." November 2. en.kremlin.ru.

———. 2016e. "Meeting with Rosneft CEO Igor Sechin." December 7. en.kremlin.ru.

———. 2017a. "Meeting with Rostec State Corporation CEO Sergei Chemezov." April 27. en.kremlin.ru.

———. 2017b. "Replies to Journalists' Questions." May 15. en.kremlin.ru.

———. 2017c. "Executive Order on Extending Special Economic Measures to Ensure Russia's Security." June 30. en.kremlin.ru.

———. 2017d. "Visit to Lebedinsky GOK." July 14. en.kremlin.ru.

———. 2017e. "Meeting with Students from Sirius Educational Centre." July 21. en.kremlin.ru.

———. 2017f. "Meeting with Permanent Members of Security Council." July 28. en.kremlin.ru.

———. 2017g. "Vladimir Putin's News Conference following BRICS Summit." September 5. en.kremlin.ru.

———. 2017h. "Unveiling of Monument to Alexander III." November 18. en.kremlin.ru.

———. 2018a. "Presidential Address to the Federal Assembly." March 1. en.kremlin.ru.

———. 2018b. "The President Signed Executive Order on National Goals and Strategic Objectives of the Russian Federation through to 2024." May 7. en.kremlin.ru.

Radio Free Europe/Radio Liberty. 2015. "Russia's Vnesheconombank to Back Suspect in Spy Case." May 13.

———. 2017. "Putin Extends Russia's Countersanctions on Western Food." June 30.

Radu, Paul. 2016. "Russia: The Cellist and the Lawyer." *Organized Crime and Corruption Reporting Project*, April 26.

Radygin, Alexander, et al. 2018. *Effektivnoe upravlenie gosudarstvennoi sobstvennost'yu v 2018–2024 gg. i do 2035 g.* [Efficient management of state property in 2018–2024 and to 2035]. Moscow: Tsentr strategicheskikh razrabotok, January.

RBC [www.rbc.com]. 2015. "Formula Millera: Chto krome zarplaty polochayut nachalniki Gazproma" Miller's Formula: What apart from salary do the managers of Gazprom get?]. October 13.

———. 2016. "Rosneftegaz Received Means from the Sale of 19.5% of Rosneft." December 16.

Reddaway, Peter, and Dmitri Glinsky. 2001. *The Tragedy of Russia's Reforms: Market Bolshevism against Democracy.* Washington, DC: United States Institute of Peace Press.

Reevell, Patrick. 2014. "Legislation Merging Russia's 2 Top Courts Stokes Worries." *New York Times,* February 6.

Reilhac, Gilbert. 2017. "Russian Opposition Leader's Fraud Conviction Arbitrary, Europe's Top Rights Court Says." Reuters, October 17.

Remington, Thomas F. 2002. "Russia's Federal Assembly and the Land Code." *East European Constitutional Review* 11, no. 3: 99–105.

———. 2006. *Politics in Russia.* New York: Pearson Longman.

Remington, Thomas F., Steven S. Smith, and Moshe Haspel. 1998. "Decrees, Laws, and Inter-Branch Relations in the Russian Federation." *Post-Soviet Affairs* 14, no. 4: 287–322.

Remnick, David. 1994. *Lenin's Tomb: The Last Days of the Soviet Empire.* New York: Vintage Press.

Reuters. 2015. "Venezuela, Russia's Rosneft Agree on $14 Billion Oil, Gas Investment." May 28.

———. 2017a. "Germany Says Crimean Turbine Scandal Souring Relations with Russia," Reuters, July 22.

———. 2017b. "Sistema Shares Plunge a Third after $1.9 Bln Rosneft Lawsuit." May 3.

———. 2018a. "Ukraine's Naftogaz Claims $2.56 Billion Victory in Gazprom Legal Battle." February 28.

———. 2018b. "Ukraine's Naftogaz Will Go After Gazprom Assets in Europe." April 9.

Reznik, Irina, and Olga Petrova. 2008. "Kak ustroen biznes Yuriya Kovalchuka" [How Yuri Kovalchuk's business is built]. *Vedomosti,* July 24.

Reznik, Irina, Ilya Arkhipov, and Alexander Sazonov. 2018. "Putin Family Split Offers Peek at Secret Dealings of Russia Inc." Bloomberg, January 25.

Roberts, Sean P., and Arkady Moshes, 2016. "The Eurasian Economic Union: A Case of Reproductive Integration?" *Post-Soviet Affairs* 32, no. 6: 542–565.

Rostec. 2017a. "About." https://rostec.ru/en/about/.

———. 2017b. "Company Organizational Structure." http://rostec.ru/en/about/structure/.

———. 2017c. "Key Companies." http://rostec.ru/en/about/companies/.

———. 2017d. "Structure." https://rostec.ru/en/about/structure/.

Rosneft. n.d. "Board of Directors." https://www.rosneft.com/governance/board/.

———. 2014. *Annual Report 2014.* https://www.rosneft.com/upload/site2/document_file/176411/a_report_2014_eng.pdf.

———. 2017. "Interim Condensed Consolidated Financial Statements (Unaudited): Three and Nine Months Ended September 30, 2017." https://www.rosneft.com/upload/site2/document_cons_report/Rosneft_FS_3Q_2017_ENG_FINAL.pdf.

Rosstat (Russian Federal Statistics Service). 2017. "Sotsial'no-ekonomicheskoe polozhenie Rossii" [Russia's social-economic situation]. Moscow: Rosstat.

Rudnitsky, Jake. 2017. "Putin Ally Wins $2.3 Billion from Sistema in Bellwether Case." *Bloomberg*, August 24.

Rudnitsky, Jake, and Sonia Sirletti. 2014. "Putin Billionaire's Assets Frozen in Italy over Sanctions." *Bloomberg*, September 23.

Russia Market Daily. 2012. "Gazprom Investor Day: Relieved about No New Negatives." Troika Dialog, February 13.

Russian Direct Investment Fund. n.d. "About Us." https://rdif.ru/Eng_About/.

Russian Economic Barometer. 2004. Vol. 13, no. 2, Spring.

Russian-European Centre for Economic Policy (RECEP). 1999. *Russian Economic Trends*, February. Moscow: Russian-European Centre for Economic Policy.

Rutland, Peter. 2008. "Russia as an Energy Superpower." *New Political Economy* 13, no. 2: 203–210.

Sabbagh, Dan. 2018. "UK to Introduce Public Ownership Registers for Overseas Territories." *Guardian*, May 1.

Sachs, Jeffrey D., and Andrew Warner. 1997. "Natural Resource Abundance and Economic Growth." Cambridge, MA: Harvard Institute for International Development.

Satter, David. 2003. *Darkness at Dawn: The Rise of the Russian Criminal State*. New Haven: Yale University Press.

Savchuk, Katie. 2016. "How Vladimir Putin's Son-in-Law Became Russia's Youngest Billionaire." *Forbes*, March 30.

Schreck, Carl. 2016. "'Five Kings': Putin Insiders Reign in Government Contract Ranking." RadioFreeEurope/RadioLiberty, February 29. https://www.rferl.org/a/putin-insiders-state-contracts-forbes-ranking/27576535.html.

Schumpeter, Joseph A. [1943] 1976. *Capitalism, Socialism and Democracy*. London: George Allen and Unwin.

Sebag Montefiori, Simon. 2005. *Stalin: The Court of the Red Tsar*. New York: Vintage.

Selyunin, Vasili, and Grigori I. Khanin. 1987. "Lukovaya tsifra" [Cunning number]. *Novy mir* 63, 2: 181–201.

Shambaugh, David. 2016. *China's Future*. Malden, MA: Polity.

The Shanghai Cooperation Organisation. 2017. "About SCO." http://eng.sectsco.org/about_sco/.

Shapiro, Judith. 1995. "The Rising Mortality Crisis and Its Causes." In *Russian Economic Reform at Risk*, ed. Anders Åslund. New York: St. Martin's Press.

Sharkov, Damien. 2015. "'Victory' for Russia's Top State Executives as They Keep Salaries Secret." *Newsweek*, March 31.

Shevtsova, Lilia. 2005. *Putin's Russia*. Washington, DC: Carnegie Endowment for International Peace.

———. 2007. *Lost in Transition: The Yeltsin and Putin Legacies*. Washington, DC: Carnegie Endowment for International Peace.

Shleinov, Roman. 2010. "Sweeping Out Palace." *Vedomosti*, December 29. (See also Shleynov.)

Shkolnikov, V. M., E. M. Andreev, and T. M. Maleva. 2000. *Neravenstvo pered litsom smerti v Rossii* [Inequality facing death in Russia]. Moscow: Carnegie Moscow Center.

Shleifer, Andrei. 2005. *A Normal Country: Russia after Communism*. Cambridge, MA: Harvard University Press.

Shleifer, Andrei, and Daniel Treisman. 2000. *Without a Map: Political Tactics and Economic Reform in Russia*. Cambridge, MA: MIT Press.

———. 2004. "A Normal Country." *Foreign Affairs* 83, no. 2: 20–38.

Shleifer, Andrei, and Robert W. Vishny. 1993. "Corruption." *Quarterly Journal of Economics* 108, no. 3: 599–617.

Shleynov, Roman. 2017. "Oberegi: U kogo ishchut zashchity Rotenbergi i Koval'chuki?" [Protection: With whom do the Rotenbergs and Koval'chuks seek protection?]. *Novaya Gazeta*, June 18.

Smith, Anthony D. 2010. *Nationalism: Theory, Ideology, History*. 2nd ed. London: Polity.

Snyder, Timothy. 2016. "How a Russian Fascist Is Meddling in America's Election." *New York Times*, September 20.

Soldatov, Andrei, and Irina Borogan. 2017. *The Red Web: The Struggle between Russia's Digital Dictators and the New Online Revolutionaries*. 2nd ed. New York: Public Affairs.

Sokolov, Vladimir, and Yulia Davydova. 2012. "Subsidizing Debt of Strategic Industry Firms: Government Target Selection Decisions and Their Consequences." Working Paper. Moscow: Higher School of Economics.

Solomon, Peter H., Jr. 2002. "Putin's Judicial Reform: Making Judges Accountable as Well as Independent." *East European Constitutional Review* 11, no. 1–2: 117–124.

Solov'ev, Vadim. "Goskorporatsii: Ne vse tochki nad 'i' rasstavleny" [State corporations: Not all dots have been put above "i"]. *Nezavisimaya Gazeta*, December 4.

Stanovaya, Tatiana. 2017. "State Capture." *Intersection Project*, January 24. intersection-project.eu.

Stent, Angela E. 2014. *The Limits of Partnership: U.S.-Russian Relations in the Twenty-First Century*. Princeton, NJ: Princeton University Press.

Stern, Jonathan P. 2005. *The Future of Russian Gas and Gazprom*. Oxford: Oxford University Press.

Stewart, Catrina. 2008. "Bank Rossiya Emerges from Shadows." *Moscow Times*, July 14.

Stewart, Heather. 2016. "Offshore Finance: More Than $12tn Siphoned Out of Emerging Economies." *Guardian*, May 8.

Stiernlöf, Sture. 2000. "Vladimir Putin, a Sly Operator." Letter to the Swedish Ministry for Foreign Affairs, January 19. Swedish National Archives.

Stockholm International Peace Research Institute (SIPRI). 2017. "SIPRI Military Expenditure Database." https://sipri.org/sites/default/files/Milex-share-of-GDP.pdf.

Stolypinsky Klub. 2016. "O Stolypinskim klube" [About the Stolypin Club]. http://stolypinsky.club/prezidium/o-stolypinskom-klube/.

"Strategiya-2020: Novaya model' rosta—novaya sotsial'naya politika" [Strategy 2020: A new growth model—a new social policy]. 2008. Mimeo. Moscow: Russian government.

Stubbs, Jack, et al. 2015. "The Man Who Married Putin's Daughter and Then Made a Fortune." Reuters, December 17.

Supreme Court of the Russian Federation. n.d. "Law on the Status of Judges." http://www.supcourt.ru/en/judicial_system/law_status_judges/.

Sutela, Pekka. 2012. *The Political Economy of Putin's Russia*. London: Routledge.

Talbott, Strobe. 2002. *The Russia Hand: A Memoir of Presidential Diplomacy*. New York: Random House.

Tarr, David, 2007. "Russian Accession to the WTO: An Assessment." *Eurasian Geography and Economics* 48, no. 3: 306–319.

———. 2012. "The Eurasian Customs Union among Russia, Belarus and Kazakhstan: Can It Succeed Where Its Predecessor Failed?" Working Paper. Moscow: New Economic School.

TASS [tass.com]. 2016. "Rosneft Privatization Deal Is Completed—Kremlin." December 7.

———. 2018. "Gazprom Increases Gas Production by 12.4%, Exports by 8.1% in 2017." January 3.

Taylor, Adam. 2015. "Is Vladimir Putin Hiding a $200 Billion Fortune?" *Washington Post*, February 15.

Taylor, Brian D. 2006. "Law Enforcement and Civil Society in Russia." *Europe-Asia Studies* 58, no. 2: 193–213.

The International Consortium of Investigative Journalists. n.d. "Igor Putin." https://offshoreleaks.icij.org/nodes/12136740.

Trading Economics. 2018. "Ease of Doing Business in Russia, 2008–2018." https://tradingeconomics.com/russia/ease-of-doing-business.

Transparency International. 2017. "Corruption Perceptions Index." http://transparency.org.

Transparency International Russia. n.d. https://transparency.org.ru/.

Transparency International UK. 2017. "Hiding in Plain Sight: How UK Companies Are Used to Launder Corrupt Wealth." http://www.transparency.org.uk/.

Transparency International UK and Bellingcat. 2017. "Offshore in the UK: Analysing the Use of Scottish Limited Partnerships in Corruption and Money Laundering." http://www.transparency.org.uk/.

Treisman, Daniel S. 2011. *The Return*. New York: Free Press.

Troika Dialog. 2012. "Russia Oil and Gas." Moscow: Troika Dialog, July.

Tsentr Strategicheskikh rasrabotok. 2017. "Perspektivy rosta rossiskoi ekonomiki" [Russian economic growth prospects]. Moscow.

United Nations. 2014. "Treaty of the Eurasian Economic Union, 2014." http://www.un.org/en/ga/sixth/70/docs/treaty_on_eeu.pdf.

———. 2015. "World Population Prospects 2015." New York: United Nations. https://esa.un.org/unpd/wpp/Publications/Files/WPP2015_DataBooklet.pdf.

United Nations Statistics Division. 2017. "National Accounts." New York: United Nations. https://unstats.un.org/unsd/snaama/.

US Congress. 2016. S.284: Global Magnitsky Human Rights Accountability Act. https://www.congress.gov/bill/114th-congress/senate-bill/284/text.

US Department of State. 2016. "Country Reports on Human Rights Practices for 2016." Bureau of Democracy, Human Rights and Labor. https://www.state.gov/documents/organization/265428.pdf.

US Department of the Treasury [www.treasury.gov]. 2014a. "Treasury Sanctions Russian Officials, Members of the Russian Leadership's Inner Circle, and an Entity for Involvement in the Situation in Ukraine." March 20.

———. 2014b. "Ukraine-Related Sanctions." April 28.

———. 2014c. "Ukraine-Related Sanctions." July 16.

———. 2014d. "Ukraine-Related Sanctions; Update of Executive Order 13662 Sectoral Sanctions Identifications List." September 12.

———. 2015a. "National Money Laundering Risk Assessment 2015." http://www.safe banking.com/DownloadDocument.ashx?documentID=115.

———. 2015b. "Ukraine-Related Designations." July 30.

———. 2017a. "Issuance of Global Magnitsky Executive Order; Global Magnitsky Designations." December 21.

———. 2017b. "Treasury Targets Individuals Involved in the Sergei Magnitsky Case and Other Gross Violations of Human Rights in Russia." Press Release, December 20.

———. 2017c. "United States Sanctions Human Rights Abusers and Corrupt Actors across the Globe." Press Release, December 21.

US Securities and Exchange Commission. 2008. "SEC Charges Siemens AG for Engaging in Worldwide Bribery." December 15. https://www.sec.gov/news/press/2008/2008-294.htm.

VEB. 2015. "Petr Fradkov Appointed as Vnesheconombank First Deputy Chairman." http://veb.ru/en/press/news/arch_news/index.php?id_19=100229&from_19=57.

———. 2017a. *Investor Presentation.* December. http://www.veb.ru/common/upload/files/veb/msfo/ir_pr_e1709_1.pdf.

———. 2017b. "Today." http://www.veb.ru/en/about/today.

———. 2018. "Supervisory Board." http://www.veb.ru/en/about/today/#supervisory board.

Vedomosti. 2010. "Priznanie Rotenberga" [Rotenberg's Confession]. October 8.

———. 2016. "Lider tamobovskoi gruppirovki Barsukov osuzhden no 23 goda" [The leader of the Tambov Group Barsukov has been sentenced to 23 years]. August 16.

Vernikov, Andrei. 2012. "The Impact of State-Controlled Banks on the Russian Banking Sector." *Eurasian Geography and Economics* 53, no. 2: 250–266.

Volkov, Vadim. 2002. *Violent Entrepreneurs: The Use of Force in the Making of Russian Capitalism.* Ithaca, NY: Cornell University Press.

———. 2008. "Russia's New 'State Corporations': Locomotives of Modernization or Covert Privatization Schemes?" PONARS Eurasia Policy Memo 25. Washington, DC: PONARS Eurasia.

von Mises, Ludwig [1920] 1972. "Economic Calculation in the Socialist Commonwealth." In *Socialist Economics,* ed. Alec Nove and D. Mario Nuti. Harmondsworth, UK: Penguin.

Voronova, Tat'yana, and Aleksei Nikol'sky. 2013. "Posledny akkord Ignatieva" [Ignatiev's last accord]. *Vedomosti,* June 20.

VTB. 2017. "Management Board." http://www.vtb.com/group/management/guide/bortnikov/.

Walt, Stephen. 1987. *The Origins of Alliances.* Ithaca, NY: Cornell University Press.

Wayne, Leslie. 2012. "How Delaware Thrives as a Corporate Tax Haven." *New York Times,* June 30.

Weaver, Courtney. 2014. "Moscow Court Seizes Yevtushenkov's Bashneft Shares." *Financial Times,* September 26.

Werning Rivera, Sharon, and David W. Rivera. 2006. "The Russian Elite under Putin: Militocratic or Bourgeois?" *Post-Soviet Affairs* 22, no. 2: 125–144.

———. 2017. "The Militarization of the Russian Elite under Putin." *Problems of Post-Communism,* 1–12.

Westman, Mattias, and Alexey Krivoshapko. 2017. "Myth and Reality: Share of the Government in the Russian Economy with the Numbers." *Prosperity Analysis,* November.

Whitmore, Brian. 2015. "The Political Heirs of Vladimir Putin." *Atlantic,* November 13.

Wile, Rob, 2017. "Is Vladimir Putin Secretly the Richest Man in the World?" *CNN Money,* January 23.

Williamson, John. 1990. *Latin American Adjustment: How Much Has Happened?* Washington, DC: Institute for International Economics.

Wilson, Dominic, and Roopa Purushothaman. 2003. "Dreaming with BRICs: The Path to 2050." Global Economics Paper 99. New York: Goldman Sachs.

World Bank. 2012. "Assessment of Costs and Benefits of the Customs Union for Kazakhstan." Report 65977-KZ. Washington, DC: World Bank.

———. 2018. *World Development Indicators* online database. http://devdata.worldbank.org/dataonline/.

World Bank and International Finance Corporation. 2017. *Doing Business in 2018: Equal Opportunity for All.* Washington, DC: World Bank. http://www.doingbusiness.org/.

Wright, Thomas J. 2017. *All Measures Short of War.* New Haven: Yale University Press.

WTO. 2012. "WTO Membership Rises to 157 with the Entry of Russia and Vanuatu." Press Release, August 22. https://www.wto.org/english/news_e/pres12_e/pr671_e.htm.

Yaffa, Joshua. 2017. "Putin's Shadow Cabinet and the Bridge to Crimea." *New Yorker,* May 29.

Yakovlev, Yevgeny, and Yekaterina Zhuravskaya. 2007. "Deregulation of Business." CEFIR Working Paper 97, February. Moscow: Centre for Economic and Financial Research (CEFIR).

Yarosh, Yuliya, and Ilya Bulavinov. 2010. "Nikto ne mozhet skazat', chto ya kogo-to unizil, u kogo-to chto-to otnyal" [Nobody can say that I humiliated anybody or that I took anything from anybody]. *Kommersant,* April 28.

Yasin, Yevgeny. 2004. "The Willful Destruction of Yukos Tells Us: Be Afraid." *Financial Times,* July 29.

Yeltsin, Boris N. 1991. "B. N. Yeltsin's Speech." *Sovetskaya Rossiya,* October 29.

———. 1994. *The Struggle for Russia.* New York: Crown.

———. 2000. *Midnight Diaries.* New York: Public Affairs.

Yeremenko, Yekaterina. 2017. "Surovy klimat" [Tough climate]. *Forbes,* August 2.

Yergin, Daniel, and Thane Gustafson. 1993. *Russia 2010 and What It Means for the World.* New York: Random House.

Yergin, Daniel, and Joseph Stanislaw. 1998. *The Commanding Heights: The Battle between Government and the Marketplace That Is Remaking the Modern World.* New York: Free Press.

Yudaeva, Ksenia V., et al. 2002. "Sektoral'ny i regionalny analiz posledstvii vstupleniya Rossii v VTO: Otsenka izderzhek i vygod" [Sectoral and regional analysis of Russia's accession into WTO: A cost-benefit analysis). Moscow: Centre for Economic and Financial Research (CEFIR).

Zakvasin, Alexei. 2015. "Zachem Sechinu trillion" [Why Sechin needs a trillion]. *Vedomosti*, April 21.

Zavadski, Katie. 2017. "Russian Spy Sent Home after Early Release from U.S. Prison." *Daily Beast*, May 4.

Zhigalkin, Yuri. 2017. "Ordenonosnaya sdelka Putina" [Putin's order-giving deal]. Radio Liberty, April 15.

Zoria, Yuri. 2018. "Hot War Still on in Ukraine's Donbas, and It's Far from Frozen Conflict." Euromaidan Press, May 15. http://euromaidanpress.com/2018/05/15/hot-war-still-on-in-ukraines-donbas-and-its-far-from-frozen-conflict/.

Zubarevich, Natalia. 2015. "Four Russias and a New Political Reality." In *Putin's Russia*, ed. Leon Aron, 22–35. Washington, DC: American Enterprise Institute.

Zygar, Mikhail. 2016. *All the Kremlin's Men: Inside the Court of Vladimir Putin.* New York: Public Affairs.

Acknowledgments

For the last four decades, I have followed the evolution of the Russian economy and the debate around it. I have spent several of those years in Russia, and I am grateful to have been a minor participant in this great Russian drama.

I have more people to thank than I can mention. My main gratitude remains with four people, Russia's great economic reformers, Yegor Gaidar, Anatoly Chubais, and Boris Fedorov, with whom I worked closely during the years 1991–94 as economic advisor to the Russian reform government, and my wife Anna who used to work as press secretary for Yegor Gaidar. Other close colleagues of mine were Mikhail Dmitriev, Tatyana Maleva, Vladimir Mau, Sergei Vasiliev, Yevgeny Yasin, and Ksenia Yudaeva.

Among my Western colleagues, I learned a great deal from Aivaras Abromavicus, Martin Andersson, Örjan Berner, Tomas Bertelman, Carl Bildt, Peter Boone, Stanley Fischer, Brigitte and Christopher Granville, Jacob Grapengiesser, Sven Hirdman, Georg Kjällgren, David Lipton, Rory MacFarquhar, Charlie Ryan, Andrei Shleifer, Christopher Smart, and Lawrence Summers.

Among journalistic colleagues, I would particularly mention Peter Baker, Chrystia Freeland, Susan Glasser, David Hoffman, John Lloyd, Edward Lucas, and Steven Lee Myers.

Several friends have read parts of this manuscript at various stages. I have listened carefully to their comments and advice and want to express my gratitude to the late Karen Dawisha, Yuri Felshtinsky, Vadim Grishin, Sergei Guriev, Thane Gustafson, Michael Mandelbaum, and Robert Otto. I have also benefited from eight anonymous reviews of my work at various stages.

Seth Ditchik, my editor at Yale University Press, made the publication of this book possible, and Laura Dooley expertly edited the manuscript.

I have discussed these topics intensely with many people and I would particularly to thank my friends, Evgeniya Albats, Sergei Aleksashenko, Leon Aron, Alexander Auzan, Harley Balzer, Charlie Becker, Anatoly Chubais, Simeon Djankov, Leonid Gozman, Daniel Fried, Yevgeny Gontmakher, Paul Gregory, Yevsei Gurvich, John Herbst, Fiona Hill, Andrei Illarionov, Vladislav Inozemtsov, Mikhail Khodorkovsky, Andrei Kolesnikov, Iikka Korhonen, Andrew Kuchins, Aleksei Kudrin, Michael McFaul, Vladimir Milov, Aleksei Mozhin, the late Boris Nemtsov, Leonid Nevzlin, Andrei Piontkovsky, Ilya Ponomarev, Stephen Sestanovich, Lilia Shevtsova, Mats Staffansson, Angela Stent, Daniel Treisman, and Alexander Vershbow.

I have greatly benefited from participating in the Rand U.S.-Russia Business Leaders Forums in Washington and Moscow thanks to kind invitations from William Courtney and in the annual Gaidar Forums at the Russian Academy of the National Economy and State Administration in Moscow. A number of Western and Russian businessmen have been most helpful, but I abstain from mentioning their names, fearing that it might not be helpful to them and their business.

I have been privileged to enjoy eminent research assistance from Antonio Weis, Amelie Rausing, and Andrey Sazonov.

This work has been possible thanks to the generous support from my employer the Atlantic Council.

Most of all I want to thank my beloved wife Anna and our children Anton, Carl, and Marianna, for their great support and understanding.

Atlantic Council,
Washington, DC
September 2018

Anders Åslund

Index

Page numbers in *italics* refer to figures.